CITIES
IN RUINS

CITIES IN RUINS

The Politics

of Modern Poetics

Cecilia Enjuto Rangel

Purdue University Press
West Lafayette, Indiana

Printed in the United States of America
Design by Anita Noble

Library of Congress Cataloging-in-Publication Data

Enjuto Rangel, Cecilia.
 Cities in ruins : the politics of modern poetics / by Cecilia Enjuto Rangel.
   p.   cm. — (Purdue studies in Romance literatures ; v. 50)
   Includes bibliographical references and index.
   ISBN 978-1-55753-571-9 (alk. paper)
   1. Ruins in literature. 2. Cities and towns in literature. 3. Poetry, Modern—20th century—History and criticism. 4. Poetry, Modern—19th century—History and criticism. I. Title.
   PN1271.E65 2010
   809.1'9358209732—dc22   2010025254

A mi padre Jorge y mi hermana Roxana, in memoriam.
A mi madre Rosario y mi hermano Fernando.
A Pedro, mi mejor lector, y a nuestra Lucía.

Contents

Acknowledgments

This book on ruins is the product of many travels, through and beyond poetry. This project owes its intellectual backbone to the vibrant dialogue I have established with many colleagues and friends throughout the years.

Among the many friends who have helped me, and encouraged me with their insightful comments, I must thank in particular Moira Fradinger, Fernando Rosenberg, John MacKay, Jill Robbins, Arturo Arias, Julio Ortega, David Castillo, Vicente Cervera Salinas, Edmundo and Carmen Vásquez, Mrinali Álvarez, Iliana Pagán, Alfonso Durán, Javier Arbona, Susan Homar, Luce López Baralt, Rubén Ríos, Esteban Tollinchi, Maruja García Padilla, Cynthia Chase, Jonathan Monroe, Carmen Dorado, Humberto Delgado, Luis Cárcamo, Doris Sommer, Luis García Montero, Teresa Gilman, and Jennifer Duprey.

I am truly grateful to Roberto González Echevarría, whose critical encouragement and moral support were fundamental in the early stages of this project during my graduate studies at Yale University. I have a clear intellectual debt to all my professors at Yale, especially Shoshana Felman, Peter Brooks, Josefina Ludmer, Nöel Valis, Paul Gilroy, Giuseppe Mazzotta, and Dudley Andrew.

Throughout the last few years I have enjoyed a constant and fruitful intellectual dialogue with Juan Armando Epple, Leonardo García-Pabón, David Wacks, Leah Middlebrook, Fabienne Moore, Gina Herrmann, Amalia Gladhart, Amanda Powell, Barbara Altmann, Evlyn Gould, and Nathalie Hester, my friends and colleagues from the Romance Languages department, at the University of Oregon. In diverse ways, they have all given me invaluable advice, and they are our family in Eugene, along with Mirtha Avalos, Sayo Murcia, Jeff Hanes, Anuncia Escala, Violet Ray, Michael Stern, Sarah Grew, Gabriela Martínez, and Lisa DiGiovanni. Our dinner parties, and the "tertulias" that go with them have nurtured us all. In particular, I must thank Carlos Aguirre, whose absolute intellectual generosity and meticulous readings have been crucial in the many stages of this book.

This project was also possible thanks to the institutional support of Yale University and the University of Oregon. At the University of Oregon, I have been able to focus on my research with the support of the office of the Vice-President for Research, the Junior Professor Development Grants, the Ernest G. Moll Faculty Research Fellowship in Literary Studies, and the Oregon Humanities Center. Elise Hansen proved to be an excellent copyeditor, and I am also very grateful to Susan Clawson and Patricia Hart from Purdue University Press for their superb editorial support.

Some chapters in this study contain material that previously appeared in somewhat different form in the following articles: "Broken Presents: The Modern City in Ruins in Baudelaire, Cernuda and Paz," *Comparative Literature* (Spring 2007): 140–57 (chapter 2); "Cities in Ruins: The Recuperation of the Baroque in T. S. Eliot and Octavio Paz," *How Far Is America From Here? Proceedings of the International American Studies Association (IASA)* Leiden 2003, ed. Paul Giles, Theo D'Haen, Djelal Kadir, and Lois Parkinson Zamora (Amsterdam, New York: Rodopi, 2005), pp. 283–96 (chapter 3); "Reaching the Past through Cities in Ruins: *Itálica* and Machu Picchu," *Colorado Review of Hispanic Studies* 2 (Fall 2004): 43–60 (chapter 5); and "Petrified Pasts: Octavio Paz and the Representation of Ruins," *Ciberletras* July 2004, http://www.lehman.cuny.edu/ciberletras/v11/enjuto.html (chapter 3). I am grateful to these journals for permission to reuse this material.

The unfailing encouragement of my family in Puerto Rico, especially Carmen Enjuto, and Antonio Luis and Luisa Ferré, has been decisive. I am deeply grateful to Diego and Camila, and Luis Fernández Cifuentes, who facilitated my work with his numerous, careful critical readings, and whose scholarship is always inspiring. This book is dedicated to my parents, Jorge Enjuto and Rosario Rangel, and my siblings, Fernando and Roxana Pagés-Rangel, for their incommensurable gifts.

Among the diverse origins of this book, I should highlight Pedro García-Caro's fascination with photographing and tracing "la muralla árabe de Murcia" and the many ruins in Spain and Mexico as the most contagious obsession. My husband Pedro has been my closest reader and the most brilliant, and challenging, interlocutor. He has read, criticized, and edited every page of this book in its multiple different stages. Our daughter, Lucía, is evidently our best work, and she has made the last few months the most joyful ones of all. Their love helped me see beyond ruins, and it always pushed me forward. This book belongs to you, Pedro.

Chapter One

Introduction

Ruins shape modern urban landscapes. They are both the effects of the real and the remains of the past.[1] Skyscrapers, with their shiny, clean, complete look characterize the modern city. But decisive historical events constantly disrupt that "finished" scenario, interrupting people's daily routines—frustrating their fantasies of tranquility and continuity. Modern poetry on ruins performs an awakening call to the lurking "real," to the violence of history in the making.

On September 11, 2001, a few months before I began this work, the world witnessed the attacks on the World Trade Center and the ruins of the Twin Towers. The twenty-first century had opened with the destruction of the symbols of globalized capitalist culture. Modernity was suddenly a vulnerable project, a finitude anticipated by postmodern architects. Suddenly ruins once again surpassed the poetic topos—they were palpable, immediate, threatening visions of reality.

But what are the differences between reading about ruins and seeing them? How do representations of ruins determine our ways of reading reality and making history? What was the difference between being a victim, witnessing the events in New York, and obsessively watching and "living" those events as they took place on our television screens? TV viewers were placed in "virtual reality"; it seemed too real to be true. It was a catastrophe of Hollywood-like dimensions in the center of New York City, the epitome of the modern city and the capital of the global world. All the images of the World Trade Center that followed showed that the American flag conquered those ruins; while reclaiming them as theirs, the flags were also a symbol of "national unity" and "victory" that penetrated the destruction and the "defeat" caused by the crumbled buildings. The attacks served to strengthen American nationalism and reinforce the military resolve to invade Afghanistan. It empowered Americans and the Bush administration, while it revealed the bleak side of the politics of fear.

However, the media coverage showed no bodies, no blood; it was a sanitized face of destruction. Slavoj Žižek comments on the coverage of the event:

> ...the "derealization" of the horror went on after the WTC collapse: while the number of victims—3,000—is repeated all the time, it is surprising the actual carnage we see— no dismembered bodies, no blood, no desperate faces of dying people... in clear contrast to reporting on Third World catastrophes, where the whole point is to produce a scoop of some gruesome detail... (*Welcome* 13)

Monuments to the victims of September 11 memorialize their names, but the rubble became a massive site of destruction, grey and opaque. Soon the ruins of the World Trade Center were one of the most visited tourist sites in New York City. Žižek goes on to associate the catastrophe with the moment in which the protagonists of the Hollywood production *The Matrix* (1999) see the ruins of Chicago after a global war and awaken to historical reality, to "the desert of the real." The "derealization" of the destruction of September 11 made "reality" or "the desert of the real" easier to digest. Nonetheless, the traumatic experience of witnessing New York in ruins provoked a collective historical awakening.

On March 11, 2004, only three days before Spain's general elections, the "effects of the real" were also felt in Europe with the attacks on Madrid's trains, an event that confirmed the powerful political effects of ruins and devastation on everyday life in the modern collective psyche. The way the trains in ruins were represented and information was manipulated proved crucial to the people's political response in the ensuing elections. A majority of the Spanish people felt betrayed by the manipulation of the event by the right-wing government, who initially blamed the Basque nationalist terrorist group ETA although much of the evidence pointed to Islamic terrorism as payback for Spain's support of the United States' invasion of Iraq. The Spanish people decisively voted in favor of opposition candidate José Luis Rodríguez Zapatero, the leader of the Socialist Party.

Like the media coverage concentrating on the monumental dimensions of the catastrophe in New York in 2001, many modern poems on ruins omit the remains of the dead and the bloody traces of war. However, there are other texts that, like the dreadful images that emerged from Madrid in 2004, disturb their readers; their portrayals of the destruction are more vivid and more evocative of dismembered bodies, literally and metaphorically. The attacks in New York and Madrid, with all their victims, highlighted the contemporary social and historical significance of the aesthetic and the political uses of ruins. As expressions of mourning or political indignation, modern poems on ruins, a somehow unexplored subject, try to cope with the "effects of the real" and interpret the violent acts committed in the name of modern progress or in defense of certain economic and cultural values.

But why mention 9/11 and 3/11 in the introduction to a book that discusses poems from the second half of the nineteenth century to the middle of the twentieth century? These events shaped the way we perceive ruins today in the United States and Europe, and they marked the beginning of my project, constantly reminding me that the ruins portrayed in the poetic texts I studied were fictional reproductions of the effects of the real. Ruins evoked an imminent sense of reality and gave these poems, these *artificial* products, a powerful scent of authenticity. Contemporary events and the modern ruins remind us of the political impact that the Spanish Civil War and the two World Wars had in the development of the poetic topos earlier in the twentieth century. For instance, Pablo Neruda's experiences in the Spanish Civil War molded his vision of the Inca ruins and Latin American politics and poetry; and the new mechanized machines of mass carnage of World War I are also unmistakably present in T. S. Eliot's metaphoric language in *The Waste Land,* itself in dialogue with soldier poets like Wilfred Owen.

This book is divided into four main chapters and an additional concluding chapter. Here, I articulate different sets of comparative analyses: Charles Baudelaire and Luis Cernuda, T. S. Eliot and Octavio Paz, the transatlantic poetics of the Spanish Civil War, and a chapter mainly on Pablo Neruda. Throughout my research I encountered diverse types of poems on human ruins, artificial ruins, and "real" ruins, products of progress or war. My analysis aims to show how through their reflection on ruins, these modern poets read, interpret, and criticize their historical and literary pasts, as well as Modernity's ever-changing present.

I conceptualize the modern topos of ruins in comparison with the Baroque and the Romantic topoi and argue that while establishing a dialogue with previous literary traditions, modern poems on cities in ruins criticize capitalist progress and the devastating effects of modern war. Modern poetry on ruins can reveal an apocalyptic vision of history, a poetics of disillusionment and of "cultural mourning" (Adorno's *Aesthetic Theory*), but it also produces a "historical awakening" (Benjamin's *Arcades Project*) that empowers the text with political and historical agency. In contrast with Romantic poems, which convey a melancholic representation of the remains of the past, modern poems *historicize* ruins, often products of modern progress or war, and avoid a narcissistic, melancholic reading of destruction. By referring to Walter Benjamin, I propose that ruins provoke a historical awakening and a conscious re-evaluation of the past. This awakening can also be triggered by urban traumatic experiences and the marginalization of physical and human ruins from the modern city. The texts I discuss tend to reject a restorative aesthetic project that monumentalizes the ruins and avoid a Romantic, narcissistic identification with the destruction. These poems on ruins distance themselves from a nostalgic reconstruction of the past, although they manifest a type of "reflective nostalgia," to use Svetlana Boym's term, in which the poets connect many different eras and places with the present. In her insightful analysis on nostalgia, Boym explains the differences between restorative and reflective nostalgia: "Restorative nostalgia evokes the national past and future; reflective nostalgia is more about individual and cultural memory… Restorative nostalgia takes itself dead seriously. Reflective nostalgia, on the other hand, can be ironic and humorous" (49). Baudelaire, Eliot, Cernuda, Paz, and Neruda tend to reveal a reflective nostalgia in their poetics on ruins. Although many of their poems avoid a nostalgic, solipsistic vision of the destruction, politically their works differ so vastly that it is crucial for the cultural critic not to homogenize their diverse poetic stages.

The five poets I compare tend to stay away from a nationalist discourse in their poems on ruins. Their complex net of literary allusions and their multiple visions of cultural identity distinguish them as poets who cross their national borders. Their poetic and political critique can be regarded as subversive when it questions bourgeois social conventions; yet Eliot, Baudelaire, Cernuda, Paz, and Neruda cannot be reduced to analogous ideological standpoints or similar aesthetic answers to their disillusionment. For example, Paz and Neruda, through very different ways, see in poetry a hopeful historical agent, while Baudelaire, Eliot, and Cernuda have more pessimistic, cynical voices.

Poems on ruins explore the decayed parts of the city: its destroyed monuments and buildings, its wreckage, and its remains. The Latin verb *ruo*, "to rush or fall," initially meant that ruin was a movement, the process of collapse. Through time, the word *ruin* also came to signify the result of the destructive motion, the remains of a historical past.[2] The etymology of the word is relevant in the development of the poetic topos, since these texts often exploit the multiple meanings of ruin. The poems I analyze often propose a rereading of the past, to condemn it, idealize it, or learn from it. "Men make their own history, but they do not make it just as they please, they do not make it under circumstances chosen by themselves, but under circumstances directly encountered, given and transmitted from the past" (Marx 15). In this passage from *The Eighteenth Brumaire of Louis Bonaparte*, Marx stresses that people are all historical products, able to change the present, but unable to escape the past and its legacy. Poems on ruins, explicitly or implicitly, project a political translation and a historical interpretation of a destroyed city, whether it is a specified city or not. Just as Marx refers to men's historical agency, we can also extrapolate from his argument that individuals *make* literary texts, products themselves of a literary and a historical context. But how can poetry speak to a contemporary audience, bombarded with narrative accounts of history? Poems, whether elusive or not, always have a story to tell, whether we learn them by heart as a rap song, a pamphlet, a sonnet, or an epic poem. However we encounter it, poetry has often been a medium of political agency and a testimony of the collective cultural memory. Still, our current fascination with ruins cannot be read in a historical vacuum; it is clearly connected to the ways ruins have been portrayed in the past. When discussing the current obsession with the ruins of Modernity as part of a reflection on war, memory, and trauma, Andreas Huyssen asks: "What shapes our imaginary of ruins in the early twenty-first century, and how has it developed historically?" ("Nostalgia" 7–8). In this essay, "Nostalgia for Ruins," Huyssen argues that we already find an "authentic ruin" of Modernity in the eighteenth century, and that in particular, Giovanni Battista Piranesi's work articulates "the ruin problematic *within* modernity rather than *after* it" (9). Just as in Piranesi's etchings, in most of the poems on ruins, Baroque, Romantic, or Modern, there is the search for, if not the finding of, authenticity, of the *real* traces of the historical past, within the fiction of the text. Huyssen pinpoints how terms such as *authenticity* and *nostalgia* are historical concepts and in the twentieth century they become obsolete. Still, if we consider the poems on ruins of the Spanish Civil War, authenticity acquires a whole different meaning from the one current in the eighteenth century, while the political significance of the text is strengthened and legitimized by the claim of the speaker as a witness and the ruins as the immediate, *real* effect of the destruction.

A historical overview of the various aesthetic and political representations of ruins is key to seeing how they are reread and re-evaluated by modern poets. Ruins have been treated as historical allegories since Antiquity, as Destiny's follies, and later on, in the Middle Ages, as part of a morally didactic discourse.[3] In Spanish Golden Age poetry, ruins reach one of their climactic moments. Baroque ruins bring up traditional motifs such as *ubi sunt* and *memento mori*, while they also portray the decayed glories of the past, of Antiquity, as examples of the power of time and nature over the works of civilization. Furthermore, the poetic representations of *le sentiment des ruines* in the eighteenth century and the Romantic ruins, whether fake or real, inauthentic or authentic, rediscover the beauty of the broken columns of Antiquity in public and private gardens and the mystery of the castles and the churches of the Middle Ages in their countryside.[4] The actual, real ruins became ideal spots for the contemplation of the melancholic self, and the Romantic poems on ruins de-historicized the remains of history.

However, modern poems on ruins historicize the city's process of transformation and elucidate its decay. Poems on modern ruins often use Baroque paradoxes or parody the Romantic melancholic self, lost in the new city, to criticize the cracks and the holes of Modernity's project. While modern poems on Antique ruins, like Cernuda's "Las ruinas," may also be read as historical allegories, criticism of Modernity is clearly found in the contrast between the city's versions of modern progress and the Antique ruins, for example in Paz's "Himno entre ruinas." Antique ruins in the modern landscape have diverse functions depending on the text, but they are usually portrayed as the historical remnants of the past, the city's museum pieces within its own open grounds.

The topos of ruins in Spanish Golden Age poetry was, at first, merely considered a mimetic project, greatly influenced by Baldassar Castiglione (1478–1529) and his famous sonnet to Rome, "Superbi colli."[5] Gutierre de Cetina (ca.1510–ca.1554) is deemed the first to "imitate" Castiglione's sonnet, although instead of Rome, he refers to Carthage.[6] Bruce W. Wardropper suggests that the interest in Carthage was motivated by Garcilaso de la Vega's sonnet "A Boscán desde la Goleta."[7] Still, in the Baroque topos, the most paradigmatic and famous echo of Joachim Du Bellay's 1554 sonnet "Nouveau venu, qui cherches Rome en Rome / Et rien de Rome en Rome n'apperçois" is in a sonnet by Francisco de Quevedo (1580–1645), "Buscas en Roma a Roma ¡oh peregrino! / y en Roma misma a Roma no la hallas," recalling his trip to Rome in 1617.[8]

In both Du Bellay's and Quevedo's poems, the traveler faces the contrast between the Rome he expects and the ruins of Rome—paradoxically the product of progress and the urban renovations promoted by Papal authorities. Ferri Coll does not believe that this poem "reflexion[e] sobre el sentido de la fugacidad de la vida o de la volubilidad de la fortuna. Para Quevedo, la idea predominante es el declive de la ciudad actual" (120). Although there is no explicit association between the Roman ruins and the fugacity of life in Quevedo's sonnet, the final paradox suggests the connection, when transient things like the river remain and permanent things disappear.[9] Quevedo carefully represents the river as a paradoxical element of flowing, fugitive water, which survives the passage of time. In the next chapters, I examine more closely the role of the river as a witness to history. For example, in Neruda's *Alturas de Macchu Picchu*, the speaker asks the personified river for the buried history of the place. The river's musicality evokes the oral nature of the Inca city's history, while it also presents the speaker's difficulty in comprehending nature's language. Nature is the survivor of history, and thus, the river is a witness, a voice and a mediator between the past and the present.

Baroque ruins also set themselves as a bridge between the Antique past and the sixteenth-century national project. A series of poems to Itálica demonstrates the search for national, cultural, and literary origins in Spanish Golden Age poetry. The archeologist Rodrigo Caro (1573–1647) spent decades rewriting his well-known "Canción a las ruinas de Itálica."[10] Caro's poem to Itálica is a national and a literary cornerstone for the topos of ruins and, as I argue, it has diverse incarnations in Cernuda's, Paz's, and Neruda's poetry, although these modern poems do not nationalize the ruins as is done in Caro's "Itálica," where what Boym calls a restorative nostalgia prevails. Even Paz's poems on ruins, which allude to Caro's text and specifically point to Mexican cultural history, express a transnational critique of modern progress.

This very brief historical summary of the topos of ruins in Spanish Golden Age poetry aims to review what has already been thoroughly studied and well documented. The reflection on death and the obsession with decay are common traits of the topos of ruins: in Baudelaire and Cernuda, ruins are often associated with the real and its specter; in Eliot and Paz, skeletons and decayed bodies can serve as metaphors of the urban landscape; and in Neruda, death is both an effect of war and a source for existential anxiety, as well as part of the natural cycle of life. The Baroque obsessions with death and decay extend the topos of ruins from the city's space to the human body, and they evidently molded the eighteenth-century depictions of destruction.

Le sentiment des ruines, nurtured by painters like Piranesi, flourishes in the eighteenth century, in particular in France,

England, and Italy. "The eighteenth century had an undeniable mania for physical representations of decay" (Goldstein 3). The fascination with ruins and decay culminated in personal journeys through the well-placed stones and the skeletons of buildings, in an effort to erase their uncomfortable historical context.[11] Yet the eighteenth century and particularly the nineteenth century paradoxically produced our modern notions of history and nation, while their conceptualization of ruins through poetry tended to empty the ruins' historical baggage.

Romanticism tightened the knot between the self and the city in ruins. The ruined site was more than a *memento mori*; it was a representation of the lost self in the lost past. Stephen Bann claims that Romanticism gives rise to the desire for history as the desire for an absent past:

> "History" is the relentless appropriation by text, figure, and scenographic representation, of what is already irretrievably lost. It is an effect of camouflage, or perhaps, in Freud's sense, a work of mourning, which achieves the displacement of one type of dispossession (the loss of centrality of "man") onto another (the loss, or absence, of the past). (*Romanticism* 10)

This notion of history is defined by the texts that convey it; "the effect of camouflage" is the tail of any tale, the effects of history as the representations of what happened. Bann implies that history is a product of nostalgia, the desire to return to the lost home, and thus, a work of mourning, which substitutes the displaced self for the slippery past. Lord Byron best exemplifies, in my view, this portrayal of the ruined self who identifies with the ruins he represents. For instance, Byron's *Childe Harold*'s protagonist inherits a ruined estate, an ancient abbey.[12] However, when Byron's speaker describes himself as a "ruin amidst ruins" in canto 4, he refers not to England, but to Italy, in particular Venice:

> But my soul wanders; I demand it back
> To meditate amongst decay, and stand
> *A ruin amidst ruins*; there to track
> Fall'n states and buried greatness, o'er a land
> Which was the mightiest in its old command,
> And is the loveliest, and must ever be... (XXV)

Byron's speaker demands that his soul—lost, melancholic, wandering, self-obsessed—turn into the soul of a historian who traces and tracks the lost glories, "the buried greatness." Yet in the poem there is really no interest in a historical scavenger hunt; as in the use of the Baroque topos, the ruins are a reminder of the fragility of imperial power. Ultimately, the speaker identifies with ruins as if he were one of them. Rather than becoming a historian, the speaker stresses his role as the beholder of beauty, the poet who recognizes the beauty of decay and aestheticizes the ruined land.[13]

Romantic poems exploited, saturated, manufactured, and crafted the ruins into emblems of the sublime. Many well-known poems on ruins abound in the works of Leopardi, Holderlin, Nerval, and Hugo, but the English Romantics particularly excel in their contributions to the topos.[14] Thomas McFarland begins *Romanticism and the Forms of Ruin* suggesting that ruins define and determine the Romantic aesthetic: "The cultural iconology of Wordsworth and Coleridge is mirrored in that of Romanticism itself. Incompleteness, fragmentation, and ruin… not only receive a special emphasis in Romanticism but also in a certain perspective seem actually to define that phenomenon" (7). The Romantic poet feels incomplete, fragmented with the social transformations of industrialization; his poetic work is a constant search for self, which is sometimes found in nature, sublime and awesome. The Romantics deified nature, and the Baroque poets saw in nature a reflection of God; in this sense, both visions of ruins portray nature as the epitome of the eternal. Nature is the ultimate survivor of time and is the symbol of time taking over the ruins, the remnants of civilization.[15]

The reflection on ruins was at the core of Shelley's aesthetics and politics. Christopher Woodward, in his book *In Ruins,* links Shelley's fascination with ruins and his democratic ideals:

> It was in the ruins of ancient Rome that Shelley found hope for the future—more specifically, in the flowers and trees which blossomed in the Baths of Caracalla… their exuberant and wild fecundity promised the inevitable victory of Nature—a Nature which was fertile, democratic and free. (66)

Shelley's political philosophy marks this representation of Nature as wild and free, taking over the ruins, the remains of the Roman Empire. Critics from Ferri Coll and Starobinsky to Benjamin and Simmel have noted that Baroque and Romantic poems on ruins portray nature as an overriding force that reclaims its space, which had been temporarily inhabited by people and their works. The invasion of nature is also sublime and beautiful because it destroys the emblems of tyranny and imperial power.

"Ozymandias" is Shelley's dramatization of the fragility of power. The ruins of the colossal statue in the desert clearly become a *memento mori* because the body of power, the statue, is broken, fragmented, reduced to a pair of legs and a face. Nevertheless, the statue evokes life in the lifeless, even when the whole work of art does not survive time:

> Half sunk a shattered visage lies, whose frown,
> And wrinkled lip, and sneer of cold command,
> Tell that its sculptor well those passions read
> Which yet survive, stamped on these lifeless things…
>
> (103, lines 4–7)

The characterization of the tyrannical king by the poet-sculptor underlines his vanity and his cold-heartedness. Ozymandias has a voice in the poem that tries to impose fear and admiration. Yet the poetic irony is evident: "My name is Ozymandias, King of Kings, / Look on my Works, ye Mighty, and despair! / Nothing beside remains. Round the decay…" (10–12). The city in ruins is no more; no works, not even ruins, remain—the desert has swallowed the remnants of his legacy. The "colossal Wreck" is condemned to oblivion and nothingness, and once again the forces of nature overpower the ruins. Shelley's political critique of totalitarian power—as well as Cuban José de Heredia's famous "En el teocalli de Cholula" (1820), whose condemnation of the Aztec empire could be read as an indictment of the Spanish empire at the end of the wars of independence—is key to understanding how Romantic poetry also looked at the past to strengthen its political critiques of the present. These texts are also echoed in Neruda's condemnation of the Inca's rigid hierarchical system and his criticism of contemporary social injustice in Latin America. Modern poetry not only reacts to or parodies the Romantic topos; it has also learned from it and has evolved into a more politically charged interpreter of the multiple historical and literary traditions.

It is surprising how very few women poets write about ruins. An exception to this trend would be Carolina Coronado (1820–1911), one of Spain's most remarkable Romantic poets. In "El castillo de Salvatierra" (1849), she, also, depicts ruins as the epitome of the speaker's loneliness, and yet she emphasizes the political and historical significance of the abandoned towers of the medieval castle: "¿Por qué vengo a estas torres olvidadas / a hollar de veinte siglos las ruinas…?" (352). Her lament echoes the cries of those female slaves of the Visigoths and Arabs, and the tower is portrayed as a witness to the peninsula's history of violence, the battles of the Reconquest. The speaker blends her desire for solitude and freedom with that of the battered women of the past and assumes animal form as a bird to reach the heights of the clouds. But the search for freedom is chastised, and the woman is left once again frail and vulnerable, scared at the power of the storm, nature, and the shadows of the towers—history.

In modern poems of ruins like Baudelaire's "Le Cygne," Eliot's *The Waste Land,* and Neruda's "Canto sobre unas ruinas," nature is not the principal force of destruction. Nature may merge with the city in ruins, and we can encounter natural and artificial elements coexisting in the modern landscape, but in modern poems on ruins, machines and bombs substitute for moss and dust. In Cernuda's "Otras ruinas," the machines of progress are evidently the agents of destruction, and in Neruda's collection of poems on the Spanish Civil War, *España en el corazón*, bombs are war's tools and the producers of the devastation. These poetic representations show the causes and the effects of the modern city in ruins, the avenues and the bulldozers of progress, the alienation and the disillusion found in human ruins, and the destructive elements of war.

Ruins are not defined merely by the abandoned building blocks and the useless broken columns of a ruined city. Romanticism recognized the difference between ruins like the statue in "Ozymandias" that are forgotten, and ruins like the Coliseum that are monumentalized to be remembered. In the modern poems about ruins, the modern city is itself the monument to progress, and ruins are treated as rubble, as the past left in the margins. Poets like Baudelaire and Cernuda do not want to mold the past into an untouchable monument to be observed and admired, and yet their criticism of modern progress reinforces the need to remember, to preserve, and not to destroy the city's historical journey. As Baudelaire's and Cernuda's works attest, ruins can have human shape; and they can also be a room without a view. Some poems on ruins, like "La chambre double" and "Habitación de al lado," reenact the tensions between the external and the interior spaces of urban life, the eternal or the ephemeral elements of Modernity, "la realidad y el deseo," "Spleen et Idéal." Poetic ruins tend to be associated with monuments, cathedrals, emblems of power that are falling apart or that have already collapsed. By analyzing a multiplicity of poems that capture the decadence, the destruction, or the frustrated desires in the urban space, I suggest several ways of defining the modern topos of ruins.

When I explore the significance of modern ruins, I also consider how these poets read each other. In certain cases, I have chosen the poems more because of their relevance to a study that compares Baudelaire and Cernuda, Eliot and Paz, or for their value in the transatlantic poetics of solidarity during the Spanish Civil War than because of their evident contribution to the theme of modern ruins. However, either directly or indirectly I have focused my analysis on the political, historical, and literary manipulation of ruins in modern poetry: their critique of modern progress, their historical re-evaluation without nostalgically representing the past, their sense of parody, and their embrace of a particular literary tradition.

Benjamin's notion of awakening marks the critique of progress found not only in Baudelaire's poetics of urban shock and trauma but in most of the poems that *see* and *envision* a different reading of the past and the present. Ruins provoke a realization—an awakening into the power of historical time and death—and yet modern ruins are not merely contemplated by the poets. The awakening can also become a traumatic experience, a reaction to the remnants of war or to vestiges left by machines that destroy old buildings so new ones may be constructed.

Nostalgia, like moss, seems to dress poems of ruins. As Huyssen explains, "In the body of the ruin the past is both present in its residues and yet no longer accessible, making the ruin an especially powerful trigger for nostalgia" ("Nostalgia" 7). Romantic ruins tend to trigger in the spectator a nostalgic feeling for the lost past—a nostalgia that often disregards the historical circumstances that aggravated the destruction or the context that situates the spectator in the ruined scene. But as I have noted, the word *nostalgia* has multiple historical specificities and diverse significations. Noël Valis, in her thorough analysis "Nostalgia and Exile," summarizes very well the history of the word:

> …[N]ostalgia as an idea can be traced back to 1688 when Johannes Hofer coined the neologism to refer to a medical condition often found in soldiers far from home and variously called *Heimweh*, regret, or *desiderium patriae*… By 1835 the term can be found in the *Dictionaire de l'Académie*. Romantic thought made nostalgia incurable, that is, a permanent condition of loss and exile, the central metaphor being childhood as a lost paradise. (120)

From the seventeenth-century depression or "homesickness" and the eighteenth-century "maladie mortelle," nostalgia became a centerpiece in the nineteenth-century Romantic sensibility.[16] Fashion and nostalgia embrace two kinds of Romantic ruins: the fake ruins and the historical ruins. Artificial ruins were intended to decorate the bourgeois garden, to give it the prestige of time and history, and to harmonize nature and culture. Fake ruins were souvenirs of colonial power. The aesthetization of ruins emptied them of their historical background.[17] On the other hand, Romantic poems on actual ruins turned to the past for questions about the self.

Nostalgia was at first conceptualized as an illness and with the Romantic sensibility it became a sense of self. As Valis remarks, "By the late nineteenth century… psychoanalysis… transformed the return home into regression, a return to the individual's own history" (121).[18] Valis argues that in the twentieth century, nostalgia is a "secularized form of cultural mourning," associated with the experience of exile. Although nostalgia and exile are not synonymous, Valis points out the "historical character" of the nostalgic, the individual who registers the past through remembrance.[19] Romantic poems on ruins feed on nostalgia, while modern poems on ruins reveal a tension with nostalgic feelings. Exiles or not, in all five poets studied here, there is a sense of loss, lost home or lost self. This emptiness may be caused by war, progress, or a simple existential crisis;

nonetheless, these poets do not automatically become nostalgic for the past, usually part of a national past, just because they feel out of place or dissatisfied with the present. Still, as Valis suggests, nostalgia can also underline the historical consciousness of the individual, his place in history, and it can also be a tool of survival in exile.

Baudelaire, Cernuda, Eliot, Paz, and even Neruda reveal a type of reflective nostalgia for another time and space in their strong criticism of progress and the failures of modernization. Boym's notion of reflective nostalgia, "ways of inhabiting many places at once and imagining different time zones," can be found in these texts (xviii). None of the poets I discuss practices a restorative nostalgia by pretending to reconstruct the past as it was, since as Boym clarifies, "Restorative nostalgia manifests itself in total reconstructions of monuments of the past, while reflective nostalgia lingers on ruins, the patina of time and history, in the dreams of another place and another time" (41). These poets' aesthetic projects are usually oriented toward questioning the nationalist discourse rather than reinforcing it. They are not opposed to political and cultural changes, but they are dissatisfied with the empty promises of a progressive narrative. In the case of the poems that stem from the Spanish Civil War, I see a transformation in the topos of ruins and, in particular in Neruda's case, a distancing from a narcissistic attitude and the existential crisis of the twenties. Neruda, Rafael Alberti, and César Vallejo, among the many poets who write on the Spanish war, evade a solipsistic vision and identification with the ruins, voicing their Marxist aesthetics within the political urgency of their work.

Baudelaire's and Cernuda's ways of escaping the traumatic experiences of daily life and the overwhelming urban scene project this need to imagine a new time zone, a form of reflective nostalgia. Eliot's and Paz's criticisms of modern progress through the topos of ruins also open up the texts to multiple frames of reading and to an intricate net of allusions—their own "cultural mourning" in the aftermaths of the World Wars. And Neruda in his search for origins in Machu Picchu reveals a reflective nostalgia that transports him to colonial times. However, he does not fall into a restorative nostalgia, an idealization and mythification of the past as a national monument.[20] Neruda sees in the ruins of the Spanish Civil War and in the Inca ruins the imperative to abandon the perspective of a speaker consumed by nostalgia. The ruins in Neruda's poems, products of the war he witnessed, express his vision of poetry as a historical agent. By transcending the nostalgic's gaze, Neruda portrays Machu Picchu and recovers the Inca ruins from poetic oblivion without idealizing the Inca's historical legacy. In this sense, he does monumentalize the Inca ruins, giving them political and cultural relevance and not treating them as historical rubble. Yet, the poem is not a restorative project since the Machu Picchu ruins are not treated as Peru's national, cultural property, and their place in the search for Latin American cultural origins is also criticized as cemented on social and gender violence.

The second chapter examines the clashing depiction of the modern city in ruins in the poetry of Baudelaire and Cernuda. The role of memory and awakening, the shock experience and the sexualization of the urban space, predominate in Baudelaire's *Les tableaux parisiens* and Cernuda's *Un río, un amor* and *Los placeres prohibidos*. How do they distance themselves from the Romantic use of ruins? Can we read the portrayals of love and desire in the modern city as a reduction to ruins? Can we pick up the pieces? In the first part of the chapter, I look at how and why the modern transformations of the city are portrayed as threatening in "Le Cygne" and "Otras ruinas." In the second part of the chapter, I move from the external sphere into the interior spaces of "Habitación de al lado," "Rêve parisien," and "La chambre double." These poems establish a drastic contrast between reality and dreams, between the real and the ideal; facing the ruins of their metaphorical and literal rooms produces a "traumatic awakening," which implicitly voices a critique of the frustrated promise of modern progress. The third part of the chapter studies the sexualization of the cityscape in "A une passante," "En medio de la multitud," and "Remordimiento en traje de noche." These poems do not portray a monumentalizing vision of ruins. They do not reconstruct the multiple stories of frustrated desire triggered by the crowd's movements; there is no complete scenario, no finished poetic statue.

The eternal and the transient as the contradictory elements of modern daily life are recurring fixations in Cernuda's and

Baudelaire's aesthetics. Finally, in my reading of Cernuda's "Las ruinas," I look at how the poem offers a reworking of Baudelaire's aesthetics in "Le peintre de la vie moderne." However, there are no modern ruins in "Las ruinas." The ruins of this unidentified city are closer to the Baroque and the Romantic topoi, yet I propose that the poem speaks to Baudelaire's aesthetics and his definitions of Modernity while voicing what I have called Cernuda's and Baudelaire's poetics of disillusionment. Max Weber's concept of the "disenchantment of the world" can be associated with this critical and disillusioned vision of reality, conditioned by the tension between religion and the increased intellectualization of society: "The fate of our times is characterized by rationalization and intellectualization, and, above all, by the disenchantment of the world."[21] In my analysis of "Las ruinas," Cernuda's hypothetical exchange with God questions "the ethical postulate that the world is a God-ordained and hence somehow *meaningfully* and ethically oriented cosmos."[22] Weber refers to science in general, not a poem, as the rational force facing religion. Cernuda did not assume a scientific position, but his rebellious stance against God and the implications that eternity does not exist pertain to the modern "disenchantment of the world." Baudelaire's revision of what is beautiful in Modernity and his ethical and moral questionings on what is considered good and evil also elicit this disenchantment.

In the third chapter, I show that Eliot and Paz share Cernuda's and Baudelaire's poetics of disillusionment and that their works can be subversive in their critique of bourgeois conventions. Nevertheless, Eliot's and Paz's poems on ruins can be politically ambiguous and culturally conservative. Eliot's interpretation of history as the "disintegration of the intellect" reads modern progress from a very conservative outlook, in which progress has weakened intellectual life because it has divided society from its major social institutions, such as the Church. Paz distances himself drastically from Eliot's idealization of a medieval mystified order. Paz's work distrusts capitalist progress as much as religious institutions that have been able to benefit and participate in the system's economic logic. However, my analysis of Eliot's and Paz's poems on ruins does not focus on the difference between their political standpoints, but rather on how in their respective ways, they both establish a critique of the development of the modern city.

In this chapter I trace how Eliot and Paz recuperate and parody the Baroque and the Metaphysical poets, Francisco de Quevedo and John Donne, to redefine their tensions with literary tradition through the portrayal of ruins. Eliot's and Paz's essays about the Baroque and the Metaphysical poets, and poems like *The Waste Land* and "Homenaje y profanaciones," show their desire to find new connections with the Old World that would legitimize their own poetic practices, establishing the basis for a neo-Baroque aesthetic that rereads the seventeenth-century literary canon, privileging juxtapositions and paradoxes. In the second chapter, Cernuda's and Baudelaire's poetics of ruins respond to the European tradition and the effects of modernization on the urban space, while in the third chapter, Eliot and Paz are revealed to be two American poets in dialogue with the European literary canon and the sixteenth century. However, Paz's poems on ruins and his "return to the origins" assert that the pre-Colombian heritage and the European tradition are decisive historical and cultural legacies, amalgamated in the constitution of Latin American poetic tradition.

This recuperation of the Baroque and the Metaphysical poets must be read in the context of a neo-Baroque aesthetic project. Eliot's and Paz's poems on ruins criticize bourgeois society as well as exemplify a form of reflective nostalgia—intending to connect with many places and various eras. The second part of the chapter maintains that Eliot's parody and homage to Donne and John Webster in "Whispers of Immortality" and the theme of human ruins relate to the vision of the city in ruins of *The Waste Land* as exemplary of the historical decay of society. In *The Waste Land*, as in Donne's "The First Anniversary," the land is portrayed as dead and putrefied; it has no water, no fertilizer. Yet unlike Donne's poem, in Eliot's text there is no idealized dead lady; only Tiresias, symbol of the modern poet's existential crisis and creative infertility.

On the other hand, Paz's "Homenaje y profanaciones" is a burlesque rereading of Quevedo's "Amor constante más allá de la muerte." Paz's theoretical standpoints, his poetics of cultural reconciliation, and his search for the mixed origins of

Latin America are revealed in the poem's insistence on the two paradigmatic cities of Itálica and Uxmal, representative of the Hispanic (and Roman) heritage and the Mayan legacy, respectively. This is further complicated in my discussion of "Himno entre ruinas" and Paz's idealization of classical Mediterranean ruins, in contrast with Aztec and modern ruins. Paz's poetics of reconciliation in "Himno entre ruinas" can be contrasted with his pessimistic historical outlook in "Petrificada petrificante." "Himno entre ruinas" underscores the merging of opposites, his vision of the heterosexual union, and poetry as a hopeful alternative to history. "Petrificada petrificante" is Paz's ultimate poetic reading of Eliot's *The Waste Land*, which leads me to reconsider Eliot's and Paz's interpretations of the mythological and the historical pasts.

The fourth chapter, "The Spanish Civil War: A Transatlantic Vision," reviews how this war politically engaged a whole generation of poets from both sides of the Atlantic. Latin American poets from Neruda and César Vallejo to Nicolás Guillén and Octavio Paz joined Spanish poets like Cernuda, Rafael Alberti, and Miguel Hernández in writing about the war in support of the Republican cause. Their representations of the war vary in tone and style, from enraged, visceral imagery to nostalgic portrayals of the past and a pessimistic view of the future. These ruins reveal a transatlantic poetics of war and in turn, they help us analyze the transformation of the topos in modern poetry.

The fourth chapter begins with a brief historical introduction to the war and its political and cultural repercussions. The politics of historical memory in Spain and Latin American are part of a global phenomenon of fighting against cultural amnesia, itself a political child of brutal dictatorships and wars in countries where we still find thousands of unidentified mass graves. The poems that I discuss, written during the thirties or early forties, are the first contributions to a poetic testimonial genre. These texts inscribe the politics of a historical memory of the war, written not only by Spaniards but also by Latin Americans supporting the Republic. The next two sections of the chapter dwell on topics crucial to understanding the Spanish Civil War: how do questions of race and gender become equally problematic and disclose complex contradictions in both the "Nationalist" and the Republican rhetorical discourses and poetics? What does the racial identification of the "other" or the feminization of Spain expose in connection with the politics of modern poetics? Cuban poet Nicolás Guillén and American poet Lansgton Hughes both served as war correspondents in Spain, and in their poems to the Republican cause, they offer their interpretations on how war changes the representation of the self, the African American volunteer, and the Moroccan mercenaries, in stark contrast with the racist ideology and the "Nationalist" rhetoric of Falangist poet José María Pemán.

Spain is also portrayed as a gendered body in ruins, as a mother, a symbol of ultimate sacrifice and life-bearing hope, in the works of Antonio and Manuel Machado, Vallejo, Alberti, and Hernández. The works of the Machado brothers, who were very close but ideologically divided during the war, reveal that the representation of the "motherland" also conveys conflicting versions of Spain. But what does the feminization of the nation evoke in the transatlantic poetics of solidarity? It provokes empathy in the reader, since Spain is the mother of all Spaniards, but its use by poets like Vallejo also demonstrates that Spain goes beyond its Spanishness, beyond the "Nationalist" definition, to signify a utopist space, the possibility of a more equal society. Cernuda's elegies in *Las nubes*, mostly written during his political exile, also feminize Spain, and along with Paz's poems to the war, provide a nostalgic historical review of the war and a sense of cultural mourning after the loss of the war. Along with Neruda's contribution to the war, they are all expressing their solidarity with the Republican cause, as well as their political testimonies to the historical memory of the war. In the context of the current polemics within the politics of cultural memory in Latin America and Spain, these poems practice what Nelly Richard believes the memory boom achieved: "Practicar la memoria… Es evitar que la historia se agote en la lógica del documento… o del monumento… (es) luchar para que el reclamo tenaz, la queja insuprimible, el radical desacuerdo, tengan siempre oportunidad de molestar… los montajes livianos de la actualidad futil, desmemoriada" (12).

The fifth chapter focuses on the political impact of the Spanish Civil War on Neruda's political and poetic projects. The aesthetic imprint of the Baroque topos of ruins, epitomized by seventeenth-century Rodrigo Caro's "Canción a las ruinas de Itálica," becomes key to both Neruda's *España en el corazón* (1938) and his *Alturas de Macchu Picchu* (1945). The representation of cities in ruins in Latin American twentieth-century poetry shows a tendency to link the historical and the mythical, the landscape and the cityscape. These texts aim to become a medium for the production of a historical memory, a means to read and translate the stones and the voices of the past. I present diverse versions of modern ruins, from the reconstruction of the modern city, and the inevitable destruction it entails, to human ruins, inhabiting the city left in shackles. In the fourth chapter, ruins are products of war when I discuss the bearing of the Spanish Civil War on both Spanish and Latin American poetry, and in the fifth chapter they become symbols of a marginalized historical and cultural tradition in *Alturas de Macchu Picchu*.

The ruined Madrid in *España en el corazón* transforms Neruda's eyesight and insight, an awakening that is more a process than an abrupt change, which culminates in *Alturas de Macchu Picchu*. The war removes the traces of melancholia, which dwell on a narcissistic vision of the self, from the poems on ruins. These texts aim to provoke political condemnation and the evaluation of history as the agent of destruction. Neruda's "Canto sobre unas ruinas" demonstrates his political reading of history, in which he distances himself from a melancholic and a nostalgic manipulation of ruins. The final section explores the aesthetic and political continuities between the ruins of modern Spain and the ruins of the Inca Empire. Neruda's *Alturas de Macchu Picchu* also sets in motion a search for the literary and historical origins of Latin America. As Enrico Mario Santí asserts, Neruda's ascent to the ruined Inca city is often read as an allegory of Latin America's recovery of its pre-Columbian past, and he eloquently notes the irony that resides in the attempt to turn the poem "into a monument to cultural identity when monumentality (in the sense of petrification of meaning) is precisely what the poem rejects" (*Neruda* 172). In *Alturas de Macchu Picchu*, the pre-Colonial ruins not only serve as an allegorical search for the historical origins of the region and a positioning against a restorative nostalgia, but the poem also reveals an allegory of Neruda's own poetic journey and evolution. The poem underscores the speaker as the interpreter of a repressed, buried past, and his work as a bridge between diverse cultural and literary traditions.

A complex net of allusions from Quevedo and Caro to Dante and Whitman links *Alturas de Macchu Picchu* to the literary canon of Western tradition. Nevertheless, the poem prioritizes workers, not canonical poets, as subjects of history whose plight confirms the historical continuity between the Inca Empire and the contemporary capitalist system. The speaker in Neruda's text purports to become a historical witness and a mediator between the past and the present. The speaker in *Alturas de Macchu Picchu* intends to recover the stories of the people buried among the stones of the Inca Empire and to be the "voice of the voiceless."

Ruins as historical allegories can make us rethink the past, but these poems tend to stress imagination as their historical tool of excavation. I examine how Baudelaire, Cernuda, Eliot, Paz, and Neruda through the topos of ruins read the effects of the real and criticize Modernity's roads to progress and war, as well as interpret the construction of their historical and literary pasts. These poems on ruins respond to the political effects of the Revolution of 1848 and Haussmannization, World Wars I and II, and the Spanish Civil War. From the poetics of disillusionment, which leads them to paradoxically portray a modern city in ruins, to the political effects of war, which distances them from a nostalgic and narcissistic vision of the past, these poets reshape the ruins of the topos into the building blocks of modern poetry.

Chapter Two

Urban Ruins in Baudelaire's and Cernuda's Poetry

The Modern City: From Ruins to Waste

Waste bothers us. Ruins overwhelm us. How can we make a distinction between waste and ruins in the urban landscape? Waste stinks, it causes disgust, though in some cases it even fascinates us; but waste almost never makes us melancholic, while ruins, on the contrary, may generate nostalgia for the lost monument or the past it represents. Nowadays, waste can be recycled, transformed into a new product of consumption, while ruins seem to permeate the modern landscape as a lingering trace of what cannot be recycled. Modern ruins provoke anguish, anger, and political indignation, a tension with nostalgic feelings, especially because modern ruins are produced for the sake of progress or as a result of war.

The portrayal of the modern city as a disintegrated, ruined entity is part of an aesthetic critique of the new pace of progress, a critical vision that bonds the literary productions of Charles Baudelaire (1821–67) and Luis Cernuda (1902–63). Architectural ruins are usually inhabited by human ruins, either literally the remains of the dead, or the individuals whom society treats as human garbage. The poetry of a modern city in ruins relocates the marginal figures of society, placing them at the center of Baudelaire's and Cernuda's historical and literary project. Baudelaire's blind men, mad swans, old maids, prostitutes, seductive women, and dreamy poets reveal the hidden, mysterious beauty of the modern city. Cernuda's phantoms, empty modern subjects eager to escape reality, also project his poetics of disenchantment. In these texts, the city constructs itself from layers of past buildings, ruined cities and unfinished maps.

In contrast to the enduring ancient ruins of Baroque and Romantic poetry, the ruins of modern urban poetry tend to be short-lived. They are the remains of the destruction and reconstruction of a city's streets, houses, public buildings, and factories rather than broken monuments and statues, abandoned churches, fragments of temples, or other remnants of a distant past. In these poems nature ceases to be the principal force that slowly overcomes the works of civilization: progress and war take over ivy and time, and *spleen* and *ennui* replace awe and nostalgia. As Georg Simmel has argued, in the modern, and often traumatic, experience of the metropolis: "The fight with nature which primitive man has to wage for his *bodily* existence attains in this modern form its latest transformation" ("Metropolis" 409). In the city, people survive traffic, crowds, and advertisements, not tigers and serpents. Modern poems on ruins differ from their Baroque and Romantic counterparts both in their reading of history and in their representation of the poetic self. The speakers in these poems are not fixed or stable in their backward gaze; they can be melancholic and nostalgic, but also humorous and ironic.

Baudelaire and Cernuda use poetic representations of the city in ruins to conceptualize and criticize Modernity. In a space that is always redefining itself, always in reconstruction, ruins can easily be treated as merely waste. Although there are temporal and cultural gaps that distance Baudelaire's and Cernuda's poetics, both these poets see in ruins the emblems of the city's historical process, and in their poems they intend to rescue the remains of the past from the bulldozers of the future. Baudelaire's work, in his powerful review of the failures of urban progress, expresses the melancholy of the Parisians who feel that their city is becoming unrecognizable; yet he also manifests a fascination with the new, bizarre versions of modern beauty. In turn, Cernuda's poetry explores Baudelaire's contradictory definitions of the modern city, but without the latter's nostalgia. Still, their poems on ruins derive from a disillusioned, pessimistic vision of the modern city, charged with social and political indignation.

There are very few thorough studies that examine in depth the connections between Baudelaire and Cernuda, and I do not want to confine this chapter to the apparent influence of Baudelaire over Cernuda. Rather, I will analyze how through these poets, modern poetry prioritizes in different ways the role of literary and historical memory and employs representations of the changing city and its ruins to reflect upon a crisis of perception.[1]

Metaphors of negativity invite readers to reconsider the political, historical, and literary implications of representing the modern.[2] Why is Modernity conceptualized through paradoxes and "negations" of itself? In this chapter, I begin by looking at Haussmann's modernization of Paris and the nostalgic responses prevalent in Théophile Gautier's preface to *Paris Démoli*, Edmond and Jules de Goncourt's journal, Victorien Sardou's play *Maison neuve*, and particularly two poems by Baudelaire, "Les Petites Vieilles" and "Le Cygne," and one by Cernuda, "Otras ruinas." Baudelaire's two poems exemplify the increasing sexualization of the city and the role of memory in Modernity. The changing city and its ruined, abandoned parts depicted in "Le Cygne" and in "Otras ruinas" introduce some of the questions of memory, perception, and awakening present in Cernuda's "Habitación de al lado" and Baudelaire's "Rêve parisien," and "La chambre double." Perception is always fragmentary, elusive; that is particularly disturbing for the poetic voice, so keen on capturing the historical memory of the present. The Benjaminian term *awakening* in some cases means a Marxist awakening into history and social reality, and in others alludes to a psychoanalytical awakening of the unconscious.[3] In the discussion of the terminology on Modernity and negativity, I examine the polemical stances and the productive dialogue among some of the scholars who have reflected upon these terms.

Cernuda's readings of Baudelaire confirm and display the connections between their texts, in particular *Tableaux parisiens, Un río, un amor,* and *Los placeres prohibidos.* An awakening from a dreamed space is used as refuge or escape from modern urban reality. Cernuda's "Habitación de al lado" and Baudelaire's "Rêve parisien" and "La chambre double" use literal and metaphorical interior space, an idealized, luxurious room, as an allegory of the dreams of economic progress—in drastic opposition to the real, the room in ruins. The shock experience is represented as a type of awakening through the speaker's encounter with a disturbing and fascinating figure in the modern city, the exterior place *par excellence.*

On the other hand, the shock experience also marks "A une passante," "En medio de la multitud," and "Remordimiento en traje de noche," where the modern individual and the crowd reconfigure the dialectics of desire and death in the city. Finally, Cernuda's "Las ruinas" evokes the antique city in ruins and explores the dialogue between the modern topos of ruins and the Baroque and the Romantic poetic representations. Although "Las ruinas" does not represent a *modern* city in ruins, Cernuda's conceptualization of the poet's social and aesthetic role responds to Baudelaire's definitions of Modernity, in between the new and the old, the permanent and the passing cultural artefacts. Ultimately, Cernuda suggests that the poet's ambitions of eternity are doomed from the start, because he senses that eternity does not exist. Although many cities abound, both abstract and concrete, in Cernuda's poetry, Baudelaire's Paris, the epitome of the nineteenth-century modern city, is constantly casting its shadow upon the evolution of urban poetry.

Broken Presents: Walking among Ruins in the Modern City

Why is Paris in the second half of the nineteenth century, at the height of its reconstruction by Baron Georges-Eugène Haussmann, paradoxically represented in modern poetry as a city in ruins? Although there are many possible answers to this question, we may start by noting that Haussmann's project to modernize the urban landscape was extremely unpopular within the working class and some sectors of the bourgeoisie. This disapproval was accompanied by a longing for the lost Paris, with its medieval quarters and narrow streets. The ruined city came to symbolize the revolutionary Paris of 1789 and 1848 that was being transformed into a well-organized structure of great stores and great avenues, trees, and lakes. Efficiency and social control were the aims; the modern city had to be both an imperial project and a grand state capital.[4] However, even as Haussmann's modernization removed the working class from the center of the city, poets like Baudelaire made marginal figures, from the prostitute and the beggar to the thief and the *flâneur*, into the central characters of imperial Paris and its process of cultural and urban deracination.

Paris in the middle of the nineteenth century was undergoing enormous changes, which produced in many an overwhelming sense of loss. Théophile Gautier in his preface to Edouard Fournier's *Paris Démoli,* indicates the changing, unfinished character of the city and the strange images it creates: "C'est un spectacle curieux que ces maisons ouvertes avec leurs planchers suspendus sur l'abîme… leurs escaliers qui ne conduisent plus à rien… leurs éboulements bizarres et leurs ruines violentes…" (2). Gautier stresses the ruined, destroyed past trampled by the construction of the city. These ruins are strange and violent; they encapsulate the violence that founds and founders modern urban planning. The stairs of this new Paris seem to lead Parisians nowhere. Several decades afterwards, Cernuda echoes this image of the metaphor of progress as a broken staircase; with it, he exposes the nihilistic, empty ideals upon which the building of Modernity rests. Gautier refers explicitly to the melancholy of the critical spectators of the new urban space: "Sans doute le penseur sent naître en son âme une mélancolie, en voyant disparaître ces édifices, ces hôtels, ces maisons où les générations précédentes ont vécu. Un morceau du passé tombe avec chacun de ces pierres…" (3). Although Baudelaire shares with Gautier that melancholic feeling toward the changing Paris, his project differs from Fournier's effort at tracing all the historical remains of the city. Instead, Baudelaire wants to capture the evanescent present and its many ghostly urban faces.

Brothers Edmond and Jules de Goncourt's journal entry of November 18, 1860, reflects the tensions and the nostalgic feelings generated by the constant transformations of the city:

> Mon Paris, le Paris où je suis né, les Paris des mœurs de 1830 à 1848 s'en va. Il s'en va par le matériel, il s'en va par le moral. La vie sociale y fait une grande évolution qui commence. Je vois des femmes, des enfants, des ménages, des familles dans ce café. *L'intérieur va mourir. La vie menace de devenir publique…* Je suis étranger à ce qui vient, à ce qui est, comme à ces boulevards nouveaux sans tournant, sans aventures des perspectives, implacables de ligne droit, qui ne sentent plus le monde de Balzac, qui font penser à *quelque Babylone américaine de l'avenir.* (346; emphasis added)

Edmond de Goncourt mistrusts a future that will disrupt gender relations and family life, which he associates with an American Babylon.[5] There is a longing for the true and authentic Paris of

Balzac's novels, versus the false and the frivolous new Paris. From this politically conservative standpoint, the Americanization of the urban landscape threatens the image of Paris as the older and wiser Europe, especially its economic, cultural, and even spiritual hegemony. It also conveys the Latin anxiety for the Anglo-Saxon superiority that characterized the Napoleonic years, marked by French imperialist ambitions in Mexico and in the American Civil War, when France sided with the South. The end of Parisian street life and the end of French family life, as the Goncourts dramatically maintained and as T. J. Clark has discussed, were some of the reactions to Haussmann's new versions of the city. This political discourse may sound familiar to a contemporary American audience in the early twenty-first century, constantly exposed to conservative fears of the demise of the *real* values of a supposedly *real* America, threatened by the change, the political alternative of those implicitly *fake* Americans. Just as the Goncourts identify with a foreigner or a stranger in Paris, in "Le Cygne" the speaker depicts himself as an internal exile and in "Otras ruinas" the urban characters are all misplaced and estranged in their own city; although in Baudelaire and Cernuda, contrary to the Goncourts, this distinction gives them a privileged critical perspective. In his analysis of this historical context, T. J. Clark also identifies Victorien Sardou's comedy *Maison neuve*, presented for the first time in 1866, which stages a family crisis triggered by the social pressures of the new Paris and its commercial culture.

Sardou's play reveals the generational gaps that divide the old revolutionary Paris from the young, new Paris. Claire, the young niece, explicitly comments on those divisions when she complains about the old house they live in: "Cette chambre, cette maison, ces portraits, tout me pèse!... Ce n'est pas Paris, c'est la province... Ce n'est pas aujourd'hui, c'est hier...Ce n'est pas une maison, c'est l'odeur humide de la cave... À deux cents pas d'ici, le Paris nouveau, brillant, vivant... !" (Sardou 16). The young couple, René and Claire, want to move to a new house and move the family store from the old traditional street, changing its name. The grand-uncle, Genevoix, opposes these changes arguing that the name of the store, *La Vieille Cocarde*, dates back to 1789 and stands for the revolutionary Paris, while the new name they propose, *Le Bouton d'or*, only emphasizes the golden principle of ostentation so rampant in this new Paris. Genevoix humorously explains his dislike:

> ...on y perd le vieux Paris, le vrai, celui-là! Une ville étroite, malsaine, insuffisante, mais pittoresque, variée, charmante, pleine des souvenirs... nous faisions là nos petites révolutions entre nous: c'était gentil! —La course à pied n'était pas une fatigue, c'était une joie... Aujourd'hui, pour la moindre course... un trottoir éternel... Un arbre, un banc, un kiosque!... un arbre, un banc... Une foule bigarrée, cosmopolite, baragouinant toutes les langues, bariolée de toutes les couleurs... *Ce n'est plus Athènes, c'est Babylone!* Ce n'est plus une ville, c'est une gare! Ce n'est plus la capitale de la France, c'est celle de l'Europe entière! Une merveille sans égale! Un monde! D'accord. —Mais, enfin, *ce n'est plus Paris... puisqu'il n'y a plus de Parisiens...* (Sardou 44–45; emphasis added)

In this comedy and especially in Genevoix's speech of condemnation of the modern city, I want to underscore the relation with the Goncourts' text and the different nationalist sentiments embedded in these discourses. Genevoix's speech prompts a criticism toward Haussmann's Paris, but not as an engaged individual who defends the working class's rights of passage to the center of the city. Genevoix's reactionary and conservative stance is very much rooted in a nationalist nostalgia for a French Paris. Karl Marx describes in his analysis of the Revolution of 1848 in the *Eighteenth Brumaire of Louis Bonaparte* the position supported by individuals like Genevoix: "It was a clique of republican-minded bourgeois... that owed its influences to the personal antipathies of the country against Louis Philippe, to the memories of the old republic... above all, however, to *French nationalism*" (27). Genevoix stands undeniably for the values of the old republic and the bourgeois establishment, united by their common Frenchness. Genevoix's speech condemns the transformation of Paris into a diverse, heterogeneous European city, and although the Goncourts are not expressing the same national, ethnic, and racial anxieties, there is a common fear: Paris is becoming a modern Babylon—the threat of progress is its Americanization. In this cultural war, the prostitute is invading the iconography of the city as suggested by Edouard Manet's famous *Olympia*, and with her, one sees the fear of sexual freedom and the selling out of the national family.

The Goncourts' journal and Sardou's play portray the atmosphere of a divided modern city, in which destruction and construction, ruins and new buildings, are all part and parcel of the same project. The Goncourts' anxious discourse stresses that women and children are in cafes threatening family life. Their interruption of and their imposition on the public sphere are expressed as catastrophic: "L'intérieur va mourir." The metaphors of the prostitute as a symbol for Babylonian Paris, the morally debased and ruined city as a result of progress, become more relevant in Baudelaire's aesthetics and his poems. Nevertheless, Baudelaire distances himself from both the nationalist discourse of nostalgia and from the capitalist discourse of progress at all costs.

The sexualized metaphor of a Babylonian city, emblem of the falls and the threats of progress, is predominant in urban poetics. As William Chapman Sharpe argues in his incisive study *Unreal Cities*: "Not only have the otherworldly cities of Babylon and New Jerusalem provided a visionary context for viewing all earthly cities as ultimately insubstantial and unreal, but the sexualization of these cities as Whore and Virgin has given a transcendent significance to a quintessentially urban incident—the male poet's sudden encounter with an unknown woman in the street" (xii). Sharpe analyzes elsewhere in his book how the sexualization of the city implies a male desire to control and master the feminized urban space.[6] The continuous process of urbanization is envisioned as a sexualized program. Women become *more visible*, more active in the public social sphere—a change that some celebrated and others condemned. Baudelaire may share with the Goncourts and Sardou's Genevoix a melancholic longing for the lost Paris, yet his poetic project distances itself from nationalist ideals. For example, in his first prose poem, "L'étranger," the poet can be identified with the stranger, the foreigner, who has no family and no country. Furthermore, in contrast to the Goncourts and Genevoix, Baudelaire tends to desire or identify with women, old or young, prostitutes or widows, emblems of a gendered city in ruins, abandoned to its own peril. In his works, there is a clear sexual tension, but ultimately, he welcomes the feminine invasion of the city. As I will discuss further on, Baudelaire's "A une passante" portrays the woman as the fleeting symbol of the new city life, the condensation of the eternal and the time-bound, the spleen and the ideal. The woman in this poem is *more visible* because she is walking alone in the crowded street and because she gazes back at the observer; and at the same time, she is *less visible*, because her image is fugitive, "un éclair." The *Tableaux parisiens* also sexualizes the city in "Les Petites Vieilles," where the old women are depicted as human ruins, an example of Baudelaire's criticism of the notions of progress.

"Les Petites Vieilles" illustrates the feminization of the city, as a space full of paradoxical faces or natures. Baudelaire depicts the old women as: "Mères au cœur saignant, courtisanes ou saintes, / Dont autrefois les noms par tous étaient cités" (*Œuvres complètes* 1: 91). In a very paternalistic tone, Baudelaire employs the dichotomy of feminine urban iconography, the prostitute versus the *donna angelicata*. These verses also project a nostalgic look at the past, in which these women had names, identities. However, the old maids are both the representatives of the city and its waste: "Débris d'humanité pour l'éternité mûrs! ... / Ruines! Ma famille! ô cerveaux congénères!" (1: 91). It may seem puzzling that the metaphoric apostrophe to the old women compares them to brains of a similar kind or of the same "gender" as that of the poetic voice. While he objectifies them, Baudelaire's speaker identifies with the old women, erasing the gender and class gaps that separate them, and underlining their common traits, their similar brains, what makes them "family." Baudelaire finds these old creatures decrepit and charming, paradoxical and sardonic epitomes of the modern beauty he associates with the changing city. The old women are emblematic of the historical memory of the city; they are the brains that condense remembrance and forgetting. They may be treated as waste by society, but Baudelaire sees in them the human ruins of the city, the traces of the past. Paradoxically, by becoming the debris of the modern city, the old women become its source, the symbols of the city's historical memory.

Just as the old women paradoxically become symbols of the new, modern Paris, in "Le Cygne" (The Swan), Andromache represents both the antique and the modern feminine figures of pain and nostalgia. In the first stanza of "Le Cygne" the speaker evokes Andromache and her artificial river, the lying Simois. The river as a mirror does not reflect her beauty but her pain and is filled by her tears. In the Baroque topos of ruins, the river is traditionally the symbol of eternity and nature, the witness of history, who survives to tell the tale. Here, however, the river does not represent nature nor is it a trustworthy witness; the Simois is actually the imitation of the river she had in Troy.[7] The river is thus a metaphor of the poem itself; it lies, and yet, it is the source that makes the speaker's memory fertile.[8] In his essay "Le peintre de la vie moderne," Baudelaire argues that perception of reality and memory nourish the imagination of the artist; and as has been thoroughly analyzed, "Le Cygne" is a sign, a self-referential poem, which signals its own process of creation when the speaker wanders through the city, and in his act of remembrance, reconstructs it.[9]

In "Le Cygne" remembrance is the creative force that links the real and the unreal, the modern and the mythical. The references to Andromache's story, and the "exoticized" allusions to an African woman, are all interconnected in a series of what we might call *imaginary memories*. The images of the mythical, timeless world are not easily accessible. This imaginary memory needs to trespass the foggy walls of consciousness: "Les cocotiers absents de la superbe Afrique / Derrière la muraille immense du brouillard" (*OC* 1: 87). In these verses the nostalgic gaze of the African woman suggests the distance between the poetic present and the mythical past and its idyllic coconut trees. The imaginary memories convey Baudelaire's definitions of the creative process, in which imagination and historical memory merge. Hans Robert Jauss avows that the power of remembrance in Baudelaire's poetics "deforms" the temporal barriers between Modernity and Antiquity. In reference to "Le Cygne," Jauss argues:

> But to demonstrate the dissonance between the spleen and the ideal, the reified chaos of the metropolis and the wordless exile of the mythical swan is not Baudelaire's ultimate object. *From the ruins of the familiar nature of old Paris, his poem gives rise to a new counterworld of the beautiful...* The harmonizing and idealizing power of remembrance is the

newly discovered aesthetic capacity, which can replace the extinct correspondence of soul and timeless nature by coincidence of present existence and prehistory, modernity and antiquity, historical now and mythical past. (Jauss, "Sketch of a Theory" 84; emphasis added)

These imaginary memories reveal the poetic coincidence of history and myth. Nevertheless, this correspondence is not necessarily portrayed as harmonious in the modern poetics of ruins. The new counterworld of the beautiful emerges from a tension, from the anguish of the internal exile. As Walter Benjamin suggests: "'Le Cygne' has the movement of a cradle rocking back and forth between modernity and antiquity" (*Arcades Project* 356). Benjamin argues that for Baudelaire, Modernity is "marked with the fatality of being one day antiquity" (22). Andromache is not a symbol of the ideal, but of pain, not only because she lost her husband Hector but also because she is not free, she is a slave, possibly like the black woman at the end of "Le Cygne," who searches for Africa on the horizon. Both women link Antiquity and Modernity in their displacement; both are characterized by the melancholic gaze that always looks back.

> Andromaque, des bras d'un grand époux tombée,
> Vil bétail, sous la main du superbe Pyrrhus,
> Auprès d'un tombeau vide en extase courbée;
> Veuve d'Hector, hélas! et femme d'Hélénus!
>
> Je pense à la négresse, amaigrie et phtisique,
> Piétinant dans la boue, et cherchant, l'œil hagard
> Les cocotiers absents de la superbe Afrique
> Derrière la muraille immense du brouillard.
>
> (Baudelaire, *OC* 1: 86–87)

The text immobilizes the women with their nostalgia of a past, buried in an empty tomb or stuck in mud, hiding in the fog.[10] "Le Cygne" foresees Modernity's own destructive nature by integrating the modern and the antique in a world where Andromache, the swan, and the speaker coexist as symbols of pain and misplacement within blocks of the new Carrousel and the Louvre.[11]

In "Le Cygne" Baudelaire describes as traumatic this nostalgic process of remembering the old city:

> A fécondé soudain ma mémoire fertile,
> Comme je traversais le nouveau Carrousel.
> Le vieux Paris n'est plus (la forme d'une ville
> Change plus vite, hélas! que le cœur d'un mortel) (*OC* 1: 85)

The comparison of the changing city with the changing heart of any mortal bestows an unsettling lack of permanence on those transformations. So, too, does the connection between Paris and the changing images of the animals and carriages of a moving carrousel. Baudelaire's "Le vieux Paris n'est plus" echoes the sentiments of many Parisians like the Goncourts and Genevoix, who felt overwhelmed by their "new" city. The city has its own mortality, its own capacity to disappear.[12] The thirsty swan is the symbol, not of a dead city, but of the chaotic Paris, beautiful and grotesque. Like the estranged figures in "Les Petites Vieilles" and "Les Aveugles" and the sphinx in "Spleen," the swan is depicted as "mythe étrange et fatal," paradoxically "ridicule et sublime" (*OC* 1: 86). The lost swan and the overwhelmed speaker are exiles within this new Paris, linked by a melancholia whose immobilizing effect causes it, as Ross Chambers argues, "to be experienced as an oppressive weight" (168).

Baudelaire's "La chambre double," "A une passante," and Cernuda's "Habitación de al lado" and "En medio de la multitud" do not refer to a specific city, unlike "Le Cygne," where Paris is the center of its architectural design. "Le Cygne" expresses with anguish the melancholic mood, so predominant in poems that use the Romantic topos of ruins; nevertheless, it also exposes the strangeness and artificiality that defines Baudelaire's "counterworld of the beautiful."[13] In this text the new Paris is constructed and destroyed by the nostalgic gaze of the speaker, whose memories weigh as much as the stones that make these new pillars:

> Paris change, mais rien dans ma mélancolie
> N'a bougé! Palais neufs, échafaudages, blocs,
> Vieux faubourgs, tout pour moi devient allégorie,
> Et mes chers souvenirs sont plus lourds que des rocs.
>
> Aussi devant ce Louvre une image m'opprime:
> Je pense à mon grand cygne avec ses gestes fous
> Comme les exilés, ridicule et sublime... (*OC* 1: 86)

The new palaces of Haussmann's Paris do not erase the "vieux faubourgs" because the metaphor of memories as stones provides the speaker with the materials to rebuild the past of his city. Benjamin puts it succinctly: "Allegories are, in the realm of thoughts, what ruins are in the realm of things" ("Allegory and Trauespiel," *The Origin* 178). The ruins are the building blocks for the construction of a historical past, the allegorical ground from which the modern city emerges. Allegories can be defined as representations of the abstract in the concrete. Benjamin suggests that ruins are like allegories, in the sense that they are representations of the past, concrete emblems of death and the passage of time. Moreover, in both Baudelaire's and Cernuda's works, the allegorical use of the modern city in ruins asserts their political and historical re-evaluation of progress.

In the second part of "Le Cygne," the speaker establishes a more clear identification with the swan when he describes himself as an internal exile of this changing Paris, the artificial forest created by Haussmann's trees: "Ainsi dans la forêt où mon esprit s'exile / Un vieux Souvenir sonne à plein souffle du cor!" (*OC* 1: 87). Both the swan and the speaker are misplaced, exiles in their own city.[14] The personified "Souvenir" in capital letters resembles the "Temps" in "Rêve parisien" and "Le Spectre" in "La chambre double." They all manifest themselves through a powerful noise, which awakens the speaker and makes him face the pressures and the frustrations of modern time. The "Souvenir" remembers the forgotten and the defeated, the emblems of the landscape of ruins. Baudelaire's criticism of progress focuses on the marginalization of common figures and icons.[15] His definition of progress as the domination of matter stems from the cultural and spiritual anxieties produced by Haussman's economic policies. Baudelaire's speaker identifies himself with the exiled, the outsider, who wanders around the modern city as a displaced, disillusioned subject.

Although "Le Cygne" expresses the melancholia so commonly associated with the Romantic topos of ruins, this poetic self is not solipsistic. He is neither stagnant nor immobile, but walks through the city. Thus, his emotional state differs from that of both the swan and Andromache, who have been interpreted as the two main figures of melancholia and nostalgia in the text. Chambers, for example, reads this poem as a critique of the Second Empire, and by connecting Andromache to the

French historical context of 1861, he politicizes the melancholia of the text:

> Andromache... thus becomes the figure for a certain sense of history—the melancholy that turns memory into a remembrance of loss and links the present to a feeling of repetition and inauthenticity. The fate of the widowed queen, wrapped in the "immense majesty" of her grief but simultaneously "fallen" with the fall of Troy... makes her symbol easily applied to the recent history of republican France. (Chambers 159)

Andromache's pain symbolizes that of France; fallen over her husband's fake tomb, her melancholia immobilizes her, but not the poem or the speaker. Just as the swan is lost in the new versions of his artificial home, a lake of dust, the speaker is lost in Haussmann's Paris, frustrated by the failures of the Revolution of 1848 and the authoritarian Second Empire. As Chambers emphasizes, the poem is dedicated to Victor Hugo, one of the most famous political exiles of the regime. Indeed, the dedication confirms the text as a "disguised expression of revolutionary regret and of solidarity shown by someone exiled within an oppressive regime toward those who were exiled outside France after 1851" (161).[16]

Does the process of destruction and construction of the city provoke and intensify the "spleen," the internal exile? Or is the melancholic looking for motives that will justify his emotional state? Baudelaire's internal exile is both a political and an aesthetic position. The speaker connects his own melancholia, determined by the space, the changing Paris, with that of multiple nostalgic figures—the swan without a lake, Andromache without Troy, the black woman without Africa, the orphans without a home, the sailors without a ship, the prisoners, the vanquished, and the exiles—who also desire the impossible: to return to their place of origin.

Richard Terdiman reads the poetics of exile and loss of "Le Cygne" as a historical production: "Memory signifies loss. The memory crisis of post-Revolutionary Europe manifested itself in feelings of exile, anxiety, and displacement" (106). All the exiles in the poem are traumatized by the "without," the absence that determines their present state, and that is why they cling to memory, because it is their only anchor to the past. But how does Baudelaire change the way we read melancholia? This is not a Romantic melancholia that emerges from his own existential conflicts; the speaker is both moved by and stuck with melancholia because Paris changes, history takes its course, and the new hollow monuments of the Second Empire reiterate the shallow façade of progress.[17] Can melancholia be a collective experience? Does he share his melancholia with the rest of the social outcasts? In *Loss: The Politics of Mourning*, David Eng and David Kazanjian claim that melancholia is a "continuous engagement with the past" and that texts that focus on what has been lost also value what remains: "This attention to remains generates a politics of mourning that might be active rather than reactive, prescient rather than nostalgic, abundant rather than lacking, social rather than solipsistic, militant rather than reactionary" (2). Because melancholia produces a politics of mourning, melancholia is not timeless. The poetic representations of ruins as remains of the past and the melancholia they provoke are in fact fundamental to the construction of historical memory; they determine how we remember and read our own memories. "Le Cygne" is a poem about remembrance; and within the context of an authoritative regime, its melancholia for the past is not a reactionary stand, but on the contrary, it is a protest against collective amnesia.

Still, one may ask, how is this approach to melancholia particularly modern? How is this different from the Romantic notion of ruins and their anxieties about industrial progress?[18] Baudelaire's aesthetics react to, but at the same time stem from, Romantic visions of the extraordinary, even as we recognize that he distances himself drastically from the Romantic vision of nature by imagining an artificial paradise and uncovering its fake nature. Metaphors of negation abound in Baudelaire's and Cernuda's works because modern poetry constitutes itself as negative as it reacts against a previous tradition. Depersonalization, disintegration, and deformation are some of the negative terms that are appropriated by this poetics of disillusionment, where the Romantic sublime and the predominant "I" tend to perish, and the spleen, the grotesque, and the strange flourish.[19]

Luis Cernuda's poems on ruins exemplify this poetics of disillusionment in twentieth-century Spanish literature. Cernuda has often been called a "neo-Romantic" or a "post-Romantic" poet, but I do not want to read his work only through those categories. Like Baudelaire, Cernuda manipulated, parodied, and played with Romantic predicaments, while he also incorporated many of Wordsworth's and Coleridge's aesthetic ideals, seeing in Bécquer a Romantic precursor.[20] Nonetheless, Cernuda's "Otras ruinas" enacts a critique of decadent modern reality without nostalgically idealizing the natural and the mythical past. Cernuda's ruins are "other" ruins, not the same, not the typical.

Baudelaire and Cernuda respond to what Paz has called "la tradición de la ruptura," modern poetry's need to react against a traditional stance, for example the Romantic sensibility, while recognizing the relevance of its predecessors. Roberto González Echevarría, in his analysis of one of the most important Modernist poems in Spanish, José Martí's "Amor de ciudad grande," writes: "Toda poesía moderna surge, entonces, de un silencio y una negación: la de la poesía que la precede, el de un lenguaje que no adquiere sustancia poética sino en el acto de su propia constitución…" ("José Martí," *Isla* 27). The poetry of negation becomes keenly modern not only because it reacts against a canonical stance, but because it constitutes itself as "negative." Friedrich's reading of Baudelaire through negative categories could be in a way too reductive; however, it can be useful in the analysis of modern Paris and the ruined city.

Despite the great temporal gap between Cernuda and Baudelaire, they both react in a similar way to modern urban progress and its social tensions. But what is the basis for comparing poets from such different literary traditions? What makes a comparative analysis of Cernuda and Baudelaire interesting and feasible are the questions and the problems their poems raise. How do they project a poetics of disillusionment in their critique of progress? How are melancholia and nostalgia problematized in their texts? How and why is the city sexualized? In 1928 and 1929, Cernuda spent an academic year as a lecturer in Toulouse. Although he was already an avid reader of Baudelaire and French literature, his visits to Paris and his year as a lecturer in Toulouse were key for his development as a poet, especially in *Un río, un amor* (1929) and *Los placeres prohibidos* (1931). Cernuda reveals his early interest in Baudelaire's poetry in his autobiographical essay "Historial de un libro" (1958) and his admiration in "Baudelaire en el centenario de *Las flores del mal*" (1959).

Manuel Ulacia explains how French Surrealist thinkers also exerted an immense impact on Cernuda's work. He refers to André Breton's first *Manifeste du surréalisme* (1924): "Le merveilleux n'est pas le même à toutes les époques... ce sont les *ruines* romantiques, le *mannequin* moderne ou tout autre symbole propre à remuer la sensibilité humaine durant un temps" (Breton 26). Ulacia comments on the fake nature of Modernity, the facade of the world of commodities and comforts: "Breton parte de las ruinas románticas... para evocar un castillo; un castillo medio en ruinas, con un interior lleno de comodidades (la edad moderna)..." (*Luis Cernuda* 51). Diverse aesthetic movements explore the use of ruins as a symbol of a terminal era; however, Ulacia's reading of modern times as a ruined castle full of useless luxuries is closely connected to Cernuda's portrayal of the modern city in "Otras ruinas." Breton points to the fascination of each era with different forms of representation, either ruins that point to an architectural project, or mannequins, the life-size representations of the ideal body, whose ultimate function is to sell an image or a product. During the late twenties and early thirties, Surrealist aesthetics determine Cernuda's reading of Baudelaire's symbolism.

When confronted with the representation of Paris, Cernuda emphasizes the subtleties that characterize Baudelaire's paradoxical poetics:

> de un lado, la vida urbana moderna, de otro, la vida elemental inalterable. No se trata de aquel viejo *poncif* sobre la oposición ciudad y campo (Baudelaire, es bien sabido, detestaba el verdor y lo natural), sino una oposición mucho más sutil entre norte y sur, entre urbanismo y primitivismo... ("Baudelaire y el centenario" 1046)

Baudelaire's wild swan symbolizes the primitive and the bizarre in the urban sphere; the swan is one of the many misplaced subjects in *Tableaux parisiens,* as are the blind, the old, the prostitutes, and the poet. In Cernuda's version of the modern city, the primitive seems to be buried among the crumbled buildings, and the marginal figures of *Tableaux parisiens* are not really the protagonists of his poems.

The main character of the poem "Otras ruinas," from his book *Vivir sin estar viviendo*, is the city itself. Its aristocrats and its crowds come and go, and its streets are made for the passerby's convenience: "Hechas para los pasos del ocioso transeúnte, / El matinal jinete o la nocturna carretela" (*PC* 402). "Otras ruinas" recaptures Baudelaire's contradictory vision of a modern city in ruins, within a clearer critical position against the ambitions of capitalist progress.[21] Machines, the products of progress, have taken over the city; they have replaced the workers; and instead of portraying machines controlled by people, the tools themselves seem to control the city in ruins. Cernuda's text lacks Baudelaire's melancholic mood in "Le Cygne," where a sense of feeling lost and nostalgic in the new city is combined with a sense of enthrallment for the ugly faces of urban beauty. In "Otras ruinas" there is no nostalgia, no melancholia, and no allure. These ruins evoke the remains of the old buildings scattered unnoticed around the many new constructions of the modern city. Luis Fernández Cifuentes stresses that Cernuda may not be the first Spanish poet touched by the French poet's modern gaze, yet he is the one who reaches in his own way the "originarios postulados de Baudelaire" ("Miradas" 167).[22] Why are these poets looking at the past, anxious at its possible disappearance, instead of being mesmerized by the future? As Fernández Cifuentes suggests, Cernuda's gaze is not "anachronistic"; it is multiple, and perplexed by the paradoxical aspects of Modernity.

The first verses of "Otras ruinas" highlight Cernuda's critique of Modernity with the contradictory consequences of progress. Machines construct and destroy buildings, constantly re-shaping the urban landscape: "La torre que con máquinas ellos edificaron, / Por obra de las máquinas conoce la ruina" (*PC* 401). Cernuda's text thus immediately distances itself from the Baroque topos of the ruins, in which time and nature overtake the symbols of power and civilization. For instance, a Baroque poem like Rodrigo Caro's "Canción a las ruinas de Itálica" portrays the ruined houses of the Roman imperial leaders as invaded by plants and inhabited by lizards. The modern city in ruins is not overtaken by nature, but by the epitome of the artificial: machines. Cernuda also eschews a Romantic vision of ruins, where the external landscape is a melancholic reflection of the speaker's internal conflicts, his ruined self.

By contrast, modern poems on ruins historicize the process of destruction. Cernuda's poem does not specify a city, but rather criticizes the modern city, with its economic, political, and social circumstances; and he blames its apocalyptic end on modern humanity's ambition.

Critics have often overlooked "Otras ruinas," yet few poems by Cernuda exemplify so well the aesthetics of the modern city in ruins, crowded yet sterile, victim of its own contradictions. The personified ruins in the second stanza claim possession of the city walls, rotten, broken, and perforated: "La ruina ha clamado por suyos tantos muros / Sobre huecos disformes bostezando" (*PC* 401). The holes in the walls are metaphors of the personified, yawning ruin. Théophile Gautier's complaint about the unfinished character of Parisian houses, "leurs escaliers qui ne conduisent plus a rien," is echoed in Cernuda's verse "O tramo de escalera que conduce a la nada." The verse ironically reveals the futile function of a staircase in a building without floors and walls—a symbol of discontinuity, of modern ruptures. In the devouring project of reconstruction, progress as a rupture between the past and the future seems like an old staircase that leads nowhere.

Although in Cernuda's text, time and nature are not the destructive elements within the city, "Otras ruinas" does have a didactic purpose in common with the Baroque topos on ruins: namely, to invite its reader not to be vain and not to take for granted the emblems of imperial power. For the seventeenth-century eye, as exemplified in Francisco de Quevedo's "A Roma sepultada en sus ruinas," the Classical ruins of Athens and Rome expose the fugitive nature of what might appear permanent and eternal. "¡Oh Roma, en tu grandeza, en tu hermosura / Huyó lo que era firme, y solamente / Lo fugitivo permanece y dura!" (*Poemas escogidos* 141). Cernuda also underlines the recurrent paradox that the apparently everlasting emblems of power inevitably disappear:

> Intacto nada queda, aunque parezca
> Firme, como esas otras casas hoy vacías,
> Hacia cuyos salones las ventanas permiten
> El vislumbre de espejos, oros sobrecargados,
> Entre los cuales discurría la vanidad solemne
> De ilustres aristócratas… (*PC* 401)

Cernuda's paradox extracts a lesson from the empty houses that were once luxurious. In the following stanza, the parody of the ladies measuring their smiles and their teacups is resonant of T. S. Eliot's "Love Song of J. Alfred Prufrock."[23] Furthermore, Emilio Barón underlines how Eliot and Cernuda share a predominant interest in Baudelaire: "Cernuda y Eliot se presentan a sí mismos como los únicos en sus respectivos ámbitos culturales, capaces de justipreciar a Baudelaire" ("Retrato del poeta" 339).[24] They all parody the artificial harmony, and the hypocrisy of the modern city's bourgeois scene.

Cernuda worked on "Otras ruinas" from January 1946 until January 1949, and he considered a variety of titles, among them "Londres" and "Babel."[25] Cernuda had in fact lived in England from 1939 until 1947 and in London for the final two years. Thus, he witnessed the effects of the German bombardments and he suffered through post-war London. Even though Cernuda decided not to particularize the city in "Otras ruinas," the metaphor of the sterile city as a desert clearly alludes to Eliot's *The Waste Land*. Indeed, Cernuda's "Como desierto, adonde muchedumbres / Marchan dejando atrás la ruta decisiva / Estéril era esta ciudad" (*PC* 402) recalls Eliot's famous lines: "Unreal city… a crowd flowed over the London Bridge, so many, / I had not thought death had undone so many" (55). Eliot's verses, in turn, allude to Baudelaire's "Les sept vieillards" as well as to canto 3 of Dante's *Inferno*, where Dante encounters a crowd of Neutrals, those who were barely admitted into Hell. Cernuda's crowd, which leaves behind "la ruta decisiva," life, could be associated with the Neutrals, who leave the city sterile, without a future.

Cernuda's critique of capitalist society sustained by colonial products is intensified by the city's inability to produce food:

> Toda ella monstruosa masa insuficiente:
> Su alimento los frutos de colonias distantes
> Su prisa lucha inútil con espacio y con tiempo,
> Su estruendo limbo ensordecedor de la conciencia. (*PC* 402)

The speaker feels lost and disturbed, like the swan in Baudelaire's "Le Cygne,"[26] and the fast pace and the deafening noise of the city numb the people's conscience, creating a crowd analogous to the Neutrals, so despised by Dante. Unlike

Baudelaire's text, where men are captive victims, Cernuda's poem finally blames people for being accomplices in the city's absolute ruin: "El hombre y la ciudad se corresponden / Como al durmiente el sueño, al pecador la transgresión oculta" (402). The city and modern humanity are joined by a destructive symbiosis; people envision the city like the dreamer who is defined by the dream and the sinner by his transgression. Cernuda's poem on the city in ruins evokes the modern identity crisis and modern humanity's destructive inclinations, but without the nostalgia for a harmonious past.

Luis García Montero comments on the hopelessness and the identity crisis in García Lorca's and Neruda's poetry of the late 1920s and early 1930s:

> La dignidad melancólica se ve desplazada por el espectáculo de las basuras, los residuos, las huellas humanas como acumulación de desperdicios. La pérdida de confianza en los orígenes convierte la belleza emocionada de las ruinas románticas en un vertedero, y la voz del poeta acaba indagando en los sótanos fríos, en las habitaciones sin decoración sentimental... (*Los dueños del vacío* 108)

García Montero suggests that Modernity has transformed Romantic ruins into an accumulation of waste. Modern poets face emptiness and hopelessness, an existential crisis, when they find themselves searching for a lost identity, a lost sense of origins, in the cultural sewers. This vision of the modern city as a sterile place is central in *The Waste Land*. Cernuda's "Otras ruinas" projects the emptiness, and disillusionment, symptomatic of "el yo en crisis." The apocalyptic end of "Otras ruinas," "Del dios al hombre es don postrero la ruina," lacks a melancholic feeling. The past, represented in the once luxurious houses, is parodied, not idealized; it epitomizes what Ulacia described as "un castillo medio en ruinas, con un interior lleno de comodidades (la edad moderna)..." (*Cernuda* 51). The idea that modern progress entails a process of disintegration and destruction, a critique to the Hegelian notions of lineal history, has been paradoxically voiced by both politically conservative poets like Eliot and Marxist thinkers and poets like Benjamin and Neruda.

Cernuda's "Otras ruinas" is an allegory of the destructive nature of Modernity. Nonetheless, the constant reinvention and reconstruction of the city contrasts with its sterility and its lack of productivity.[27] In her book on Benjamin, Susan Buck-Morss indicates that for Baroque allegorists "the ruin was... emblematic of the futility, the 'transitory splendor' of human civilization, out of which history was read as a 'process of relentless disintegration'" (164). Buck-Morss quotes Benjamin to comment on how the Baroque ruin differs from his use of the ruin in *The Arcades Project* as "an emblem not only of the transitoriness and fragility of capitalist culture, but also its destructiveness" (164). Baudelaire and Cernuda convey through different lenses and diverse poetic traditions similar preoccupations in their portrayal of the modern city in ruins; they both want to prevent the historical remains of the city from being treated as waste. Baudelaire's conceptualization of Modernity's destructive nature provides the allegorical ground from which Cernuda's poetics of disillusionment stems.

But why is progress in its economic and cultural reconstruction of the city conceived as threatening and destructive? What roles do awakening and shock play in the aesthetization of the modern urban experience? Why is this further complicated with the sexualization of the city space and the representation of human ruins? So far, I have discussed the transformations of the public, exterior space, and how these poeticized ruins serve as a critique of the ideological discourse of progress. In the next section of this chapter, I will examine the interior space, the private rooms of Cernuda's "Habitación de al lado" and Baudelaire's "Rêve parisien" and "La chambre double" that stress the experience of awakening and the conflict between the real and the ideal, *spleen et ideal, la realidad y el deseo*—so crucial in both Baudelaire's and Cernuda's poetics. The human ruins, the phantoms of this modern city are also the leftovers of the discourse of progress. In Baudelaire and Cernuda aesthetization of collapse represents both an affirmation of the historical changes of the city and a critique of the bulldozers of modern progress.

The Other Room: The Shattered Dreams of Baudelaire and Cernuda

Hugo Friedrich writes in *The Structure of Modern Poetry*: "Reality, dismembered or torn to shreds by the power of imagination, becomes, in the poem, *a landscape of ruins*. Forced unrealities lie above it. Yet the ruins and unrealities convey the mystery and the secret for whose sake the poets write" (169; emphasis added). Cernuda's "Habitación de al lado" and Baudelaire's "Rêve parisien" and his prose poem "La chambre double" illustrate this evasion of a reality in shambles through a dream or an idealized space.[28] For example, "Rêve parisien" reconstructs an unreal space filled with abandoned castles and walls, surrounded by dreamy lakes and cascades. The only thing Parisian about this Parisian dream is that the "terrible paysage" of the city deforms it.

In these poems the shattering noises of time in the form of a pendulum and shocking knocks at the door of consciousness signal a deteriorated, unjust social reality. Cernuda's "Habitación de al lado," "En medio de la multitud," and "Remordimiento en traje de noche," and Baudelaire's "Rêve parisien," "La chambre double," "A une passante," and "Les Petites Vieilles" all evoke that imprecise, hidden mystery to which Friedrich alludes, a paradoxical reaction to urban beauty that both fascinates and disgusts. However, in this first stage of Cernuda's poetry one does not find the social critique of the urban space that permeates his later works and Baudelaire's *Tableaux parisiens* and *Le Spleen de Paris (Petits poèmes en prose)*. Baudelaire's spleen, revealed through the use of negative terminology, is produced not only by the emptiness and banality of modern expectations, but also by the impossibility of inhabiting the desired space, the dream. This juxtaposition between desire and reality, in its multiple evocations (social, emotional, economic, sexual), will also have its own voice in Cernuda's subsequent poetry books, as suggested by the title of his collection *La realidad y el deseo*.

Jonathan Culler and Jauss re-evaluated Friedrich's polemical argument about modern poetry's structural unity based on negativity. Indeed, Culler reconsiders Friedrich's theories on negativity when he analyzes Baudelaire's "Spleen" and the poet's tendency toward a depersonalized consciousness or subjectivity. Both "Rêve parisien" and "La chambre double" depict a loss of consciousness and an awakening, and Culler invites us to rethink their negative terminology:

> I want here to note simply that the predominance of negative categories in describing the experience of consciousness portrayed in these poems—loss, absence, destruction, alienation, banality, ennui, fragmentation, disintegration—leads

> to an association of value with operations of consciousness
> or the imagination, which endow this "landscape of ruins"
> with an aura of mystery, or which move toward self-aware-
> ness in their condition of desolation. ("On the Negativity of
> Modern Poetry" 194)

Culler's insight proves to be particularly useful for my reading of "Habitación de al lado," "Rêve parisien," and "La chambre double." The dreamed spaces represent an escape from reality and consciousness; they fill all the emptiness and the absences of the real urban place. Awakening becomes a traumatic experience precisely because it leads the speaker(s) to "self-awareness in their condition of desolation." "La chambre double" describes the real room as a "landscape of ruins," where everything is chaotic and rotten. The darkness, the shadows, and the nocturnal imagery of these poems contribute to what Culler called the "aura of mystery." Terms such as *mystery, beauty, reality, imagination*, and *memory* are often too vague or too abstract, but they can also be useful because of their lack of precision. Friedrich, Culler, and Jauss incorporate these terms, which are not necessarily always linked to negativity, intending to avoid the simplification of Baudelaire's aesthetics into dichotomies. Furthermore, Baudelaire in *Le peintre de la vie moderne* employs those terms to conceptualize a Modernity that emerges from economic and cultural crisis.

The crisis of perception in the nineteenth century defines modern ways of seeing, and it is determined by a crisis in the collective historical memory. In "Le peintre de la vie moderne," Baudelaire underscores the gap between perception and memory, where he asserts that both memory and imagination are the sources of all artistic work. In his seminal essay on Monsieur Guys, he explains an aesthetic and ethical imperative: to "capture" the marginal, grotesque, "new" faces of the period. In an attempt to further clarify the elusive term *modern*, Paul de Man and Marshall Berman propose divergent readings of the concept and of Baudelaire's poetics. Baudelaire to some extent had to deal with the paradox that "there is nothing modern about Modernity" while reacting to the disparities and disillusionments that arise from the economic, social, and political process of modernization (De Man 161). De Man maintains that Modernity is a temporal concept and that modern literary work has to be analyzed as part of a "continuous historical movement" (161) De Man highlights that whoever asserts his own Modernity has to recognize that his "claim to being a new beginning turns out to be the repetition of a claim that has always already been made" (161). The quest for originality and legitimization induces the poets to subscribe their work to new beginnings. This suggests a sceptical reading of modern poetry's pretensions to be original and new.

Certainly, the topos of ruins is not original or new. But what gives it a new interesting twist is how Baudelaire and Cernuda used it to describe the construction, and the destruction, of the modern city. Nevertheless, Berman's reply to de Man's claim is persuasive when he indicates that it "empties the idea of Modernity of all its specific weight, its concrete historical content" (133). Berman's analysis focuses on the inner contradictions of Baudelaire's aesthetics and how the process of modernization cannot be overlooked when discussing his poetry. In the flux between progress and decadence, each modern artistic movement reveals continuity with the past and a reaction against a tradition, a consecrated aesthetics. Baudelaire and Cernuda respond to different contexts, but they tackled similar challenges: how to capture the ephemeral and the permanent elements of their era and their respective cities, which situated their poetry within a particular historical framework. Ruins evoke the fragility of cities, as well as the fantasmagoric, eternal aura that remains. Throughout this book, I argue that the poetry of the modern city in ruins, which is often not particularized as Paris, Madrid, or Mexico City, provokes a tension in the poetic self. In these texts melancholia and nostalgia for the past are problematized, and we sometimes find a mythification of the poetic personae.

Philip W. Silver avows that Baudelaire and Cernuda ultimately share a sense of self, the aesthetic conscience of creating a poetic persona with every poem:

> Para Cernuda, como para Baudelaire, cada ataque contra la sociedad no es sino un medio más de definir el ser propio y mostrar cierta imagen del ser de los demás... Pero ya tengan como tema la figura del artista, la sociedad en que vive o la propia poesía, todos se encaminan al mismo fin: el de hacer inmanente en el poema el yo mítico del poeta... (*Luis Cernuda: El poeta en su leyenda* 215)

Their rebellious voices against the literary canon and social conventions define Cernuda's and Baudelaire's poetic personae and their myths. For example, Baudelaire's speakers are immersed in French cultural politics, and the mythification of the poet as a *flâneur,* as a visionary, as an internal exile of Paris, also situates the artist within a particular historical moment of Modernity.

Baudelaire, far from being lost in a distanced past, was for Cernuda very much part of the modern present. In 1959, Cernuda underlines in a conventional manner Baudelaire's international canonization: "Baudelaire no pertenece ya solamente a la tradición poética y literaria de Francia, sino a la de todo el occidente... es el primer poeta moderno" ("Baudelaire y el centenario" 1037). In this homage, Cernuda complains that the Hispanic literary tradition has not been appreciative of its debt to Baudelaire.

Cernuda's readings of *Spleen et Idéal* and *Tableaux parisiens* have left their mark on the surreal and clashing images of his collections, *Un río, un amor* and *Los placeres prohibidos.* But why read Cernuda with Baudelaire's aesthetics as an influential source? Would these literary borrowings diminish Cernuda's originality or the value of his poetry? I will let Cernuda himself answer this question. In a letter to Jaime Gil de Biedma, Cernuda reacts to the incorporation of one of his verses by the younger poet:

> No necesitaba disculpa alguna por utilizar un verso mío en un poema suyo. Un verso de otro poeta nos ofrece a veces nuestra propia visión o nos parece iluminar nuestra manera de ver un poema, de ahí lo natural que es incluirlo en el mismo. Eso es cosa legitimada por el uso de no pocos poetas, entre los cuales me limito a recordarle a Baudelaire y a Eliot. Yo lo he hecho también en alguna ocasión. ("Carta a Jaime Gil de Biedma," *Epistolario inédito* 66–67)

Coincidentally, Cernuda alludes to Baudelaire and Eliot as the main figures that "authorize" such intertextual poetic practice. Ulacia remarks on the constant intertextuality present in Cernuda's poetry: "Cernuda metafóricamente 'canibaliza' la tradición poética europea en sus diferentes expresiones desde el romanticismo hasta los diferentes movimientos de vanguardia" (*Luis Cernuda* 12). This form of cannibalization can be analyzed as appropriations, redeveloped inheritances, and in some cases, its study can shed some light into the enigmatic verses that abound in *Un río, un amor* and *Los placeres prohibidos.*

The fantastic and nightmarish scenery of Cernuda's "Habitación de al lado" (1929) can be even more enlightening and striking if reconsidered in connection with Baudelaire's "Rêve parisien" and his prose poem "La chambre double" (1862). The manuscript of "Rêve parisien" is dated March 1860, and it is dedicated to Constantin Guys, the painter who inspires "Le peintre de la vie moderne." The dedication already suggests that, just like the essay he would write in 1863, this is a poem more about his aesthetic vision than about Guys.[29] Nearly sixty years later, in July 1929 in Madrid, after he had spent nearly eight months as a lecturer in Toulouse, Cernuda wrote "Habitación de al lado." The three poems enact a moment of revelation or awakening through the metaphoric images of a dreamed space. The title of Cernuda's poem reminds me of "La chambre double," where the ideal, dreamlike room clashes with the putrid space of reality. The prose poem enacts an encounter with the Real, in connection with Jacques Lacan's definition of the term. Lacan's reflection on an awakening from a dream through a knock on the door highlights the gap between perception and consciousness and echoes Baudelaire's "La chambre double" and its own account of a traumatic awakening (Lacan 66–67). However, unlike Baudelaire's texts where the traumatic awakening becomes the climactic moment in the sphere of reality, Cernuda only represents "the other room," the place where the "durmientes" encounter death and the Ideal.

The first verse in "Habitación de al lado" coincides with the speaker's situation in Baudelaire's poems, when a dream, a "sudden night" of the mind, interrupts the middle of the day: "A través de una noche en pleno día / Vagamente he conocido a la muerte" (*PC* 151). These verses recall the first stanza of "Rêve parisien," where the encounter with a deathlike place is a "vague" memory that fascinates the speaker:

> De ce terrible paysage,
> Tel que jamais mortel n'en vit,
> Ce matin encore l'image,
> Vague et lointaine, me ravit. (*OC* 1: 101)

The vagueness of the image manifests the sensations of dreaming or remembering a dream in broad daylight. It evokes the metaphysical interlude that "La chambre double" illustrates with the metaphor of the eclipse: "un rêve de volupté pendant une éclipse" (280). The eclipse suggests a darkening, an interruption in consciousness, where dreaming becomes the manifestation of subconscious desires. The metaphor of the eclipse appears in "Habitación de al lado" in the first verse: "A través de una noche en pleno día" (*PC* 151)—a moment of darkness that becomes a revelation of death in the dream.

In "Habitación de al lado," the personification of death, through a highly charged adjective "lunática"—"moonlike and lunatic, having a metallic gaze"—alludes not only to the mythological figure of Diana in a hunting scenario, but also echoes the seductive, mysterious feminine eyes that encapsulate Eternity in "La chambre double." The power of the gaze of "l'Idole" in "La chambre double" projects both the speaker's attraction toward Ideal beauty and to Eternal death—another instance where *eros* and *thanatos* meet. In Cernuda's poem, death is portrayed as a solitary huntress; the fact that no whippet accompanies her is emphasized twice: "No la acompaña ningún lebrel" (*PC* 151). Death merges with the natural landscape, although she seems to suck the color out of the dunes and lakes of the dreamed space.

The natural landscape depicted in "Habitación de al lado" has more striking similarities with the fantastic world of "Rêve parisien" than with the furnished room of "La chambre double." The first section of "La chambre double" represents the room, its furniture, and its windows through a different light, beautified and idealized. The second part of the prose poem portrays the real, sordid room, from which the speaker wants to escape. "Habitación de al lado" and "Rêve parisien" do not describe the real, physical space in much detail. They concentrate on a subconscious room, painting only a ghostly landscape with "L'enivrante monotonie / Du métal, du marbre et de l'eau" (*OC* 1: 101). The first stanza of Cernuda's poem depicts disturbing images of the ruined place, inhabited by death: "Vive entre los estanques disecados, / Fantasmas grises de piedra nebulosa" (*PC* 151). Cernuda's ponds and stones have clear resonances of "les étangs dormants" and "des pierres inouïes" so prevalent in Baudelaire's "Rêve parisien" (*OC* 1: 102). In Cernuda's poem, death and its ghosts are also evoked in the "sombras blancas," the "pálidas dunas," and the "blancas lagunas" (*PC* 151). The transparency and the whiteness exalted by these images, similar to the greyish landscape paintings of J. A. McNeill Whistler, are different from Baudelaire's colorful poetic dreams, where blue, green, and pink predominate, despite the speaker's acknowledgment that "Et tout, même la couleur noire, / Semblait fourbi, clair, irisé" (*OC* 1: 102). In Cernuda's poem, death absorbs all the colors of the birds' feathers with her metallic gaze: "Con sus grandes colores formando un torbellino / En torno a la mirada fijamente metálica" (*PC* 151). Obviously, vision plays a fundamental role in the reading of these "painted poems" or "poetic paintings."

"Rêve parisien" emphasizes this desire to be read as a painting explicitly when the speaker describes himself: "Et, peintre fier de mon génie, / Je savourais dans mon tableau…" (*OC* 1: 101). The synaesthesia underlines the delight the speaker feels when he remembers and reinvents his dream, his own painting. Baudelaire acutely shows the constructed nature of this landscape: "Architecte de mes féeries / Je faisais, à ma volonté…" (1: 102). The poet's memory, his imagination, and his will are acknowledged as the creative forces that mold the text, in consonance with his aesthetics in "Le peintre de la vie moderne."

The magnetic imagery and the significant silence of "Rêve parisien" link the poem with the dreams of the prose poem and Cernuda's text. In "Rêve parisien" only the eyes allow us the revelation: "(…Tout pour l'œil, rien pour les oreilles!) / Un silence d'éternité" (*OC* 1: 103). The desire to capture the eternal elements of Modernity is one of Baudelaire's essentialist aesthetic prerogatives. The representation of death and the "Idole" evoke eternity, also foreshadowed by metaphors of silence in "Habitación de al lado" and "La chambre double."

Nature is mute in these poems. In Cernuda's verses, death only loves silent birds (birds are mute as is the secret nature of this space): "Ella con mucho amor sólo ama a los pájaros, / Pájaros siempre mudos, como lo es el secreto" (*PC* 151). The beings or the personified objects that inhabit these texts have a language of their own that contributes to the mysterious opaqueness and the semantic difficulties of reading a dream. In "La chambre double," the furniture of the room attains the qualities of that "vie somnambulique." The personification of the fabrics (probably curtains) attempts to reconcile the closed and the open, the private and the public space, the artificial and the natural, or as Cernuda put it, the urban and the primitive: "Les étoffes parlent une langue muette, comme les fleurs, comme les ciels, comme les soleils couchants" (*OC* 1: 280). Like Cernuda's birds, Baudelaire's fabrics in "La chambre double" speak a silent language, a visual language.

The inorganic in these poems paradoxically illustrates a natural landscape, or vice versa; as in the case of "La chambre double," Baudelaire develops metaphors of nature to depict furniture in a fantastic manner. Friedrich argues:

> In Baudelaire's eyes, the inorganic achieves its supreme significance when it is used as artistic material... such a strong equation of art and the inorganic can at best be found in the... baroque poetry in Spain and Italy... But even that era could never have produced a poem like Baudelaire's "Rêve parisien," the chief text of his spiritualization of the artificial and the inorganic. Not a real metropolis, but a dreamed city, deliberately artificial... (35)

Friedrich remarks on the absence of external, natural light, the stars and the sun, and the absence of humans and vegetation, to sustain the predominance of the inorganic. However, I am more inclined to interpret this imagery as a combination of the organic and the inorganic, the natural and the artificial. For instance, the "nappes d'eau s'épanchaient" (*OC* 1: 102) convey the longitude and the stillness of the water through the metaphor of the inorganic sheets.

"Rêve parisien" stresses the fusion of liquid and solid elements, metaphors that both contrast and complement each other: "L'enivrante monotonie / Du métal, du marbre et de l'eau" (*OC* 1: 101). Water is both personified and objectified, both still and restless, and it is everywhere in the poem: "Plein de basins et de cascades," "des cataracts pesantes," the "étangs dormants," "flots magiques," and "un ocean" (*OC* 1: 102). In Baroque poems of ruined cities, the river is always a symbol of the eternal elements of nature, which paradoxically survive the solid, but ephemeral constructions. These images of liquidity contrast with the abundance of stones and pillars in the ruined, dreamed city: "Babel d'escaliers et d'arcades, C'était un palais infini" (*OC* 1: 102). "Rêve parisien" depicts a solid city, made of "des murailles de métal," "des colonnades," and "des pierres inouies" (*OC* 1: 102), surrounded by water. But what makes this dream particularly Parisian? Baudelaire inscribed the dream in contrast to the Parisian landscape, where the anxieties and the pressures of modern reality provoke the need to escape to an ideal and surreal space. Although I do not want to imply that there is nostalgia for a pre-modern past in Baudelaire's dreams, there is a prevalent frustration with the Parisian process of modernization.

Baudelaire's disillusionment and the modern crisis of perception are also shown through the metaphors of blurred vision and lack of clarity found in these texts. The elusiveness of a dream and the need to remember it are part of the modern mnemonic crisis, before it changes with the blink of an eye. "Rêve parisien" merges the organic and the inorganic, the liquid and the solid as exemplified by: "Des cataractes pesantes, / Comme des rideaux de crystal, / Se suspendaient, éblouissantes / A des murailles de metal" (*OC* 1: 102). The representation of windows, curtains, and rain provide a framework of perception in both this text, the prose poem, and "Habitación de al lado." The speaker's eyes, like the windows or crystals of the poem, could be blurred and transformed by the layers of water and fabrics that fall like waterfalls, "des cataractes." The actual double meaning of *cataractes* raises the question of blurred vision, by pointing also to the medical term of the eye disease, cataract; in French, it is the same, *cataractes*.[30] Therefore, the rain through the windows is both a metaphor of the reading process and a visual metaphor for the deformation of reality.

Fabrics, as emblems of the inorganic, abound in both "La chambre double" and "Habitación de al lado." The imagery of "La chambre double" captures the pouring rain and the distorted windows of the room: "La mousseline pleut abondamment devant les fenêtres et devant le lit; elle s'épanche en cascades neigeuses" (*OC* 1: 280). The silk fabrics refer to the imagined white curtains in front of the windows, exploiting the metaphor of rain or cascades that fall like tears. When the speaker wakes up and recognizes the decrepit furniture, the fancy curtains disappear, with "les tristes fênetres où la pluie a tracé des sillons dans la poussière" (*OC* 1: 281). The traces of the rain and the dust accentuate the murky ways of looking at reality through those windows. The silky curtains that framed the speaker's encounter with his Idol in his bed are also metaphors of the multiple layers of vision prevalent in the prose poem.

Clearly, what lies beneath the covers of the dream are the commodities of the bourgeois ideal, the material luxuries of silk not only dress and cover the *real*, but even the windows, the text that frames the real. Part of the frustrations of both Baudelaire and Cernuda with the modern project is that the ideal of economic success is only reachable for some in the form of an unattainable dream. In Cernuda's text, velvet like "mousseline" is illustrative of the idyllic, soft beauty: "con sus bosques, / donde el cazador si quiere da caza al terciopelo" (*PC*: 151). The enigmatic image of a hunter in this dreamed forest hunts "terciopelo," which can refer to both the meaning of the elegant, exotic fabric, or to a type of serpent called *macagua terciopelo*. Although the idea of hunting serpents makes more sense than hunting fabrics, in the oneiric logic of the poem I propose that "terciopelo" is used as velvet, the soft fabric. The final verses describe the sleepers as clouds, resembling the very nature of the ghosts they encounter in the first stanza:

> Y los durmientes desfilan como nubes
> Por un cielo engañoso donde chocan las manos,
> Las manos aburridas que cazan terciopelos o nubes
> Descuidadas. (*PC* 151)

The image of hands that attempt to touch the impossible, the clouds, is a metaphor for the aesthetic project of capturing that ideal beauty. If we consider Baudelaire's "La chambre double" in this reading of Cernuda's poem, it is not difficult to visualize the windows as the "cielo engañoso donde chocan las manos." In a metonymic relationship the hands of the bored spectators "hunt" or try to catch the velvet pieces, which I read as possible curtains covering the windows that frame the deceitful sky. As in Baudelaire's prose poem, the fabrics are covering and dressing the ideal, the unapproachable.

The final verse in "Habitación de al lado" alludes neither to death nor to the bored hands, but to the speaker himself: "Sin vida está viviendo solo profundamente" (*PC* 151). The paradox of living without life underlines the experience of dreaming and discovering a face of death. Even if in the verse he used the third person and not the first, the adjective *solo* points to a masculine figure, who could be "el durmiente" or the speaker himself. The final adverb *profundamente* also alludes to the act of sleeping deeply. C. G. Bellver's reading of death in Cernuda's Surrealist texts ties them to T. S. Eliot's poetry:

> Eliot suggests that having lost its contact with the past and because of its spiritual sterility, our age may know only an existence synonymous with death. This same Baroque conceit of death-in-life appears in Cernuda's poetry, especially in his surrealist pieces, where paralysed or corpse-like beings… illustrate both his own and mankind's suspended existence. ("Luis Cernuda and T. S. Eliot" 113)

The Baroque paradox "sin vida está viviendo," alluding to San Juan de la Cruz's and Santa Teresa de Jesús's mystic poems, both titled "Vivo sin vivir en mí," points in Cernuda's text to a very different form of alienation and to the anxiety of the modern city. The paradox of life without life can also be read in connection with the poem in the same collection, "Estoy cansado." There, Cernuda underlines the link between the speaker's state of apathy and his critique of the city in ruins: "Estoy cansado de las casas, / Prontamente en ruinas sin un gesto…. / Estoy cansado de estar vivo, / Aunque más cansado sería el estar muerto…" (*PC* 152). On a humorous note, the speaker prefers to be tired of being alive than tired of being dead. Cernuda's "Estoy cansado" echoes the frustrations of an existential crisis and the lack of energy, also evoked in Neruda's "Walking Around." Bellver's notion of suspended existence signals how the speakers are dreaming in a state of suspension from reality. However, in "Habitación de al lado" the sleeper or the speaker does not wake up. Unlike the traumatic awakenings in Baudelaire's poems, Cernuda chooses to represent only the dreamed vision of death. The trauma occurs inside the dream, when full of fear the sleeper faces death: "¿Por qué soñando, al deslizarse con miedo, / Ese miedo imprevisto estremece al durmiente? / Mirad vencido olvido y miedo a tantas sombras blancas" (*PC* 151). The speaker invites us and the sleepers to face those ghosts, conquering fear and forgetfulness. In Cernuda's poem the fear that we sense in "La chambre double" and "Rêve parisien" when the speaker wakes up is experienced before, in the dream itself; Cernuda's dream is a form of awakening, a revelation.

The awakening in "La chambre double" and "Rêve parisien" stages one of the most traumatic issues of Baudelaire's urban poetics: the dictatorship of Time, often personified as a ruthless force. In "Rêve parisien" there is no specific Idol or feminized death as in Cernuda's poem, since the eyes that appear are the speaker's, and when he awakes, it seems that his eyes still show the remnants of that luminous vision: "En ouvrant mes yeux pleins de flamme / J'ai vu l'horreur de mon taudis" (*OC* 1: 103). Friedrich's concept of empty ideality in "Rêve parisien"—images "glittering to the eye and uncanny to the soul"—refers to the speaker's awakening, which proves to be even more shocking because of his sordid feeling of emptiness. Awakening becomes a traumatic experience because he has to return to himself and his reality: "rentrant dans mon âme" (*OC* 1: 103).

Baudelaire's poems reflect an acute sense of temporality, highlighted by the speakers' awakenings and disturbing encounters with Time. De Man, in his critique of Friedrich's historicist project, quotes his *Structure of the Modern Poetry*: "in Baudelaire 'idealization no longer, as in the older aesthetic, strives toward embellishment of reality but strives for loss of reality'" (172). De Man links this loss of reality with both the loss of representation and the loss of the self, characteristic of modern poetics. In "Rêve parisien" awakening to reality means a return to the self, a return to temporality.

In both "La chambre double" and "Rêve parisien" the dreamed space is characterized by its silence, while modern reality is marked by the sounds of the clock, the pendulum whose voice we hear. The contrasts between vision and sound, dream and reality, ideal space and the urban space ultimately depict time as fissure. The first part of "Rêve parisien" privileges metaphors of vision, in contrast to the last two stanzas, marked by sound.[31] In "Rêve parisien," the dictatorship of time provokes a traumatic awakening:

> La pendule aux accents funèbres
> Sonnait brutalement midi,
> Et le ciel versait de ténèbres
> Sur le triste monde engourdi. (*OC* 1: 103)

Time is linked to death when the pendulum produces funeral sounds. In "Rêve parisien" time does not arrive as in "La chambre double" with "un coup terrible," a knock at the door, but it is also violent. However, in contrast to these two poems, in "La habitación de al lado" a different face of death emerges, one that lives in a timeless place.

For Cernuda, death is encountered in sleep, in dreams. For Baudelaire, awakening from the ideal is traumatic because it makes him see life as a time bomb and reality as a vehicle that will lead to death. It is frequent to find in several of Baudelaire's poems *funèbres* rhyme with *ténèbres*; but here these adjectives are particularly suggestive because they describe the sky in the middle of the day, possessed by a metaphoric night or invaded by the multiple clouds that we also find in Cernuda's "cielo engañoso." The cloudy, dark sky responds to a break with consciousness manifested in the dream. This darkness, which characterizes many modern poems on ruins, allows another form of vision, the awakening that both Cernuda and Baudelaire seek in their poems.

Baudelaire's "La chambre double" represents the speaker's awakening as a shocking, mnemonic experience: the dream is shattered into pieces. Benjamin emphasizes that "indeed, awakening is the great exemplar of memory: the occasion on which it is given to us to remember what is closest, tritest, most obvious" (*Arcades Project* 389). Therefore, remembering can also be a way of awakening. In "La chambre double" it is with horror that the speaker remembers his reality, his room in ruins, and the traces of time: the dusty furniture, the dirty fireplace, "l'almanac où le crayon a marqué les dates sinistres!" (*OC* 1: 281) Time and reality can be heard in the knocking at the door, the sound of the clock, or as Benjamin suggests, the ringing of the hand bell. In reference to the Dream House, Benjamin comments: "The despotic terror of the hand bell, the terror that reigns throughout the apartment, derives its force no less from the magic of the threshold. Some things shrill as they are about to cross a threshold" (*Arcades Project* 88). In the threshold of awakening, dream and reality border with each other; in "La chambre double," it is the speaker who shrills with horror at the realization that he has regained consciousness of Time.

The dictatorship of Time and the modern shock experience in Modernity is what divides the ideal from the spleen in

Baudelaire's "La chambre double," where duality is emphasized by the title itself.[32] The prose poem begins with the dream-like description of a room, where objects and furniture fuse with nature and its language. The room seems to represent a wish-fulfilling space. The Idol, who controls that universe, is a woman, "queen of dreams," whose eyes like the sun's flames "traverse le crépuscule," or "pierce the twilight." Her eyes devour: "Elles attirent, elles subjuguent, elles dévorent le regard de l'imprudent qui les contemple" (*OC* 1: 280). The speaker recognizes the "black stars" of this female gaze that attract and subjugate, a recurrent poetic motif in "A une passante," "Les yeux de Berthe," and "Les promesses d'une visage."

The Idol, the symbol of this "supreme life" in the eroticized room, contrasts with the Spectre, the shadow of time and social responsibilities. The dichotomy between the Idol, the epitome of desire, and the Spectre, a metaphor of reality, enacts the tension arising from the title of both Baudelaire's *Spleen et Idéal*, and Cernuda's *La realidad y el deseo*. Nonetheless, just when the speaker realizes that in the dream world of "La chambre double," time has disappeared and the desired "Eternity reigns," time makes its grand appearance in the form of a knocking at the door—"Un coup terrible, lourde, a retenti à la porte" (*OC* 1: 281)—and the speaker receives it as a violent "coup de pioche dans l'estomac" (*OC* 1: 281). Reality is suddenly a nightmare that knocks at the door of the unconscious to bring him back to the real chamber. With his brutal blow the Spectre strikes the Idol, and the ideal room. The decadence of the furniture, the coldness of the place, and the fetid odor contrast with the harmony, the warmth, and the perfumes of the luxurious room. The dream should be read as a representation of a bourgeois space that contrasts with the poverty of the furniture, the mess of the unfinished manuscripts, and the disgusting smell of stale tobacco. The only thing that the speaker welcomes when he wakes up is "la fiole de laudanum," the bottle of opium that will help him evade reality again. The traumatic awakening is not only represented by the shock of the violent knocking at the door, but also by the effects of coming back into consciousness. From the disappearance of time ("Le temps a disparu"), we pass to a sudden "le Temps a reparu; le Temps règne en souverain maintenant" (*OC* 1: 282). The capital letter emphasizes the shift from time to a personified, all-powerful Time. He awakes to "Souvenirs, de Regrets, de Spasmes, de Peurs, d'Angoisses, de Cauchemars, de Colères" (281). The repetitive sound of the seconds, strongly and solemnly, that from the pendulum say "Je suis la Vie, l'insupportable, l'implacable Vie!" announces the dictatorship of time, intensified by the alternative reality that results from hallucinatory drugs. Then, the speaker's awakening to the implacable Life in the form of Time makes him realize the imminence of Death. The portrayal of an internal space, the crumbled and ruined room, highlights Baudelaire's critique of modern progress. The avaricious city enters in the form of a Spectre, a vision of Death and the machine of Time, which disrupts any dreams of escaping his decadent reality. Commenting on another of Baudelaire's poems, Benjamin asserts that: "This time is outside history, as is that of the *mémoire involontaire*. But in the *spleen* the perception of time is supernaturally keen; every second finds consciousness ready to intercept its shock" ("On Some Motifs," in *Illuminations* 184). To be conscious of the "real" chamber he needs to remember; to see he needs to recognize first: "Horreur! Je me souviens! Je me souviens!" "La chambre double" depicts the violent knocking at the door of consciousness as the provoker of a traumatic awakening, as a blow not just to the stomach but also to the mind.[33]

In "La chambre double" the speaker recognizes and remembers the objects in his room, which reiterates the split between those two clashing worlds. When Baudelaire speaks of the "true artist," embodied in Constantin Guys, he maintains that: "Il dessine de mémoire, et non d'après le modèle... En fait, tous les bons et vrais dessinateurs dessinent d'après l'image écrite dans leur cerveau, et non d'après la nature..." ("Le peintre de la vie moderne," *OC* 2: 698) In the *Arcades Project* Benjamin associates the moment of awakening with the moment of remembering, and "La chambre double" literally reenacts that encounter. However, here Benjamin refers to a way of "doing history that presents itself as the art of experiencing the present as waking world" (389).

Can we read Baudelaire's prose poem as one that implies a collective awakening into history? This dreamlike, luxurious, a-temporal room can be associated with the collective desires of economic progress, but the speaker's awakening cannot be read as one that has collective historical dimensions. The speaker of "La chambre double" realizes that he has stopped dreaming when he feels the existence of time. More than an awakening into history, one finds an awakening into time and death. In this sense, his regaining consciousness of reality is a kind of temporal awakening, where one can read an implicit political critique of the marginalization of the artist in the urban space and how he is reduced to no space of his own.

An analysis of "La chambre double" and "Rêve parisien" in comparison with Cernuda's "La habitación de al lado" attempts to introduce the links between their modern poetic projects and their representations of the dreams and the ideal place. These three texts are characterized by an internal space, a room (literally and metaphorically) in which we find the tensions of modern reality, its ruined landscape, and the dreams produced by the expectations of progress. In modern poetics, the topos of the city in ruins is not limited to an architectural space, as we see through these texts the ruins of progress invade the mind, the ultimate interior landscape. The metaphorical implications of ruins in these imaginary landscapes can also be connected to Baudelaire's and Cernuda's debt to Romantic aesthetics. The effects of modernization and the urban space in the representation of the body, and in the case of these three poems, its traces in the subconscious, can be read as another way of portraying the speaker as *a ruin amidst ruins*. And yet, these poems convey a political and social critique of the causes of those ruins; the trauma of an unjust, devouring reality is what provokes the dreams of escaping or losing reality. Therefore, the dream of an alternative space to the modern city and an awakening into reality become crucial steps toward the construction of the topos of ruins in modern poetics.

The poems I will discuss now represent an exterior space, the street. Baudelaire's "A une passante" in *Tableaux parisiens* and Cernuda's "En medio de la multitud" in *Placeres prohibidos* and "Remordimiento en traje de noche" in *Un río, un amor* also enact in the urban scene the shock experience and a sudden awakening. The awakening to reality complicates the poetic topos, where ruins are not merely contemplated or observed, but experienced and lived. These poems situate the speaker in the middle of the crowd, both present and absent. The encounter and loss of gazes conveys the fleeting and the eternal, expressing Baudelaire's aesthetic notion of "la mémoire du présent" ("Le peintre," *OC* 2: 696). Through this notion, memory is a sponge that absorbs both the emblems of modern beauty—a woman in black or a ghost—and the feelings of frustration and fear faced by the individual lost in the urban crowd. Cernuda and Baudelaire explore the modern ruins through both dreamed and real rooms, public and private spaces.

In the Middle of the Street: Revisiting Baudelaire's and Cernuda's Modern Urban Poetics

"Baudelaire dedicó una parte de su atención a la existencia de la gran ciudad donde vivía, París, y a las formas de vida que presentaba... la modernidad como detalle" (Cernuda, "Baudelaire en el centenario" 1045). Cernuda emphasizes Baudelaire's intention: the depiction of Modernity needs to focus on certain details that may seem marginal or unimportant at a distance, but in his aesthetic project they constitute its core. Modern details such as the displaced swan, the muddy aura, the deformed old maids, and the passerby's gaze portray, more than an urban landscape, the embodiment of the unseen, the unspoken character of the modern city in ruins.

Baudelaire's "A une passante" has been compared to some of Cernuda's poems, in particular by Emilio Barón Palma and Luis Fernández Cifuentes. But Barón Palma, in contrast to Fernández Cifuentes, limits his study of the influence of Baudelaire on Cernuda to a juxtaposition of poems, without textual analysis. Barón Palma's simplistic commentary refers to "En medio de la multitud" as an example of the theme of loneliness: "Tema esencial en la poesía de Cernuda es la soledad: amor a la soledad, horror a la compañía no deseada... Alguien que despierta nuestro deseo más hondo, para desaparecer, al instante, entre esa muchedumbre anónima que nos oprime y nos hace perder la posibilidad de ese ansiado contacto. Tema propio de Baudelaire..." ("Baudelaire en Cernuda" 84).[34] Barón quotes Baudelaire and suggests that the interrelations between the poems are so obvious that they do not need explanation. Even if loneliness is permanently present in Cernuda's urban poems, it does not automatically follow that he despises crowds.

In Baudelaire and Cernuda, the speakers are able to extract the beautiful and the disturbing from their immersion in the crowds. Barón comments that Baudelaire's poems are characterized by "soledad del cuarto… oscuridad, horror hacia los otros y hacia el mundo urbano exterior…" (84). In my view, Barón misread these texts; Baudelaire is not horrified by the crowd. As Benjamin stresses: "As regards Baudelaire, the masses were anything but external to him; indeed, it is easy to trace in his works his defensive reaction to their attraction and allure" ("On Some Motifs," in *Illuminations* 167). In both "En medio de la multitud" and "A une passante" we find that the crowd is an integral part of the poem, a central character; rather than an obstacle, the crowd promotes human encounter.

In a quite different project from Barón's work, Fernández Cifuentes analyzes the relevance of "A une passante" as a foundational text in modern poetry and examines its presence in Cernuda's poetics. Fernández Cifuentes explores the links between Baudelaire's poem and Cernuda's "En medio de la multitud":

> Es evidente, a primera vista, que los atributos fundamentales de la mirada urbana y amorosa de Baudelaire se despliegan aquí con parecida explicitud: la multitud; el suceso o la escena del insistente "pasar"…; la movilidad de la mirada amorosa; la "ciudad" que ya no sólo se nombra como tal sino que se sugiere casi infinita, en ese "sin rumbo" y "anduve más y más"… ("Miradas" 168)

The gaze becomes a medium of communication in a space that triggers the alienation of the individual, navigating in the overwhelming city crowd. Movement and fluidity are emphasized by the rhythm and the imagery of these poems, where instances and figures vanish as quickly as they appear. The encounter of the gazes in "A une passante," "En medio de la multitud," and "Remordimiento en traje de noche" stages diverse forms of awakening.

"A une passante" reproduces a typical scene of the *modern* city and exemplifies Baudelaire's conceptualization of Modernity, where Modernity is embodied by both the transitory and the eternal as he explains in "Le peintre de la vie moderne." "A une passante" catches the fugitive moment of the meeting of gazes.

The shift from perception to memory is the first step in the creative process. The poem enacts both the desire to remember and the desire to know. As Peter Brooks explains in *Body Work*: "The drive for possession will be closely linked to the drive to know, itself most often imaged as the desire to see. For it is sight, with its accompanying imagery of light, unveiling, and fixation of the gaze, that traditionally represents knowing, and even rationality itself" (9). Brooks refers to the desire to possess and know the body by the predominantly male gaze in Western artistic and philosophical tradition. Vision, the most abstract of the senses, is the highest and most valuable in the Platonic hierarchy. Baudelaire's penetrating gaze wants to capture Modernity, and in a parallel act, he wants to control the feminized urban landscape. In poems like "A une passante," "Les yeux de Berthe," and "Promesses d'un visage," the male gaze desires to know and master the eyes, the face, the body, which seem so mysterious and unknowable. It is through the meeting of gazes that "A une passante" dramatizes the appearance and disappearance of love and desire in the modern urban scenario. Griselda Pollock in her feminist reading of vision indicates, "The gaze of the flâneur articulates and produces a masculine sexuality which in the modern sexual economy enjoys the freedom to look, appraise and possess, in deed or in fantasy" (79). She recalls Benjamin's reading of "A une passante" and remarks, "The poem is written from the point of view of a man who sees in the crowd a beautiful widow; he falls in love as she vanishes from sight" (79). Pollock's insightful reading on the sexual tensions projected in the spaces of Modernity points to a revealing factor in Baudelaire's poem: the male gaze is the medium, the translator, the narrator of the meeting of gazes. Yet she obviates the relevance of the female gaze in the text; by looking back the woman passerby is also enjoying the freedom to look and possess. Nonetheless, the reader is only left with the effect of her look: her "regard" is like an "éclair," a flash of light that leaves the speaker hanging in the night once she vanishes.

The meeting of gazes has a shocking effect on the speaker, but we do not know how the woman reads his gaze. This impossibility disturbs Janet Wolff, who discusses how women are invisible in the nineteenth-century public spaces and how Baudelaire's depiction contributes to the misogynistic literature of Modernity, even as he tries to incorporate marginalized women as central characters of the city:

> The prostitute, the subject of the poem *Crépuscule du soir...*
> elicits a similarly ambivalent attitude of admiration and dis-
> gust... More unequivocal is Baudelaire's sympathy for those
> other marginal women, the old woman and the widow; the
> former he "watches tenderly from afar" like a father, the lat-
> ter he observes with sensitivity to her pride, pain and poverty.
> But none of these women meet the poet as his equal. They
> are subjects of his gaze, objects of his "botanizing." (42)

Wolff criticizes the literature of Modernity and its sociology as limited to the experiences of men. She argues that by equating the modern with the public, male thinkers such as Baudelaire, Benjamin, Simmel, and recently Berman and Sennet, have ig-nored the experiences of women, restricting them to the private space. Nevertheless, she signals the relevant role of women in Baudelaire's poetics, particularly his fascination with the pros-titutes, the old women, and the widows. These women were not "flâneuses," but they participated in the city life, although it is obvious that women did not have the same freedom to stroll around the streets of a metropolis as men did. I do not want to imply that Baudelaire's discourse is not misogynistic, but I do not want to disregard it or dismiss it just because it is. Baude-laire's ambivalence toward women as subjects of Modernity complicates his discourse and permits him to write a text like "A une passante," which Wolff recognizes as exceptional:

> The nearest he comes to a direct encounter with a woman
> who is not either marginal or debased is in the poem "A une
> passante"... The tall, majestic woman passes him in the busy
> street; their eyes meet for a moment before she continues
> her journey, and the poet remains to ask whether they will
> meet in eternity. Her return of his gaze is confirmed in the
> last line. (42)

As Wolff recognizes, the lady in "A une passante" is dressed in black, which implies that she is a widow. Nonetheless, the speaker's gaze is full of desire, not compassion nor a fatherlike, condescending tenderness. Wolff's is a legitimate critique, and yet when she complains that the literature of Modernity only narrates the male experience, she only alludes to George Sand and she fails to discuss the works of other nineteenth-century women writers who have become part of the modern literary canon, such as Renée Vivien, Flora Tristán, Emilia Pardo Bazán, Rosalía de Castro, and Elizabeth Browning, among others. The meeting of gazes in "A une passante" may not represent a sexual revolution, or even a scent of sexual liberation, but it does convey the possibility that the speaker, the ultimate subject of the poem, becomes also an object of the other's gaze. She is lost in the crowd, where we sense the fugitive face of Modernity.

But is she lost in the crowd? What does this mean in the context of nineteenth-century Paris? Pollock suggests that for the bourgeois woman "to maintain one's respectability… meant not exposing oneself in public. The public space was officially the realm of and for men" (69). Is the passerby, the possible widow, exposing herself to the menace of the male gaze? If she is a widow, does this mean that she has more freedom to walk alone among the city crowds? Her dress and her movements identify her as a bourgeois woman, yet she is also a transgressor of the masculine space. She is walking alone and dares to look back at the speaker, the flâneur, the consumer of eyes. Pollock highlights, "The spaces of modernity are where class and gender interface in critical ways in that they are the spaces of sexual exchange" (70). The urban crowd is emblematic of the modern space; sexual exchange is not only materialized when female bodies are treated as commodities, it is also powerful in the meeting of gazes, in the manifestations of desire. The passerby will remain imprinted in his memory and in his text because she is just that, a passerby; her disappearance intensifies the speaker's frustrated desire to see, to know, to possess.

Eyes and gazes, sight and vision point to the presence of time and desire in the modern city, the painting of Modernity in "A une passante." In the poem, the city might not be represented explicitly as in ruins, since it is mainly the force behind the encounter, the background that determines the outcome of the frustrated love story. However, Baudelaire's critique of the modern city dominates the text when we think of the implications of the end of love or lack of love in the urban space. The hustle and bustle of the city, its lights and movements, re-created in this poem may also remind us of Edgar Allan Poe's "Man of the Crowd" and Wordsworth's "Residence in London." "La rue assourdissante autour de moi hurlait": the street is howling like an uncontrollable beast. Still, the animalization of the city is perceived not so much through the visual image, but through the sounds that arise from the street. Through the atmosphere drawn in the first verse of "A une passante," as in "Rêve parisien" and "La chambre double," sound signals the city and its untamed pace, while vision responds to an interruption, a moment of complicity and desire, attached to Baudelaire's notions of an ideal flash of beauty. The pressures of time and the movements of the crowd aggravate the rapidity of the instant when the speaker casts a glance upon the passerby and meets her gaze.

In his analysis of the shock experience in Baudelaire's poem, Benjamin also comments on the anonymity of the crowd:

> In the sonnet "A une passante" the crowd is nowhere named in either word or phrase. And yet the whole happening hinges on it... this very crowd brings to the city dweller the figure that fascinates. The delight of the urban poet is love—not at first sight, but at last sight. It is a farewell forever, which coincides in the poem with the moment of enchantment. Thus the sonnet supplies the figure of shock, indeed of catastrophe. ("On Some Motifs," in *Illuminations* 169)

Benjamin refers to this lady in "A une passante" as a figure of shock because she incites the speaker's realization that eternal love and beauty are found and lost in an instant in the modern city. Here, the shock experience is closely tied to "Rêve parisien" and "La chambre double," where the awakening to reality is a traumatic moment.

"A une passante" distinguishes itself from other poems because it tells a story; it is not merely the description of a seductive woman, it is also an anecdote of the encounter. But within the anecdote, the speaker depicts the passerby. The poem re-creates the moment seemingly as it flees. As the woman approaches the speaker, we perceive her figure, then the color of her costume, "la douleur majestueuse" associated with mourning clothes, her elegant movement, and finally her gaze. The woman appears to embody the harmony that Baudelaire avows belongs to the era she represents: "chaque époque a son port, son regard et son sourire" (*OC* 2: 695). Her "jambe de statue" underscores the paradox and the tension between the moving figure and the unmoving statue. This tension also projects her symbolic significance, the ephemeral nature of her movements versus the eternal image of her static leg. Her body is as beautiful as a sculpture, and her agile and noble movements seduce the eye of the beholder. She is in continuous action: "Une femme passa, d'une main fastueuse / Soulevant, balançant le feston et l'ourlet." The poem transcends the pictorial limits of description and re-creates the action by becoming a sort of camera that follows her own particular way of walking and moving. Benjamin also evokes the power of the returned gaze. This is not the passive, objectified woman; she is observed and she dares to look back.

Jonathan Crary in his historical analysis of vision in Modernity considers that "the problem of the observer is the field on which vision in history is said to materialize, to become itself visible" (5). Although Crary is not referring to literary texts in his work, some of his theoretical standpoints can shed light on "A une passante," a poem in which vision becomes visible. The gaze in "A une passante" is the protagonist of the text, and by materializing the field of vision in the crowded streets of Paris, Baudelaire also depicts the gaze as a historical product. It is not only the subjective encounter of gazes, since it is placed within a context, marked by the loud noises, the rapid movement, the sea of people which permits the meeting, but which absurdly triggers its frustration. By making vision visible in the poem, Baudelaire also cements his aesthetic ideas of "Le peintre de la vie moderne": the work of art begins with a visual experience—perception molded by memory and imagination, although ultimately the urban space reduces love to a fleeting, ruined, doomed desire.

Still, her gaze will always be remembered, and therefore it will live in "l'éternité" of his memory and of the poem itself. In the poem the gaze is the only form of communication in the modern city. The apostrophe to the woman "Ô toi que j'eusse aimée, ô toi qui le savais!" establishes her absence. In reality her gaze has disappeared with the crowd, and the speaker alludes to the ephemeral nature of that instant and the irrevocable power of time with the violent image of "un éclair," a metaphor of an awakening or vision. The modern crowd gives rise to these fugitive encounters, both a cause and a consequence of the modern city in ruins, urban anonymity, and the fast pace of progress. Ultimately, the modern city is in a constant process of destruction and reconstruction, making what is fugitive, and ephemeral, a permanent trait of its space. "A une passante" stages Baudelaire's aesthetics of the memory of the present, and the frustrations that emerge in a modern city, often represented as paradoxically in ruins.

The passerby in Cernuda's "En medio de la multitud" also represents the fugitiveness of Modernity. This prose poem does not dwell on the description or the encounter of gazes; instead, Cernuda concentrates on the effects of the passerby in the speaker's body. Interestingly, the poem seems to be dated April 14, 1931, the day the Spanish Second Republic was proclaimed. However, Cernuda's sympathy for the Republican, democratic ideals is not voiced in the poem, where politics do not seem to dominate the urban crowd. The poem's structure and surreal style differ greatly from Baudelaire's sonnet; and the incorporation of a woman's reaction to this specter opens and complicates the field of vision:

> En medio de la multitud le vi pasar, con sus ojos tan rubios como la cabellera. Marchaba abriendo el aire y los cuerpos; una mujer se arrodilló a su paso. Yo sentí como la sangre desertaba mis venas gota a gota. Vacío, anduve sin rumbo por la ciudad. (*PC* 176–77)

There are considerable differences between "A une passante" and this prose poem. For example, the passerby is a masculine figure, and the only features that distinguish him are his eyes and his hair, both blond. The specter or ghost, as suggested at the end of the poem, arouses an immediate reaction from a woman, who upsets the dual structure of the speaker and the passerby prevalent in Baudelaire's "A une passante." Her admiration for his beauty makes her kneel, treating him as a divine vision. The speaker's reaction is less sudden. Cernuda represents the speaker's livid state as the product of this shocking experience. In a metaphorical leap, the specter like a vampire sucks the speaker's blood, or to be closer to the poem, his blood abandons his veins, as if life deserted his body.

The woman who kneels in the middle of the street is a figure of disruption. Unlike in "A une passante" there is no reciprocity in the gazes, and desire is complicated further with Cernuda's homoerotic imagery and his portrayal of both male and female forms of desire and awe. Like the lady in Baudelaire's poem, the quick pace distinguishes the specter's movements and the violence he causes: "Marchaba abriendo el aire y los cuerpos" (*PC* 176). Yet the specter seems unaware of the rest of the world. José María Capote Benot's study of Cernuda's Surrealism mentions this poem's oneiric imagery yet he foregoes a thorough analysis because he considers it too hermetic and difficult.[35] Nevertheless, he underscores an important aspect of the text, it is written in the past, and this suggests a past, dreamed experienced.

The crowd molds the urban space in this poem. The "multitud" is not only emphasized by the title and the first verse, but also in the feeling of emptiness produced by the vision and the speaker's immersion in the crowd: "Gentes extrañas pasaban a mi lado sin verme" (*PC* 177). The ambiguous meaning of the verse portrays a realistic situation in the modern city, in which an alienated subject feels ignored and erased in the crowd; the speaker can see but cannot be seen. The imperfect verb *pasaban* shows an action in progress. The strange people seem odd because there is a barrier of visibility between them and the speaker. Ironically, the field of vision is made visible in this poem by the speaker's invisibility. The speaker's journey in Cernuda's poem leads him to a literal emptiness of the body, his metamorphosis into a ghost. It is interesting that he transforms himself through a walk around the city: "Anduve más y más" (177). In another vanishing act like the specter's disappearance in the crowd, the speaker stumbles upon a body that melts at his touch: "Un cuerpo se derritió con leve susurro al tropezarme" (177). The disappearance of the speaker's body may be related to de Man's argument that the loss of reality is linked to the loss of representation and the loss of the self (172).

Death is manifested by this gradual loss of the body. The feet, the hands, the voice that fade away announce his final shocking realization: "No sentía mis pies. Quise cogerlos en mi mano, y no hallé mis manos; quise gritar, y no hallé mi voz. La niebla me envolvía" (*PC* 177). His journey around the city seems to stop when he discovers he has no feet to walk with and when he feels that the fog blurs his vision. A similar state of blurred vision characterizes the speakers of all the poems discussed. C. G. Bellver has analyzed this imagery as signs of Cernuda's obsessive sense of loneliness in the city: "The fog that envelops this specter suggests his spiritual annihilation, and his loss of vigor and of sensory perception serves not as a social comment on the city but as a poetic reproduction of the disorientation and the impotence that constitutes Cernuda's loneliness" ("The City as Antagonist" 160). I agree with Bellver in that "En medio de la multitud" is not a poem about social condemnation. Resentment does play, however, an important role in this text, as an abstract feeling that acquires literal and metaphorical weight. The speaker's body has ceased to exist, and what bothers him is his heavy life, his past. There is no turning back. Paradoxically, he cannot liberate himself from life because he is dead: "estaba muerto y andaba entre los muertos" (*PC* 177). In a similar ending to "La habitación de al lado," roaming through the city enables him to face a death-in-life experience in another form of awakening.

The speaker in "En medio de la multitud" becomes the ghost, similar to the figure with an aura he perceives in the first verse. In comparison to "A une passante," there is a different form of representation of death and desire in the urban space. The lady in black in "A une passante" is a symbol of both the ideal and death; her gaze produces both light and darkness: "Un éclair… puis la nuit!" The moment of vision both kills and restores to life: "le plaisir qui tue…Fugitive beauté / Dont le regard m'a fait soudainement renaître / Ne te verrai-je plus que dans l'éternité?" (*OC* 1: 92–93). She embodies both the fugitiveness of life and the eternity of death and the enduring vision engraved in a poem. Fernández Cifuentes alludes to these verses in particular, in his analysis of "A une passante" and "En medio de la multitud":

> Desde luego, a través del poema de Cernuda, el centro de gravedad parece situarse más bien en "le plaisir qui tue," pero no sólo por el mismo "jamais" pueda arrastrar connotaciones de muerte y el resto del poema resulte, entonces, densamente poblado de señales de mortalidad—desde el luto de la "passante" o la estatua luctuosa que se identifica con ella, hasta la noche y la eternidad—sino también… porque

> ese "renaître" que parece colmar de vida la escena urbana
> de Baudelaire y justificar la interpretación de Benjamin...
> contiene, sin embargo, para Cernuda un inesperado mensaje
> de muerte. ("Miradas" 170)

In rebirth we can sense another form of death; as Fernández
Cifuentes notes, in Cernuda's "Lázaro" we find the final verses
of "En medio de la multitud": "que yo era un muerto / andando
entre los muertos" (*PC* 177). Paradoxically, the awakening of
the resurrection is an awakening to death. Neither "A une passante" nor "En medio de la multitud" is a poem that depicts a
city in ruins, but they both capture the fleeting encounters with
desired subjects in the urban scene, stirring the traditional topos
eros and *thanatos*, and transgressing the palpable divisions
between death and life, the ephemeral and the eternal, conventional paradoxes in the modern topos of ruins. Baudelaire's
attempts to portray the city and its forms of desire in ruins lead
him to use contradictory terms, which seems to indicate that
it is impossible to constrain Modernity to one definition. As
I indicated previously, Capote Benot dismissed "En medio de
la multitud" precisely because of the difficulty in finding defi-
nite answers to the poem's oneiric and surreal logic. However,
Capote Benot does recognize the text's similarities with "Remordimiento en traje de noche": "Si comparamos este poema
con 'Remordimiento en traje de noche,' por ejemplo, vemos que
el tema de uno y de otro son similares; la niebla, la presencia de
la muerte, ese cuerpo vacío que pena de amor, la soledad y la
incomunicación entre los hombres" (153–54).

Naturally, Cernuda's "Remordimiento en traje de noche," the
poem that introduces *Un río, un amor* (1929), has closer connections with "En medio de la multitud" than with Baudelaire's
"A une passante." Thus, the discussion of "Remordimiento en
traje de noche" may clarify some of the enigmatic images in
"En medio de la multitud." The poem begins with "Un hombre
gris avanza por la calle de niebla" (*PC* 143). Unlike "En medio
de la multitud," this poem seems to evoke an empty foggy street,
but the second line "No lo sospecha nadie. Es un cuerpo vacío"
reveals that there are others that see him but do not see his emptiness. However, unlike Baudelaire's poem and "En medio de la
multitud," the crowd does not have real predominance here. The
specter of Modernity in this poem is not the crowd, but the grey

man, the shadow, the ghost, the hollow body, ultimately consecrated in its title, "Remordimiento en traje de noche."

The body of the grey man is empty just as nature for Avant-
garde poetics has become empty. His body is "Vacío como la
pampa, como mar, como viento. / Desiertos tan amargos bajo
un cielo implacable" (*PC* 143), an echo of Eliot's *Hollow Men*.
Manuel Ulacia makes an interesting point about the title of the
collection *Un río, un amor*: "Inicialmente esta colección iba a
llamarse 'Cielos sin dueño'... El título es revelador porque...
Aquí no hay dios: el cielo ha quedado sin dueño. Tanto el
hombre como las geografías simbólicas ('pampa,' 'mar,' etc.)
están vacíos como el cielo. En esta composición la divinidad
no puede ser más el modelo deseado" (*Cernuda* 144). It is
particularly striking if we remember the woman's reaction in
"En medio de la multitud" to the specter as if he was the emblem of a divinity. Although kneeling could be both a sign of
adoration and of plea, it suggests his power over her. Unlike the
prose poem, in "Remordimiento en traje de noche" there is no
first person and there is no other woman; the poem seems to be
"narrated" in third-person singular, and it refers to its readers
in second-person plural. The natural spaces that are evoked, the
pampa, the sea, the desert, are all part of the emptiness and the
loneliness of these figures.

The night is the temporal space that predominates in both
"En medio de la multitud" and "Remordimiento en traje de
noche," as in many of Baudelaire's *Tableaux parisiens*. The
darkness and the opaqueness of the night symbolize the internal
state of the speaker and highlight the visual metaphors of reading dreams or surreal images. The night becomes the biggest
shadow of all, the resentment that follows the speaker in his
journey through the city. The grey man with wings is like Benjamin's "angel of history," in this case the shadow of a personal
past, the metaphorical night of resentment:

> Es el tiempo pasado, y sus alas ahora
> Entre la sombra encuentran una pálida fuerza
> Es el remordimiento, que de noche, dudando,
> En secreto aproxima su sombra descuidada. (*PC* 143)

The personification of resentment as an anonymous grey man, a
doubt-ridden being who pursues his own shadow, echoes life as
a heavy load to bear in "En medio de la multitud": "Me pesaba

la vida como un remordimiento, quise arrojarla de mí. Mas era imposible, porque estaba muerto y andaba entre los muertos" (*PC* 177). Resentment does not vanish with death. The grey man of resentment continues to linger, unperceived. Time and life seem to continue their course without being bothered, and as in many poems about ruins, nature takes over: "La yedra altivamente / Ascenderá cubriendo los troncos del invierno" (143). Although this is not a poem about the city in ruins, it shares some of the characteristics of the topos; here, nature's invasion and power is over nature itself, not over the monuments of the past.

Time, dressed as a grey man or a shadow, dominates reality and nature. However, it seems to be impossible to be felt, to touch or to approach: "No estrechéis la mano" and "¿No sentís a los muertos?" (*PC* 143). These are the only instances when the speaker refers directly to the readers, and they point out our inability to react or even to comprehend. Although I cannot avow that Cernuda had Dante in mind when he wrote this poem, these verses remind me of Dante's *Purgatorio* VI and XXI. In canto VI, Virgil and Sordello embrace each other when they recognize themselves as fellow poets and fellow Mantuans. The embrace provokes an intermission and Dante's digressive speech about the corrupt state of Italy. The problems of representation explored in the *Divine Comedy* are once again dramatized: poets tend to confuse shadows with reality. In canto XXI, the situation is restaged when another poet, Statius, wants to embrace Virgil in a gesture of admiration, but he refuses:

> Già s'inclinava ad abbraciar li piedi
> al mio dottor, ma el li disse: "Frate,
> non far, chè tu se' ombra e ombra vedi."
> Ed ei surgendo: "Or puoi la quantitate
> comprender dell'amor ch'a te mi scalda,
> quand'io disiento nostra vanitate,
> tratando l'ombre come cosa salda."
>
> (353, lines 130–36)

> Already he was bending to embrace my teacher's
> feet, but he (Virgil) told him: "Brother, do not, for you are
> a shade and a shade is what you see."
> And he (Statius), rising: "Now you can grasp the
> greatness of love that burns in me toward you,
> when I forget our emptiness,
> treating shades as solid things."
>
> (353, lines 130–36)

This sign of humility from Virgil marked by the "brother" implies that they are equals as shadows and that Statius does not have to honor his feet. Nonetheless, the relevance of the scene lies in Virgil's wise recognition of who they are and their situation. The imperative in Cernuda's poem, "No estrechéis la mano," responds to the same futile gesture of attempting to have contact with a shadow. The challenge of poetic representation is difficult to meet when shadows must embody the empty, the disembodied death. The paradox of the empty body, also developed in Rafael Alberti's *Sobre los ángeles* and Federico García Lorca's *Poeta en Nueva York,* alludes to the Baroque conceit in "Habitación de al lado": "Sin vida está viviendo solo profundamente" (*PC* 151). Cernuda's poems portray an encounter with death and time in the form of a dream or of a surreal vision.[36] The hollow men, and their emptiness, depicted in these poems respond to a political critique of Modernity and its effects on the individuals, who become an anonymous mass in the urban space. Baudelaire and Cernuda, as well as Eliot, Paz, and Neruda, represent the city as one in ruins to criticize modern progress's ventures, but they also insist that their speakers assume responsibility and face, with resentment, the emptiness that consumes them.

Cernuda's and Baudelaire's works dramatize the loss of the body within the clash of the ideal and the real in the modern city. The preponderant role of vision as a source of knowledge and creation inserts modern poetry in the tradition of Platonic philosophy; yet, it also reveals a crisis in representation in the impossibility of grasping the passing elements of the modern city, constantly changing. By analyzing visual metaphors of desire and death, trauma and awakening in the modern city in ruins, I reconsider Baudelaire's aesthetic project and how it is read and manipulated in Cernuda's poetic work. "A une passante," "En medio de la multitud," and "Remordimiento en traje de noche" are not paradigmatic of the topos of ruins but, as I suggest in this book, the topos does not consist only of broken or destroyed architectural spaces. The body in ruins, described as empty or fragmented, is key in the representation of the topos in modern poetics, as exemplified also by Eliot, Paz, and Neruda. These three texts portray a decadent atmosphere, and they may even respond to the tension of death and human ruins in the urban sphere; however, these poems' relevance in the context of my discussion here resides in their depictions of the crowd, in how love and desire end in ruins in the modern city.

But let's be more explicit, why then are these poems pertinent to the analysis of the topos of ruins in modern poetry? These texts lay the groundwork for Baudelaire's and Cernuda's critique of modern progress, and they further complicate the detailed web of correspondences in their portrayal of a modern city and its traumatized, invisible, and visible subjects. Although Crary is mostly considering the connections between science, technology, and art in the construction of vision, he poses a poignant question: "How is the body, including the observing body, becoming a component of new machines, economies, apparatuses, whether social, libidinal or technological?" (2). In these texts, Cernuda and Baudelaire portray their speakers not just as subjects but as observing bodies, interacting in a social and libidinal sphere, marked by the crowd and the city's development. The modern subject's perception and memory are manipulated by the social economy of the city. These three poems show how desire is transformed by the changing modern city and how it is complicated by the tension of the permanent and the fleeting in Modernity.

Cernuda's "Ruins": The Ultimate Historical Allegory?

Cernuda's "Las ruinas" best exemplifies his rereading of the Baroque and the Romantic ruins, from a modern perspective and through a "rebellious" discourse. "Las ruinas" was written in England in 1941, twelve years after the poems I have just discussed in *Un río, un amor* and *Placeres prohibidos*, but before "Otras ruinas." Rather than comparing this text with Baudelaire's poems, I find that his essay "Le peintre de la vie moderne" articulates his aesthetic ideas about Modernity and is key in Cernuda's conceptualization of the eternal and the fugitive in Modernity. Cernuda's "Las ruinas" evokes ancient and absent ruins; the imaginary journey brings them to life, and the poem reconstructs the city. But this reconstruction does not imply a restorative nostalgia in Cernuda's project. There is no nationalist sentiment that calls for the restoration of the past. "Las ruinas" does not specify which city it refers to, although some critics have suggested that it is "una visita imaginaria a

Pompeya" (Silver, *Luis Cernuda* 212).[37] Despite the fact that it can be read as an allegory of Modernity and that it is clearly about the ruins of history, this is not a poem on the modern city in ruins. Still, Baudelaire's aesthetics complicate Cernuda's reading of the topos and his reaction to the social, religious construction of God as the symbol of eternal life.

Cernuda wrote "Las ruinas" with an alternative title, "Campos de soledad" (*PC* 799). It is the second poem of *Como quien espera el alba* (1941–44), a collection written between his time in Oxford and Glasgow and during World War II. Some critics and contemporary poets often tend to read Cernuda's poetry as a literary biography, a product of his melancholic, lonely, tortured self.[38] I will avoid that line of reasoning because Cernuda's distance or lack of it when it came to his poetic production is difficult to measure with precision, which some critics purport to possess. In a similar note, he has been called a Romantic poet. Luis Antonio de Villena suggests that Cernuda's poetry is characterized by his "gusto por la soledad" and his "continuo idealismo" (75). These characteristics could also be attributed to Góngora, Garcilaso, Dante, Donne, or T. S. Eliot; thus, in my view, solitude and idealism should not be the cornerstones for the argument that Cernuda is a Romantic poet.

Philip Silver has approached this issue from a more soundly methodological and convincing standpoint. He asserts that Cernuda's solipsistic vision of the world and his readings of Holderlin, Leopardi, and the English Romantics recast his poetry and confirm him as a High Romantic poet.[39] The problem with Silver's interpretation of Cernuda as a High Romantic is that it seems to encompass a great part of his poetry, and although there are solipsistic, melancholic poems with a strong Romantic vein, there are many others that do not fit the description. Poetry constantly defies this impulse to categorize it. Poems like "Otras ruinas" distance themselves from the Romantic version of the city, and even a poem like "Las ruinas," in dialogue with the Romantic topos of ruins, also alludes to the Baroque tradition, to Symbolist aesthetics, and to Cernuda's own modern prerogatives.

"Las ruinas" begins with the description of nature usurping the ruins covered by grass. The first stanza represents nature taking over the works of civilization, which could be read close to both a Romantic and a Baroque conception of the topos. The alternative title Cernuda gave to this poem, "Campos de soledad," is a direct quote from the first verses of Rodrigo Caro's "Canción a las ruinas de Itálica": "Estos, Fabio, ¡ay dolor! que ves ahora / *campos de soledad*, mustio collado / fueron un tiempo Itálica famosa" (in Rivers, *Poesía lírica* 289; emphasis added). It is possible that Cernuda changed the title either for the sake of originality or because there are already many references to Caro's classic text.[40] It may also be that he did not want to emphasize so much the word *soledad*, especially considering that his first verse depicts a lonely site: "Silencio y soledad nutren la hierba" (*PC* 323). Nature is nurtured by silence and solitude, by the absence of humans and culture. On a different note, there is another wink to the reader, an allusion to Bécquer's "Volverán las oscuras golondrinas" ("Rima 53," *Rimas* 20) with the lines: "Mientras la golondrina con grito enajenado / Va por el aire vasto…" (Bécquer, in Cernuda, *PC* 323). Bécquer's famous poem established the swallow as a symbol of the Romantic sensibility in the Spanish tradition. Cernuda's verse can be read as a way of honoring Bécquer as well as a transformation of the image, a parody of the swallow, not playful and melancholic as in Bécquer's text, but alienated and disturbed. In this sense, the swallow's "grito enajenado" is comparable to the poem itself; the poet and the swallow both seem to be lost, exiled from the group, witnesses to the ruins.[41]

Luis García Montero, in his analysis of the city in modern poetry, compares Bécquer's role in the Hispanic tradition to Baudelaire's in the French: "Bécquer representa en la cultura española el papel urbano de Baudelaire" (*Los dueños del vacío* 105). Although I would not go so far—I consider Bécquer aesthetically tied to Romantic metaphors from which Baudelaire wants to break free and distance himself—García Montero is right in interpreting Bécquer's letters as insightful readings of the pace of modern reality:

> En las *Cartas literarias a una mujer*, Bécquer defiende una lírica seca, breve, eléctrica, versión estilística de la velocidad. Por eso, en la "Carta IV"… El paseante "sólo se tropieza con rotas columnas y destrozados capiteles, mudos sarcasmos de la loca aspiración del hombre a perpetuarse." La síntesis y el simbolismo son la versión lírica de la velocidad, de una

realidad sometida a la alegoría infinita y precipitada de encarnar la ausencia. (105)

García Montero's revealing analysis undeniably focuses on an anxious Bécquer—the disillusioned reader of the failures of progress and its aspirations of eternity. Just as Baudelaire's *Tableaux parisiens* depicts the daily performances of the city's quick pace and its pressures, Bécquer also seems to abhor the emptiness of its reconstructing project and its rhythm. As García Montero suggests, poetic symbols such as ruins aim to concretize, embody the absence; poems on ruins intend to represent what remains, but they also point to what is missing. Why do I emphasize Bécquer's role as a bridge between Baudelaire and Cernuda, especially when I claim that Cernuda cannot be categorized as a High Romantic? Mainly, because I want to show the Bécquer to which Cernuda reacts; not to assert that Cernuda was a descendant of both Bécquer and Baudelaire, but to argue that he is interested in the various critical versions of progress when he consciously explores the topos of ruins. In his essay "Bécquer y el poema en prosa español," Cernuda situates Bécquer in the French tradition of the prose poems. Bécquer is just like Bertrand, Baudelaire, and Rimbaud, "cansados de la versificación mecánica" and, like them, tries to "crear para la poesía un instrumento libre de las convenciones": the prose poems (Cernuda, "Bécquer y el poema en prosa español" 986). Cernuda delves into the genre of prose poems in *Ocnos*, but he has already explored it in poems like "En medio de la multitud." "Las ruinas" is not a prose poem, but there are stanzas with strong prosaic undertones, and the allusion to Bécquer in the beginning announces the poem's intertextual dialogue.

In "Las ruinas," along with Caro's site of solitude and Bécquer's swallow, the grass, the leaves, and the silver moonlight paint the ruined scene. There is a great silence that weighs upon the place, yet the ambiguous personification of the leaves seems to suggest the presence of the absent, the ghosts who inhabited the city in ruins: "Las hojas en las ramas tiemblan vagas / Como al roce de cuerpos invisibles" (Cernuda, *PC* 323). From these ghostly, abstract presences we perceive the concrete, marble ruins in the second stanza. The ruins are illuminated with the foggy, dreamlike light of the night: "...las ruinas de mármol, / construcciones bellas, musicales, / que el sueño completó" (323). The marble ruins could be sculptures, emblematic of Greek and Roman art, but they could also be grandiose monuments, now incomplete, torn apart by time and history. Nonetheless, the poem portrays itself as an act of imagination from the very beginning. The dreamlike journey into the ruins is a journey into the past; it is a process of reconstruction.

The third stanza states the didactic purpose of the Baroque poems on ruins: "Esto es el hombre." This verse marks the beginning of the core of the poem and its final repetition announces its dénouement. The reader is called upon to look, just as Caro did with the apostrophized Fabio. Humanity is equal to its remains and its works: "Mira / la avenida de tumbas y cipreses, y las calles / Llevando al corazón de la gran plaza" (Cernuda, *PC* 324). The imagery indicates a vertical and a horizontal landscape, an avenue made both of tombs, symbols of death, and of trees, symbols of life. These metaphors describe a natural landscape that may have replaced the city, yet it continues to reveal its presence: "Todo está igual, aunque una sombra sea / De lo que fue hace siglos, mas sin gente" (324). The didactic purpose of the poem reappears once again in the paradox: the cycle of life leads into a cycle of ruins—the certainty of death. As in a dream, the poem must rebuild the city, a shadow of what it was, with the shadows of its inhabitants.

The representation of the river as the witness of history is a recurrent element in the topos of ruins. The apostrophe to the Guadalquivir River in Góngora's "A Córdoba" and the reference to the Tiber in Quevedo's "A Roma sepultada en sus ruinas" both remark on the Heraclitian paradox of the river, whose flow is permanent and eternal in comparison with the fugitive nature of human constructions. The fourth stanza in "Las ruinas" echoes this traditional representation of the river, clearly contrasted with the "titánico acueducto" and the "arcos rotos y secos" (Cernuda, *PC* 324). The aqueduct and the arches are symbols of the Roman civilization in Spain; they represent the control of water, its distribution, and its manipulation once it goes through the architectonic construction, the aqueduct. But in the poetic present, the aqueduct and the broken, dried arches are all covered with plants, "el mirto" and "la anémona." They lie in ruins while the personified river fools death: "En tanto el agua libre entre los juncos / Pasa con la enigmática elocuencia / De su hermosura que venció a la muerte" (324). Just as in Neruda's *Alturas de Macchu Picchu*, the river is a vehicle of communication with the past, even though it lingers on, mysterious and impenetrable. In "Las ruinas," the only survivor of death and time is the water, which remained free from the constraints of the aqueduct, "agua libre."[42] In this well-structured poem, the life embodied by the river, an emblem of nature, is in the fifth stanza in juxtaposition with death, encapsulated in the empty tombs and urns.

Individuality disappears; the dead inhabitants are all a vast, anonymous mass of death. Only the receptacles survive, but empty of their contents: "En las tumbas vacías, las urnas sin cenizas, / Conmemoran aún relieves delicados / Muertos que ya no son sino la inmensa muerte anónima" (Cernuda, *PC* 324). Unlike Caro's poem, in which we don't have the stones with the written names of the dead, the history of Itálica's people—"Casas, jardines, césares murieron / y aún las piedras que de ellos se escribieron" (in Rivers, *PL* 290)—in Cernuda's text, they do have names. But Cernuda's speaker chooses not to focus on the meaning of those "relieves delicados." Instead the dead in "Las ruinas" are absorbed by death itself, and their names as well as their tombs become anonymous, classless, and sexless. In Caro's "Itálica" there are heroes and saints to name and remember; it is not a classless society that mourns its city. Cernuda, in contrast, decides to portray death as anonymous and as an equalizing force. In Baroque aesthetics, as I will discuss in the third chapter on Eliot and Paz, there is a continuation between the city in ruins and its human ruins. In his essay on ruins in Cernuda's poetry, Antonio Colinas emphasizes how "La ruina se desdobla en los versos de Cernuda. La ruina humana (el *niño muerto, Lázaro*) aparece junto a una determinada ruina-piedra: la tumba" (136).[43] The city of tombstones highlights the preponderance of human ruins in Cernuda's work. The tombs are compared in Cernuda's "Las ruinas" to the other empty and useless remains humans have left behind—their jewelry, their perfume bottles, and their sexual talismans. Colinas indicates that Cernuda's lesson, learned from the ruins, "es la dura y vacía lección del tiempo histórico," and that is why the individual "se ve obligado a gritar con la mirada… y a través de ella recibir… borrosas respuestas—signos, símbolos—en el pasado arrasado… en un tiempo sin fechas y sin nombres: es la lección de las ruinas" (136). Cernuda's "prendas," "pomos," "sortijas y joyeles" are all remnants of the past, without the specificity of dates, but marked by the intransigence of time.

Ironically, stones have replaced humans. The only path that connects us with the past is reached through the stones, symbols of the construction of the city and its destruction. The stones, the columns, the square, the altars, the city walls are not only what constitutes the city in ruins, they are depicted as silent witnesses of both public and private history: "… las columnas / En la plaza, testigos de las luchas políticas, / Y los altares donde sacrificaron y esperaron, / Y los muros que el placer de los cuerpos recataban" (Cernuda, *PC* 324). The personified columns are witnesses of their political conflicts, the altars can give testimony of their religious rites and brutality, and the walls are the accomplices of their erotic lives. As in Caro's "Itálica," "Las ruinas" describes almost architectonically the city, "lo que resiste al tiempo." But as the speaker denotes in the seventh stanza, men embrace the strongest paradox; they are able to conceive the eternal, the surviving elements of time, yet they themselves are mortal: "hechos de esa materia fragmentaria / Con que se nutre el tiempo" (325). Cernuda's vision is slightly macabre; instead of remarking that life nurtures and constitutes humanity, he concentrates on death as its backbone: "Ellos en cuya mente lo eterno se concibe / Como en el fruto el hueso encierran la muerte" (325). Ultimately, Cernuda refers to the poet himself as someone who dreams of eternal works, yet his body is as doomed to die as anyone else's.

The eighth stanza signals a change in tone. Cernuda abandons the description of the ruins and his dialogue with the Baroque and the Romantic topos, and he reproaches God for the mortal nature of human beings. The use of apostrophe is often found in poems on ruins, and its function is to claim the presence of the absent. This part marks the speaker's rebellious attitude against the possibility of an eternal life beyond this one, but ironically and interestingly, it is the most prosaic moment of the poem. The speaker's rhetorical questions challenge God in a move similar to Baudelaire's swan in "Le Cygne," convulsively moving its neck upward to the sky, "Comme s'il

adressait des reproches à Dieu!" (*OC* 1: 86). Cernuda first affirms that God made humans and in the next stanza he negates
His existence. When in the eighth stanza he addresses God,
he stresses our mortality as the stamp of our humanity: "Oh
Dios. Tú que nos has hecho / Para morir, ¿por qué nos infun-
diste / La sed de eternidad, que hace al poeta?" (*PC* 325). The
speaker confronts God's sense of irony; poets are doomed to a
frustrated desire for eternity. Cernuda's position is not close to
Huidobro's "creacionismo"; the speaker's desire is conscious
of its own incapacity to infuse eternity in his poetic, earthly
works. Thirst for eternity hurts precisely because he is certain
that there is no water. Silver also emphasizes the relevance of
this poem in Cernuda's *ars poetica*: "'Las ruinas' es un poema
decisivo, pues también contiene el credo del poeta, en el cual
afirma que es la sed de eternidad lo que hace al poeta, esto es, el
impulso de hacer permanente lo efímero" (*Luis Cernuda* 212).
Cernuda and Baudelaire both specify in their poems and essays
that the tension between the eternal and the fugitive elements
of Modernity is at the core of the modern poet's aesthetic questions. Baudelaire argues in his essay on modern aesthetics that
the duality of men is projected in art: "Considérez… la partie
éternellement subsistante comme l'âme de l'art, et l'élément
variable comme son corps" ("Le peintre de la vie moderne," *OC*
2: 686). Nevertheless, Cernuda's perspective is much more pessimistic. Art, just like ruins, is determined by its concreteness,
its body, and therefore, it is always vulnerable to the passage of
time and history.

In "Las ruinas" Cernuda creates a surprising effect in the beginning of the ninth stanza. The text's rhetorical questions cannot be answered because they are just attempts. Nevertheless, if
God does not exist, why continue to talk to Him?:

> Mas tú no existes. Eres tan sólo el nombre
> Que da el hombre a su miedo y su impotencia,
> Y la vida sin ti es esto que parecen
> Estas mismas ruinas bellas en su abandono:
> Delirio de la luz ya sereno a la noche,
> Delirio acaso hermoso cuando es corto y es leve. (*PC* 325)

When Cernuda's speaker declares that God does not exist and
is just a name, not only does he overpower His shadow, but he
defines Him as fiction, a dream that brings consolation, easing

humanity's fear of death. Cernuda seems to imply that people need to believe in God because of their fear of facing time, and the present. Ruins represent life without God, a city without its inhabitants. Cernuda's defiant attitude toward God and religion can also be linked to his criticism of progress and its social values. As Paz suggests in his essay on Cernuda, "La palabra edificante," "La poesía de Cernuda es una crítica de nuestros valores y creencias; en ella destrucción y creación son inseparables... Su hostilidad ante el cristianismo no es menor que su repugnancia ante las utopías políticas" (139). Paz underlines the paradoxical representation of the modern city in ruins. For instance in "Otras ruinas," destruction and reconstruction are two faces of the same coin. In "Las ruinas," the aesthetic experience of beautiful and abandoned ruins reveals the hollowness of death and of religious belief. Life is like the delirium provoked by the aesthetic experience of the ruins, beautiful and endurable as long as it lasts a few moments in time.

The last verse of the ninth stanza presents the aesthetic principle of finding beauty and eternity in the instant. Paz also voiced this poetics of the instant in his *El arco y la lira,* stating that poetry becomes itself in the instant in which time stops: "Ese instante contiene todos los instantes. Sin dejar de fluir, el tiempo se detiene, colmado de sí" (25). In that instant when time ceases to exist in poetry, Paz finds his possibility of eternity. This notion of poetic time is not necessarily neglecting the historical time and its process. Cernuda acknowledges the fragility of the instant, even in the poem itself; the joyous moment passes, and it becomes *history.*

Baudelaire defines Modernity through this dichotomy of the instant that signifies eternal, as the correspondence of these two visions of time: the modern artist "...s'agit... de dégager de la mode ce qu'elle peut contenir de poétique dans l'historique, de tirer l'éternel du transitoire" (*OC* 2: 694). Cernuda reflects upon the interaction of historical time and poetic time, yet in this text, poetry is also transient: "mis obras humanas que no duran" (*PC* 325). Nevertheless, Cernuda is not searching for the new and the particular beauty of the modern landscape in "Las ruinas." The tenth stanza echoes the traditional *carpe diem* discourse:

> Todo lo que es hermoso tiene su instante, y pasa.
> Importa como eterno gozar de nuestro instante.
> Yo no te envidio, Dios; déjame a solas

> Con mis obras humanas que no duran:
> El afán de llenar lo que es efímero
> De eternidad, vale tu omnipotencia. (*PC* 325)

One of the didactic principles of the Baroque poems on ruins is the *carpe diem*, enjoy the instant and do not be vain, because grand cities and strong empires have been easily destroyed. The speaker addresses God once again to underline his lack of envy and lack of desire for omnipotence and eternity. The consciousness of solitude and the mortality of his own poetic works give him a sense of self. The eleventh stanza repeats the didactic purpose of this diatribe: "Esto es el hombre. Aprende pues, y cesa / De perseguir eternos dioses sordos…" (*PC* 326). The reader must now see himself in the context of the city in ruins: the lesson of the ruins is that we must not search for the eternal in God or in our monuments, but in the instant.

The metaphors of human life as fragile and beautiful as a flower, embracing death, and the personification of the night in the last stanza may be associated with the Romantic sensibility. These metaphors explore the speaker's ways of facing his own mortality in a contemplative mode: "…me reclino / A contemplar sereno el campo y las ruinas" (326). This poem is not about the modern city in ruins, but the antique city in ruins. "Las ruinas" is not paradigmatic of the poems I have been discussing in this chapter because it seems to take place outside the modern sphere. However, Cernuda incorporated Baudelaire's aesthetics and his contradictory definition of Modernity as a fundamental tension in his poem: "La modernité, c'est le transitoire, le fugitive, le contingent, la moitié de l'art, dont l'autre moitié est l'éternel et l'immuable" (Baudelaire, *OC* 2: 695). Baudelaire highlights, throughout "Le peintre de la vie moderne," this duality of art and men, this creative need in lyrical poetry to differentiate and merge the historical and the poetic.

Marshall Berman reiterates the duality, the contradictions of the modern subject: "To be modern is to find ourselves in an environment that promises adventure, power, joy, growth, transformation of ourselves and the world—and at the same time threatens to destroy everything we have, everything we know, everything we are" (15). Baudelaire's anxiety toward Modernity and his criticism of progress is charged with the social frustrations of unfulfilled promises, but it is also complicated by his desire to grasp the historical, to represent the destructive, revolutionary elements of his present; art is what he calls "la mémoire du présent" (*OC* 2: 696). In the beginning of "Le Cygne," Baudelaire alludes to a small, mythical river that fed his memory, "ma mémoire fertile," and made him realize that: "Le vieux Paris n'est plus (la forme d'une ville / Change plus vite, hélas! que le cœur d'un mortel)" (*OC* 1: 85). Just as in "Otras ruinas," when city and man are connected to each other, Baudelaire points to the constant transformations of the modern city and he suggests that the modern poet must represent those external, historical changes.

Although Baudelaire wants to capture the transient particularities of his age, "Le Cygne" reveals a nostalgic gaze at the mythical past. Does Cernuda's "Las ruinas" project nostalgia for a lost, ideal city in reaction to war and modern alienation? "Las ruinas" expresses a pessimistic, disillusioned vision of the future, yet the ruins are neither idealized nor mythologized. This poem voices what I have called a poetics of disillusionment, in touch with Weber's "disenchantment of the world" and Eliot's vision of history as a process of disintegration. Years before this poem was written, Juan Ramón Jiménez parodies Cernuda's male muse, his interest in ruins, and his prevalent disillusionment: "La inspiración de Luis Cernuda es un Adonis errante entre ruinas clásicas, que tornan por el suelo todas las formas de ilusión…."[44] But this parodic reflection on Cernuda's work obviates the critique of certain social and cultural values he develops in his poetics of disillusionment.

The ruins leave the speaker in a contemplative mode at the end, but they ultimately provoke in him a confrontation with God, with the illusions of eternity, and a realization of the modern poet's desires and frustrations. Valis suggests the Spanish Civil War intensified feelings of nostalgia for a lost Republic. Still, in Cernuda's poem, more than nostalgia, there is anguish over death, embodied in the unalterable future of ruins:

> In the context of the *fin de siglo*, nostalgia as a sign of modernity seems to be mourning not only of the past but also, strangely enough, the future. The nostalgic is, metaphorically and affectively, truly an "out of place," operating as a narrative of loss and memory and centered upon a phantom topography of desire… The historical weight of nostalgic

> feeling is specially acute in times of rapid change and cata-
> strophic events such as war and exile. In the case of the Span-
> ish Civil War and the Republican exiles, the passage of time
> has not only intensified such feelings but also created them.
> (Valis, "Nostalgia" 124)

Even if in this essay Valis does not comment on Cernuda's
work, this quote seems to describe his situation as a Republican
exile in England, the United States, and Mexico. When Cernuda
wrote "Las ruinas" he was very much "out of place," marginalized and isolated in England, but he often felt like this; his na-
tive Sevilla was never a warm, welcoming home. His gloomy
perspective can be connected to his war experiences and his
state of mourning for the past and the future, as Valis indicates.
"Las ruinas" uses the topos to meditate upon the role of the
poet, the menacing fear of death, and to criticize how the desire
for eternity upholds both religious and aesthetic discourses.
Cernuda's poem transports the reader to an abandoned, ruined
landscape, which could be read as an allegory of the effects of
World War II in Europe or the Spanish Civil War. But the lack of
specific references to modern times stresses an awakening into
history through death, time, and reality, more than a product of
the urban shock experience and the failures of progress that I
have discussed throughout this chapter.

"Otras ruinas" (1949) follows "Las ruinas" (1941), and they
both establish a sense of historical continuation among the diverse eras. After a few years of alternative titles, Cernuda chose
to characterize the antique ruins as the original "ruinas" and the
modern ruins as the "other," the alternative, the continuation of
"Las ruinas." War is not explicitly named in these poems, but
they are both reflections of the destruction Cernuda witnessed
in Europe. Even if "Otras ruinas" highlights the machines of
progress as the destroyers of the city's past, both this poem
on modern ruins and his poem on the abandoned Baroque
and Romantic landscape share the common premise: "Intacto
nada queda, aunque parezca / Firme." Moreover, in both "Las
ruinas" and "Otras ruinas" there is no nostalgia for the lost
city, no desire to return to the past and to change the historical
predicaments that determine it. Unlike "Le Cygne," where there
is a melancholic vision of the lost Paris and a fascination with

the new Paris, Cernuda's cities are not named, and they do not reveal the desire to return.

Baudelaire's and Cernuda's criticism of modern progress does not claim to be a conservative standpoint against electricity or other technological advancements. Cernuda's and Baudelaire's works, just like Eliot's and Paz's, can be read as subversive critiques of bourgeois social and economic values. Their review of the past can be characterized as nostalgic, but while it emphasizes modern poetry's ties to traditional and canonical poets, it also conveys an ironic, humorous tone, and the critical distance of parody. While Eliot and Paz parody the Baroque ruins, Baudelaire and Cernuda also project a similar tension with the Romantic tradition.[45]

In this chapter, I have not concentrated on how the topos of modern ruins differentiates the Romantic ruins, although I have alluded to some of the drastic differences between both aesthetic enterprises. Romantic poems on ruins, either fake or real, tend to dehistoricize the past, the context that produced those ruins, to focus on the self as the main subject of the poem. Baudelaire's and Cernuda's poems intend to historicize the remnants of the past. The historical is not only prevalent in the specification of dates and names, but also captured in their reflection on time and decay.

So far, I have examined poems that depicted a room in ruins, a ruined dream, desire in ruins, antique ruins, human ruins, and the modern city in ruins. The city's turmoil, the threat of collapse, and the critique of modern progress seem to distinguish all of them. As I remarked in the beginning of this chapter, ruins and waste are vastly different. Waste smells and disgusts, while ruins are usually covered by nature's dress. Yet modern ruins can also be ugly, dusty, and covered by bricks and broken pieces of cement. What differentiates modern ruins from urban waste in Baudelaire's and Cernuda's works are their allegorical significance and their historical implications. Baudelaire's and Cernuda's poems on ruins suggest that they do not want the remnants of the city to be treated as waste.

Cities in Ruins

The Burlesque Baroque in
T. S. Eliot and Octavio Paz

In Search of Neo-Baroque Pearls

The etymological definition of *barroco* points to something extravagant or bizarre, a pearl with an irregular shape.[1] The *pérola barroca* is the product of the Portuguese commerce with pearls in the East, a result of their explorations abroad in the early sixteenth century.[2] In a headlong dive, searching for irregular pearls in the traditional corpus of enigmatic conceits and paradoxical images, Octavio Paz and T. S. Eliot immerse themselves in the poetic and critical endeavor of recuperating from critical oblivion the Baroque and the Metaphysical poets. This is palpable in T. S. Eliot's critical and aesthetic ties with the English Metaphysical poet John Donne, in particular his influential "The First Anniversary," as well as in Paz's homage and rewriting of Francisco de Quevedo's sonnet "Amor constante más allá de la muerte." Both Paz and Eliot use the Baroque tradition in the historical sense and as an "objective correlative" to rethink metaphors of death and decay, decomposed bodies and ruined cities in post-war Europe and America. I will discuss how they balance their desire for modern formal innovations in a "tradition against itself," to use Paz's expression, and the intertextual dialogue they establish with the Baroque and the Metaphysical poets, in *The Waste Land* and "Whispers of Immortality," and *Homenaje y profanaciones,* "Himno entre ruinas," and "Petrificada petrificante."[3]

The connections between the Spanish Baroque poets and the English Metaphysical poets are various and multilayered. Helmut Hatzfeld argues that the Spanish Baroque had an immense influence over all European poetry of the seventeenth century, especially in England: "Por lo que toca a la literatura inglesa, parece más difícil aún comprender cómo fue posible que un país protestante y sajón pudiera adoptar durante medio siglo los elementos espirituales de otro país que era precisamente su adversario en lo político y en lo religioso" (445).

Although Hatzfeld suggests that the Metaphysical poets were more Mannerist than Baroque, he specifically emphasizes the influence of the Spanish Baroque on Donne: "Un poeta como John Donne con su educación católica y su viaje a Cádiz (1596) conoce bien España y sus juegos de palabras y agudezas de ingenio" (448).[4] In an essay on Donne, Paz proposes a comparative study between the English poet and Quevedo.[5] Paz underlines that:

> la poesía de Donne se inscribe dentro de la llamada escuela "metafísica," tendencia no sin analogías con el conceptismo y el gongorismo españoles. Sabemos que el poeta inglés leía con facilidad nuestra lengua. Visitó España en su juventud y participó en la expedición y saqueo de Cádiz. En 1623 escribe a Buckingham, entonces en Madrid: "I can thus make myself believe that I am where your lordship is, in Spain, that in my poor library, where indeed I am, I can turn my eye towards no shelf, in any profession, from the mistress of my youth, Poetry, to the wife of mine age, Divinity, but that I meet more authors of that nation than any others." ("Un poema de John Donne" 96)[6]

Paz uses Donne's private confession to make a relevant point on the transnational facet of the Baroque and Metaphysical poets.[7] Like Hatzfeld, Paz indicates that an aesthetic movement such as the Baroque is never a national enterprise.[8] On the other hand, Eliot's poetic and critical work concerning the Metaphysical poets was mainly written in the nineteen twenties, while Paz wrote his in the fifties and sixties. Paz's perspective is not only chronologically different from Eliot's vision of the past. Paz is a kind of crucible; he wants to absorb the Metaphysical, the Baroque, and the Modernist poetic discourses. He is more interested in inscribing the Spanish tradition in a more *mestizo* culture of international exchanges, of which he claims to be the heir.

Yet, both these poets elaborate a poetics that favors a historical continuity between eras. In their quest for the eternal, these texts allude to the Classical or the Baroque tradition, exemplifying Lois Parkinson Zamora's notion of an "anxiety of origins." Parkinson Zamora explains her idea in contrast to Harold Bloom's "anxiety of influence": "American writers search for precursors rather than escape from them; to connect to traditions and to histories (in the name of a usable past) rather than dissociate from them (in the name of originality)" (*The Usable Past* 5). Eliot and Paz intend to resuscitate seventeenth-century poetry as a "usable past" without idealizing it or presenting it as sacred and untouchable.

However, one of the problems with concepts such as resuscitating, recuperating, and recovering is that they enclose a strong dose of nostalgia. Svetlana Boym describes it as the "incurable modern condition" and the "historical emotion" of our era. Eliot and Paz could easily identify with the nostalgic "rebellion against the modern idea of time, the time of history and progress" (xv). As I have remarked in the Introduction, Boym distinguishes two categories: restorative nostalgia and reflective nostalgia. Restorative nostalgia thinks of itself as "truth and tradition," it feeds on nationalist sentiments with a desire to "return to the origins"; while reflective nostalgia "explores ways of inhabiting many places at once and imagining different time zones" (xviii). Eliot and Paz are both anti-nationalists; and although they had different notions of origins, they did look for a sense of lost self in the Baroque tradition.[9] Still, complex works like *The Waste Land* and "Homenaje y profanaciones" evoke many places, many times, in their authors' aim to universalize their poems. They both recognize that which attracts them to the Metaphysical and the Conceptualist poets: their disillusioned tones, their cynicism, their acute awareness of the failures of early Modernity. Yet Eliot's and Paz's nostalgic visions of the ruined past have undeniable burlesque tones and an overtly subversive critique of the present social and cultural order. Therefore, Eliot and Paz manifest a firmer bond to a reflective nostalgia, which dwells on a sense of loss while both are "ironic and humorous" about it. Boym clarifies that "restorative nostalgia manifests itself in total reconstructions of monuments of the past, while reflective nostalgia lingers on ruins… in the dreams of another place and another time" (41). Although Eliot's and Paz's poetry could be characterized as monumental, they are more interested in portraying fragments than a whole totalizing vision of a historical and a literary reality. The parodies of Donne and Quevedo in Eliot's and Paz's poems show the split of consciousness, the fractured modern self, that oscillates from nostalgically paying homage and critically distancing the poets from their literary models.

Eliot's and Paz's return to the past is also read by different critics, and for diverse reasons, as a subversive act. Raymond Williams in *The Politics of Modernism* stresses that Modernism amalgamated various extreme political views; while Expressionists like Brecht defended leftist ideas, Pound and Yeats tended to the right:

> in Britain... literary Modernism moved explicitly to the right... Pound's characteristically total avant-garde position ended in Fascism, and Yeat's version of the "people," sustained at first by a broad and diverse movement, became a right-wing nationalism. The most interesting because most influential case is that of Eliot, seen from the 1920's [*sic*] to the 1940's [*sic*] as the key modernist poet. Eliot developed what can now be seen as an Ancient-and-Modern position, in which unceasing literary experiment moved towards a conscious elite, and in which an emphasis on tradition (so distinct from earlier Modernist and avant-garde rejections of the past) was offered in effect subversive of an intolerable because shallow and self-deceiving (and in that sense still bourgeois) social and cultural order. (61)

Williams is arguing that Eliot's recuperation of the past should be seen as subversive because it served as a way to criticize the present, the bourgeois social order. However, although both the left and the right political versions of Modernism coincide in their attack on bourgeois society, they strongly differ in their visions of the alternative social order: one defends a communal society, the other an organic, almost feudal system. While Eliot's poetry is formally subversive, his revision of the past and its incorporation through tradition remains profoundly conservative and nostalgic. Nevertheless, his positions remained ambiguous in many aspects. In his well-known biography of Eliot, Peter Ackroyd stresses this point: "The essential problem was the peculiar ambiguity of his work and personality: he seemed too radical to conservatives, and too conservative to radicals" (157).

Still, horrified by Fascist versions of an organic, racially purified society after World War II, Paz based his nostalgia on a historical reading of Latin America as the melting pot of cultural diversity and racial impurity. Neo-Baroque poetics, theorized by writers like Carpentier and Lezama Lima, and later on by Paz, defends the idea that Latin America is the product of a *mestizaje*, symbolized by the coexistence of multiple artistic styles during the "Barroco de Indias." Parkinson Zamora refers to the Baroque as subversive because "it provides the very structure with which to subvert" the repression of the Spanish Counter-Reformation in Latin America. "The baroque provides the space necessary for the complex processes of transculturation to create distinctly Latin American cultural forms" (93). In this sense, Paz's return to the Baroque past is not a nostalgic act, but rather a subversive take on Latin American history and literary tradition.

Paz explains the political agenda of a "return to the origins" throughout his reading of Mexican history in *El laberinto de la soledad* (1950). He describes Mexicans as sons of La Malinche, the indigenous woman who became Hernán Cortés's lover and translator. He asserts that Mexicans disowned La Malinche as a traitor, but by doing so they repudiated their own origins, the cultural synthesis that she epitomizes: "Al repudiar a la Malinche... el mexicano rompe sus ligas con el pasado, reniega su origen y se adentra solo en la vida histórica" (*El laberinto de la soledad* 225). Paz argues that the Mexican Revolution changed the way Mexicans defined themselves. In an incomplete way, they were able to reconcile themselves with their indigenous heritage and its synthesis within the Hispanic Mexican nation. He underlines that the Mexican self-search is manifested in their search for a form that defines and expresses them. However, the subversiveness of Paz's claims is highly contentious since it ultimately plays into the rhetoric of national unity founded in that cultural synthesis. Paz often describes it as a strange or bizarre form, characteristically associated with the Baroque. Furthermore, in *El laberinto de la soledad*, Paz tends to be a cultural essentialist, and his reading of history is also marked by a totalizing vision:

> *Toda* la historia de México, desde la Conquista hasta la Revolución, puede verse como una búsqueda de nosotros mismos,

> *deformados* o enmascarados por instituciones *extrañas*, y de
> una *Forma* que nos exprese... La Revolución fue un descu-
> brimiento de nosotros mismos y *un regreso a los orígenes*,
> primero; luego una búsqueda y una tentativa de síntesis,
> abortada varias veces; incapaz de asimilar nuestra tradición,
> y ofrecernos un nuevo proyecto salvador, finalmente fue un
> compromiso. (312 and 314; emphasis added)

Throughout his essays and poems, Paz avows that the Mexican
Form is a deformity. The governing institutions, the state and
the church, are strange in the sense that they are not autochthonous. But then in a nation whose origins are not only the
Aztec pyramidal empire, but also the Spanish conquest and
colonization, where can one find the "autochthonous" or the
"original" self? The Baroque artistic expressions are not only
symptomatic of the wonderful deformity and the bizarre nature
that the conquistadors encounter and describe; the Baroque sensibility also allows the coexistence of contrasting cultural and
artistic elements, representing the synthesis Paz describes as an
existential and a national search for a collective identity. The
Mexican Revolution's attempts to find that synthesis are frustrated because the social inequities are still divisive and incisive.
The national project still bears the marks of the Revolution in
its search for a new social and economic (re)Form. However,
one should clarify that now the return to the origins, the reconciliation with the past, and the desire to reach "universality"
seem essentialist, almost futile enterprises, but in the context
of the nineteen fifties, *El laberinto de la soledad* questioned
the historical, the national, and even the sexual discourses that
predominated.

Eliot and Paz are two American poets who seek the presence
of the past in the European literary tradition. Their essays and
poems about the Baroque and the Metaphysical poets reveal
their desire to find new roots within the Old World that would
legitimize their own poetic practices. Eliot explains that "Tradition... cannot be inherited, and if you want it, you must obtain
it with great labour. It involves, in the first place, the historical
sense, which we may call nearly indispensable to anyone who
would continue to be a poet beyond his twenty-fifth year... (it)
involves a perception, not only of the pastness of the past, but of

its presence…" ("Tradition and Individual Talent" 49). Eliot's and Paz's definitions of tradition and its malleable boundaries have been amply discussed by other critics.[10] Tradition, in particular for American writers, is not inherited, it is acquired and manufactured. I will explore how Eliot and Paz use canonical Baroque works and the topos of ruins to redefine the value of literary tradition in their experimental Modernist poetry.

Yet, unlike Eliot's, Paz's search for cultural origins leads him to the buried past in Aztec and modern ruins, where the pre-Colombian and the European traditions coincide: "México buscaba el presente afuera y lo encontró adentro, enterrado pero vivo. La búsqueda de la modernidad nos llevó a descubrir nuestra antigüedad… era un descenso a los orígenes…" ("La búsqueda del presente" 389). In "Homenaje y profanaciones" the allusions to the ruined cities of Itálica and Uxmal exemplify the conjunction of both heritages. Paz places himself in the tradition of Lope and Quevedo, yet maintains that Mexicans are and are not literally Europeans, "Somos y no somos europeos" ("Manierismo" 14). This quest for the lost origins in both the European and the indigenous heritage links Paz's work to a neo-Baroque poetics. As he states in relation to the Baroque poets of Nueva España (what would become Mexico), such as Sor Juana Inés de la Cruz, "Respiraban con naturalidad en el mundo de la extrañeza porque ellos mismos eran y se sabían extraños" ("Manierismo" 14). Paz hints that the grotesquely beautiful pearl of the Baroque represents the New World itself. Defining the American Baroque as the epitome of what is bizarre is also a way of essentializing those origins as unique and deformed.[11]

While Paz defines himself as a Mexican poet, caught in between Modernity and Antiquity, the Americas and Europe, Eliot considers that he is more part of the European literary tradition than the American canon. Still, Eliot also participates in the articulation of a neo-Baroque poetics, not limited to Latin American writers.[12] Eliot is particularly interested in the Metaphysical poets, privileging the English over the French or the Spanish seventeenth-century poets. And although Eliot also evinces an anxiety of origins, without disregarding his admiration for Dante and Baudelaire, he chooses to find his political, religious, and literary models in British culture, not New World aesthetics.

This is mainly reflected in his poetic and political tension with Walt Whitman, the epitome of the democratic voice and the nationalist poet of American literature.

Eliot's interest in the English Metaphysical school over poets like Whitman could also be related to American New Criticism and its ideological prerogatives. Fredric Jameson discusses how: "The New Critics, following mentors like Irving Babbit and Charles Maurras, explicitly repudiated English Romanticism and its radical tradition and returned for models to Metaphysical and Cavalier poetry" (46). Jameson contrasts the New Critics with the Russian Formalists and their dialectical attitudes toward history.[13] Eliot's revaluation of the Metaphysical poets is tied to a conservative political agenda, evident in many of his essays, even though his poems are anything but political pamphlets. On the other hand, the study of the Baroque and the Metaphysical schools that reappeared at the beginning of the twentieth century can also be related to left-wing literary circles in Spain and Latin America, searching for new ways of rebelling against the nineteenth-century's nationalist literary criticism and positivist literary values.

The cultural traffic between the European Baroque and the Americas was at first revealed by scholars like the Mexican Alfonso Reyes, one of Paz's most admired teachers and friends. In *Cuestiones gongorinas* (1927) Reyes discusses, among other issues, Góngora's influence on Latin American seventeenth-century poetry (12).[14] His study of the Baroque poets is framed within the Spanish literary context of the Generation of '27.[15] Federico García Lorca also denounces the constant marginalization of Góngora:

> El Góngora culterano ha sido considerado en España… como un monstruo de vicios gramaticales cuya poesía carece de todos los elementos fundamentales para ser bella… Y Góngora ha estado solo como un leproso lleno de llagas… esperando las nuevas generaciones que recogieran su herencia objetiva y su sentido de la metáfora. ("La imagen poética de Don Luis de Góngora" 240)

García Lorca's beautiful image of Góngora as a literary leper is a reaction against Spanish academic figures like Marcelino Menéndez Pelayo, whose disdain for Góngora echoes that of many of the poet's seventeenth-century rivals. Menéndez Pelayo accuses Góngora of obscurity and intellectual emptiness; the famous "Soledades" is for him a poem "sin asunto, sin afectos, sin ideas..." (324). He comments on Góngora's and Quevedo's poetry: "medio bucólica, medio petrarquista, la cual voluntariamente se aisló del arte popular... lanzó sobre todas las literaturas de Europa una plaga peor que la langosta, la plaga de las églogas, de los madrigales, de los sonetos, de las canciones metafísicas al modo toscano" (327). Although he is evidently not fond of locusts, Menéndez Pelayo's preference for playwrights like Lope de Vega is strongly influenced by nineteenth-century nationalistic notions of the "pintoresco español."

Many poets in the nineteen twenties fought vigorously against Menéndez Pelayo's disregard of Góngora and Quevedo.[16] Dámaso Alonso gives the best explanation of the resurgent appreciation of these Baroque poets. Alonso goes back to Ignacio de Luzán, the Spanish critic who wrote *La poética* in 1737, to show how the eighteenth century critically buried most of the Baroque writers. The nineteenth century does unearth Calderón and Lope de Vega, but mainly because they appealed to its Romantic sensibilities and had been already canonized by the Germans. Thus, why did the beginning of the twentieth century see a revival of interest in poets like Góngora? Alonso is one of the few who successfully attempts to answer this question:

> En el primer cuarto del siglo XX... se produce un cambio total en la manera de considerar la vida como materia de la ciencia o de arte. Al nuevo modo de entender el fenómeno estético, acompaña una nueva valoración crítica de la literatura del pasado. Y vuelve a adquirir importancia un poeta como Góngora, cuyo central empeño fue la creación de un cosmos poético en el que la realidad del mundo está traducida... en materia irreal, orden, sistema, nitidez, depuración... ("Notas a la Antología en honor a Góngora" 397)

Alonso adequately describes a historical change in aesthetic reception and conceptualization provoked, I believe, by French Symbolists like Baudelaire and Mallarmé. In the beginning of the twentieth century, Borges and Reyes alluded to works of comparative analysis on Góngora and Mallarmé to emphasize the continuity between the Spanish Golden Age and the French use of modern poetic artifice.[17] The exploitation of metaphor and the imagistic exploration encouraged both the admirers of Mallarmé and the practitioners of Surrealist aesthetics to reread poets like Góngora. The revalorization of the unreal, or the surreal, transformed Góngora into a poetic model. Therefore, "lo pintoresco español" that was exalted by Romantic aesthetics became less relevant, less of a literary challenge.

René Wellek, who does not discuss at length the twentieth-century Spanish poets' interest in the Baroque, maintains that the German revival of seventeenth-century poetry in the nineteen twenties is essential for the literary study of the term. Wellek suggests that among the causes for this resurgent interest in the Baroque, there is a misunderstanding: "Baroque poetry was felt to be similar to the most recent German expressionism, to its turbulent, tense, torn diction and tragic view of the world conduced by the aftermath of war" (76). Yet like Dámaso Alonso, he specifies that it was also linked to a change of sensibility and taste: "part was a genuine change of taste, a sudden comprehension for an art despised before because of its conventions, its supposedly tasteless metaphors, its violent contrasts and antitheses" (76). However, Wellek is dissatisfied with any form of stylistic definition of Baroque aesthetics because he argues that paradox, asyndeton, and oxymoron are not peculiar to the term. While it is problematic to delineate literary categories through literary terms, I use conceits and paradoxes, cynicism and pessimism, as tools for reading into the philosophical and poetic insight of these texts. The categories of Baroque and neo-Baroque are problematic because they are categorical, resting on generalizations and conventions, tones and terms. Yet they serve not only as a way of historicizing literary periods, they provoke a discussion of how we conceptualize the interrelations between literary movements and its individuals, crossing national and temporal boundaries. These categories help rethink Eliot's and Paz's poetry in relation to seventeenth-century poets, without limiting their work to the traces of influence and the search for the origins of Modernity.

Despite the fact that Eliot does not refer frequently to Góngora or to his Spanish contemporaries, he is a key figure in the European and the American re-evaluation of a Baroque poetics. Eliot begins his Clark Lectures, delivered at Cambridge in 1926, identifying himself and his own aesthetic project with the Metaphysical school: "There are no wanting voices to declare that the present age is a metaphysical age... If likeness exists, then it is valuable to understand the poetry of the seventeenth century, in order that we may understand that of our own time and understand ourselves" ("The Clark Lectures," in *Varieties* 43). Why is the present metaphysical? Why is Eliot ascribing himself to a historical discourse of almost lineal continuity between the past and the present? The post-war environment of the twenties provoked a re-evaluation of ideas and situations. When Eliot suggests that we will understand more thoroughly our time by studying seventeenth-century poetry, his statements may be stretched to the political and the cultural spheres, but in narrowing them down to the literary sphere, Eliot is indicating that poets are, above all, readers. Thus, their readings of traditional texts shape their poetic sensibilities. The Metaphysical conceit acquires a particular relevance because it takes metaphors to the extreme and provokes an effect of shock and awe, similar to what is proposed first by the Symbolists and later on by the Surrealists.

Eliot's criticism of the Metaphysical poets is a crucial step toward the re-conceptualization of an aesthetics that Sumil Kanti Sen describes as intrinsically anti-Romantic in its desire to "externalize emotion" and to find an "objective correlative." Sen attributed Eliot's use of "non-poetic material" and dramatic verse to the influence of the Metaphysical poets. Eliot's treatment of rhythm and imagery is also linked to the French Symbolists.[18] On a similar note, F. O. Matthiessen addresses those characteristics that join Eliot with Donne and Baudelaire, but he takes it a step further when he alludes to what joins both seventeenth- and nineteenth-century poets:

> The principal quality which drew Eliot to the symbolists is one they possess in common with the metaphysicals, "the same essential quality of transmuting ideas into sensations, of transforming an observation into a state of mind"... "the presence of the idea in the image"... In both schools there is a demand for compression of statement, for centring on the revealing detail and eliminating all the inessentials... (16–17)

The correspondence of thought and feeling, the abstract and the concrete, the imaginary and the real, is ultimately what Eliot and his critics indicate when synthesizing the aesthetic ideas that tie the Metaphysical school and the Symbolist poets. In this quote, the obsession with the essential and the inessential is merely a reflection of Baudelaire's and Eliot's insistence on capturing the "essence" of their respective eras: the detail most people overlook, the image that reveals the ambiance, the mind-frame of a generation.

Eliot's earlier work might be considered a constant challenge of the Metaphysical conceits, which he valued and emulated. Both "Whispers of Immortality" and *The Waste Land* frequently wink an eye to poets like Donne and Baudelaire with extravagant metaphors and difficult wordplays that try to capture the new visions of death and cities in ruins. How are these poems revolutionizing, deforming modern aesthetics? And what are their allegorical implications?

Paz compared the strange curves and the bizarre imagery of Eliot's *The Waste Land* to a cubist painting or a collage, but Paz was predominantly drawn to elements that we also associate with Baroque aesthetics. In an essay about Eliot's influence on his work, "La vuelta de los días, T. S. Eliot," Paz explains in detail how *The Waste Land* fascinated him when he first read the translation by Enrique Munguía in 1930: "El imán que me atrajo fue la excelencia del poema, el rigor de su construcción... también su novedad, su extrañeza... el carácter fragmentario de cada parte y la manera aparentemente desordenada en que se enlazan" (40).[19] Indeed, Paz's comments on Eliot in turn echo Eliot's early praise of John Donne's ability to maintain poetic order while integrating diverse moods and feelings, "rapid alterations and antithesis" ("John Donne" 331). The fragmentary structure of *The Waste Land* reveals the strange metaphors and transitions that give the poem coherence and unity, an order within the disorder. Paz focuses on the bizarreness of *The Waste Land,* implicitly attaching it to his neo-Baroque "estética de la extrañeza." Paz feels attracted to the poem because he can identify Eliot's aesthetic project with his own search for the bizarre and the exceptional in Mexico.

Paz underscores that one of *The Waste Land*'s main contributions resides in its incorporation of history and history-making: "La novedad de *The Waste Land* está tanto en su forma cuanto en la aparición de la historia humana como (con/in)stancia del poema. La poesía regresa a la épica. Como toda épica, ese poema cuenta una historia transfigurada en un mito" ("La vuelta de los días" 41). This perspective is consistent with how Latin American writers like Paz and Neruda conceptualize modern poetry as the integration of the historical and the mythical in the structure of the poem. They incorporate formal aspects associated with the epic genre in order to historicize and politicize lyric poetry. The historical context of World War I is deeply embedded in *The Waste Land*'s cities in ruins, but Paz is referring to a specific historical context fused with an image of continuous cultural decrepitude. Eliot's poem is indeed reflecting upon a wider historical interpretation: the social and cultural decay of Western civilization, which he calls the "disintegration of the intellect." As Northrop Frye declares, Eliot believed that "the disintegration of Europe began soon after Dante's time," and that "history since represents the degeneration of the (this) ideal," a European community with shared values (8). For Eliot, Dante was the ideal poet, who integrated intellectual and emotional wisdom, diverse philosophic and religious currents, in a well-constructed poetic system. Of course, Dante was not only a poet but a politician in exile when he wrote the *Divine Comedy*. Dante searched in his poem not only for coherence and understanding, but also for integration and unity on many levels. Eliot's appreciation of the medieval era is based on his notion of a unified society, where the church, the arts, and the state shared common values. Thus, this explains his opposition to a reading of history as a progression, which has led to divisions, multiple nations, and diverse Christian institutions. Without referring to Eliot, Benjamin signals what attracts Eliot to both Baroque and Medieval Christianity: "There is a threefold material affinity between baroque and medieval Christianity. The struggle between the pagan gods, the triumph of allegory, the torment of the flesh, are equally essential to both" ("Allegory and Trauespiel," *The Origin* 220). Baroque poems on ruins like Rodrigo Caro's "Canción a las ruinas de Itálica" frequently opt for the destruction of pagan gods and their monuments and the endurance of the immortal Christian relics. Eliot's "waste land" is also an allegorical space that represents the spiritual emptiness of the modern city, subject to destruction like the empires of Antiquity. The torment of the flesh is more prevalent in Eliot and Quevedo than in Donne and Paz, where playfulness and enjoyment are very much embedded in their erotic poetry. Still, Benjamin's insight indirectly reveals Eliot's motives to reinvigorate the study of both Dante and the Metaphysical poets.

In his "La vuelta de los días, T. S. Eliot," Paz finally emphasizes the political differences between him and Eliot and considers that as a self-confessed rebel what ultimately joined him to the more conservative poet was their mutual anguish at Modernity's ruins and disasters.[20] Ultimately, Paz's political stances in the nineteen fifties diverge from Eliot's conservative views. However, even if Paz wants to distance himself politically from Eliot, their common horror before the modern world situates him in a pessimistic, cynical position, which has often justified the nostalgic idealization of the past.

Eliot's Donne: "Expert beyond experience"

Eliot's critical and poetic readings of Donne shed light into the gloomy, fractured, and dead bodies that become symptomatic of a world in ruins. Eliot's fascination with Donne's aesthetics, developed in his 1926 Clark Lectures, is also substantiated by two of his earlier essays, "The Metaphysical Poets" (1921) and "John Donne" (1923), where he underlines Donne's complex unity of different emotions and moods: "with Donne... (it is) impossible to isolate his ecstasy, his sensuality and his cynicism" ("John Donne" 332).[21] Eliot compares Donne to Baudelaire and how his new moods were foreshadowed by previous moods. Predominantly, he values the way these poets tie diverse metaphors and conceits into a coherent system of thought. Eliot's admiration of Donne's cynicism and scepticism also reveals his attitude toward the literary recuperation of the Metaphysical school—both a poetic alliance and a parody of conceits.

Written between 1917 and 1918, Eliot's "Whispers of Immortality" (*Collected Poems* 45–46) illustrates the poetic revaluation of the Metaphysical poets—thus, it is not just a reaction to World War I. The poem is divided into two parts, each made up of four stanzas. The first part revolves around questions of death and the body, explicitly referring to Webster and Donne. In contrast, the final four stanzas distil exuberance and desire, provoked by the mysterious Grishkin, the exotic Russian woman who surpasses a Brazilian jaguar's feline qualities. Richard Bradford offers an accurate reading that connects the erotic aspects of the second part with Eliot's ruminations on the Metaphysics: "Donne's and Webster's treatment of sex has an odour of death about it—Eliot's point is that in their poetry, love and physical attraction are continually and relentlessly attended by a morbid anxiety" (106). The morbid anxiety in the second part of the poem is primarily perceived in the final stanza, where "our lot" prefers to cuddle up with dry bones rather than succumb to the temptations of Grishkin's warm lustful promises.

This morbidity is suggested as well in the very first verses of "Whispers of Immortality": "Webster was much possessed by death / And saw the skull beneath the skin."[22] Death possesses John Webster's imagination. Ironically, the poets whom we call Metaphysics do not transcend the physical or go beyond the body. In Eliot's poem, Webster *sees* death by *foreseeing* it. Webster sees the physical manifestation of death, which has also become its symbol: the skeleton. Eliot represents the idea of death through the skull of the dead man. Although "Whispers of Immortality" presents the body as a human ruin, and not the city in ruins, this poem is the key to introducing how Eliot reads the Metaphysical poets and their obsessions with decay and death, also explored in *The Waste Land*.

The representation of the body in the first part of "Whispers of Immortality" expresses a morbid preoccupation with the "skull," "the breastless creatures," the "lipless grin," "the dead limbs," the "skeleton" and its bones. The image of nature taking over the human remains is a disturbing image, characteristic of the paradoxical conceits of the Metaphysical: "Daffodil bulbs instead of balls / Stared from the sockets of the eyes!" The bulbs refer both to the plant growing from such a bud, the daffodil, and to the incandescent electric lamp. The daffodil flower and the electric bulb share a particular brightness, a yellow that unites the natural and the artificial. The flowers replace the gaze of the dead by invading the hollow sockets of their eyes. Here nature occupies the skeletons of the dead bodies as in Baroque ruins, when nature takes over the remnants of the city.[23] In this case, Eliot integrates into the image of the daffodil bulbs, the Metaphysical poet's use of natural metaphors with modern "clinical and analytical" metaphors, the mechanized versions of death.

World War I determined how Eliot describes death in this poem. New killing machines made Eliot's generation see and judge war with different lenses. Although there is no reference in the poem to the fields of poppies, the red flower symbol used by the British for commemorating the end of World War I shows how, just as in the text, the social reaction to the war tried to counterbalance the bombs, the gas masks, the fields of blood with emblems of nature and its life cycle. The representation of the body in its decayed forms is not only a product of death; in "Whispers of Immortality" it is mainly the product of the imagination. How we think the body transforms itself in death is manipulated by thought and imagination. Eliot constantly tries to recapture Dante's balance on thoughts and emotions, and therefore, his verses on how Webster and Donne favor thought over emotions could be read as a critique. For Eliot's Webster, thought seems to be a repressive force, aiming to control the body, and at the same time, dependent on the body: "He knew that thought clings round dead limbs / Tightening its lusts and luxuries." In these verses thought seems to overpower erotic desire. These verses have to be read in relation to the final stanza, where the Abstract Entities "circumambulate" Grishkin's charm to evade the seductive smell of desire. Like Webster, "our lot crawls between dry ribs / To keep our metaphysics warm," playing with the myth that intellectual production has to distance itself from sexual reproduction or simple pleasures, and hence, concentrate on reading dead men's works.

Eliot underscores in a 1931 essay, "Donne in Our Time," how much Donne "felt" his ideas. Thought seems to be materialized, concretized in his poetry. He synthesizes Donne's aesthetics: "His attitude towards philosophic notions in his poetry may be put by saying that he was more interested in ideas themselves as objects than in the truth of ideas... Donne was, I insist, no sceptic: it is only that he is... interested in the way he feels an idea; almost as if it were something he could touch and stroke" (11). Eliot represents death as something palpable or perceivable in the poem with the references to Webster and Donne, to the skull and the fever of the bone. Still, Eliot's poem does differentiate between Webster's fascination with the physical metaphors of death and Donne's more conceptualized reactions to death: "he knew the anguish of the marrow."

For Eliot's Donne, thought seems to equal experience:

> Donne, I suppose, was such another
> Who found no substitute for sense,
> To seize and clutch and penetrate;
> Expert beyond experience.

Eliot incorporates the colloquial "I suppose" as a way of satirizing the critics who pretend to have literary authority. But it also serves as a way of recognizing Donne's revolutionary use of "natural conversational diction instead of a conventional tone" ("Donne in Our Time" 14). Peter Carpenter notes on these verses that the polysemous word *sense* evokes both sex and understanding (280). The sexual undertones of "to seize" and "penetrate" are also projected in *sense*.[24] Nevertheless, Donne is characterized as an "expert beyond experience," a subtle mockery of his lack of actual physical, material experience. Eliot remarks in his essay "The Metaphysical Poets" that: "A thought to Donne was an experience; it modified his sensibility. When a poet's mind is perfectly equipped for its work, it is constantly amalgamating disparate experience..." (117). Eliot's comments are also linked to his own aesthetic project and *The Waste Land*'s layers of literary experiences.[25] As in Paz's "Homenajes y profanaciones," memory for Donne is the creative source of experience; it remembers, reinvents, relives. Eliot's parody of Donne's and Webster's obsession with ideas is a way of synthesizing the common way of defining the Metaphysical school and the Spanish *conceptista* aesthetics. The representation of thought and memory in both Donne and Quevedo is linked to the Baroque topos of ruins because the portrayal of ruins often evokes memory as the creative force that thinks and imagines what is lost, filling the gaps between the past and the present.

The fourth stanza of "Whispers of Immortality" describes Donne's ability to metaphorically penetrate the core of things, reaching the "anguish of the marrow." Eliot remarks how the Metaphysical poets shared a peculiarity that united them: "their attempts were always analytical" (Wolf 115). They were exploring the limits of imagination and our intellectual potential, which obviously challenged Eliot and Paz. Like Webster, who knew how thought clings to the body, Donne only knows what we feel: "He knew the anguish of the marrow." Yet, the only possibility of relieving the morbid anguish, "the fever of the bone," is to have no contact with flesh, to conceive of sense as understanding and thought as experience.[26]

The second part of the poem is devoted to a parody of the feminine symbol of modern eroticism, Grishkin. B. C. Southam in his notes to "Whispers of Immortality" clarifies that Grishkin refers to Serafima Asfieva (1876–1934), a Russian dancer who opened her own ballet school in London: "Pound introduced her to Eliot," intending that a poem would result from that encounter (110). In the poem, her Russian eye and her "uncorseted bust" offer a promise of sexual pleasure and availability, which is characterized by the image of "pneumatic bliss." Southam indicates that this is a reference to the pneumatic philosophers (from the Greek *pneume*) who "regarded the spirit as no less a subject of study than the body" (111). Therefore, the poem alludes to Grishkin's faculties of attracting both the spirit and the body, the ideal form of desire for the Metaphysical poets. Southam continues to stress the experimental, humorous aspects of the image: "In 1918, the phrase was remarkable, since while pneumatic tyres and pneumatic drills were familiar, the 'pneumatic bliss' of Grishkin's 'friendly bust' was Eliot's own innovation" (111). Although the "pneumatic bliss" and the "daffodil bulbs" are different types of metaphors, they are both playing with ambiguous meanings and the mechanization of nature and of feelings.

The comparison of Grishkin to a jaguar depicts her as both wild and in control of her private space: her maisonnette and her drawing room. She surpasses the Brazilian jaguar with "her feline smell." Grishkin is portrayed as exotic not just because she is foreign, being Russian, but because she is reminiscent of the largest South American cat that preys on little monkeys, American marmosets. Pound and Eliot may feel some sort of humorous identification with those monkeys. On the other hand, Donne and Webster are the emblems of the Old World Baroque, the European poetic tradition. The Brazilian jaguar could be read as an enigmatic reference to the animals that make the Americas "strange." The strangeness and the exoticism of Latin America is precisely what is manipulated and occasionally parodied in the New World Baroque. The jaguar's lack of domesticity is opposed by inference to the European notions of controlled femininity—the placid, comfortable, indulgent cat. Grishkin's animalization is contrasted to the intellectualization, the reduction to abstractions of the Metaphysical poets. Grishkin's purpose in the poem is difficult to pinpoint. However, her presence serves to develop a burlesque tone in this "homage" to the Metaphysical poets, and at the same time, allows Eliot to joke around with Pound, who desired the creation of a poem inspired by Grishkin.

The most revealing verses are the final ones:

> And even the Abstract Entities
> Circumambulate her charm;
> But our lot crawls between dry ribs
> To keep our metaphysics warm.

Grishkin's charm seems to be especially powerful, a magnet for both abstractions and real bodies. The previous allusion to the "pneumatic philosophers" announces the Abstract Entities, which could stand for thoughts or poems revolving around Grishkin. In this sense, the final stanza parodies both Grishkin and those abstract beings by taking the conceit of "pneumatic bliss" even further. Southam emphasizes how Pound's multiple corrections of the poem make the text almost collaborative. This also explains why Pound would be part of "our lot," as Southam corroborates: "Hence we have to visualize the Abstract Entities, captivated by Grishkin's 'charm,' circling her in admiration. Whereas, the stanza continues, 'our lot'—i.e. poets such as Webster and Donne; you, Ezra, who introduced me to her; and myself—are left to find what comfort we can with fleshless bones" (113). The final verses show that "our lot" opt for "dry ribs" and empty skeletons instead of falling for her seductive, though maybe overrated, body. These poets move through poetry like the jaguar or the cat. They crawl into a dead, desiccated body to keep the Metaphysical poets warm, alive, valuable in the literary canon—whispering words of immortality.[27]

The Metaphysical poets reappear in *The Waste Land*, although not as explicitly as in "Whispers of Immortality," for example in the striking verses in "The Burial of the Dead":

> That corpse you planted last year in your garden,
> Has it begun to sprout? Will it bloom this year?
> Or has a sudden frost disturbed its bed?
> O keep the Dog far hence, that's friend to men,
> Or with his nails he'll dig it up again! (55, lines 71–75)

In Eliot's notes, where he revealed some of his literary allusions, he affirms that "O keep the Dog far hence…" is a reference to Webster's *White Devil*.[28] In the context of Webster's play, these verses echo Cornelia's words:

> And with leaves and flowers doe cover
> The friendlesse bodies of unburied men…
> But keep the wolfe far thence, that's foe to men,
> For with his nailes hee'l dig them up agen.
> (*White Devil* 182, lines 91–92, 97–98)

Cornelia is lamenting the murder of her son Marcello, killed by her other son Flamineo. In this edition, F. L. Lucas suggests in his notes that Cornelia's madness alludes to Shakespeare's Ophelia, but he does not indicate the more Classical reference to Sophocles' *Antigone* and the fratricide that leaves one of the brothers unburied. However, Lucas's comments on those verses prove to be very useful: "Again the suggestion of murder breaks through Cornelia's raving. For superstition believed that it was murdered bodies which were thus dug up… The animal ate the other parts of the flesh, but left the face undisfigured so that identification should be easy" (Webster, *The White Devil* 263n). Murder was a disgrace on both the victim and the perpetrator, while the untouched face makes the crime even more palpable, even more unforgettable. Eliot's verses suggest that both the poet and the reader have the role of the digger dog, maintaining the memory of the dead—as in the end of "Whispers of Immortality" to keep the Metaphysical poets warm. I should also point to the image in "Whispers of Immortality" of the daffodils blooming out of the skeleton's eye sockets. The imagery of the Metaphysical is both buried and revealed. The corpse is both a symbol of death and of life; it is both a buried crime and a seed that announces the seasonal rebirth. Eliot's poetic rereading of Donne and Webster metaphorically represents how criticism may bury some dead bodies, yet poets like Eliot and Pound keep them warm, so that they will bloom in their creative works.

These verses assign the poet the duties of the dog, who will dig out history's corpses from the ruins of the modern city.

The desert zone of Eliot's *The Waste Land* strikes me as being particularly in touch with Donne's *First Anniversary*, where the world is represented as being in a lethargic, convalescent state since the death of a young lady. Donne's poem is dedicated to the daughter of Sir Robert Drury, Elizabeth Drury, who died suddenly at the age of fourteen. Eliot's comments on this poem in his Clark Lectures humorously remark on the Metaphysical qualities of Donne's reflection on death:

> From one point of view it is merely a couple of insincere funerary poems on the daughter (whom he had never seen) of a rich man whose favor he wished to cultivate... It is a meditation upon death. But what a meditation! It has no philosophy, no structure or unity, no "central idea," no beginning and no end, but it is the most metaphysical of all of Donne's metaphysical poems. ("Lecture V: Donne's Longer Poems," *Varieties* 151)

Eliot complains that in comparison with Dante, his ideal poet, Donne is the poet of chaos, "a voluptuary of thought." In his lecture on Crashaw he compares the three poets, asserting that Dante had the best system of thought and feeling, whereas Donne created a "sequence of thoughts which are felt," and Crashaw developed "a sequence of feelings which are thought" (*Varieties* 183). In essays such as this, Eliot maintains that Donne's poetry has no structure but in others that it has a unique order. In his essay on "John Donne" in 1923, he compares him with Baudelaire in that "every new mood is prepared by and implicit in the preceding mood—the mind has unity and order. And so with Donne" ("John Donne" 332). Yet in 1931 he writes about Donne's lack of organization, to argue that he was not a medieval poet: "Donne is the antithesis of the Scholastic, of the mystic, and of the philosophical system maker. The encyclopaedic ambitions of the schoolmen were directed always towards unification... In Donne, there is a manifest fissure between thought and sensibility, a chasm which in his poetry he bridged in his own way" ("Donne in Our Time" 8). Although it would be easy to accuse Eliot of contradicting himself, these statements reveal what he considered to be the main Metaphysical qualities of Donne's school. Donne redefines the notions of unity by creating a poetics that associated dissimilar elements or opposing forces. In his final Clark Lecture on nineteenth-century poetry on Laforgue, Corbière, and Baudelaire, Eliot emphasizes their ties with Donne's poetics of relativity with the aim of linking contradictory elements. He states that "the *real* metaphysical poetry of the nineteenth and the twentieth centuries springs from the belief in Good and Evil, and consists in a conscious and deliberate contrast *and* confusion of the moral and intellectual with the non-moral and unintellectual" (Lecture VIII, "The Nineteenth Century: Summary and Comparison," *Varieties* 211). It is playing with the malleable boundary between extremes that Eliot both condemns and emulates.

Eliot idealizes Dante's sense of unity and poetic structure, yet he recognizes that the fragmentary Modernist aesthetics is closer to Donne's work. He is particularly interested in Donne's role in the process of the "disintegration of the intellect in modern Europe" (*Varieties* 158). Eliot emphasizes that he speaks with regards to poetry and not modern Europe's decline. His choice of words like "disintegration" and "decay" supposedly does not respond to their moral or historical significance, but to poetic values and structure, in contrast with Dante's model of integration. However, what really lies behind his theory is his aesthetic aim to reconcile the intellect with emotions; and even if he washes his hands of moral questions, he is very much criticizing and judging Western society and its historical course. Like Paz, Eliot sees himself as a re-builder of the ruins of tradition.

To analyze the topos of ruins in Donne may seem far-fetched because no poem of his is explicitly dedicated to a ruined city. Nevertheless, Donne uses the metaphor of ruins on multiple occasions, which encourages the discussion of Eliot's notions of disintegration in Metaphysical poetry. Thomas Docherty explains how the scientific discoveries of the era change the relation of poetry to history, which may be enlightening when considering Donne's *First Anniversary*: "With the Copernican revolution in astronomical thought, there occurs a fundamental 'displacement' of the Earth and of the privileged position accorded humanity. Centrality and stable certainty are lost..." (8). Eliot's characterization of Donne as a poet of chaos is precisely reflecting the spatial displacement of his poetry. The uncertainty that Docherty emphasizes is what Eliot perceives as part of the "disintegration of the intellect."

Donne's *First Anniversary* depicts a deformed world, which could also be connected to the New World Baroque aesthetics of bizarreness and deformity. Although Donne is not referring to the Americas, but rather to the beginning of the world as narrated by the Christian tradition: "The world did in her cradle take a fall, / And turned her brains, and took a general maim / Wronging each joint of th' universal frame" (275, lines 96–98).[29] The personification of the world as a fallen child, whose deformity disrupts its frame, determines its future as doomed to decay instead of progress. On the other hand, the portrayal of the New World as deformed in texts from the "Barroco de Indias" underscores the discourse of its exceptionality. Being a deformed world does not necessarily lead up to decay or the apocalypse; it may simply be a metaphor for a world that needs to be reshaped, giving it a new form. However, Donne uses American exoticism not so much in comparison to Europe, but as a way of praising the dead lady's charm: "she whose rich eyes, and breast, / Gilt the West Indies, and perfumed the East; / Whose having breathed in this world, did bestow / Spice on those isles…" (276, lines 229–32). With her beauty she supposedly surpasses the value of gold and spices, extracted from both East and West corners of the world. She becomes the ideal form that gives body, brightness, and perfumes to the New World— the exotic, far away Other.

Just as Eliot criticizes Donne's lack of structure and unity, Donne is protesting the lack of unity and coherence in the world's deformed social sphere. Wolf states that "John Donne's often quoted lines from the 'Anatomy of the World' complain not only of the cosmological and epistemological decay of the dominant world-view but also of social disintegration" (31).

> 'Tis all in pieces, all coherence gone;
> All just supply, and all relation:
> Prince, subject, father, son, are things forgot,
> For everyman alone thinks he hath got
> To be a phoenix… (276, lines 213–17)

The patriarchal structure of power is also crumbling along with many seventeenth-century edifices, and her death is just another symptom of the rotten world he describes. One of Donne's apostrophes to the world in the *First Anniversary* also exposes the morbid anguish evoked in "Whispers of Immortality": "Sick world, yea dead, yea putrefied, since she / Thy intrinsic balm, and thy preservative, / Can never be renewed thou never live" (272, lines 56–58). Docherty also pinpoints how women become the symbol of historical mutability by threatening to change masculine order. Yet paradoxically, women are used as the motives for poetic creation. Through their idealization, that longed-for order can be restored (9).[30] Elizabeth Drury was the "pure angelic element that gave the world sense, direction, shape and meaning. With her dead, the world is in a state of decay, confusion and chaos. The poem is to work as a talisman, restoring order with the return of this ghostly genius, the name of Elizabeth Drury" (228). As a *donna angelica,* she becomes a symbol of certainty and faith that protects us from the world of ruins and chaos. The sterile body, death, and disillusionment are recurrent topics and images in both Donne and Eliot. Their use of these themes also connects them to the poetics of disenchantment that I pinpointed in Baudelaire and Cernuda. In Eliot's *The Waste Land*, as in Donne's poem, the land is described as dead and putrefied; it has no water, no fertilizer, and no preservative. Yet there is no idealized dead lady, no Beatrice; only the lonely Tiresias, emblem of the poet's infertility, remains.

In *The Waste Land,* Tiresias exposes the poet's blindness, his infertility as part of a city in ruins. William Chapman Sharpe indicates that Eliot's metropolis represents "the ruin of Western civilization." Tiresias seems to be scavenging the pieces. Sharpe argues that *The Waste Land* is a poem about the process of reading and Tiresias is the "hypocrite lecteur" frustrated with his lack of literary insights. Sharpe explains how Eliot's text is integrated into the tradition of Baudelaire, Whitman, and Wordsworth's urban poetics:

>...in the nineteenth century the urban poet of *Tableaux parisiens, Leaves of Grass,* or *The Prelude* represents his encounter with the other in a mimetic way, as an incident spawned by the new social and physical conditions of the great city. But the twentieth century poet encounters the other—and the city—as already written, as a figure already displaced into quotation, pastiche, collage, poetic text. Eliot destabilizes time, space and mimetic effect, so that his

metropolis becomes a polyphonic... multivoiced, unabashedly literary artefact... (118)

Tiresias reveals the importance of pastiche in the poem, both
as a Classical character from Sophocles' tragedies and as the
representative of the modern reader; he is both woman and
man, subject and object, producer and product of the spaces of
waste.

In "The Burial of the Dead," winter covers death's marks with
its snow: "Winter kept us warm, covering / Earth in forgetful
snow" (53, lines 5–6). The dead land is dressed in white like the
white sheet of paper—evoking the beginning of the poem. Tradition is far from being a readable mirror of the past: "A heap of
broken images, where the sun beats" (line 22). Donne's decayed
world is also exposed through images in the second stanza like
the "dead tree" and the "dry stone." Eliot's search for origins in
the Metaphysical poets could also be contained in his rhetorical
question: "What are the roots that clutch, what branches grow /
Out of this stony rubbish?" (lines 19–20). After resettling all the
stones from his literary edifice, Eliot's roots—Dante, Donne,
Webster, Shakespeare, and Baudelaire, among others—will be
recovered. *The Waste Land*'s final verses—"These fragments
I have shored against my ruins" (69, line 431)—allude to all
the voices and the literary fragments that compose its intricate
nest. In this text the topos of ruins is a pretext to incorporate and
parody in a fragmentary fashion all the hierarchical figures in
Eliot's poetic canon.

The "tumbled graves," the "falling towers," and the ruined
cities of "What the Thunder Said" portray a landscape linked
to Donne's apocalyptic vision of the future, where "This
world, in that great earthquake languished" (Donne 270, line
11). Donne's poem is an elegy to a young lady; supposedly, its
ultimate goal is to pay homage to her memory and to express
his pain in confronting death. A few verses earlier in the poem,
Eliot quotes the famous Provençal poet Arnaut Daniel, who tells
Dante in *Purgatory 26* to remember his pain, before hiding himself again in the fire: "Poi s'ascose nel foco che li affina" ("Then
he hid himself in the fire that refines them" [canto XXVI, 445]).
Eliot's work also traces his own pain, his own modern anguish.

This modern anguish may be the product of a split of
consciousness, which seems to be both dissected and cured in

the medical project of Donne's *Anatomy of the World.* Yet why did Eliot choose Donne's work over other English canonical poets to ponder upon his own poetic practice and existential anguish? Docherty asserts that Donne's poetry had therapeutic qualities for Eliot's generation:

> The poetry of Donne thus becomes a means of therapy for the modernist poet or reader, suffering from our split of consciousnesses and the need of restitution, wholeness and pure individuality. The immediacy and unity of Donne's poetry, then, are construed as therapeutic devices... But Donne's poetry is also difficult, as it dislocates language into meaning: obscurity of the medium rather than clarity... (5)

Docherty pinpoints why Eliot reconsiders Donne's poetry in the context of the twentieth century: it is a model of the lost unity the Modernist poet nostalgically longs for. However, just as Docherty reveals that Donne's work is not exactly a pure and clear manifestation of a poetic wholeness, but is full of obscure conceits and enigmatic metaphors, I would stress that Eliot's reading of Donne does not limit the Metaphysical poet to a homogenous notion of unity. Quite the contrary, Eliot's Clark Lectures and his 1931 "Donne in Our Time" underline Donne's obscurity and the chaotic nature of his poetry. Eliot's criticism often exposed the contradictions that make both Donne and his poetic works difficult to decipher.

Conversely, Paz does not read in Donne and Quevedo an escape from or a therapy for the modern split of consciousness. In opposition to Docherty's argument, Paz emphasizes that Donne and Quevedo are the originators of modern poetic sensibility precisely because of their awareness of the split of consciousness. For Paz, the fissure of consciousness is a form of identification, a stamp of Modernity, which is represented in the cities in ruins. Paz shares Eliot's modern disenchantment and sense of distress.[31] When Paz compares Quevedo's and Donne's works, he holds that their consciousness of the fractured self is strikingly modern. Unlike Eliot's lamentation of the fissure, the disintegration of society, Paz seems to be celebrating it:

> Quevedo... nos muestra la visión de la caída de la conciencia en sí misma, una caída que revela nuestra fractura interior...

el primer poema realmente moderno de la literatura española
es *Lágrimas de un penitente*... Y si pienso en la poesía europea de esa época, sólo encuentro en Donne una premonición
semejante, en un pasaje de *The First Anniversary, An Anatomy of the World*. ("Reflejos: Réplicas" 74–75)

Paz indicates that the Metaphysical and the Conceptualist poets
share a consciousness of a fallen conscience, although there is a
poignant difference between them in their representation of the
universe. Donne meditates on the decay and the fragmentation
of the universe, incorporating the revolutionary scientific theories of his time, while Quevedo does not venture into explicit
reflections about the cosmos. Nonetheless, I would reiterate
that Quevedo's sonnet "Avisos de la muerte," which begins
with "Miré los muros de la patria mía," for instance, is a poem
that compares the devastation of the city with the decay and the
mortality of the body. It could well serve as a microcosm for
the universe, although the homeland is not the universe.[32] But
the problem of attributing to Donne and Quevedo the category
of originators of Modernity is that once again it obviates many
great poets and diverse ways of defining modern sensibility.
It signals the neo-Baroque obsession with discovering origins
and attributing originality to certain originators in their literary
labyrinth. Paz's reading of Quevedo in comparison with Donne
becomes relevant in the analysis of how he intends to parody
"Amor constante más allá de la muerte" and also how he trans-
lates one of Donne's poems.

Paz's reflection on Donne and Quevedo as initiators of the
modern tradition is not limited to his essays. In 1958, he translated Donne's "Elegy 19, To His Mistress Going to Bed." José
María Rodríguez García challenges Paz's intention to honor
Donne through his translation: "Paz deliberately sets out to an-
tiquate Donne—to cause him to become outdated—rather than
modernize him as he claims" (156). Rodríguez García argues
that Paz's translation becomes more than a "transculturating"
practice: it censures the erotic and philosophic defiance of
Donne's "Elegy 19" by domesticating its language. He maintains that Paz misrepresents and misreads Donne in his translation by not recognizing that the erotic experience described in
the poem is an imagined, voyeuristic, autoerotic act. He finally
indicates that "Paz uses Donne to create a convenient other, the

false consciousness of a literary periodization against which he can define himself as unequivocally modern" (173). Thus, Paz's poem is a beautiful piece that nevertheless misrepresents Donne's text and context. Paz's parodic homages to Donne and Quevedo embrace the topos of ruins through human remains; the modern split of consciousness literally ruptures the body, but may find solace in poetry.

Paz's Quevedo: From Love to Ruins, a Parody of Conceits

"Homenaje y profanaciones" could also be read as a form of translation and a transculturating practice. It could be read both as a bridge between the Spanish Baroque and the neo-Baroque and as a wall between eras, styles, and poets. Paz's excavation into Donne's and Quevedo's poetry aims to find the roots of modern sensibility, the vestiges of a fallen conscience. The main difference between the translation of Donne's poem and "Homenaje y profanaciones" is that in the latter the insistence on deforming, misrepresenting, and profaning Quevedo's sonnet is blatantly obvious, while in the translation there seems to be a desire to be faithful to the "essence" of the poem. Whatever their purpose, both Paz and Eliot make us reread Donne and Quevedo, redefined by a Modernist poetic tradition, and turn them into originators of that very Modernity.

"Homenaje y profanaciones" is Paz's ultimate poetic reading of Quevedo's famous poem "Amor constante más allá de la muerte," where he both pays homage to and, like so many literary sons, attempts to parody Quevedo's sonnet. Paz's title underscores that paradoxical intention. However, I suggest that Paz's "Homenaje y profanaciones" does not successfully parody Quevedo's poem. Paz's piece exposes a more pessimistic, more sceptical view of death and the remains of the body. The poem is divided into three parts, reflecting the structure of the sonnet. Paz indicates that the poem is a disfiguration of Quevedo's classic text: the first quatrain serves as introduction, the second presents a conflict, and the two tercets provide a solution. *Aspiración* stands for Quevedo's first quatrain, and in Paz's words, it expresses "inhalación, afirmación y homenaje"; *Espiración* represents the second quatrain, and it implies "interrogación, negación y profanación"; and *Lauda* stands for the two tercets that point to a sense of beyond, "más allá de la afirmación o la negación, la eternidad o muerte."[33] Both *Aspiración* and *Espiración* point to the act of breathing, inhaling or exhaling; they imply that the poem is part of a living body and its final goal is to express its own vivacity. Paz explains *Lauda* as a "piedra sepulcral," which alludes to the praise of the dead in their own tombs. This last stone may refer to the literary dead that need to be remembered, similar to Eliot's attempt to keep the Metaphysical poets warm. The purpose of these three parts is to evoke the structure of the sonnet, while pondering upon each stanza of Quevedo's poem with its respective imagery and metaphors.

Both Quevedo and Donne play with bizarre and bold conceits, the typical antitheses of temporality and eternity, body and soul that are prevalent in all Metaphysical poetry.[34] Paz's poem plays with these dichotomies, but especially in the final stanza, he desires to transcend them through the enumeration of the senses and the profusion of temporal adverbs. This is part of his attempt to create a poem of totalizing dimensions, distancing himself from the excessive use of antitheses in Baroque poetry.

In his essay "Quevedo, Heráclito y algunos sonetos," Paz discusses his reading of Quevedo's poem: "El famoso soneto de Quevedo *Amor constante más allá de la muerte*, que Dámaso Alonso considera 'probablemente el mejor de la literatura española,' es un ejemplo extraordinario de la cristalización del deseo en idea fija. La imaginación deseante se afirma con una suerte de blasfema obstinación, no frente a la vida y sus mutaciones sino ante la muerte" (130). In both Quevedo's and Paz's poems, death is only confronted and transcended through memory and the poetic imagination. The poem serves as a tool, a weapon against death and oblivion. Love is expressed and materialized through the body, which death can transform but not obliterate. Paz's reading emphasizes the resurrection of the body in the sonnet:

> Quevedo se aparta del platonismo y del petrarquismo: no afirma la inmortalidad del alma sino la del cuerpo, literalmente reanimado por la pasión... Pero... el agente de la resurrección no es Dios sino el amor humano hacia otra criatura humana... no hay realmente resurrección del cuerpo sino reanimación de sus despojos. (131)

It is not divine love but human love that awakens the remains of the dead body. However, the reanimation of the body is provoked by the soul's connection to another being who remembers and loves that dead body. Quevedo's portrait of the dead body is strikingly modern and disturbing. Yet in a lecture in 1996, Paz oversimplifies the first part of his "Homenaje y profanaciones": "*Aspiración* recoge los temas neoplatónicos de Quevedo aunque en un lenguaje moderno: la memoria, el amor y la inmortalidad del alma" ("Reflejos: Réplicas" 78). If we compare these two essays, Paz seems to contradict himself. I would argue that Quevedo's modern idiom relies precisely on his ability to combine neo-Platonic themes with the concreteness of secular love, confronting and surviving death. Paz explores the paradoxical representation of *eros* and *thanatos* in his "Homenaje y profanaciones," more a tribute to Quevedo than a parody of his work. On the other hand, "Homenaje y profanaciones" has been compared by Manuel Ulacia to a collage or a deformation of Quevedo's sonnet, parallel to Picasso's parody of Velázquez's *Las Meninas*, in the context of the revalorization of Baroque aesthetics in twentieth-century poetry and painting ("Francisco de Quevedo" 207). In this sense, it recalls Eliot's "Whispers of Immortality" and its ironic tone. Memory and imagination are the creative sources of both poems.

"Homenaje y profanaciones" could be read as a metaphor of how to write a poem, a sonnet about sonnets, and so the whiteness of the first stanzas, just as in the snow of "The Burial of the Dead," resembles the whiteness of the blank page: "Yo no veo nada sino lo blanco... el alma desatada del ansia y de la hora" (341). The whiteness of the page evokes the blinding light of Quevedo's "blanco día," as well as the multiple possibilities of poetic re-creation, without time as a limitation. The white light created by the paradoxical shadows of the day imposes on the speaker a physical and a metaphorical blindness; thus, just as in Baudelaire, vision is only possible through memory and imagination. The act of reading and re-creating through memory also gives these artists the needed temporal distance of any parodist.

The second part of *Aspiración* reveals that remembering the beloved's body gives it meaning and life. As in Eliot's poems, remembering the dead is an act of creation that secures the literary immortality of both the subject and the object of remembrance. In Quevedo's sonnet, death triggers a fire, which fuses memory and body. Paz alludes to Quevedo's metaphor of the body as a God, "Alma a quien todo un Dios prisión ha sido," when he describes the dead body as "Cuerpo de un Dios que fue cuerpo abrasado, / Dios que fue cuerpo y fue cuerpo endiosado" (340).[35] Although it is easy to misread these verses and interpret a reference to Christ, if we consider Paz's essays on Quevedo's sonnet, we would recognize that the body evoked is deified by love and memory.

The third part of *Aspiración* aims to be the center of the homage to Quevedo. Nevertheless, the wordplays, the paronomasia, meant to capture the Baroque are actually too elaborate: "Sombra del sol Solombra segadora," "el nudo desanuda," "el ánima desanimada," and "la memoria desmembrada" (342). These wordplays create a stylistic distance between Paz's poem and Quevedo's sonnet. Still, Paz successfully transforms Quevedo's oxymoron of memory: "nadar sabe mi llama el agua fría." Paz's verses, "nada contra corriente y mandamiento / nada contra la nada," suggest that memory must swim against nihilism, holding on to the belief in the immortality of the soul (342). Memory oxymoronically fuses fire and water, defying the river of forgetfulness. Along with memory, imagination is the other source of creativity in *Aspiración*, with the verses "pensar que transfigura la memoria / el resto es un manojo de centellas" (342). The poetic imagination transforms memory and gives it a particular energy or brightness. The roles of imagination and of memory in these poems underline the manipulation and the distance Paz and Eliot want to establish in their burlesque recuperation of Quevedo and Donne.

In contrast to *Aspiración*, *Espiración* presents us with real doubts about the immortality of the soul and the power of memory to survive: "Tiempo de luz: memoria, torre hendida…Todas tus piedras vueltas pensamiento / la ciudad se desprende de sí misma…" (342–43). These verses allude to *The Waste Land*'s falling towers and the ways Eliot develops metaphors of time passing: "Falling towers / Jerusalem Athens Alexandria / Vienna London / Unreal /… And upside down in air were towers / Tolling reminiscent bells, that kept the hours / And voices singing out of empty cisterns and exhausted wells…" (67, lines 374–77;

68, lines 383–85). These towers in "What the Thunder Said" represent lost empires and societies such as the Greek, the Austro-Hungarian, and the British. The bells remember the past and signal the passing hours, while the voices recapture a typical characteristic of the topos of ruins: the evocation of the phantoms, the voices of the past. The lack of water distinguishes Eliot's dry, cracked landscape; and all the forms of saving water, the main ingredient for life, are exhausted. In Paz's poem the topos of ruins—ruined bodies, cities in ruins, ruined literary gods—is materialized in the recurrent presence of stones. As in Rodrigo Caro's "Canción a las ruinas de Itálica," not even the stones that tell the story remain untouched by time. The city disintegrates when the stones become thoughts, memories of vanished buildings. These verses evoke Eliot's cities in ruins, illustrating that literary memory is a fragile construction. This apocalyptic vision is introduced by "Cielos de fin de mundo," which seem to seclude the world, "el mundo no es visible. / Se lo comió la luz" (342). In an attempt to secure his own immortality, the speaker paradoxically evokes his own mortality and imagines his own death as bright light, "tiempo de luz"—a moment in time that dissipates all space, his body, city, and world.

It is his own immortality that is in question in the second part of *Espiración*:

> Vana conversación del esqueleto
> con el fuego insensato y con el agua
> que no tiene memoria… y con la tierra
> que se calla y se come sus palabras. (343)

This skeleton does not bloom with nature like the ones in "Whispers of Immortality" and *The Waste Land*. In a pessimistic tone, the speaker plays dead, frustrated by his own decomposition. Nature does not speak in this poem; the poem speaks for nature. His own immortality is only secured through poetry, Paz's textual body. In the third stanza of this second part, time is written in "mi suma," "la huella," "el sello de los ayes y los años" (343). His poetic memory is maintained in "el trazo negro de la quemadura / del amor en lo blanco de los huesos." Much as death transforms the body, "el trazo negro" of the ink marks, paints, "burns" the white paper, "el blanco de los huesos" (343).

The wordplay and empty conceits of the third part of *Espiración* accentuate Paz's burlesque tone. The repetition of sounds, the internal rhyme, and the use of homophone words pretend to ridicule Quevedo, but they ultimately highlight the reverence to the stone, a sepulchral praise for the dead poet. This part is intended to be a profanation of Quevedo, his tomb, his style. The repetition of the paradoxical verse "Sol de sombra Solombra cegadora" (343) accentuates the burlesque attitude. This stanza implies that death imposes another way of seeing and in this sense is another act of imagination. But ironically, this part of the poem raises a much more remarkable issue, the temporality and atemporality of death. His eyes have to imagine, to see the invisible: "lo que miraron sin mirarlo nunca" (343). They saw, in past tense, making the act of imagining one of remembrance. This is a meta-poetic instance, since Paz is remembering and imagining Quevedo and at the same time seeing the unforeseeable: his own death.

In one of his essays on Quevedo, Paz emphasizes that imagination is a historical construction ("Quevedo, Heráclito" 132). With "El entierro es barroco todavía / en México," he upholds that the burial of the dead—our ways of imagining, remembering, or paying homage to our dead—is a historical and cultural endeavor, with temporal, "todavía" and "barroco," and spatial, "México," particularities (343–44). Just as in Eliot's "The Burial of the Dead," the Mexican funeral rites are portrayed as ways of engraving the traces of the dead. However, the only "universal" certainty, without temporal or spatial particularities, is death itself: "Morir es todavía / morir a cualquier hora en cualquier parte" (344). Thus, Paz tries to reconcile both Mexican death and universal death. These verses are particularly revealing because they assert that contemporary Mexican culture has its roots in Baroque aesthetics. The historical and poetic continuity Paz establishes in these verses attests that, like Eliot, he is trying to understand and conceptualize the present through the past.

In between the first and the third stanzas discussed lies a second stanza that focuses on the "profanation" of Quevedo's Baroque style. The alliteration of "Los laúdes del láudano de loas" points to the musical instruments in a *loa*, praise for an honorable man, used to introduce a play that can calm down the audience with an opiate effect (343). The "dilapidadas lápidas y laudos" (343) refers to the squandering of commemorative stones for the poet, and "la piedad de la piedra despiadada" describes the tomb of the poet. Death is "despiadada," while the stone itself shows pity by recalling the buried person. The final verse of the stanza, "las velas del velorio y del jolgorio" (343), ironically portrays through its internal rhyme the religious and cultural ritual of the funeral and is connected to the next stanza, where the Mexican burial is characterized as Baroque. The emphasis on the stone as the permanent sign of identity and death creates a contrast with the ephemeral nature of the body. The representation of the stone is another form of aspiring to immortality when nothing but a name is left of our remains.

In *Lauda* the disintegration of the body, portrayed in Quevedo's sonnet as reanimated by love's power, is actually recalled later on as "polvo de los sentidos sin sentido / ceniza lo sentido y el sentido" (344).[36] As in Donne's and Quevedo's poems, these verses stress the conceptualist play with the double meaning of sense or "sentido," as signaled by the abstract "lo" and the more specific "el." Quevedo's famous verses "serán ceniza, mas tendrá sentido; / polvo serán, mas polvo enamorado" (179) are truly "profaned" as sense and feeling become mere ashes. The next two stanzas exemplify the ravages of death. They go from the particularity of the deterioration of the body to the remains of the cities in ruins.

The eyes of the corpse are the main focus of this stanza: "los dos ojos / atónitos, los dos ojos vacíos… / la visión sin visiones entrevista, / los dos ojos cubriéndose de hormigas" (344). The Surrealist imagery of a decomposed body and the metonymy of the dead, blind eyes also remind me of the eye sockets in "Whispers of Immortality" and the blind reader Tiresias in *The Waste Land*. The eyes invaded by the minuscule ants—an imagist allusion to *Un perro andaluz*—also recall the Baroque topos of the ruins overpowered by nature, and Caro's "Itálica": "La casa para el César fabricada / ¡ay! yace de lagartos vil morada."[37] The similarities between these two poems are not coincidental, since Paz gives us an obvious allusion to Caro's poem in the next stanza: "Itálica famosa, madriguera de ratas / y lugares comunes, muladar de motores, / víboras en Uxmal anacoretas" (344). Caro's hymn to "Itálica famosa" epitomizes the Baroque poems of ruins. Although "Homenaje y profanaciones" is in honor of Quevedo, Paz also remembers and parodies Caro's poem, among others, in condemning its profusion of commonplaces.

The continuity between the decrepitude of the body and that of civilization is also signaled by the invasion of the ruined cities by strange and misplaced animals: rats, vipers, crabs, and octopi. Paz tries to critically escape those emblematic representations of cities in ruins in his incorporation of contrasting surreal images and elements from different historical eras. The "muladar de motores" shows a modern landscape of abandoned motors, decrepit machines in a rubbish dump, near the city walls. The image of Modernity's obsolescence is contrasted with "el emporio de centollas o imperio de los pólipos," both symbols of power and commerce but ridiculed by the new owners, crabs and octopi. Itálica and Uxmal, representative of the Roman and the Mayan heritages, are also united by the metaphors "el emporio de centollas o imperio de los pólipos." Two ruined cities of both the European and the American continents, Itálica and Uxmal, emphasize the continuity between two historical traditions that still influence current Hispanic culture. The rats of the south of Spain and the vipers of the ancient Mayan city in Mexico's Yucatán seem to be pathetic remnants of those two powerful empires. The two cities are now made of layers of diverse eras and architectural projects. "Sobre los lomos del acorazado," the layers of history settle: labyrinths, cathedrals, bicycles, and broken gods. Ancient, medieval, and modern traditions are all integrated into these spaces of waste from the past and the future, symbolizing the impossible recollection of ruins.

The final part of "Homenaje y profanaciones" recaptures the repetitive style and continues to insist on death's constancy in both the historical life of cities and city dwellers. These cities in ruins are the footprints of "la muerte immortal de la historia." Paz denotes the meaning of these verses: "entre la historia y sus fechas (la historia como productora de ruinas) y la inmortalidad anónima de la naturaleza (mata a los individuos para que sobreviva la especie) están el hombre y la mujer" ("Reflejos: Réplicas" 79). History and nature are the only forces that defy death; their immortality produces a constant, a cyclical time that merges the construction and destruction of cities. However, even if Paz's comment suggests that ruins will always be produced as long as history continues to evolve, he seems to situate in a different sphere the role of men and women. The emphasis on the unification of the almost abstract, "universal" bodies of the man and the woman at the end of "Homenaje y profanaciones" intends to conclude the poem with a hopeful message. This idealized heterosexual bliss reinforces Paz's poetics of reconciliation, as I will discuss in the following section. The union of the lovers' bodies as the answer to the imminent future of ruins is implicitly tied to Freud's ideas in *Civilization and Its Discontents* on sexual reproduction as the force that fights off our death instinct—deeply connected to Paz's reflection on history as a producer of ruins. In this sense, this final move toward the fusion of bodies leads Paz's poem into an exaltation of the natural, in contrast with the historical.

Poetry becomes a handcrafted enterprise: "Hoy… esculpimos un Dios instantáneo / tallamos el vértigo" (345). These verses celebrate the union of two lovers' bodies, where the sexual act is compared to the poetic practice itself and its creation of gods. Paz himself corroborates this reading: "el dios es un dios instantáneo creado por la unión de los cuerpos y que se deshace cuando éstos se separan" ("Reflejos: Réplicas" 79) The lovers search for the lost body, the vanished instant:

> Nos buscamos perdidos
> dentro de ese cuerpo instantáneo
> nos perdemos buscando
> todo un Dios todo un cuerpo y sentido
> otro cuerpo perdido. (345)

In *Espiración*, Paz tries to extend Quevedo's poetic reflection on a universal death through the iconography of cities in ruins. However, in these last stanzas, Paz goes back to Quevedo's sonnet. The evocation of the lovers' union defies history and its ruins, time and its temporal adverbs. The reconciliatory move of love and death through poetry is Paz's consolation when he faces the spaces of waste that Eliot's poetry uncovers. This explains why he chooses Quevedo's "Amor constante más allá de la muerte" instead of "A Roma sepultada en sus ruinas" when it comes to rewriting a Baroque poem, which will be fundamental for the neo-Baroque aesthetic project.

In the final part of *Lauda,* the two bodies that become one, "Festín de dos cuerpos a solas," project the neo-Platonic notion of love. The erotic imagery of an embrace that creates "un Dios instantáneo," "todo un Dios todo cuerpo y sentido," desires to distort the spiritual union. Paz refers to Quevedo's metaphor of the body as a God who imprisons the soul, "Alma a quien todo un Dios prisión ha sido." In this way, Paz eroticizes even further Quevedo's poem. *Lauda* finally disrupts all notions of temporality, eternity, and death, by fusing the lovers' bodies and their memories: "los cuerpos abolidos en el cuerpo / memorias desmemorias de haber sido / antes después ahora nunca siempre" (345). The lack of conjunctions and commas re-enacts the breathlessness of this collage of temporal paradoxes.

The Neo-Baroque Chiaroscuro of Paz's "Himno entre ruinas"

Paz's "Himno entre ruinas" is also a hymn to the literary ruins and edifices of the Baroque tradition. As Paz himself points out in *Los hijos del limo*, neo-Baroque poets want to be identified with their precursors. In this poem, Paz distances himself from the literary tradition of the ruins "al no evocar las glorias del pasado y fijar su atención más en la naturaleza que en la historia," as John Fein asserts ("Himno entre ruinas" 165).[38] Paz does not mention in his "Himno entre ruinas" any specific historical event or proper name, except for Polifemo, a mythical figure. Fein also remarks the tension between nature and history, maintaining that Paz privileges nature. As I previously proposed regarding "Homenaje y profanaciones," in the topos of ruins nature tends to be the survivor of time, the embodiment of eternity. Further than that, for José Lezama Lima, American nature symbolizes culture itself. Its monstrous landscape is the *agent provocateur* of all its cultural expressions. But in Paz's poem, nature is not necessarily American; in the first few stanzas, we are transported to the Old European World. The tension between nature and culture, history's ruins, is materialized through the structure of Paz's "Himno entre ruinas," divided into two types of stanzas: the odd-numbered stanzas are characterized by the luminosity of the Mediterranean natural landscape and the Classical ruins, while the even stanzas, highlighted by italics, are marked by darkness and a pessimistic tone, alluding to the decadence of the modern city. Paz's text manifests a desire to honor a mythical, natural world and condemn the historical reality of social oppression and corruption.[39]

The poem is introduced by an epigraph from Góngora's "Fábula de Polifemo y Galatea," emphasizing the chiaroscuro we will encounter throughout the text. The first stanza opens with the sunrise, "¡Alto grito amarillo...!" and "la herida cárdena del monte resplandece," an image that will be crucial to close the temporal cycle at the end of the poem (233). The odd stanzas that portray a bright sun and the even stanzas placed under the shadows of "un sol anémico" or "un sol sin crepúsculo" evoke the chiaroscuro. Jason Wilson notes how the change of scenery relates to Baroque aesthetics: "The physical landscape of Sicily, with its... fertile nature, enters Paz's poem from Góngora, as does the notion of the uncorrupt world of poetry, opposed to the mindless violence of World War II, the rivalry between Galatea and Polifemo modernized" (45). As in "Homenaje y profanaciones," Freud's theories on society's tension between the death instinct and the life instinct could also be considered to discuss Polifemo and Galatea. In Góngora's poem, Polifemo is overwhelmed and overpowered by what Freud calls the "instinct of aggressiveness and destructiveness," while Galatea represents *eros*, the emblem of love and beauty, through which arises those uncontrollable desires (78). In contrast with the fusion of lovers in "Homenaje y profanaciones," the two characters personify the antithetic elements of human nature that Freud ponders. The metaphors of light and darkness that respectively embody Galatea and Polifemo also project the structural division of Paz's "Himno entre ruinas."[40]

The Classical ruins depicted in the first stanza are contrasted with the Mexican ruins and the young people's indifference toward the remains of their cultural heritage: "¡Estatua rota, / columnas comidas por la luz, / ruinas vivas en un mundo de muertos en vida!"[41] The broken statues are molded by time, symbolized by the sun and its devouring light. Some may associate the broken statues with Paz's and Eliot's fallen towers and cities in ruins, but in "Himno entre ruinas" the Classical ruins do not represent decay or destruction. These ruins are alive, as opposed to the human beings who surround them. They may be broken and abandoned, but in Paz's poem they are one with the natural landscape, the sun, the sea, the cliffs and its goats. The verse that precedes the broken statue verse is "Todo es dios." The statues that used to represent the Roman mythical gods do not represent them anymore. The broken statue and the decayed columns serve as a paradoxical contrast to the Mexican youngsters, smoking marijuana, alive but dead.

Similarly to the situation in Caro's "Canción a las ruinas de Itálica," the speaker must embark on an archaeological project: "¿dónde desenterrar a la palabra?" Is there a "word"? Do those pyramids have buried voices that want to tell their story? We don't know. Unlike Neruda in *Alturas de Macchu Picchu,* Paz does not even attempt to speak for the voices of the Aztecs. He only evokes the nostalgic, desperate "canto mexicano... piedra que nos cierra las puertas del contacto" (234). As I will suggest in my discussion of "Petrificada petrificante," the stones symbolize the social and economic immobility in Mexico. The Mexican song, in contrast with this poem's intentions, becomes a stone that divides the past and the present—it impedes any form of reflection, any contact zone. The second stanza reveals a strong critique of the lack of communication in contemporary Mexican society. It is a city of "muertos en vida"; the image of sterility prevalent in *The Waste Land* is captured in the last verse, "sabe la tierra a tierra envejecida." The speaker is like a buried corpse, tasting the leftovers of the earth. The land is fruitless and therefore futureless. In her essay "Nostalgia and Exile," Noël Valis discusses Paz's *El laberinto de la soledad* and remarks: "Paz's Mexico becomes a metaphor of modern alienation, the feeling of displacement and dispossession which flooded the geographies and the hearts of the post–World War II era. In Paz's vision of things, we are all living in exile, expelled from the present, from the fullness of time and space" (128). Although Valis does not specify any poem, her reading of Paz's *El laberinto de la soledad* accurately describes the role of Mexico in "Himno entre ruinas." The Mexican youngsters are on top of the pyramids, in the middle of the Aztec city in ruins, alienated from modern society and yet oblivious to the past, to the edifices of their cultural history.

In the odd stanzas, the speaker finds eternity in the delight of the senses and the abundance of nature. As in Caro's last stanza of "Itálica," where the only permanent remains are San Geroncio's, the eternal in the third stanza of "Himno entre ruinas" is also evoked with religious language: "resurrección," "vino, pan solar," "esbelta catedral," and "templos en el mar." Nevertheless, the fourth stanza situates itself in the urban landscape and the shadow that surrounds the superpowers: "Nueva York, Londres, Moscú. La sombra cubre al llano con su yedra fantasma." The ruins of post-war Europe are now divided between the communist and the capitalist countries, the "escalofrío" of the Cold War. The reference to the paradigmatic modern cities alludes to Eliot's "What the Thunder Said" and the enumeration of cities that were once great but whose brightness is now opaque: "Jerusalem Athens Alexandria / Vienna London / Unreal" (67, lines 375–77). Paz's description of a shadow that covers the city not only responds to time and the overpowering of nature's ivy, but to the repeated verse in *The Waste Land:* "Unreal city, / Under the brown fog of a winter dawn." However, although the brown fog of pollution and of nightfall corresponds to Paz's shadow, these cities in "Himno entre ruinas" are not portrayed as unreal. Quite the contrary, they represent what is "real"—what Žižek has called "the effects of the real" (*Welcome* 7).

In "Himno entre ruinas," the fragility of power and the omnipotence of time, so embedded in the poetic tradition of the ruins, are also suggested by the second reference to Góngora's work: "Acodado en montes que ayer fueron ciudades, Polifemo bosteza" (234). Polifemo is the witness of history. He is bored by the predictable cycle of destruction and cities in ruins that will merge with the natural landscape of the first stanza. Change and repetition are manifested in the metaphor of "rebaño de hombres," an echo of the first stanza: "Un puñado de cabras es un rebaño de piedras" (233). In a strong criticism of social exploitation, the image of the ruins reminds us how easily humans can be turned into stones.

The crowds of rats that inhabit these modern cities recall the Itálica and the Uxmal in "Homenaje y profanaciones." The rats may represent the businessmen in control of the large cities, an idea reinforced by the crawling "rebaño de hombres." As we see in the verses:

> Abajo, entre los hoyos, se arrastra un rebaño de hombres.
> (Bípedos domésticos, su carne
> —a pesar de recientes interdicciones religiosas—

es muy gustada por las clases ricas.
Hasta hace poco el vulgo los consideraba animales impuros.)
(234)

The ironic tone and the parody of the Mexican economic elite are obvious. Paz criticizes the double cannibalism of Mexican history and the animalization of the working class. The cannibalism practiced by the Aztec priests as a religious sacrifice and the economic cannibalism performed by the inheritors of the European system make religious and moral laws into ridiculous and decorative pronouncements. The parody of the privileged feasts of the economic elite emphasizes the way tastes change depending on the cultural practices of the place and the era—what some consider today impure, such as rats and worms, others deem sophisticated, like escargots and frog legs.

As part of its identification with neo-Baroque aesthetics, "Himno entre ruinas" is organized by paradoxical imagery and contrasts. For example, the vitality of the sea opposes the urban waters of the sixth stanza: "¿y todo ha de parar en este chapoteo de aguas muertas?" (235). The phallic symbols of the green pines or the "espiga henchida de minutos" (235) point to an elevated form that predominates in the mythical stanzas and contradicts the vertical shape of the speaker's thoughts, associated with serpents and rivers. The poetic voice is frustrated: "mis pensamientos se bifurcan, serpean, se enredan... al fin se inmovilizan... ríos que no desembocan..." (235). But his thoughts do lead up to a final stanza, where the sun unifies the poetic structure and its juxtapositions.

In the poems that represent ruins, time is related to death as a symbol of destruction. However, by using the idea of eternal return and circular time, materialized in the sun, Paz makes time a symbol of creation: "Día, redondo día, / luminosa naranja de veinticuatro gajos" (235). The poem's last stanza provides a synthesis of the opposing worlds of the pastoral and the urban, myth and history, nature and the city, Classical and modern ruins: "se reconcilian las dos mitades enemigas." The sun as a symbol of time can become an orange, and the "manantial de fábulas" will continue to flow because through poetry, words become deeds.

The notion of a circular time, linked to a mythical world, and its clash with a historical reality is projected in Paz's poem. In reference to Paz's insistence on the myth of the universal man and his allusions to the Spaniards' faces in the Civil War, Valis criticizes this discourse:

> Myth-making may compensate for the disappointments of history (and a secularized world). What it cannot do is *replace* the historical. Such mythologizing prevents Paz from moving beyond myth. There is, as the constant conversion and interchangeability between myth and history, singularity and universality implies, a certain circularity in his thinking. Paz, who repeatedly rejected historical determinism, nevertheless straitjackets history by making it a prime cause of our feeling of orphanhood and exile. (128)

Valis's criticism of the circularity in Paz's thought makes me reconsider the tensions between myth and history in "Himno entre ruinas." The final stanza suggests the fusion of opposing forces, the power of poetry to connect the mythical and the historical, not that myth should replace history. However, Valis's insight precisely questions the politics that support that fusion, the "interchangeability between myth and history." Can poetry historicize the mythical? What are Paz's aims in the mythologizing and the idealization of the ruined Sicilian landscape, so harmonious with its natural space?

The odd stanzas of "Himno entre ruinas" that portray the idealized, natural landscape seem to suggest that the "origins" lie in the Classical ruins, in the Mediterranean rediscovery of the senses, rather than in the Aztec or the modern ruins, which are associated with decay and death. Could we read these ruins as emblems of a literary tradition, symbols of the Classical and the Baroque legacy? The incorporation of Góngora's Polifemo and the allusion to the Classical ruins is not only a literary move toward a certain past that should serve as an aesthetic model. It is also a political choice, used to criticize the present and its discourse of modern progress. Paz's idealization of a distant place and a mythical time is part of his anti-nationalist critique of the Aztec and the European legacies, which left violence as the cornerstone of the Mexican nation. Paz's poem ends by encouraging faith in the power of poetry; the idea that words become actions that create political and historical awareness. His poetic idealization of a mythical natural landscape does not necessarily mean that he wants to erase or forget the literal and metaphorical cannibalism and history of genocide. In an idealist positioning, Paz desires to break with that cycle of violence through poetry. Finally, he sings to the poetic imagination as the medium to contribute to historical and literary memory. "Petrificada petrificante" also criticizes the violence and the anger encapsulated in the Mexican well of historical origins, but unlike "Himno entre ruinas," this poem does not offer any consolation, no reconciliatory move toward the union of opposites, no satisfaction for the unquenched thirst at the end.

Among Stones: Eliot's *The Waste Land* and Paz's "Petrificada petrificante"

"Petrificada petrificante" is Paz's definitive poetic reading of Eliot's *The Waste Land* and a dim re/vision of Mexican mythological and historical contexts. Often overlooked, this text addresses the longer poem, beginning with "Terramuerta" as a clear allusion to Eliot's dead land.[42] I will focus on a comparative analysis of this poem with Eliot's *The Waste Land,* not discussing in detail the neologisms and the mythological symbolism that abound in the text, which have already been thoroughly analyzed by Martha Nandorfy and Alejandro González Acosta, but focusing instead on the topic of ruins.

As part of Paz"s collection *Vuelta* and its section titled *Ciudad de México,* "Petrificada petrificante" evokes Eliot's desolate landscape but specifically illustrates Mexico's literally asphyxiating reality. The poem cites its own title:

> Valle de México
> boca opaca
> lava de bava
> desmoronado trono de la Ira
> obstinada obsidiana
> petrificada
> petrificante
> Ira
> torre hendida. (608)

Nandorfy explains the title's dual dimensions, underlining that "petrificada" may signal an effect, or the object of an action, and "petrificante" points to the cause as well as the process of turning into stone (573). The title refers to Anger, an allegory of Mexico, as being both the object and the subject of a petrifying history. In these verses Mexico is portrayed as the symbol of anger coming from a volcanic grotto or a hollow pit. The common metaphors in the topos of ruins describing empires through elevated buildings or fortified thrones are turned into symbols of decay and destruction. The stones that built the Aztec empire, the angry México, have fallen and are themselves immobile, petrifying history and progress. Paz's poetic style in these verses also corresponds with wordplays that abound in "Homenajes y profanaciones." In this case, the wordplay "petrificada petrificante" can point to the stones of literary and historical traditions, which not only seem petrified and untouchable, but also have the power to petrify the viewer or the reader. In this sense, Nandorfy's reading of the Virgin with a "corona de culebras" (609) as a reference to Medusa, "cuya mirada petrificaba al mirado," proves very revealing. Mexico, in the disguise of Anger, Medusa, or the Virgin, is feminized, and portrayed as chaotic and sterile, petrified and petrifying.

However, Paz's allusions to *The Waste Land* open the semantics of this poem to the modern city in ruins; Mexico is not the only possible background of the text. Paz's cracked tower, "la torre hendida," has a strong chain of echoes from the Babel tower to Eliot's falling towers. The broken cultural phallic symbol of the tower is an intrinsic part of the spaces of waste and sterility explored by both Paz and Eliot. The barren, dry landscape is obviously not only reminiscent of Eliot, it also echoes Juan Rulfo's *Pedro Páramo* and *El llano en llamas*. Nevertheless, here I will focus on how Paz reads Eliot in this poem, as part of his neo-Baroque aesthetics. The metaphysical conceits in all these texts indicate the crude, paradoxical vision of modern nations as ruined spaces. Uncomfortable with their own complacency, Paz and Eliot are morally and culturally criticizing and judging Modernity, which explains as well their particular interest in recapturing the Metaphysical poets and Baroque aesthetic values and oxymorons.

In the critique of modern progress in "Petrificada petrificante," men bring on the ecological disaster: "los hombres fueron los ejecutores del polvo" (607). The personification of the wind makes it a witness to the passage of time and the destruction of cities. Similar to the river in the Baroque topos of ruins that is the only constant element among ruined cities, the wind survives the land and the water: "el viento / en la tumba del agua / recita sus letanías" (607). The wind, like the thunder in Eliot's "What the Thunder Said," is described with an impressive image as both a poet and a priest: "el viento / cuchillo roto en el crater apagado" (607). The broken knife also corresponds with the shape of thunder, but without its noise or its light. As in Eliot's poem even thunder is sterile; it comes without rain, in silence.

Although in Eliot's text, Tiresias has a predominant role, in this text Paz decides to underline a nameless, mutilated body, symbolizing the sterility imposed on the land. The metaphors of knives and blades acquire a more poignant signification when he paints a picture of Mexico as "un país de espinas y de púas." The mutilated body parts, the hand, the tongue, the breasts, and the penis, are the product of those cutting images:

> salta la mano cortada
> salta la lengua arrancada
> saltan los senos tronchados
> la verga guillotinada. (609)

The disturbing fragments of the body in ruins also point to images of lack of productivity. Without their hands, the people cannot work; without their tongues, they cannot speak and communicate; without their breasts, women cannot feed their children; without their penises, men cannot reproduce. The traumatized body is not only sterile, but it has no possibility of enjoyment.

Among other tropes, "Petrificada petrificante" also shares with "What the Thunder Said" the use of onomatopoeia: "drip drop drip drop…" and "tristrás en el polvo tristrás" (609). In "The Burial of the Dead," Eliot incorporates a series of characters from the Tarot cards—the Phoenician sailor, the Belladonna, and the Hanged Man. Paz attempts a similar enumeration of characters, yet his correspond to the religious, cultural, and mythological heritage of Mexico: "La Virgen… / El Desollado / El Flechado / El Crucificado…" (609). These icons of Catholic culture are just some of the desiccated images, forgotten and abandoned. These symbolic figures could also be read as the catalogue of heroes in the topos of ruins, exemplified by the Roman heroes in Caro's "Itálica" and the Inca workers in Neruda's "Alturas de Macchu Picchu." Nevertheless, Paz's catalogue is not limited to the Judeo-Christian tradition; he also includes Aztec mythological figures. As Nandorfy indicates, the "colibrí representa a Huitzilopochtli, el dios de la guerra y también de la vida y la renovación del solsticio" (581). And as González Acosta affirms, the rabbit alludes to the Spanish conquest: "el Conejo (en el Ometochtli, Año del Conejo, llegó Cortés a Tenochtitlán para cumplir la profecía)" (522). However, in this catalogue, the figures are definitely not characterized as heroic, particularly the feminine characters. The Virgin is characterized by a "corona de culebras," analogous to Christ's crown of thorns and, as I have mentioned, reminiscent of Medusa's head. The "Señora" has "pechos de vino y vientre de pan / horno / donde arden los muertos y se cuecen los vivos" (609). The feminine body, in particular the breasts and the womb, emphasizing its reproductive capacities, is paradoxically portrayed as an oven, a cave where death reproduces itself. Femininity, and its traditional connotations with fertility, is replaced by a feminized Anger as the producer of ruins and the sterile landscape.

In "Himno entre ruinas," the speaker asks himself "¿dónde desenterrar a la palabra?" In "Petrificada petrificante," the speaker turns to the images of these religious and mythological icons and unburies them:

> Imágenes enterradas
> en el ojo del perro de los muertos
> caídas
> en el pozo cegado del origen. (610)

González Acosta comments that the dog with one eye refers to "Xolotl, el dios 'doble' de Quetzalcoalt" (521), and Nandorfy considers that it alludes to "un Cerberus perdido, perro que en la mitología griega guiaba a los muertos a Hades... aquí los conduce a la luna, destino último de muchas mitologías indígenas" (576). Nandorfy refers to the lines "el can tuerto / el guía de los muertos... / en... la luna." The blind eye of the dog is like the well where the images of the past are encapsulated and buried. The dog who likes digging up corpses also appears in Eliot's "The Burial of the Dead" (55). Paz's imagery is surreal and obscure; the images of the historical and mythological past are paradoxically amalgamated in the blind eye of the dog that snoops about graves, but cannot see those images. They are part of the buried heritage that lies inside the blocked, dry well. The repeated verse "Hemos desenterrado a la Ira" suggests that the well of origins only contains a history of anger and violence. Unlike "Homenaje y profanaciones" and "Himno entre ruinas," which conclude with a poetics of hope and reconciliation, "Petrificada petrificante" ends with the impossibility of quenching the thirst; from the broken men and the broken stones emanates the "agua que alarga más la sed." I agree with Nandorfy's criticism of the problems presented in this text: "la única posibilidad de cambio parece ser la degeneración… en dar la apariencia de comprometerse con la historia nacional cuando en realidad su configuración viene a ser un petrificado mito de negación petrificante" (578). "Petrificada petrificante" ends with a petrified apocalyptic landscape that leads nowhere. The historical and mythological past that needs to be unburied seems not to produce any sort of revelation. The final ritual, when stones are broken, presents a paradoxical form of bitter water that prolongs the thirst of the community; and the final question remains unanswered. Although this poem does not address the Baroque topos of ruins as explicitly as "Himno entre ruinas," it clearly exemplifies the intertextual dialogue between Eliot and Paz in their anguished versions of the modern city in ruins.

Neo-Baroque poets reread the Spanish Golden Age and Latin American literary tradition, privileging juxtapositions, paradoxes, intertextuality, and the opposition to an authoritative system.[43] Alejo Carpentier, José Lezama Lima, Severo Sarduy, and Carlos Fuentes have defined in different ways neo-Baroque aesthetics. Lezama Lima emphasizes that the European Baroque is usually interpreted as the art of the Counter-Reformation, while he maintains that the Latin American Baroque should be regarded as an art of Counter-Conquest (*La expresión americana* 181–82). The return to the sources of the past leads many seventeenth—and twentieth-century Latin American writers to the mythical background and the aesthetic values of the Aztec, Mayan, and Inca cultures.[44] Roberto González Echevarría's argument regarding Juan de Espinosa Medrano, el *Lunarejo*, suggests that the originality of these poems is not a product of "an anxiety of influence": "...the Baroque issues from an impasse in the doctrine of imitation, it leads to the enthronement of 'ingenio,' of 'wit,' which is, briefly, the self-conscious shuffling of models and the creation of poetry from this reflexive activity" (*Celestina's Brood* 191). Eliot's and Paz's neo-Baroque aesthetic projects recover this notion of an American originality that is not intimidated by European poetic models, but quite the contrary, establishes a dialogue with their seventeenth-century counterparts, full of wit and paradoxes, irony and hyperboles. Frank Warnke also comments on how the Baroque poets' emphasis on wit and "ingenio" as a creative source is part of their aesthetic project: "The chief poetic faculty, then, is what seventeenth century English called 'wit' (Spanish *ingenio*, Italian *ingegno*), the capacity for perceiving likeness beneath seeming unlikeness, and the essence of poetry becomes not so much the imitation of the phenomenal world as the imaginative modification of it" (*Versions of Baroque* 19). Warnke synthesizes what many critics like Eliot have been suggesting all along: the metaphysical wit joins the disjointed aspects of nature, which explains the frequent use of the paradox and the oxymoron. As González Echevarría pinpoints, that is how the Baroque poets escape the traps of imitation, not only of the reality they perceive but also of the literary tradition that precedes them.

However, the criticism of modern progress and the search for origins, or lost pearls, in the representation of cities in ruins cannot overshadow the ideological complexities that lie behind a discourse that desires to rescue an idealized past. The problem with Eliot's disenchanted theory of the "disintegration of the intellect" is that there never was an integrated intellect or an integrated social system in the first place. Although one may want to read Eliot's and Paz's apocalyptic visions of Modernity as literary moves toward a future where progress is not attained through war and devastation, they are really calling to move toward an unreachable, mythical past. Still, in contrast to Eliot, Paz insists on both a cultural synthesis and a reconciliatory synthesis of past and present, symbolized in the union of man and woman that transgresses all time frames in "Homenaje y profanaciones."

The literary discourse that defines the exceptional and the originality of American artistic expressions through the notion of cultural synthesis is obviously linked to Lezama Lima's "metaphoric subject." However, Lezama Lima's "metaphoric subject," associated with Baroque aesthetics, opposes what he calls the "crepuscular critic," epitomized by Eliot. Lezama Lima asserts that Eliot's pessimism directly relates to his incorporation of myths and literary classicism:

> Sabemos que en el caso de Mr. Eliot, el método mítico era más bien mítico crítico, conforme con su neoclasicismo *a outrance*, que situaba en cada obra contemporánea la tarea de los glosadores para precisar su respaldo en épocas míticas, pues él es un crítico pesimista de la era crepuscular. Pesimista en cuanto él cree que la creación fue realizada por los antiguos y que a los contemporáneos, sólo nos resta el juego de las combinatorias... Nos acercamos a esos problemas de las formas, con el convencimiento de que el sujeto metafórico... destruye el pesimismo encubierto en la teoría de las constantes artísticas. (*La expresión americana* 15, 20)

Lezama Lima is implicitly referring to Eliot's famous description of himself in 1927 as a classicist, a royalist, and an Anglo-Catholic.[45] This clarifies Lezama's characterization of Eliot as a neoclassicist and a pessimist—the antagonist of the Baroque American artist who synthesizes the European, the African, and the indigenous heritages. Gustavo Pérez Firmat further explains the dichotomy: "The crepuscular criticism of neoclassical aesthetics recycles old myths, an attack that Lezama traces backs to Eliot's mythical method. Matinal hermeneutics, on the contrary, invents new myths by the happy and even mutation of old ones" (318). Although Eliot's pessimism is evident in his theory of the "disintegration of the intellect" and in his poetic apocalyptic visions of the future, I would not limit his work to that of a "crepuscular critic" and a conservative classicist. Eliot's dialogue with Donne, Baudelaire, and Pound is also complemented by his admiration for Hindu aesthetics and Medieval Christian myths. Lezama Lima and Pérez Firmat claim that Eliot opposes the metaphorical subject, who "commands Western culture without being dominated by it. This combination of foreignness and familiarity allows him to play freely, even irresponsibly, with literary and cultural tradition..." (Pérez Firmat 318). Even if his constant pessimism and scepticism were to distance him from Lezama's exceptional American artist, nurtured by the overwhelming American landscape, Eliot's intertextual poetry could not be read as a mere recycling of old myths and Classical, canonical poems. Eliot's interests cannot be reduced to a neoclassical aesthetic trend, ignoring his admiration for the Baroque and the Symbolist poets. Still, I do not want to imply that Eliot is like the metaphorical subject in every way; he had no interest in defining himself as an American or as a product of diverse cultural and ethnic backgrounds. Paz is much closer than Eliot to representing what Lezama calls the American artist with a "baroque curiosity" who finds the "authentic" in the synthesis of diverse cultural elements.

Eliot and Paz explicitly signal and parody the Baroque and Metaphysical poets to ponder upon their own poetic practice. I avoid falling into the quicksand of intertextual presuppositions and hierarchical genealogy because although I focus on Donne's and Quevedo's influences, I amply discuss the multiple precursors that join these two, like Webster, Dante, Góngora, and Caro. There are many origins and a plurality of texts that conform and deform our readings of the literary canon. I choose to narrow this study to canonical poets that influence other canonical poets. I hope that my analysis is not limited to doing only that. The point of examining neo-Baroque poetry is precisely to try to understand why twentieth-century poets incorporate a particular consciousness of intertextuality into their own poems. I do not want to imply that Baudelaire is less important than Donne in *The Waste Land*. And I do not want to limit each text to the category of neo-Baroque when I explore how it pertains to this aesthetic movement. Yet, Eliot and Paz rethink the Baroque tradition in many of their essays and poems, searching for the ways it has molded their modern sensibilities. Like the dogs that dig out the buried pearls of the Baroque, the first half of the twentieth century witnessed the appropriation of aesthetic values that would legitimize and support a Modernist discourse within its search for origins.

Eliot's *The Waste Land* captures the semiotic relevance of the Baroque quality of pearls. The verse "Those are pearls that were his eyes. Look!" is at first used to describe the image of the Phoenician Sailor in "The Burial of the Dead," and it reappears later on in "A Game of Chess" (54, line 48; 57, line 125). The substitution of pearls for eyes strikes me as particularly symptomatic of the modern crisis of representation. The fertility god, whose image is thrown into the water to signify the end of summer, is eyeless. The pearls will go back to where they came from. It seems that, for Eliot, the Baroque artifices *par excellence* were pearls that covered our vision and deformed our perception of reality.

In his Clark Lecture on Crashaw, Eliot develops the metaphoric association of the Baroque style with pearls when he explains that Santa Teresa's *Autobiography* is a great book of "transparent honesty": "When, for instance, she tells of how the Lord took her crucifix from her, and returned it adorned with pearls, she adds conscientiously that no one was ever able to see the pearls except herself. (Seventeenth century poetry is much like a crucifix ornamented with pearls... except that we are able with some trouble to perceive the pearls)" ("Lecture VI, Crashaw," in *Varieties* 166). Eliot's conceit is particularly revealing when one reads the footnote that quotes *The Life of St. Theresa* and how instead of pearls, she describes a crucifix of supernatural stones, more perfect than diamonds. The natural, real quality of pearls makes Eliot's confusion even more suggestive, since seventeenth-century poetry, overcrowded with conceits, needs to be carefully analyzed to discover those obscure pearls.

Pearls are a metaphor of Baroque aesthetics because they could be conceptualized as both natural and artificial. Taken out of their natural frame, they are "deformed," "aestheticized," manipulated, and amalgamated to become a necklace or a crucifix. Like Baroque pearls, ruins in the nineteenth century also became a fashionable trend where the natural and the artificial coexisted, to create a more prestigious, fake, historical background in bourgeois households. If you did not have "natural," "authentic" Roman ruins in your backyard, you could always construct them to fit the size of your stylish garden.[46] However, these artificial ruins were emptied of their historical and political significance, and in that sense they contrast with the modern representation of a city in ruins, charged with the political implication of manifesting historical change in its most concrete ways.

The appreciation of ruins changes through time and through diverse artistic movements. Boym summarizes very accurately the development of the topos of ruins:

> ...the value of the ruin itself changes through history. In
> the baroque age, the ruins of antiquity were often used di-
> dactically, conveying to the beholder "the contrast between
> ancient greatness and present degradation." Romantic ruins
> radiated melancholy, mirroring the shattered soul of the poet
> and longing for harmonic wholeness. As for modern ruins,
> they are reminders of the war and the cities' recent violent
> past, pointing at coexistence of different dimensions and
> historical times in the city. The ruin is not merely something
> that reminds us of the past; it is also a reminder of the future,
> when our present becomes history. (79)

Yet the Baroque fascination with antique ruins does not only reflect an admiration for their great monuments. The Baroque representation of ruins is also aimed to grasp the "eternal," what survives the destruction of pagan culture. As Boym points out, the Baroque, the Romantic, and the modern ruins project diverse significations and preoccupations. But what all the representations of ruins have in common is a visceral search for the "eternal," the fascination of what remains after everything is destroyed. Modern ruins portray the scars of war or violent history, as well as what Baudelaire designates as the eternal and the fugitive elements of Modernity. *The Waste Land* and "Himno entre ruinas" are poems marked by World War I and World War II, respectively; but that does not mean that their ruined landscape is only a product of a recent war or catastrophe. These poems evoke a modern city in ruins that has been part of a process of destruction and construction, of natural and mechanical fatalities; its ruins are part of the project of progress marked by constant regression.

Ruins are the witnesses and the victims of time, history, nature, war, pollution, oblivion, and melancholic fascination. In the poetic landscape of ruins, one encounters multiple metaphors of waste and an overwhelming accumulation of literary and historical echoes. In his study of allegory in German Baroque drama, Benjamin explains the connection between allegory and ruins. Benjamin states that allegorical representations such as statues or poems "concretize" ideas in the same way ruins "concretize" historical change: "The allegorical physiognomy of nature-history, which is put on stage in the *Trauerspiel*, is present in reality in the form of the ruin... Allegories are, in the realm of thought, what ruins are in the realm of things. This explains the baroque cult of ruin" ("Allegory and Trauerspiel," *The Origin* 177–78). The ruined city reveals how the natural elements overpower and invade the historical space. Benjamin does not view in that menacing nature the emblems of the eternal, but quite the contrary, he perceives the ruins as signs of destruction, not of endurance: "In the ruin, history has physically merged into the setting and in this guise history does not assume the form of the process of an eternal life so much as that of irresistible decay" (177). Still, ruins are frequently portrayed as traces of the "eternal," always remainders and reminders of the "presence of the past."

"Whispers of Immortality" and "Homenaje y profanaciones" evoke the conventional Baroque dichotomies of the eternal and the temporal in experimental and grotesque ways. Eliot and Paz critically insert themselves into the tradition of Donne and Quevedo; and they recover the seventeenth-century poets' fame, their immortality, while securing their own. Eliot's and Paz's recuperation of the Baroque and the Metaphysical poets in their twin labors as poets and critics is an essential step for the conceptualization of neo-Baroque poetry in the twentieth century. Their consciousness of the "presence of the past," the meeting point of Modernity and Antiquity, lead Eliot and Paz into the making of new, irregular, deformed poetic pearls.

Chapter Four

The Spanish Civil War

A Transatlantic Vision

> Hoy celebro nuevamente a una España empeñada
> en rescatar su memoria histórica, único camino para
> construir una conciencia cívica sólida que abra las
> puertas al futuro… Hay quienes vilipendian este es-
> fuerzo de memoria. Dicen que no hay que remover
> el pasado, que no hay que tener ojos en la nuca, que
> hay que mirar hacia adelante y no encarnizarse en
> reabrir viejas heridas. Están perfectamente equivo-
> cados. Las heridas aún no están cerradas. Laten
> en el subsuelo de la sociedad como un cáncer sin
> sosiego… La memoria es memoria si es presente y
> así como Don Quijote limpiaba sus armas, hay que
> limpiar el pasado para que entre en su pasado.
>
> Juan Gelman
> *Acceptence Speech of Premio Cervantes*
> *April 2008*

"Hay que tener ojos en la nuca": Toward a Transatlantic Historical Memory of the War

How can we address the broken historical memory of Spain? Can we cure that wounded collective self through the reconstruction of the past? Can we really "clean" the past to see its dirty hidden spots? Before facing those questions that arise from Juan Gelman's speech when he won the prestigious Premio Cervantes, a brief historical overview of the Spanish Civil War is necessary. But which events shall be prioritized as antecedents to the war? One could mention the nineteenth-century *guerras carlistas*, wars for the throne of Spain that confronted the conservative, Catholic landowners with the liberal, bourgeois establishment. Besides the civil wars in the peninsula, the Spanish American War in 1898 epitomized the end of the Spanish colonial presence in the Americas, "losing" Puerto Rico, Cuba, and the Philippines, which produced a national and an existential crisis. How can we talk about the Spanish Republic and the Civil War without mentioning the Disaster of Annual in 1921 when the Spanish army was grossly defeated by the Moroccans under Abd el-Krim, as a result of its incompetence, corruption, and lack of economic and military resources? The subsequent military dictatorship of General Miguel Primo de Rivera (1923–30) is also key to understanding the roots of fascism in Spain and the political turmoil and frustrations that led to the declaration of the Second Republic. Should we approach history as a fragmentary tale, a series of patches we put together according to our reconstructions of the past? Of course not, but in this brief historical introduction, I will only draw certain connections that will help us contextualize the transatlantic literary movement and the poetics of solidarity triggered by the Spanish war.

The Second Spanish Republic (1931–39) emerged with the abdication of King Alfonso XIII and the implementation of a democratic system, with diverse political parties, from the Monarchics and the right-wing Coalición Católica to the Socialist and Communist parties. In the first years of the Republic, the Socialists were in power and they tried to implement a series of social reforms (land reforms, the secularization of the public education system, the right to divorce, female suffrage) that would make Spain a lay, modern state. When the Catholic Coalition won the elections of 1933, many of those social and political reforms were halted, and Spain became more and more divided. As Gabriel Jackson explains: "In October 1934, a divided and fearful Left rose against a government which seemed to be drifting in the direction of clerical fascism" (Introduction ix). Armed miners had fought for two weeks in Oviedo, Asturias, but their rebellion was suppressed by the Moroccans and the Foreign Legion, and among its military officers, Francisco Franco stood out. The miners and the political organizers were brutally persecuted. "The class and ideological confrontations in Asturias prefigured those of the Civil War" (ix). In February 1936, the leftist coalition, el Frente Popular, won the elections and defeated the right-wing coalition, el Bloque Nacional. The tensions escalated, and street violence was rampant.

The Spanish Civil War (1936–39) began with a *golpe de estado*, a military coup on July 17–18, 1936 against the democratic regime of the Republic. The *coup d'état* developed into a full-scale civil war, largely because of international intervention, or lack thereof. As Jackson succinctly explains:

> The Republican cause depended heavily upon Russian armaments, aviators, tank drivers, and staff officers. Between thirty and forty thousand anti-fascist volunteers, flocking to Spain against the will of their governments, fought in the Republican ranks. The forces under General Francisco Franco, known variously as Insurgents and as Nationalists, depended increasingly throughout the war on the armed aid of Italy, Germany and Portugal. (Jackson, Introduction vii)[1]

The war was both a national crisis and an international event with multiple repercussions beyond the Spanish boundaries. Even though the Soviet Union and, in the first year of the war, the International Brigades committed their efforts to support the Republic, the majority of the international community abandoned the Spanish democratic system.[2] The Republicans were struggling to arm and train the people, in contrast to the Insurgents, who relied on the experience of a great part of the professional army and on the financial and military support of Hitler and Mussolini. Furthermore, the Foreign Legion approached the war in Spain, on the mainland, as another colonial war, where Moroccan mercenaries were used and abused, trained to carry out the same violent, military tactics their Moroccan counterparts had been subjected to by a Spanish military that tried to hold on to the remnants of its crumbled imperial status.[3] The Catholic Church, paradoxically so deeply politicized and so estranged from the democratic political process, also blessed the Insurgents as a whole—the Fascists, the Catholic conservatives, and the Falangists. The Church became an institutional buttress that offered a spiritual justification for the "Nationalist" cause; and as we know, the war was often referred to as a *crusade*. Throughout this chapter I will refer to the troops led by

Franco as Insurgents, or as "Nationalists" in quotation marks, because I find, along with many other scholars like María Rosa de Madariaga, that the term *Nationalists* is how the Insurgents liked to call themselves to imply that they were the ones fighting for the "nation," and to easily extrapolate that the "anti-Nationalists" were anti-Spanish. As Madariaga also argues, she does not refer to them as "Nationalists" because there were Basque and Catalan Nationalists fighting for the Republic (17).

Summarizing the complexities that entangle the Spanish Civil War and its historical, political, and cultural repercussions in just a few pages is, to say the least, a difficult task. But as Helen Graham describes: "the military coup unleashed what was in effect a series of culture wars: urban culture and cosmopolitan lifestyles versus rural tradition; secular against religious; authoritarianism against liberal political cultures; centre versus periphery; traditional gender roles versus the 'new woman'..." (*Spanish Civil War* 2). Although reducing the culture wars to a group of opposing factors can also be a contentious task, and those juxtapositions do not always help us explain a very divided left and right, these factors can be useful when it comes to trying to situate the war beyond the political, military sphere.

Throughout the war, General Francisco Franco tried to unite the various conservative "families" under the rubric of an anti-Republicanism that merged with the protection of Catholic, traditional values and the abhorrence of their common enemies: Communists, Freemasons, Atheists, Jews, Basque, Catalan, Galician Nationalists, and Democrats. Officially the war ended in April 1939, when the "Nationalist" victory constituted its New State, Franco's dictatorship. Yet, the Republican *guerrilleros* or *maquis*, with the support of the Communist Party, continued to wage war on the regime under really precarious conditions for almost twelve years after the end of the war. To this day, the numbers vary, but most historians agree that political prisoners by the end of 1939 were 270,000, of which many were sentenced to prison or death, and around 20,000 were sentenced to a slow death, forced labor in El Valle de los Caídos (Valley of the Fallen), the sheer rock monument to the victors. Franco's regime implemented a totalitarian system, under which between 140,000 and 200,000 people were executed and hundreds of thousands imprisoned.[4] Half a million

Spaniards went into exile in Mexico, Chile, the United States, other parts of Latin America, and Europe, especially France and England.[5]

Franco's military dictatorship and his authoritarian regime was "by far the most centralized in Spanish history" (Payne 231). Its centralization and totalitarian practices were cemented in a terrible system of state repression: from linguistic and cultural repression in the case of speakers of Catalan, Basque, and Galician to ideological and military persecution of anyone who could be suspected of treason against the new regime. Franco continuously legitimized his use of absolute control by delegitimizing the democratic distribution of power through an electoral system. As he said in 1962: "We did not win the regime we have today hypocritically with some votes... We won it at the point of the bayonet and with the blood of our best people."[6] Franco's vision of Spain clearly continued to divide the country into two camps: the best and the worst, the Spanish and the anti-Spanish, the victors and the vanquished, and ironically the loyals and the traitors.[7] The "Nationalists," dead or alive, had a *place* in that social sphere; while Republicans, the vanquished, were vanished and banished, ostracized, persecuted—literally and metaphorically *displaced*.

The story of the victors was historically engraved throughout Spain: from street names and public monuments to honor the Insurgents, among them, the famous Valley of the Fallen, the cemetery for the "heroes" of the war, to carved slogans in churches all over the country saying "Presente!" or "José Antonio Presente!" as part of the hagiography of the Falangist leader, José Antonio Primo de Rivera. Throughout history, ruins are always manipulated, preserved, or abandoned; their symbolic value served Francoist propaganda. Although in this chapter, I mainly focus on the ruins of the Spanish Civil War and their poetic representation by Republican poets, it is relevant to point out how the Franco regime exploited two approaches to the ruined landscape. For example, the Alcázar of Toledo had been a battleground in the beginning of the war and was destroyed in July and August 1936. After the war, Franco decided to reconstruct it and maintain it as a symbol of the "Nationalist" resistance to the Republican attack. To this day, there are many articles or notes to the editor in *El País*, one of the biggest newspapers in Spain, complaining that the Francoist version of the battle of the Alcázar is still present in el Museo del Ejército, in Toledo. The Republicans bombed the Alcázar almost to the ground, and although it has frequently been referred to as a bastion of the Insurgents, who fought for seventy days, we still have voices that see it as stones with more than one history to tell. At the inauguration of the library in the Alcázar, Felipe González, the Spanish *Presidente del Gobierno* from 1982 until 1996, poetically begins by recalling its historical rollercoaster: "Reconstrucción, ruina, reconstrucción, ruina... Historia. Mil setecientos años: romanos, visigodos, musulmanes, judíos, cristianos. Armas y letras. Todo en torno a estos muros de piedra. Piedras que nos cubren y nos soportan generación tras generación. Nos sobreviven y están a nuestra merced para desordenarlas, quemarlas, volverlas a ordenar."[8] González responds to the traces of history in those stones and the arbitrary nature of its constant destruction and reconstruction. However his speech does not linger on the majestic grandeur of the past or how to interpret it as a symbol of the Civil War; he wants to use the opportunity to signal how the library keeps the historical memory alive. He presents himself as part of a democratic Spain, that aims to "recuperar las libertades individuales y reconocernos en la diversidad de identidades que siempre han compuesto el mosaico de España."[9] For González, the Alcázar acquires a very different significance from the meaning Franco's regime gave it.

Bruce Wardropper argues that the English and the Spanish have strong cultural differences in their treatment of ruins: "When Coventry Cathedral was bombed in the Second World War, a new cathedral was built beside the ruins. When the Alcázar of Toledo was bombarded by artillery in the Spanish Civil War, it was… reconstructed in its original form. The Spaniards, like their continental cousins never learned to like ruins. They remained for them a grim reminder of the fragility of man's life" (305). Wardropper is keen on establishing that there are various forms of seeing in ruins an emblem of cultural memory, but he does not point out that the ruins of the Alcázar would politically weaken the Fascist project—its reconstruction represents the Fascist reinvention of the country after the Spanish Civil War and its intent to erase history's footprints. Nonetheless, the regime's reaction to ruins is revealingly not homogeneous.

Franco visited both the ruins of the Alcázar of Toledo and the ruins of Belchite, a town in the province of Zaragoza, where from August 24 until September 6, 1937, the Republican forces fought the Insurgents who had taken over the town. The siege made Belchite another symbol of "Nationalist" bravery in the eyes of the Francoist regime, but in contrast to the reconstruction of Toledo's Alcázar, this time the Caudillo decided not to rebuild the town. The ruins would remain visible to all as a way to remember the destruction of the war. The new town would be a substitute for the lifeless ruins of the older town, but as Antonio Marín suggests, the ruins also speak of the post-war repression:

> El general Franco quiso mantener intactas las ruinas del viejo Belchite como símbolo de su victoria, para que nadie nunca se olvidara, y mandó construir un pueblo nuevo, homogéneo, sobrio, de casas clónicas, en formación casi militar. Ahora que las ruinas del pueblo viejo prácticamente han desaparecido debido al desgaste del tiempo y los saqueos, empezamos a conocer la otra cara de la historia, la que ha sido silenciada: gran parte del pueblo nuevo fue construido por presos políticos republicanos.[10]

Marín explains how the division of the past and the present, the old and the new towns, persists in the narrations of the history of the war and the symbolic nature of the ruins. Franco intended to keep some ruins ruined and others masterfully reconstructed in his enterprise to write the history of the victors' resistance, but as Marín argues at the end, the Republican soldiers are the ones who were resisting and defending the legal democratic system.

The Spanish exile meant the displacement of hundreds of thousands of Republicans who left their families, the remnants of their past, and everything they owned. Much has been written on the intellectual exodus that dramatically transformed the cultural production in Latin America, especially in Mexico.[11] The Spanish exiles tightened the biological, cultural, and ideological ties between sectors of the Latin American and Spanish communities. In the last twenty-five years, we find a series of contemporary works that evoke those transatlantic connections from the perspective of the grandchildren in Latin America, the United States, and Spain. This generation is interested in recovering the ruins of the past—rereading and reclaiming them. Among the eruption of texts and films, there are novels like Mexican writer Jordi Soler's *Los rojos de ultramar* (2004), where the story of the Catalan Republican grandfather, exiled in Mexico, delves into a journey through the past, full of nostalgia, misery, solidarity, and conspiracies; documentaries like *Death in El Valle* (1996) by C. M. Hardt, where the American filmmaker recounts her experiences and her family's tensions as she tries to find out how her grandfather was killed during the Francoist dictatorship; and historical biographies based on unpublished manuscripts, like the one on Vicente Rojo, the famous Republican military leader who was exiled in Bolivia and in 1957 returned to Spain, *Vicente Rojo: Retrato de un general republicano* (2006), written by his grandson, *El País* journalist José Andrés Rojo.

What triggers this memory boom and is it a transatlantic phenomenon? Does it only fascinate the grandchildren of Republican exiles? What about Mexican filmmaker Guillermo del Toro's *El espinazo del diablo* and *El laberinto del fauno*? Del Toro has no Spanish grandfather, but he was greatly influenced by Emilio García Riera, a Spanish film historian exiled in Mexico. Almudena Grandes suggests that one can ideologically adopt a lineage and choose how to pay homage to that legacy. The commemoration of the Second Republic's seventy-fifth anniversary is the product of a whole generation in touch with and proud of their grandparents and their struggle for democracy:

> Los nietos, biológicos o adoptivos, de los republicanos del 31, nos hemos hecho mayores también en experiencia, en seguridad y en la definición de nuestra propia identidad. Somos la primera generación de españoles, en mucho tiempo, que no tiene miedo, y por eso hemos sido también los primeros que se han atrevido a mirar hacia atrás sin sentir el pánico de acabar convertidos en estatuas de sal... Este fenómeno... no tiene tanto que ver con la memoria del pasado como con nuestro propio presente, la memoria que legaremos a nuestros descendientes. (Grandes 124–25)

Grandes speaks of and for a generation without fear, unlike the generation of her parents, the children who grew up under Franco's dictatorial regime and the fears during the transition to democracy of Spaniards who dreaded to relive the Civil ..... and its bloodbath. In her essay, she points out that the commemoration of the Second Republic has to do not so much with the nostalgic revision of the past, but with the reconfiguration of the present in Spain, and the community's decision to remember their democratic tradition as part of their historical legacy.

The memory boom in Spain and Latin America, which emerged after the brutal dictatorships that had murdered so many, is also a global phenomenon. The need to come to terms with the past and the anxiety of a collective amnesia are palpable in every continent from Australia and Latin America to South Africa, Eastern Europe, and the former Soviet Union, China, Japan, the Middle East, and the United States. But as Andreas Huyssen so eloquently notes in his reflections on the "culture of memory": "it is important to recognize that although memory discourses appear to be global in one register, at their core they remain tied to the histories of specific nations and states... the *political* site of memory practices is still national, not post-national or global" (*Present Pasts* 16). Although by suggesting a transatlantic approach to the rewriting of the historical memory of the Spanish Civil War, it may seem that I am proposing a post-national gaze, I absolutely agree with Huyssen in that "the *political* site of memory practices is still national." *La guerra sucia* in Argentina or Franco's dictatorship in Spain is not easily comparable to the practices of apartheid in South Africa or the genocide during the Holocaust. These historical events and moments are too complex, too varied and multifaceted, for them to be remembered in similar ways. However, even within the confinements of the politics of memory in the national space, and because history has no borders, it is revealing how historical memory is not always preserved by the "nationals" who lived and survived those events. That is why the nightmare of the Holocaust has more than one political site. Huyssen comments on the issues that join the Holocaust and the *desaparecidos* of Latin America, since they "share the absence of a proper burial site" (18). Interestingly, Spain's *Asociación por la Recuperación de la Memoria Histórica* is also born from that collective angst with mass graves and the need to literally excavate the past of the Spanish Civil War and the post-war regime. Huyssen argues that the culture of memory tries "to counteract this fear and danger of forgetting with survival strategies of public and private memorialization." In this sense, the rewriting of the historical memory is a form of survival, a way of dealing with and facing a traumatic past.

Still, Huyssen pertinently asks himself and us: "Why this obsession with the past and why this fear of forgetting?" (*Present Pasts* 18). He brilliantly ponders upon the multiple answers to that question and suggests that it is more fruitful to read the political layers of history and the changing notion of temporality itself, rather than to use trauma or historical trauma as a central category (8). I also consider that one of the many possible answers to this question may reside as well in the crisis of identity. Memory is hard to pinpoint, elusive, full of dark patches that suddenly see the light, but it is ultimately attached to our collective and our individual experiences, the need to identify who we are by what we have become. Almudena Grandes situated the commemoration of the Spanish Republic within the context of a generation that is finally sure of itself: "nos hemos hecho mayores también en experiencia, en seguridad y en la definición de nuestra propia identidad" (120). The notion that a country can grow and mature is as old as the notion of the country itself; progress is often determined by that process of reaching a collective adulthood, and therefore, "our own identity." Memory is so malleable and unpredictable. It seems that we must always be searching for the footprints of the past in this memory boom that projects our fears of forgetting, because our social, cultural, historical, and national identities are always changing, and in this movable feast the modern subject needs something to hold on to, to reclaim as ours. The generation of grandchildren embraces its ideological legacy, choosing whom to commemorate by reclaiming, among other things, the bodies of the Republican victims who have no tomb, no site of remembrance. Of course, this memory boom in Spain has also been attacked and manipulated by right-wing historical revisionists like Pío Moa and César Vidal, who blame the Spanish Civil War on the Republicans and voice once more the Francoist historical propaganda. The practice of rewriting the historical memory of the war is clearly politicized, but fortunately respectable historians such as Gabriel Jackson, Paul Preston, Helen Graham, Santos Juliá, and Julián Casanova are not alone in their attempts to salvage the interpretation of the past through key archival work.

In October 2007, Spain's socialist government approved "La Ley de la Memoria Histórica" ("The Law of Historical Memory"), to remember the victims of the Spanish Civil War and the Francoist dictatorship. It was a political and a legal attempt to literally contribute to the excavation of the past, the archeology of mass graves, and to distance itself from the polemical stand of the transition to democracy, the so-called *el pacto del silencio* ("the pact of silence").[12] Even though this law has been amply criticized by diverse ideological viewpoints, it reveals the need to methodically structure and support the very politicized memory boom. As I have previously noted, comtemporary writers and filmmakers, along with professional and amateur historians, are at the center of the culture of memory that has triggered a debate about the role of amnesia and remembrance in society. In this chapter I will discuss how Latin American and Spanish poets rewrite the history of the Spanish Civil War and provide a testimonial voice of the past. But the texts I will discuss are not by contemporary writers retrieving their historical legacy; I will focus on the poems on ruins written during the Civil War or in its aftermath and how this historical event defined the ideological identity of that generation of writers. Still, what could a transatlantic approach bring to the table? Besides signaling once again the international dimensions of the war, it provides a new way of redefining Spain from poets who were and were not Spanish.

Although the "rebels," the Fascists and Conservative Catholics, labeled themselves as "Nationalists" and therefore reduced Republicans to *anti-españoles*; the Republican rhetoric also used the nationalist discourse to represent the war as an invasion, as a struggle against traitors who wanted to "colonize" the Spanish soil. José Alvarez Junco argues that both the Republicans and the "Nationalists" used the same essentialism of Spain, and even echoed similar mythical histories of the nation. The Republicans seemed to intensify this trend as they felt that their version of Spain was slipping away: "El discurso nacionalista no hizo sino acentuarse a lo largo de la Guerra, sobre todo en los momentos en que la situación militar de la República se volvió angustiosa" ("La guerra civil" 586–87). The nationalist discourse only intensified during the war.[13] But even though Republican poets like Cernuda, Neruda, and Antonio Machado addressed the "essence" of Spain in connection with the working people or with an abstract umbilical cord that connects all Spaniards, the transatlantic reading of the nation helps us see how Latin American poets like Nicolás Guillén represent the war as a fight against the imperialist nation that the fascist Insurgents embraced. These competing ideological visions of the past, where the Republicans recall the wars of independence in both Spain and Latin America, and the "Nationalists" nostalgically idealize the legacy of the Reconquest of Spain, the Catholic Kings, and the Spanish Empire, revealed the main differences between both nationalist discourses. Still, we find some Republican newspaper articles and popular *romances* in which the nationalist discourse embraces the right-wing rhetoric of the Reconquest in order to criticize and condemn the presence of the Moroccans in the "Nationalist" troops.[14]

The Spanish Civil War became a political and a poetic call to arms against fascism. The assassination of Federico García Lorca in August 1936 marks the violent beginning of the war, and in February 1939, the death of Antonio Machado, who had just crossed the frontier into France, foreshadows the tragic end of the war. Throughout the war, a net of transatlantic solidarity was formed; Tristan Tzara, Langston Hughes, W. H. Auden, and Nicolás Guillén, among other poets, participated in Nancy Cunard and Pablo Neruda's Republican magazine against the fascist movement, *Los poetas del mundo defienden al pueblo español*. From both sides of the Atlantic, Latin American poets such as Neruda and Vallejo joined Spanish poets such as Cernuda, Rafael Alberti, and Miguel Hernández in writing in support of the Republican cause. Their representations of the war vary in tone and style, from enraged, visceral imagery to nostalgic portrayals of the past and a pessimistic view of the future.

Roberto González Echevarría explains how the Civil War gave this generation of poets a sense of cohesion:

> Antes de la Guerra Civil el vínculo entre la acción política y la poesía había sido... distante en el tiempo y el espacio... La intervención poética en un presente pletórico de acción apenas existía... La Guerra Civil le dio foco, dirección y sentido a la rebeldía que las vanguardias habían heredado del romanticismo... el arte tenía una causa que defender, y en el Fascismo un enemigo que atacar. ("Guerra de los poetas" 1)

Romantic poetry elevated political and social rebellion against injustice and oppression, promoting the "Nationalist" discourses of the nineteenth century. Yet, as González Echevarría suggests, with the Spanish Civil War, poetry lost its abstract rebellious background and became a political act against a very real and concrete fascist threat. Along with *España en el corazón,* César Vallejo's well-known *España, aparta de mí este cáliz* manifests the immense sense of solidarity among Latin American poets with the Spanish people, as well as their strong political and poetic commitment to defend the Spanish democracy. Neruda emphasized how the Civil War "moved" poetry itself: "No ha habido en la historia intelectual una esencia tan fértil para los poetas como la guerra española. La sangre española ejerció un magnetismo que hizo temblar la poesía de una gran época" (*Confieso que he vivido* 177). Although Cernuda and Paz did not collaborate in Cunard and Neruda's project, they did participate in different ways in the international effort that supported the Spanish Republic.[15]

In Paris, in July 1937, Neruda organized with Louis Aragon, among other notable writers, an international congress of antifascist writers that would take place in Valencia and Madrid: el "Segundo Congreso de Escritores Anti-Fascistas."[16] On the fiftieth anniversary of that congress, in 1987, Paz underlined the fraternity and solidarity among the writers who had participated, as well as the lack of collective self-criticism: "La fecha que nos convoca es, simultáneamente, luminosa y sombría" (*OC* 9: 438). In that essay, Paz constantly remarks on the contradictory tensions of modern reality and how the modern poet is frequently trapped in its entangling net. In contrast to Paz's position, Neruda did not want his political vision to be overshadowed by the grey areas of contradiction and in certain ways he opted for a more dogmatic, less ambiguous stance. Still, Paz's reflections on the rhetoric of the war are clearly tinged by his conservative gaze five decades after that meeting.

Also in 1937, Cernuda participated along with Antonio Machado, Rafael Alberti, and Miguel Hernández in an anthology of poems that defended the Republican cause, *Poetas en la España leal.*[17] Cernuda could be seen as politically closer to Paz than to Neruda, because the Chilean poet would later become a member of the Communist Party and a more outspoken political voice against the capitalist system and neocolonial practices.[18] Nonetheless, Cernuda also criticized the effects of capitalist progress in, among other texts, "Otras ruinas," as I indicated in the second chapter. The political implications of Cernuda's portrayal of the modern city in ruins and its links with Baudelaire's poetics suggest a strong criticism of modern versions of progress—a criticism he also expresses in *Las nubes*, the collection of poems that he wrote from 1937 to 1940, which he began in Spain and concluded in political exile in England. Like Neruda's *España en el corazón* and Vallejo's *España, aparta de mí este cáliz, Las nubes* denounced the injustices of the war with its merciless mercenaries, and the abandonment of Republican Spain by other democratic countries such as France and Great Britain, as well as expressed a painful and nostalgic vision of his country.

Cernuda's *Las nubes* retakes his vision of Spain, his Spanishness, from the nationalist discourse; and even though his poetry is more nostalgic and pessimistic than Neruda's and Vallejo's, we find that they all share the use of Spain as a symbol of freedom and hope, social justice and political solidarity. The ruins of Spain provide both a lesson of endurance and a threat of the ultimate destruction that they foreshadow. In a way, Cernuda, Alberti, Vallejo, Neruda, Hughes, and Nicolás Guillén are determining the contemporary culture of memory in the Hispanic world, because through their works they construct a notion of identity defined by their ideological bonds.

The politics of memory that are so prevalent and vibrant in current affairs and in contemporary cultural projects have been molded by those poets whose texts serve as historical testimonies of the past. Let's go back to the epigraph in the beginning of this chapter. Juan Gelman is a famous Argentine poet, who was exiled in 1976 during the Argentine coup and military dictatorship that killed around 30,000 people, the well-known *desaparecidos*. Among the many missing persons, his son and his pregnant daughter-in-law were tortured and subsequently killed and his baby granddaughter, born during captivity, was given to one of those families who sided with the state. Finally, in 2000 Gelman found his granddaughter and they were able to reunite. Therefore, Gelman's words when he won the Cervantes Prize in 2007 transcend the conventional rhetoric of a speech that shows gratitude for an award. Gelman uses the opportunity not only to talk about *Don Quijote* and what literature means to him, but to place it in the context of the politics of memory and the need to remember the disappeared. He not only recalls the Southern Cone *desaparecidos* (those of Chile, Argentina, and Uruguay), but also the multiple anonymous dead in Hiroshima, to emphasize that those unnamed victims deserve to be remembered. He reminds us of Antigone's plight and her persuasive arguments that the burial of the dead is an inalienable right. It is in this context that Gelman commends Spain's embrace of the past, clearly alluding to the law that had recently been passed. He responds to right-wing politicians and citizens, who condemn the recuperation of the historical memory: "Hay quienes vilipendian este esfuerzo de memoria. Dicen que no hay que remover el pasado, que no hay que tener ojos en la nuca, que hay que mirar hacia adelante y no encarnizarse en reabrir viejas heridas. Están perfectamente equivocados. Las heridas aún no están cerradas" (Acceptance Speech). When Gelman describes those who voice their fear against disturbing the ghosts of the past, those who only look at the future ignoring the old wounds that cover the national body, he is also reminding us of Benjamin's angel of history. His critique coincides with Benjamin's reflections on the fascist notions of progress, where the historical past is just a disturbing obstacle in this storm, this blind and senseless race toward the "future," when he reiterates once more the need to have "ojos en la nuca," "eyes in the back of the neck." The ruins of the past will not be pieced together with amnesia, and the open wounds will not be closed and mended with the band aid of progress. Gelman's provocative imagery reinforces our need to look back and learn from the past through this memory boom, but it also defies us to *see*, to have open eyes, just as we face those collective open wounds.

The Racial Other: The Transatlantic Poetics of Solidarity of Langston Hughes and Nicolás Guillén

Why is war poetry often underestimated as propagandistic? How are social, cultural, and racial tensions addressed or not addressed in these poems? Is there a transatlantic poetics of the Spanish Civil War? The literature that emerges from the

Spanish Civil War testifies to the transnational character of the conflict and its international repercussions. These poems wanted to provoke what Benjamin calls a "historical awakening" in the reader. They intended to mobilize their readers through an anti-hegemonic poetic discourse, so that those readers would become historical agents, rather than passive observers.

The redefinition of cultural and racial identities in the transatlantic political and aesthetic discourses of the Spanish Civil War cannot be understood only through Spanish writers and a nationalist discourse from both ideological sides.[19] Langston Hughes's "Song of Spain" (Hughes, in Mullen 162–64) and Nicolás Guillén's "España" (181–92) contribute in diverse ways to this redefinition of Spain and of the war as an international event. Hughes's poem prioritizes the working class as the main agent of history, and Guillén underlines the speaker's racial and cultural identity to legitimize his poetics of solidarity. In his poems and articles, Hughes also deals with the many contradictions and racial questions that emerge from the presence of Moroccan mercenaries in the rebel troops fighting the African American volunteers in the International Brigades. In his poem "Letter from Spain Addressed to Alabama" (156–57), Hughes explores that encounter and the empathy with the black "other." In contrast to this treatment of race and these representations of the war, the fascist aesthetics of José María Pemán's "La Bestia y el Ángel" demonize the religious and ideological "other," the epitome of the machine, and show the problematic incongruities of the "Nationalist" discourse. These poems emerge as cornerstones of the way we reconstruct the collective memory and the history of the war.

The transatlantic politics of solidarity during the war does not imply that we forget the Spanish imperialist history in the Americas and how it is still present in Spain's postcolonial relations with Latin America. However, it is interesting how the "anti-Spanish" sentiment, which had haunted the American academy and inflamed nationalist rhetoric in Latin America in the nineteenth century, was questioned and theorized during the war.[20] Octavio Paz in an essay he wrote in 1938, "Americanidad de España," addresses this new solidarity:

> La guerra de España, aparte de su esencial y dramática
> significación para el presente de todo el mundo y para su

> inmediato porvenir, ha señalado, en Hispanoamérica, el
> despertar de una nueva solidaridad, nutrida no sólo en la her-
> mandad democrática y de clase, sino en la unidad histórica
> de lo hispano. El hispanismo, en América y España, parecía
> una tesis desprestigiada, reaccionaria. Era natural. Con el
> hispanismo se hacía defensa de todo aquello, antiespañol y
> antiamericano… la defensa del régimen de encomenderos,
> clero y Corona…(*Octavio Paz en España* 69–70)

Paz went on to argue that the fight against fascism is precisely against that imperialist heritage that the right upholds and reveres. He avowed that this was not only the war of the Spanish; it was a war that defended democracy itself, and thus, "La defensa de España es la defensa de América" (74). As we know, the Fascists' political and aesthetic discourse is marked by a nostalgic vision of their glorious imperial past as an anti-modern utopia; they dressed their insurrection as *La cruzada,* and their recuperation of history clearly privileged the *Reconquista* and the *Conquista* as the ideological backbone of their war. Therefore, Paz's claim that this was a war against an imperialist fascism that threatened all the democratic nations is well grounded. The fascist rhetoric, and later on, Franco's dictatorial regime supported the racist discourse of the Conquest, in favor of the homogenization of the nation: "una, grande y libre." And in "Nationalist" propaganda, the Republicans were traitors, financed by the Soviet Union—a paradoxical stand, since the "Nationalist" crusade survived and succeeded precisely because of the financial and military support of foreign forces, such as Hitler's Germany and Mussolini's Italy.

Langston Hughes was one of the representatives of the United States in the Second International Congress of Writers against Fascism in Valencia in 1937. He gave a speech entitled "Too Much Race," in which he argued that racism is just another form of fascism: "We represent the end of race, and the Fascists know that when there is no more race, there will be no more capitalism, no more war… because the workers of the world will have triumphed" (Hughes, in Mullen 96). Hughes and Nicolás Guillén's Marxist poetics emphasized that the Civil War was an international and a social struggle, in defense of the working class and the Spanish Republic. Hughes and Guillén were great friends, who traveled together throughout Spain as journalists covering the war and promoting the Republican cause. Guillén was the editor and a reporter of Cuba's *Mediodía*, and Hughes wrote for Baltimore's *The Afro-American*.[21]

In his speech, Hughes reiterates the connection between racism and fascism, which has been amply discussed.[22] As we know, the "Nationalist's" military support came from Hitler and Mussolini, and therefore their propaganda was anti-Semite, anti-Negro, anti-liberal thinking. It is interesting that after they won, Franco anonymously authored the script for the famous film called *Raza*, where the Hispanic race is conveniently delimited to his followers, since Republicans, and everyone who supported them, were "anti-Spanish." At the end of the film, the victorious march glorifies this vision of a new militarized Spain, a purged nation that suppressed or erased from the map any cultural, ideological, or racial diversity, although the "Moorish" mercenaries appear as the proud soldiers in the back of the line. Although "Moor" was used as a pejorative way of describing the Moroccans, I use it sometimes in reference to these poets' poems or their own prejudicial way of referring to the mercenaries.

This imperialist and racist discourse is also under attack in some of the poems that supported the Republic. In this speech as in his many articles and poems, Hughes showed he was "pro-Spanish Republican" and defined himself as the voice of Negroes and poor people. Most of his articles in *The Afro-American* were directed toward narrating the role of African Americans in the war, but he became more and more interested in the role of the Moors as "Nationalist" mercenaries. A poem such as "Letter from Spain Addressed to Alabama" exemplifies his need to empathize with and understand the Moorish soldiers as colored and oppressed victims of imperialist policies. However, while in many articles he stresses his role as a Negro reporter, in his famous poem "A Song of Spain," he privileges his working-class status. Here Hughes evokes a poetics of simplicity and accessibility, just as Neruda did in *España en el corazón*. This poetry should not be easily dismissed as propagandistic or less poetic; he simply incorporates the political dialectic into the structure of the text and reiterates an oral, informal tone. The poem begins as a dialogue, an apostrophe to all who are singers, on how to define the song of Spain. Is the song of Spain marked by its cultural identity? Can Spain be defined by the stereotypical imagery of a tourist brochure? Is Spain's song based on flamenco, gypsies, the traditional bullfight, famous painters, or literary masterpieces like *Don Quijote*? The poetic voice continuously interrupts the flow with "I do not understand," "What's that?," "You wouldn't kid me, would you?" The incorporation of slang or a colloquial tone into the text stresses the dialogue and intensifies the speaker's voice, which identifies with the worker and popular culture, not just with singers.

In Hughes's poem, Spain and its national identity are not determined by its cultural products, but by the people's spirit, and their struggle: "A bombing plane's / the song of Spain. / Bullets like rain's / the song of Spain... Toros, flamenco, paintings, books— / Not Spain. / The people are Spain" (163). The speaker does not identify himself as an African American; he privileges class identity over national or racial identities. But the speaker here is not an innocent, superior moral voice. He acknowledges his own role of complicity and indifference: "I, worker, letting my labour pile / up millions for bombs to kill a child" (163). The poem moves from an outcry against workers' contributing to make the Fascists' bombs to a demand to become active, historical agents: "Workers, lift no hand again / to build up profits for the rape of Spain! / Workers, see yourselves as Spain!" (163). Therefore, the workers must identify themselves with Spain and the victims of the war, to understand that it is not an isolated fight. As I have mentioned, Guillén and Hughes both went to Spain as reporters; their articles and their poems aim to politicize their readers, not only to inform them.

But unlike Hughes, who only identifies with the worker in this text, in his poem "España," Cuban poet Nicolás Guillén chooses to emphasize his racial and cultural identity; thus, he represents the voice of Latin Americans and their Spanish and African heritage. The poem clarifies from the very beginning that his is not the Spain of Cortés or Pizarro and the Spanish Conquest, but the Spain of the Republican "milicianos," "los cercanísimos hermanos."

In the first stanzas, Guillén uses the imperative to demand that the reader become a witness to history: "Miradla, a España, rota!" The insistence on the word *see*, "mirar," recalls Neruda's "Explico algunas cosas," the famous testimony of his war experiences in Madrid. Neruda's poetic voice addresses the fascist generals: "mirad mi casa muerta, / mirad mi España rota" (*Tercera Residencia* 41). He insists that we all see the destruction of his "casa muerta," a symbol of the country itself. When at the end, he repeats, "Venid a ver la sangre por las calles," he challenges us, just like Guillén, to become witnesses to history. In *Remnants of Auschwitz: The Witness and the Archive,* Giorgio Agamben alludes to two definitions of the word *witness* in Latin, one that stands for a third person in a trial and the other for the person who has lived a certain experience and feels the urgency to give testimony (15). The emphasis on "seeing" and witnessing in the poetics of the war emphasizes that these poems are also historical testimonies.

Neruda's autobiographical details in "Explico algunas cosas" give veracity to his poetic testimony, while Guillén's "La voz esperanzada" in "España," provides fewer personal details to dress up as a poetic "I" who goes beyond the individual self. He wants to stand for all colonial subjects who value, defend, and fight for freedom: "Yo, hijo de América, / hijo de ti y de Africa, / esclavo ayer de mayorales blancos... / hoy esclavo de rojos yanquis... / yo, corro hacia ti, muero por ti" (189). Just as Hughes, in his speech "Too Much Race," connected racism and white supremacist culture in the United States with fascism, Guillén legitimizes his voice as one of the oppressed by recalling a heritage of violence and slavery. Thus, the struggle against fascism is a struggle against a common history of oppression. Guillén emphasizes with pride the speaker's racial features—"con mi cabeza crespa y mi pecho moreno"—enabling him to speak as a product of Cuba's *mestizaje.*

Guillén is constantly distancing the past from the present and the war's historical immediacy. He revisits the Spanish Conquest to legitimize the current struggle against the imperialistic ambitions of fascism: "Con vosotros, brazos conquistadores / ayer, y hoy ímpetu para desbaratar fronteras..." (190). Just as in Neruda's and Vallejo's poems, solidarity with the Spaniards is also revealed through language and the use of *vosotros.* In these verses, Guillén suggests that Latin American writers can and should support Spain, and its democratic Republic, without having to forget or historically erase the brutal past of the Spanish Conquest. It is not a question of forgetting Cortés and Pizarro, it is a question of realizing that Franco and the Fascists represent those imperialistic, totalitarian values. Instead, Guillén stresses that the post-imperial Spanish arms have the "impetus to break down borders," in dialogue with a transatlantic poetics of solidarity that aims to break down the national, racial, and cultural barriers, for a common cause.

Why do I talk about race when my work focuses on ruins, remnants of a broken past, stones that are not supposed to be defined by racial or cultural identities? But aren't some ruins more valuable than others? Aren't we all the time determining which ruins should be appreciated in a museum and which ruins should be considered waste? The same happens with certain questions or historical subjects. Although these poems are not specifically addressing the topos of ruins, they are key in the discussion of a transatlantic poetics of the war, and I believe they shed light on how Americans and Latin Americans read the war as an international struggle. As I have suggested, the topos of ruins is not limited to texts that portray broken buildings; damaged bodies and their racialization are crucial for our understanding of these poetic critiques of modern warfare and fascist ideology. Furthermore, the racist discourse in the Spanish Civil War rhetoric and poetics is seldom discussed in comparison with other aspects of the war, and it is very much a part of the ruined social landscape. As Michael Ugarte states in his essay on race in the war: "Indeed, racial and ethnic conflicts and tensions have received little attention in the otherwise multilayered social and literary historiography of the Spanish Civil War" ("The Question of Race" 108). The topic may make us uncomfortable because racial tensions during the "good war" were complicated further when the "Nationalists," as they called themselves, used and abused Moroccan mercenaries. Susan Sontag in *Regarding the Pain of Others* reminds us that: "General Franco was using the same tactics of bombardment, massacre, torture and the killing and mutilation of prisoners that he had perfected as a commanding officer in Morocco. Then, more acceptably to ruling powers, his victims had been Spain's colonial subjects, darker-hued and infidels to boot; now his victims were compatriots" (9). Sontag stresses how the Spanish Civil War was also determined by the history of the colonial war in Morocco and by how warfare techniques were transferred from Africa to the peninsula. But this becomes a particularly complex issue when, to persuade the Moors to fight for them, the "Nationalists" would try to hide their racist ideology and emphasize their religious zeal. They condemned the Republicans, their hated internal Other, not so much on racial grounds, but on religious and ideological premises. As Sebastian Balfour explains in *Deadly Embrace: Morocco and the Road to the Spanish Civil War*: "What had been the external Other was mobilized against the internal Other. From a Christian war against the infidels of old tradition, the Civil War was portrayed as a religious war against atheism waged together by the two dominant religions of the Mediterranean" (280). He goes on to argue that this transposition also has a class dimension, the external Other, before associated with the infidels, the uncivilized "hordes," were now the Spanish workers against whom the "Nationalists" would be fighting. Therefore, "la España rota" of both Guillén's and Neruda's poems stresses not only the literal and material ruins, as the effects of a very real war, but the metaphorically broken Spain, where the past is in pieces, molded, and reshaped according to the ideological perspective of the speaker and the "destinatario."[23]

However, questions of race and gender become equally problematic and reveal complex contradictions in both the "Nationalist" and the Republican rhetorical discourses. On the one hand, women become *compañeras* and in the beginning of the war they were able to fight as *milicianas*, but the controversial initiative was quickly questioned and defied, and throughout most of the war they were asked to continue serving the cause in the traditional social roles assigned to women.[24] When it came to racial tensions, not only did the "Nationalists" racialize and demonize their ideological other, but some of the Republican representations of the Moors also echoed that reactionary discourse. As Michael Ugarte argues, there were inconsistencies "on both sides of the ideological divide," and he points out how ironic it was that during the war "the Spanish left used the rhetoric of reactionary nationalism to discredit Franco's insurgency" ("Question of Race" 111). Here he refers to Madariaga's analysis of the Republican representation of the Moors in newspaper articles in *El Sol* and popular poems in the *Romancero Libertario*, where Moors are depicted as brutal, uncivilized hordes, the traditional enemy of Spain (Madariaga 364–69). Some of those *romances* like "Mater Nostra" paradoxically defend Republican Spain by recalling the traditional "heroes de la patria": "El Cid... Isabel la Católica, Pizarro... Hernán Cortés" (367). However, I find this to be an exceptional reading of history among the poems that support the Republic; usually, poets were much more politically conscious of the ideological implications of returning to those very questionable heroes. Ugarte reminds us of the Neruda verse in "Explico algunas cosas," "Bandidos con aviones y con moros," in which he conglomerates all the enemies of the Republic into three verses, never alluding to those questionable patriotic heroes. Ugarte also discusses Emilio Prados's "El moro engañado," where the poetic voice treats the Moors in a patronizing, paternalistic way. Still, one can always find a text like Juan Gil Albert's poem "Lamentación (Por los muchachos moros caídos ante Madrid)" in *Son nombres ignorados* (1938), which stands out as a Republican poem where the speaker empathizes with Moroccans, victims of the deceiving maneuvers of the "Nationalists."

Within the context of this discussion on race during the war and in agreement with Gil Albert's poem, Hughes's critique of the use by the "Nationalists" of the black other, the Moor, as "carne de cañón" or "living bait" is crucial. In an article he wrote on October 30, 1937, for *The Afro-American,* he states: "Naturally, I am interested in the Moors, too... As usually happens with colored troops in the service of white imperialists, the Moors have been put in the front lines of the Franco offensive in Spain—and shot down like flies" (in Mullen 109). Hughes, like many Republican militants, especially from the Communist Party, thought of the Moroccans as victims of the fascist system, often betrayed, lied to, and used in the front lines. But Hughes is intrigued by what their presence can cause in the psychic of the Republican side:

> What I sought to find out in Spain was what effect, if any, this bringing of dark troops to Europe had had on the Spanish people in regard to their racial feelings. Had prejudice and hatred been created in a land that did not know it before? What has been the treatment of the Moorish prisoners by the loyalists? Are they segregated and illtreated? Are there any Moors on the government side? (in Mullen 109)

Hughes's questions are thought-provoking and key, and there are still very few studies that try to answer them. His idealization of the Spanish people to the point of suggesting that it was a land that did not know racial "prejudice and hatred" until then may sound naïve and definitely misguided, but what he is questioning is precisely the ideological effect of those contradictions. How can the Moors be helping the very militiamen they were fighting against as colonial subjects? What will this do to the representation of the racial other in the People's Army? The effects of the use of Moroccans in the war has already been studied; the Insurgents exploited the fears that Moors provoked in the Spanish psyche.

Hughes's poem "Letter from Spain Addressed to Alabama" posits the contradictions and ideological inconsistencies that appear when the poetic voice, an African American volunteer from the Abraham Lincoln Battalion, finds himself face to face with a wounded and captured Moor. The poem is structured as a letter, written on "November something 1937," addressed to "Dear Brother at home," and signed with the traditional Republican salute, "Salud, Johnny" (in Mullen 157). Therefore, Hughes's poetic personae becomes the common African American volunteer, who narrates this encounter as if he were telling a story, where the informal, oral tone and slang predominate. The speaker signals the racial identification of blacks and Moors from the first stanza: "We captured a wounded Moor today. He was just as dark as me." The speaker tries to establish a dialogue with the prisoner, but of course, the language barriers interfere at first, until: "somebody told me he was sayin' / They nabbed him in his land." His story is that of the typical Moroccan who does not know what he is fighting for and feels betrayed by the Fascists. Hughes's text connects European imperialist interests in Africa with the Spanish Civil War, where volunteers are fighting for "freedom" versus those who want to "enslave." The end aims at another form of transatlantic solidarity, when the African American speaker empathizes with the Moroccan, paradoxically a victim of both the "Nationalists" and the Republican forces, and through the apostrophe, he hopes to make amends with him: "Listen, Moorish prisoner, hell! / Here, shake hands with me!" But it was too late, "the wounded Moor was dyin' / And he didn't understand." I agree with Ugarte that this gesture is "replete with pathos," and that the poem itself is "a resounding cry against war" ("Question of Race" 115).[25] The need for a translator is key; the African American, the Moroccan, and the Spaniards don't share a common language, and yet they find each other fighting on the same battlefield and dying in each other's arms. The difference between the African American soldier and the Moroccan mercenary is one of ideological conviction. The volunteers of the International Brigades were moved by their own ideals, their need to participate in the struggle against fascism; the Moroccan mercenaries were moved by economic need, and the fascist propaganda of instant gratification.

These poems start building the historical memory of the war and shape the struggle against fascism with its racist, ultra-nationalist, and male-chauvinistic agenda. They emerge from a transatlantic politics of solidarity and the ethical imperative to tell the story of the war. The legacy of their struggle remains one of the uniting factors of a multicultural, democratic society. Benjamin also saw the ethical imperative to critique progress from the historical materialist perspective. In the spring of 1940, just months before he killed himself in the frontier between Nazi-occupied France and Francoist Spain, Benjamin wrote his *Theses on the Philosophy of History*. There he explains how historicists always echo the victor, and therefore we must all read our "universal history" with scepticism: "There is no document of civilization which is not at the same time a document of barbarism" ("Theses," in *Illuminations* 256). Thus, the historical materialist must "brush history against the grain," analyze its manipulative texts, and try not to freeze or retain a static image of the past.

Poems also write history and determine our historical memory of the past, and not always do we find a historical materialist perspective in these texts. Juan Cano Ballesta, in dialogue with Manfred Lentzen's reflection on José María Pemán's famous "Poema de la Bestia y el Ángel," maintains that in contrast to Republican poets who tend to evoke the bloody, tragic reality they face, in fascist poets like Pemán an evasive idealization of reality predominates: "Sus versos 'antes que referencia histórica, [son] acto de fe' que convierte la guerra civil en un acontecimiento de la historia de la salvación, de amplia transcendencia providencialista, orientada a valores supremos como unidad, grandeza imperial y catolicismo, y totalmente desinteresada por la problemática social de obreros y campesinos" (*Las estrate-gias* 78–79). In these poems, which echo the fascist rhetoric, elitism, individualization, abstraction, and idealization of the "supreme" spiritual self reign; they try to evade the repercussions of social warfare.

Pemán's "Poema de la Bestia y el Ángel" clearly projects a fascist vision of progress, disguised as a spiritual renovation; the Angel was ultimately proclaimed as a metaphor for the Fascist's victorious outcome of the war. In Pemán's poem, the Republicans are demonized; they are the Beast, the machine, evil in its purest form *versus* the Angel, the symbol of the Fascists, who are aligned to God and His Spirit. However, it does not end with that; both the Beast and the Angel are racialized enemies. In Pemán's text, the external Other reappears as part of the nostalgia for the glorious imperial past: "Cuando hay que descubrir un Nuevo Mundo / o hay que domar al moro… los ángeles que están junto a Silla / miran a Dios… y piensan en España" (*Poesía de la guerra civil* 308). But the real enemy is once again the internal Other, where the "rojo" and "ateo" join the stereotype of the materialistic Jew; furthermore, the war is repeatedly conceptualized as "la cruzada," with the "Cruz" as its main weapon: "Es inútil, judío. / Cruces de hierro doblarán tu hoguera" (320). In contrast, how do you imagine he portrays the Angel? Well, he's lovely… so Spanish in his demeanor: "Es rubio como una espiga / a punto de madurar" (326). The young, blond soldier is clearly racialized as well, but the difference is that he is white; in the fascist, anti-Semitic rhetoric, whiteness is an ideal image of the self—an ideal that is more connected to the Aryan race than to the very racially mixed, sometimes "off-white" Spaniard.

In his article "The Two Totalitarianisms," Slavoj Žižek reminds the reader that in the current culture of memory, where there was the possibility of banning communist symbols as if they were just as bad as Nazi symbols: "It is necessary to take sides and proclaim Fascism fundamentally 'worse' than Communism" ("The Two Totalitarianisms"). Pemán's poem animalized and demonized the ideological and racial other, once more stressing the strong ties that link Franco's fascism with Hitler's Nazism. As Žižek points out:

> Nazism displaces class struggle onto racial struggle and in
> doing so obfuscates its true nature. What changes in the pas-
> sage from Communism to Nazism is a matter of form, and it
> is in this that the Nazi ideological mystification resides: the
> political struggle is naturalised as racial conflict, the class
> antagonism inherent in the social structure reduced to the
> invasion of a foreign (Jewish) body which disturbs the har-
> mony of the Aryan community.

The disruption of a "spiritual" and "social" harmony is precisely in jeopardy in Pemán's text, where the machine incarnates
the "red" and "foreign" invasion. Pemán's rhetoric voices and
adheres to the Nazi racist struggle; its threatening apostrophe to
the Jew, who will be burned at the stake, also reminds us of the
Spanish Inquisition and the era of 1492, when the Reconquest
of Spain ends with the conquest of Granada, the expulsion of
the Moors and the Jews, and the Conquest of what would be
known as the Americas.

Although I believe that Pemán's poem reveals a biological,
cultural, and ethnic racism in his portrayal of the Jewish people
and the blond Angel, in homage to Hitler's and Mussolini's fascist ideology, I absolutely agree with Cristina Moreiras-Menor
when she argues: "There is a significant difference between the
racism of Nazi Germany and that of Italian and Spanish fascism.
While the first is largely a biological racism based on the superiority of the Aryan race, the other two share a cultural racism
based on tradition and national imaginaries" (n129). In connection to Etienne Balibar's reflections on a "racism without race"
that takes place in modern anti-Semitic discourse and responds
to the Reconquista and the Inquisition in Spain, where the Jew's
"essence is that of cultural tradition, a ferment of moral disintegration" (23–24), Moreiras-Menor explains that the "Spanish
raza" meant "the national spirit, or the notion of hispanidad"
(124). This is key when we read Antonio Machado's, Vicente
Huidobro's, or even César Vallejo's use of *raza* as a form of
unity through language and solidarity with the Spanish working
class and their struggle; this reminds us that the Hispanic "race"
was not necessarily seen as the private property of the "Nationalist" and the fascist discourse. Still, Machado, Huidobro, and
Vallejo, among others, refer to the "Spanish *raza*" with very

different connotations and implications if you compare them to Pemán, Rafael Sánchez Mazas, or even Franco's use of *race*. As Moreiras-Menor points out: "The *franquista* project to regenerate the race is racist in that it believed blindly in the spiritual superiority of the Spanish race" (126). The Francoist rhetoric would lean on a hierarchical vision of society, in which the "Nationalists" were not only spiritually superior, but the *only* ones who were politically, culturally, and economically able to lead Spain to salvation.

To conclude this line of thought, and although I do not want to imply that Benjamin had read Pemán, I do want to contrast his use of the allegory with Benjamin's angel of history. Unlike Pemán's Angel, Benjamin's is not racially identified, and it seems to be more like an abstract, deformed, grotesque ghost. Inspired by Paul Klee's "Angelus Novus," Benjamin imagines the angel of history: "His eyes staring, his mouth open, his wings are spread... His face is turned toward the past" ("Theses," in *Illuminations* 257). The angel sees piles of "wreckage upon wreckage," but even though he wants to "make whole what has been smashed," he can't because "a storm irresistibly propels him into the future to which his back is turned, while the pile of debris before him grows skyward. This storm is what we call progress" (257–58). The angel of history has a redemptive quality that seems to be destroyed by this vision of progress, which is a continuum that propels us but does not let us reflect upon where it leads us. In contrast, Pemán's Angel is more like young Adonis, the idealized soldier who reminds us of the "angels" of José Antonio Primo de Rivera, the famous leader of the Falange, and his description of Paradise: "un Paraíso donde no se descanse nunca y que tenga, junto a las jambas de las puertas, ángeles con espadas" (Pérez Bowie 138). Unlike Benjamin's angel, who is the ultimate witness of history, these angels seem to be the ultimate "terminators," never relaxing in the fluffy clouds, always on guard. As soldiers, they guard the doors of Heaven to "protect" it and "terminate" whoever stands in their way to "salvation." Although one cannot oversimplify the Falange's ideal of an industrialized modern society, it seems to stand opposed to Benjamin's critique of modern progress and the historicist's vision of a homogeneous, empty time. Benjamin's critique of the violence done in the name of progress is also voiced by the poets who support the Republic, in their poems on the ruins of the Spanish Civil War.

Nowadays, we are redefining our ways of remembering in Latin America and Spain. After decades of dictatorships and the politics of fear, there came the politics of forgetting and silence in the name of a peaceful transition into democracy. And now in Spain, just as in many countries of the Southern Cone, the politics of remembering are really gaining ground in literally and metaphorically excavating the past. The so-called generation of grandchildren of the Civil War, from both sides of the Atlantic, needs to participate in the historical reconstruction of the war. Are these poems distant from our modern prerogatives? Can they still talk to us after seventy years? Obviously, they do, and a film like *El laberinto del fauno,* written and directed by Mexican Guillermo del Toro and filmed in Spain, is one of the best examples of a transatlantic aesthetics. Set in Spain, 1944, after the Fascists won the war, the film captures the armed resistance to the regime and its suppression.[26] Through the eyes of a girl, the historical narrative interweaves a fantastic, alternative reality. In a world where the fascist monsters are more treacherous than the faun, the giant frog, or the child-eating creature, the tragic ending is paradoxically a happy one. I am not really ruining the film with this disclosure because it has a circular structure. Death is preferable to life in a fascist society; her sacrifice opens the doors to her fantasyland, an underworld kingdom that transgresses and defies the Catholic notions of heaven, in which her gods are her father and mother.

El laberinto del fauno, a visual poem in itself, takes us into a journey of the self, not only into the historical past. The metaphor of the dead tree, rotting from the inside, just like Franco's Spain, tells us about the necessity to go underground, to dig into the past and face it with its very human monsters. Transatlantic poetics, just like this film, aims to provoke a "historical awakening" and a "real state of emergency," to echo Benjamin. Hughes's and Guillén's works become a political weapon against fascism, political testimonies that redefine identity politics and defy "Nationalist" discourses. Throughout this chapter I argue that along with these three poets I have just discussed, Luis Cernuda, Octavio Paz, César Vallejo, Miguel Hernández, and Pablo Neruda, and their poems to the dead, the broken bodies, the rotten buildings, the ruins of the Spanish Civil War, determine the transatlantic politics of solidarity.

But what is Transatlantic Studies? It sounds like a big boat, the cruise that will take us back and forth from one coast to the other, from the old to the new worlds. Is it merely a redefinition of the way we teach Spanish in the United States, in which we join two positions into one? Is it a "way in" for Peninsular Studies, when some fear that the Spanish boat is slowly sinking with fewer teaching positions because of the powerful Latin American wave in the US academy? Some read Transatlantic Studies with scepticism, the product of a long process of reconfiguration of Hispanic Studies. As Sebastiaan Faber eloquently explains in "Fantasmas hispanistas y otros retos transatlánticos," the study of Spanish and Latin American literatures has gone through diverse phases in the academic world in the US; during the nineteenth and early twentieth century, Peninsular Studies had the upper hand in the battle for prestige and cultural relevance, and Hispanism came to prioritize Spanish as the language of economic and cultural value, without questioning the hegemonic discourse it voiced, but with the Cold War, and the US interventions, cultural, political, and economic projects in Latin America, there was a shift of interest. Peninsular Studies became more and more entrenched in a conservative vision of historical and literary tradition, and Latin American Studies would be connected to progressive outlooks. Among other factors, the battle for resources and power within academic circles created certain rivalries between Peninsular and Latin American Studies. Transatlantic Studies intends to file down those rivalries and strengthen the bridges between both fields, clearly opposing the imperialist legacy of Hispanic Studies, and proposing a theoretical framework, where texts, among other cultural products, are read through a transnational perspective.[27]

Transatlantic Studies was initially associated with English and American comparative analyses, and in Hispanic Studies it began with the discussion of Latin American Colonial and Spanish Golden Age literature. How can we read Sor Juana without having read Quevedo, or vice versa? But in the past fifteen years, departments of Spanish and Romance Languages are more and more interested in considering the common history of Latin American and Spanish literature, crossing the boundaries of national and regional perspectives. But is this really a new approach to the way we read? Yes and no. After all, we study writers who travel, through and beyond the book, and who establish intellectual and artistic dialogues, from Unamuno and Darío to Neruda and Alberti. If their national origins would never limit their discussions, why should we? The academic discipline is constantly redefining itself, and what the Transatlantic approach provokes is a discussion and a reconfiguration of our traditional ways of dividing Peninsular and Latin American Studies, particularly with regards to nineteenth- and twentieth-century literatures. Thus, Transatlantic Studies reconstructs the field to be able to address political and literary questions, and topics, without dehistoricizing or decontextualizing the texts we analyze. Guillén's and Hughes's contributions to the poetics of the war, and the questions they raise on the racial incongruities that emerge from the war, fervently oppose the racist rhetoric of Pemán's text. The Transatlantic approach revitalizes the discussion, where a Cuban and an American poet defy the Spanish Nationalist discourse.

In *The City of Words*, Alberto Manguel suggests that: "Caught between definitions of nationality and globalization, between endemic loyalties and a chosen or enforced exodus, the notion of identity, personal and social, has become diffuse, uncertain" (2). The Transatlantic approach addresses that unstable notion of identity. It may be a way of raising more questions than answers. But it is clearly a path that leads us to question how, through the American academy, United States identity politics imposes a way of reading Latin America and Spain. Transatlantic Studies does not aim to privilege either Peninsular or Latin American literatures; it aims to reflect upon the complex bridges that connect them.

In a multicultural society, we need to defrost our notions of identity. Are we not redefining the ways Spanish is taught, read, and lived in the United States, which increasingly is becoming a bicultural, bilingual nation? Manguel in his reflections on identity claims that the language of poetry has "no labels, no borders, no finitudes" (25–26).[28] The transatlantic politics of solidarity in the poems that emerge from the Spanish Civil War challenge us to become historical agents and to rethink how we read ourselves and our communities, the past and the present, our historical imperatives and our ruins.

The Feminization of Spain and Its Ruins:
Antonio and Manuel Machado, Rafael Alberti,
César Vallejo, and Miguel Hernández

Why is the *patria* or the nation often represented in poetry as a mother? What does the feminization of a Spain in ruins evoke? In colonial times, Spain would be called the motherland, "la madre patria," to emphasize the condescending attitude toward its children and their subaltern status in the distribution of power; this situated the colonies and its subjects in the immature infantile stage and depicted imperial Spain as a giver of life, a provider. The feminization of the nation often intensifies certain characteristics we expect from the country, which is supposed to give us a sense of self and a sense of protection. It is key to note that with the wars of independence in the Americas, the young republics, or even countries that still can be categorized as colonies such as Puerto Rico, writers often feminized the *patria* in their national poetry, although "la madre patria" is inherently (and ironically) still associated with Spain. Nowadays with our global economy, the neoliberal markets, and the constant migration of people, the nation is not always united by the illusion of a common bloodstream; but in the beginning of the twentieth century, the forces of nationalism responded to the need to be part of a collective with shared cultural roots. The metaphor of the "madre patria" centers on the notion that a "good" mother is always self-sacrificing and loves her children unconditionally; the ability to give birth makes the mother the epitome of life. She, therefore, symbolizes the energy that connects all her children, all the national subjects. In the prints and caricatures that react to the loss of the empire in the Spanish American War of 1898, Spain is often represented as a young queen with her lion by her side, as a mother in mourning after the death of her children, Cuba, Puerto Rico, and Guam, or as in a cartoon in the *Syracuse Herald*, an old woman throwing stones at a menacing hat/submarine carrying the US Navy flag.[29]

The representation of Spain during the twentieth century as the motherland underlines the national fratricide that erupted with the Civil War. My grandfather was a judge loyal to the Republic, and his brother was a proud Monarchist. They did not see eye to eye in the political battlefield, and like our family, with the war the "national" family was broken, divided, and hurt. The use of Spain as a mother in the poetry of the supporters of the Republic shows their desire to hold on to their Spanishness, their sense of belonging to the nation. However, the personification of Spain as a mother and a teacher in César Vallejo's "España, aparta de mí ese cáliz" indicates that Spain did not belong only to the Spaniards, but its political repercussions went beyond the national arena; for Vallejo, the war materialized the people's plight, their revolutionary struggle for social justice. But why do politically committed poets, such as Rafael Alberti, Miguel Hernández, and César Vallejo personify Spain as a mother figure? Is it merely a literary convention, which provokes an emphatic reading? Are there conflicting visions of the mother Spain?

Antonio and Manuel Machado became the symbol of brothers, who loved and worked with each other, and yet when the war broke out they adhered to opposing ideological camps. During the Republic, Manuel and Antonio Machado had worked together on three plays, which never reached the stage.[30] But Manuel remained in Burgos where he was on July 18, 1936, and Antonio followed and supported the Republic, from Madrid, Valencia, and Barcelona to his last days when he crossed the French border to Collioure in 1939. In their work, both poets represent Spain as temporal space, a body who engenders the future—imagery that reappears in Alberti, Hernández, and Vallejo, among many other poets. Antonio Machado suggests that the cultural construction of the nation is under a tense rope: on one end, the historical memory of the past, and on the other, the possibility of a revolutionary tomorrow; while Manuel Machado insists on the need to maintain the chain of command, where the past, the present, and the tomorrow of Spain are joined by the high-horse rhetoric of glory and tradition.

Antonio Machado's "El mañana efímero" in *Campos de Castilla* was written in 1913, twenty-three years before the beginning of the Civil War, and in this parodic and ironic depiction of Spain, he is foreshadowing the two visions of Spain that face each other during the conflict.[31] The poem sets the tone from the very first lines, where the picaresque, popular Spain coincides with its devout community: "La España de charanga y pandereta, / cerrado y sacristía... / ha de tener su mármol y su día / su infalible mañana y su poeta" (*Campos de Castilla*

213–14). The Spain he parodies will have its light of day, where poets and artists will try to give it permanence through marble statues; still, the immobility of marble and its association with luxurious tombs may also announce its infallible tomorrow, death. At the end of the poem, we find a new Spain where the chisel of the artist and the worker take over its future, to mold it and transform its social reality. The text can be divided into five parts, separated twice by the repetition of the verses "El vano ayer engendrará un mañana / vacío y ¡por ventura! pasajero." The speaker stresses the traditional representation of time, the future as a product of the past, and through his ironic tone, criticizes the banality of the nation-state: the vain yesterday will give birth to an empty, and fugitive, tomorrow.

"El mañana efímero" shows the nineteenth-century Galdosian parody of the provincial bourgeois young man, corrupt and superficial, looking at France for a fashionable model to follow. Michael Predmore examines the social type depicted here: "Estos son tipos representativos de sectores de la burguesía que han perdido sus raíces históricas y su función social, corrompidos y reducidos a la impotencia por el sistema de la Restauración. No poseen tradición, no tienen un estilo propio... una clase de gente que ha nacido vieja..." (176–77). Spain is also "Esa España inferior que ora y bosteza, / vieja y tahúr" (232), where boredom and religious zeal go hand in hand. But as in Galdós's *Doña Perfecta*, this conservative, dogmatic, ultra-Catholic Spain clearly at the center of this burlesque portrayal is not necessarily associated with the marginalized working class:

> esa España inferior que ora y embiste,
> cuando se digna a usar de la cabeza
> aún tendrá luengo parto de varones
> amantes de sagradas tradiciones
> y de sagradas formas y maneras;
> florecerán las barbas apostólicas
> y otras calvas en otras calaveras
> brillarán, venerables y católicas.
>
> (Machado, *PC* 232)

This parody of the provincial Spain also depicts the Carlists, with their pretensions of being the protectors of traditions, and their self-righteous, dogmatic, anti-intellectual attitudes, who pray while they threaten to attack. Indeed, the Carlists literally attacked the crown; the *guerras carlistas* in the nineteenth century destabilized the monarchy and stirred the cultural, social, and economic turmoil that has often been pointed to as the roots of the Spanish Civil War. In Antonio Machado's "El mañana efímero," Spain is feminized as a body that will give birth to many men, who paradoxically find in a bald head and a long beard emblems of respect.

Although the image of the past as the family tree of the future responds to a lineal reading of history, the repetition of the verses "El vano ayer engendrará un mañana..." underlines the speaker's critique of the circular motion of time and finally proposes a rupture with the cycle. The following depiction of Spain responds to the early twentieth-century urban reality and Valle-Inclán's aesthetics of the grotesque: "Como la náusea de un borracho ahíto / de vino malo, un rojo sol corona / de heces turbias las cumbres de granito" (233). The visceral imagery paints a gruesome, reddish Madrilenian sky, darkened by the excrement of yesterday's banalities, and evokes the new day "estomagante escrito" ("written with the stomach"), product of the drunk's bad hangover and nausea. However, the ironic, burlesque tone ceases in the last verses. Machado ends his diatribe with a vision of a hopeful Spain, young, proletarian, revolutionary: "España del cincel y de la maza, con esa eterna juventud que se hace / del pasado macizo de la raza" (233). The chisel and the mace, just like the ax, are the working tools that will become weapons of "Una España implacable y redentora." The speaker acknowledges that this hopeful Spain does not emerge from a historical vacuum. Machado conveniently rhymes *maza* and *raza* to identify the Spanish "race" with the working class. The use of *maza*, a "drop hammer" or "mace" to evoke the workers is an example of metonymy, but it is also a way of confronting the solidity, the strength of Spain, with the fragility, the ephemeral nature of the "vano ayer." As Predmore suggests, there is a stark contrast between this young Spain and the "España inferior," born old and corrupt (178). There is a sense of ultimatum, of final redemption when the intellectual discourse of social justice is put into *praxis*: "España de la rabia y de la idea."

Almost twenty-five years later, during the Civil War, Antonio Machado wrote a sonnet (Sonnet 78), which nostalgically alludes to his childhood past, "Otra vez el ayer," and fears of tomorrow's "Nationalist" victory. Unlike "El mañana efímero," there is no irony or parody in this sonnet. In the first stanza, the speaker evokes an idealized image of "yesterday's" *locus amenus*: behind the blinds, the window is the threshold that transports him to the childhood garden, full of music and light. Through the apostrophe to his natal city, the speaker is also nostalgically holding on to a sense of belonging:

> Mi Sevilla infantil, ¡tan sevillana!
> ¡Cuál muerde el tiempo tu memoria en vano!
> ¡Tan nuestra! Avisa tu recuerdo, hermano.
> No sabemos de quién va a ser mañana. (*PC* 457)

The adjective once used so often in "El mañana efímero" to describe a vain yesterday, here has another connotation. Time is personified or animalized as a destructive force that tries to bite into the power of memory, but this is in vain because even though time passes by quickly the speaker protects his memories of Sevilla. In the third verse of this stanza, he changes his addressee and speaks directly to his metaphorical brother, the Spaniard, or literally to his brother Manuel, to take care of and take notice of their memories, of those experiences that connect them because tomorrow's fate is uncertain. Although the tone and the style of the poem is dramatically different, the verse with its sense of urgency reminds me of a line in one of César Vallejo's most moving poems to the war: "¡Abisa a todos compañeros pronto!" (*Obra poética* 461). Machado is not paying tribute to Pedro Rojas, or to a particular fallen soldier, but the speaker is clearly concerned with the manipulation of the past, the construction of the historical memory once the war is over.

The pessimistic tone, as well as the fierce political critique of the Fascists, is intensified in the tercets: "Alguien vendió la piedra de los lares / al pesado teutón, al hambre mora / y al ítalo las puertas de los mares" (457). Antonio Machado responds here to the exploitation of the Moroccans, and the economic interests of the Germans and the Italians. As Helen Graham reiterates: "Hitler and Mussolini intervened in Spain because they saw it as the most effective way of changing the balance of power" (*The Spanish Civil War* 39). But in exchange for military support,

Franco also convinced the Germans by giving them privileged access to the mining industry in Spain, as well as giving the Italians unlimited access to the Mediterranean Sea. Thus, Machado denounces Franco's policies of selling the "stones" and the "sea gates." The final verses portray the fascist insurrection as an anti-populist movement that with its politics of fear promotes hate among the people, the working class, who "¡…ayuna y labra, y siembra y canta y llora!" The speaker ends with a lament, a cry; a metaphor of the poem itself as a song that started as an individual cry for a long-lost past and culminates in the evocation of a collective voice that plows and sows the earth.

Manuel Machado's poetry in support of the "Nationalists" and Franco's cause also frequently alludes to this tension between the past and the present and the need to strongly tie tomorrow to yesterday. His sonnet "Tradición" precisely evokes this National-Catholic appropriation of the Spanish "glorious" historical past and its tradition:

> ¡Ay del pueblo que olvida su pasado
> y a ignorar su prosapia se condena!
> ¡Ay del que rompe la fatal cadena
> que al ayer el mañana tiene atado!…
> … ¡Goza de su herencia / gloriosa!…
> ¡Vuelve a tu tradición, España mía!
>
> (Manuel Machado 163)

Manuel Machado accuses those who forget the past of being ignorant and defiant of Spain's "glorious" tradition. From very different perspectives both this poem and his brother's Sonnet 78 argue that the past must not be forgotten. But Manuel Machado accuses the Republicans of forgetting their past in their goal to change the present. Spain must return to its imperial glory, to its tradition, and must not pretend to be godlike: "¡Sólo Dios hace Mundos de la nada!" Manuel Machado criticizes the Republic as a revolutionary and utopian project that intended to create a new world. One of the main dissonances between the texts is the past they respectively cherish; while Antonio nostalgically depicts his childhood Sevilla, Manuel politically chooses to echo the rhetoric of the "Nationalists," where *tradition* means their long-lost imperial projects. Once more in the second sonnet of "Tradición" Manuel reiterates that forgetting equals death and that the chain that connects the past and the present should not be broken. This is ultimately not necessarily a reactionary stand, since we find this premise in most poems on ruins, but the ideological message and the desired effect of the poem is to exalt the imperial past as tradition, as the *status quo* that must be defended and preserved. The Spanish glorious past and the evocation of the Spanish Conquest as the decisive "poem" is more explicit in another text by Manuel Machado, "Los conquistadores" (The Conquistadors), where Pizarro and Cortés are elevated as the epitome of greatness; this fits well with the Francoist propaganda of the insurrection as a crusade and as a way to rescue the imperial tradition.

The insistence on connecting today and tomorrow with yesterday in Manuel Machado's poetry, especially in "Tradición" and "Blasón de España," goes back to his literary and ideological dialogue with his brother and with Antonio's "El mañana efímero." In Antonio Machado's 1913 text, the vain yesterday engenders the ephemeral tomorrow, in an unbearable cycle, until the ritual is broken by "la España de la rabia y de la idea." In Manuel Machado's second sonnet of "Tradición" this cycle is unbreakable: "Los astros van caminos circulares… / Nunca nada será que no haya sido" (164). It suggests that regardless of the possibility of political change, a glorious fate is already written. This poem clearly responds to "Blasón de España," where Manuel Machado, instead of exposing his vision of a glorious past in an abstract way, alludes to the famous ruins of the Alcázar de Toledo. In the Alcázar, fought for from July 19 until September 27, the Fascists found a symbol of resistance to the democratic Republican forces. The construction of the Alcázar began in the eleventh century under Alfonso VI, and it was reconstructed under Carlos V in 1535. Therefore, the place has known a few phases of ruins and reconstructions. Manuel Machado's poem stresses its ruins and stones as the representative of a larger, heroic struggle and a glorious past: "Hoy, ante su magnífica ruina… / ¡Mirad, mirad cómo rezuman gloria / las piedras del Alcázar de Toledo!" (165). The speaker echoes "una voz de gesta peregrina" as if his was the voice of the traditional *cantares de gesta*, as the voice who demands that we witness the magnificence of its ruins. The aftermath and the destruction, here, become idealized as an emblem of honor.

The fact that most of Manuel Machado's poems are sonnets reveals a particular tendency in the poets who support the cause of the Fascists and the Nationalist-Catholics. This is not to say that the sonnet was taken over by these poets, since Antonio Machado wrote around nine sonnets about the war, and other poets such as Rafael Alberti also explore the sonnet form, but in the Republican front the *romance* is predominant.[32] As Juan Cano Ballesta explains, Francoist rhetoric found formal constriction an effective way to carry their message: "La misma forma del soneto, severa y ceñida, es control, contención, estructura; es también el rechazo del 'verso libre' surrealista que sugiere caos, anarquía, desorden, ímpetu desbordado; como la retórica franquista exalta el orden y la jerarquía, mientras condena la anarquía y el caos" (*Las estrategias* 63). However contentious, as Cano Ballesta suggests, while the Republican poets, famous and anonymous, tended to the "verso libre" and the popular *romance,* the Francoist poets privileged the sonnet as the ideal, elitist form, emblem of the hierarchical and structured society they envisioned.

In contrast to the anonymous heroes of the *romances*, in another sonnet, "¡España!," Manuel Machado continues to exalt the insurrection, but this time mentioning it as a possession of Franco, "the leader":

> ¡Oh!, la España de Franco, baluarte
> contra la plaga asiática en Europa…
> Madre de Mundos, de titanes tropa…
> España única y grande ¡Arriba España! (172)

Franco's Spain is portrayed as the only one who can resist the "invasión" of the Soviet Union, represented in a very racist way as an Asiatic plague. The feminization of Spain, evident in the apostrophe "Madre de Mundos," implicitly refers to the conquest of the Americas as if the continent was a *tabula rasa* when they "found" it, and it shows the condescending attitude toward the existing civilizations of the Aztecs, the Mayans, and the Incas. The depiction of Spain as a mother who gives birth to new worlds contradicts his own argument in "Tradición" when the speaker claims that "¡Sólo Dios hace Mundos de la nada!" But ultimately, Manuel Machado uses the conventional feminization of the nation as *madre patria* to reiterate Francoist propaganda slogans of "¡Arriba España!" and "una, grande y libre," interestingly omitting the "libre," the "free" part of the coined phrase.

In contrast to this vision of a "Nationalist" Spain, the Republican poets embrace a visceral depiction of their *madre patria* tied to the search for origins in the land itself. Spanish historian Santos Juliá suggests that the metaphor of the nation as mother predominates in the second and final years of war, as the Republican troops start losing ground and Spanish poets begin their political exile. He clarifies that while political speeches hold on to the Republic, the poets evoke Spain: "patria, libertad, tierra, pueblo no son República, son España, que tiene su representación en todo lo que evoca el origen, todavía cercano a la tierra" (*Historia de las dos Españas* 272). Among the many poets he quotes, Cernuda, Vallejo, Hernández, he reiterates Antonio Machado's sonnets, in which Spain is attached to a varied landscape: "llano, loma, alcor y serranía." Juliá also addresses how Antonio Machado feminizes the Spanish land in these verses: "Mas tu, varona fuerte, madre santa, / sientes tuya la tierra en que se muere, / en ella afincas la desnuda planta, / y a tu Señor suplicas ¡Miserere!" (457). This disturbing sonnet portrays a motherland who pleads to God, the Father, for her son the traitor. In conjunction with the representation of the Virgin as a mediator, the nation is the "madre santa"; but it is also "varona fuerte," a masculinization of the mother intended to stress her strength and valor. Juliá concludes that the "mito omnipresente de la madre" is explained through the people's intrinsic connection to the land, and the anguish of a lost common place. Still, the trope cannot be read in merely literal terms, as César Vallejo's *España, aparta de mí ese cáliz* demonstrates, Spain becomes much more than Spain.

For Peruvian poet César Vallejo, Spain is a teacher, a mother, a book that is born from a dead body; its struggle is a decisive moment for modern history. Vallejo—who had lived in Paris since 1923, had visited Spain frequently, and lived in Madrid in 1931—worked tirelessly for the Republican cause during the war. He was deeply affected by the war, and his book *España, aparta de mí ese cáliz*, captures like no other in poetic *praxis* his Marxist ideals and the vision of humanity being fought for in the social struggle of the war. Vallejo fell ill and died in April

1938, his last words: "España... Me voy a España" (Vélez and Merino 16). Vallejo's elusive title has been read as an emblem of God, the Father: "Dios y España se confundían en una misma imagen...: lo atestigua meridianamente la sustitución de Padre por España en la famosa frase pronunciada por Jesús en su oración de Getsemaní: 'Padre si quieres, aparta de mí este cáliz' de donde procede el título" (Forgues 59). Furthermore, Julio Vélez and Antonio Merino explain that the title emerges from the passage in the Bible when Jesus denies and rejects death, which is a constant topic in Vallejo's poetry collection. Spain has to hold on to the hope of its resurrection through a working class that never dies (16).[33] Spain becomes the idealized space of social justice, the utopia. In this poetry book, religious and political language merge in these texts that aim to find redemption in violence.[34]

In the Second International Congress of Writers Against Fascism, Vallejo—like many Latin American writers, especially Nicolás Guillén, Juan Marinello, and Vicente Huidobro—stressed the cultural and political bonds that unite the Americas and Spain.[35] In his speech, "La responsabilidad del escritor," Vallejo argues that writers have the ethical imperative to use the word, the "verbo," as a weapon of action; thus, to face history is their political responsibility. Vallejo's use of *raza* and the aggrandized depiction of Spain may sound polemical nowadays, but it is crucial to read it within the historical context:

> Camaradas: Los pueblos iberoamericanos ven claramente en el pueblo español en armas una causa que les es tanto más común cuanto se trata de una misma raza, y sobre todo, de una misma historia, y lo digo, no con un acento de orgullo familiar de raza, sino que lo digo con un acento de orgullo humano, y que sólo una coincidencia histórica ha querido colocar a los pueblos de América muy cerca de los destinos de la madre España. (*OC* 642)

Vallejo explains that Spanish Americans identify with Spain because they share a common race and history, but he clarifies that his pride is in humanity. Therefore, *race* can be read here as the human race. As a general term it can also be defined as a cultural bond, rather than the biological or ethnic identity mark of a group. And yet, Vallejo reiterates that a shared race and history stems from the historical coincidence of the conquest that connected Spain and the Americas and responds to the colonial rule by recalling the filial bond with "la madre España." Vallejo once again alludes to Spain as a mother figure and develops this reflection: "América ve, pues, en el pueblo español cumplir su destino extraordinario en la historia de la Humanidad, y la continuidad de este destino consiste en que a España le ha tocado ser la creadora de continentes; ella sacó de la nada un continente, y hoy saca de la nada al mundo entero" (*OC* 642). Vallejo suggests here that Spain is the "creator" of the Americas, aggrandizing its role as a cultural and political power to set it as an example for the world. These instances in his speech are easily misunderstood if we do not contextualize them. Jean Franco interprets this discourse as showing how "Vallejo saw man's only hope as the union of individuals within a socially just 'body politic'… That is why Spain became, for him, the matrix of a qualitatively different future, the inventor of an America from which the new man could emerge" (*César Vallejo* 230). Jean Franco's analysis, without referring directly to this segment, responds to Vallejo's claim that Spain is a creator and inventor. She points to the right direction when she signals Vallejo's aim to be the future, not the past; his vision of emerging from "nothingness" into a new social order is at the basis of the transatlantic solidarity that results from the Spanish Civil War.

Vallejo was not politically naïve about the use of language and the ideological manipulation and appropriation of a common race and history in the opposing rhetorical discourses of the war. He knows that Francisco Franco's "Nationalist" quest represents the imperialist interests that once justified the conquest and the colonial subjugation of the Americas. He attacks General Franco in an article that appeared in 1937 in both *Nuestra España* and *Repertorio Americano*, "América y la 'Idea de Imperio' de Franco":

> Respuesta más elocuente no podría dar América a los repetidos llamamientos dirigidos por Franco a nuestros países para fundar un imperio hispanoamericano diz que sobre la base de los "lazos de la sangre y el idioma, de la historia y la civilización." Desde luego, ignoramos lo que Franco entiende por imperio hispanoamericano… y sólo la registramos para

notificar… que América rechaza, en nombre precisamente de
los auténticos destinos de la raza, todo vínculo siquiera fuera
momentáneo y circunstancial, con los lacayos de la invasión
extranjera en España y destructores de los pueblos y ciudades
en que tuvieron cuna ese mismo idioma y esa misma civiliza-
ción que nos son comunes. (*OC* 636)

The rage and indignation, transparent in the tone of this article,
intensify the emotional implication of Vallejo in this cause.
Vallejo accuses Franco of trying to trick Spanish Americans and
manipulate the Spanish legacy through the promise of a common imperial project. He also retakes from their lexicon the use
of words like *race, common language,* and *civilization*, by arguing that the Francoist troops were lackeys of foreign imperial
powers (Germans and Italians) who were destroying the places
that served as a cultural cradle. It is interesting that Vallejo
emphasizes his voice as a Peruvian, as a Spanish American, so
frequently in his articles and speeches, and yet in his poetry, his
first person speaker is not geographically identified. The collection begins with: "Voluntario de España, miliciano / … cuando
marcha a morir tu corazón… / no sé verdaderamente / qué hacer,
dónde ponerme; corro, escribo, aplaudo…" (*Obra poética* 449).
Vallejo's speaker is in anguish, and his need to take action can
only find refuge in the written word. Yet *España, aparta de mí
ese cáliz*, in contrast to what some critics assert, is not a personal, solipsistic vision of the war.[36] The poetry collection aims
to value the notion of sacrifice for a noble collective cause that
goes beyond the self and its personal tragedy. The religious connotations and allusions in the poems portray Spain as a Christ
figure or the representation of a sacrificed god. As I mentioned
earlier, the title's response to "Padre, aparta de mí ese cáliz,"
an attempt to evade death on Jesus's part, suggests that for the
poet, Spain took the place of the Father, God, and the echo of
those words can represent a rejection of death and an embrace
of hope and life. Thus, one can understand the recurrent obsession with a collective and an individual resurrection that comes
with the social revolution. Still, the poem that titles and ends the
poetry collection does not represent Spain as a father or a Christ
figure, but as a mother, a teacher, a role model to all.

The feminization of Spain as a mother is particularly palpable in the last poem, "España, aparta de mí ese cáliz." The

poem begins and ends with the apostrophe to the children of the world, "Niños del mundo." The addressee becomes an instant reference to both the children of the war and future generations; a reference that also determines the tone and the metaphors that evoke a war whose violence disrupts any sense of normalcy and progress, and which also explains the personification of Spain as a mother and a teacher, the main educators in both the private and public spheres. As in the case of Cernuda and Hernández, Vallejo feminizes Spain as a mother to intensify the sense of *pathos* in the poem. The fear of failure is stressed from the very beginning with the conditional verb: "si cae España —digo es un decir," verses that will be repeated and structure the poem through the possibility of a fallen Spain. In the first stanza, the war interrupts the learning process of those children and makes them suddenly grow up. If Spain falls: "niños, ¡qué edad la de las sienes cóncavas! / ¡qué temprano en el sol lo que os decía! / ¡qué pronto en vuestro pecho el ruido anciano! / ¡qué viejo vuestro dos en el cuaderno!" (481). The defeat of the Spanish Republic, already possible at the end of 1937 when Vallejo wrote this collection, marks in the text the era of "concave" temples, or hollow minds.[37] Without the power of education, the mind is easily formed and deformed. Paradoxically, the children turn old, ripe, when they are still green. Ruins in this poem take shape in the abandoned emblems of a lost childhood when the speaker complains that the children already have the broken bodies of elderly people and that the number two in their notebook has aged, lonely without the other numbers, useless in the disrupted learning process.

The second stanza becomes a cry for help, an apostrophe that demands that the children (and the readers) become witnesses to the sacrifices of the national body in ruins, the wounded mother Spain:

> ¡Niños del mundo, está
> la madre España con su vientre a cuestas
> está nuestra maestra con sus férulas,
> está madre y maestra,
> cruz y madera, porque os dio la altura,
> vertigo y división y suma, niños;
> está con ella, padres procesales! (481)

Spain is depicted as a woman wounded, carrying her womb, precisely a symbol of her femininity and her maternity, as if it were her cross. The third verse also feminizes Spain as a teacher "con sus férulas," which means in both English and Spanish a splint used to straighten a broken bone, and a cane or rod, often used by the teacher as a way to implement authority and chastise disobedience in the classroom. *Férula* also means "authority" itself, and in this verse the fact that it is plural may suggest that it is referring to both meanings: Spain can have both a broken cane and a needed splint, and she can be both mother and teacher, the symbol of sacrifice, the cross and the material of what it is made, wood—the signifier and the signified.

Throughout Vallejo's book, language itself is under attack during the war. Spain becomes a text, and the defeat of the Republicans means a regression in language. The third stanza implies that when the intellectual process of development is cut short, even the physical development of the children is paralyzed: "niños, ¡cómo vais a dejar de crecer! / ¡cómo va a castigar el año al mes! / ¡cómo van a quedarse en diez los dientes, / el palote el diptongo..." (481). Personified time represents the social violence of war, where adulthood, the year, seems to punish the month, the child, with a half-toothless mouth, whose time has stopped. As Julio Ortega explains: "No solamente el desarrollo intelectual de los niños puede interrumpirse ('en palote el diptongo'); además, en lugar de ascender por el lenguaje para ejercer su poder, sufrirán una regresión; y hasta sus dibujos ('el corderillo') señalarían las ataduras de la imaginación" (*La teoría poética* 84). The war has intercepted the infantile language and world. The children, still learning the alphabet, suffer a literal and metaphorical regression captured in the moving imagery of the text: "¡cómo vais a bajar las gradas del alfabeto / hasta la letra en que nació la pena!" Language gives us the tools to express intense emotion, and yet it also falls short; the children go back to feeling the pain and the sorrow without knowing how they got there. Instead of going up the ladder of knowledge and through the multiple steps that give us the power of letters, words, and discourse itself, they are left empty-handed.

In the fourth and fifth stanzas, the speaker seems to plead, and at the same time to assume the voice of the teacher, who repeatedly uses the imperative on her students: "Bajad la voz" (482). The children are now identified as the "hijos de los guerreros," the children of the soldiers fighting the war, and they should be quiet for Spain, who contemplates its own skull, its own "to be or not to be" moment. The verses, "bajad la voz, el canto de las sílabas, el llanto / de la materia…," may actually allude to an anecdote that Alejo Carpentier recounts where some of the delegates of the Congress of Writers in Defense of Culture found themselves in a meeting, and the windows of the salon were open. A group of children who were playing in the plaza started asking who the foreigners were, and when they found out, they started singing for them as a sign of gratitude, "un milagro de espontaneidad" (qtd. in Vélez and Merino 121).

Vallejo's speaker in this stanza seems to also bring to mind the degradation of language and an evanescent process wherein the voice becomes the "canto," "llanto," "rumor," and "aliento." The last stanza closes with a reapropriation of the metaphors and imagery of the first stanza. Through the use of the imperative and the conditional verbs once again, Vallejo depicts the defeat of the Republic as a catastrophe for humanity: "Bajad el aliento, y si / el antebrazo baja, / si las férulas suenan, si es la noche…" (482). Now that the temples are hurt, the speaker demands the impossible: not only lower your voice, but your breath. When the ferules or canes sound, the children hear the noise of repression and torture—a foreshadowing of the use of force inside and outside the classroom during Franco's dictatorship. Sound becomes crucial at the end of the poem, where the end of the war seems to announce the beginning of a horror film:

> si hay ruido en el sonido de las puertas
> si tardo,
> si no veis a nadie, si os asustan
> los lápices sin punta, si la madre
> España cae —digo en un decir—
> Salid, niños del mundo; id a buscarla…!

The shrieking noise of doors and the subtle and innocent imagery of blunt pencils reveals the very visceral fear of the most vulnerable victims of the war. The pencils not only point to the tools of learning, they are also the weapons of the poet, the tools of writing, and the broken pencils reiterate the war's attack on language itself. And yet, the speaker, instead of aiming to protect the children, as a mother would do, entices them not to let fear stop them from taking action: if you lose your mother, your country, go find her, retake her. The roles are therefore reversed, and the children are asked to save the motherland.

Spain is a book that sprouts from a cadaver to give resurrection a different meaning. As in the last verses of "España, aparta de mí ese cáliz," where hope prevails in the appeal to children and future generations not to let it die, Vallejo's poems, from "Masa" to " Pequeño responso a un héroe de la República," reiterate the need to believe in a social and political resurrection. In "Pequeño responso," the book is a symbol that gives a sense of natural recycling and political hope, and it is a material remnant of history, a way of maintaining the historical memory of the war. The text ends with: "y un libro, yo lo vi sentidamente, / un libro, atrás un libro, arriba un libro / retoñó del cadáver ex abrupto" (*OP* 470). The poem narrates the story of this book and how it emerges from the dead body, "retoñaba," and at the end, the speaker becomes a witness of how it blooms. Without trying to conglomerate all these poets in a strict categorical framework, most writers who participate in the transatlantic poetics of solidarity of the war evoke the testimonial genre and stress the poets' need to become witnesses to history, who testify their visions of poetic truth. From the ruins of the dead body emerges hope in the shape of a book; just as in Alberti's "Madrid-Otoño" from the battered body of the pregnant city emerges hope in the cry of a newborn. Still, Jean Franco eloquently explains how "Pequeño responso" and Vallejo's work in general differentiates itself from Alberti's poetics during the war:

> There is a world of difference between Vallejo's book and the dead heroes of Alberti's poems whose bodies return to earth and are metamorphosed as plants. This alter kind of immortality allows no cultural transmission from one generation to the next whereas the "libro" of the "Pequeño responso" is both a cultural product and etymologically related to nature. The Latin *liber,* derived from the same root as a tree bark; hence it can readily be thought of as "sprouting." Yet the book is also separate from nature and no longer subject to its laws. Thus the analogy between the new man who

> overcomes death and the text which is born out of life but
> does not simply return to nature with the death of its creator
> is both exact and far-reaching. (*César Vallejo* 234)

As Jean Franco avows, Vallejo's poetics of resurrection aim to produce immortality; the word, the book itself is an achievement of cultural transmission that goes beyond nature's cycle. And yet, in "España, aparta de mí ese cáliz," the speaker rejects the chalice, rejects the blood of Communion, because he does not want to give in; he still wants to find hope in the children's journey and search. Even though in this poem, the process of cultural transmission has derailed, and the *two* in the children's notebooks has aged with the struggle between the two Spains, for Vallejo the children can actually give Spain its life back. Jean Franco reiterates the difference between Vallejo's books sprouting from the cadaver, its creator, and Alberti's Baroque vision of dead bodies that return to nature, to become natural fertilizers. Both poets were committed Marxists, who integrated their political ideals into their poetic projects; and yet, for both, there is a need to find some sort of immortality or resurrection after death.

The need of ecological renewal, versus the religious resurrection, is a topos that reappears throughout Alberti's poetry collection, *Capital de la Gloria*, and in a way, it also signals his nationalist rhetoric of Spanish resilience in moments of ultimate crisis. In "El Otoño y el Ebro," the poem dedicated to Enrique Líster, a famous Republican commanding officer who fought in the Battle of el Ebro, Alberti also explores the metaphor of autumn. The poem compares the resilient Republican soldiers to the trees in the fall, without leaves, naked, vulnerable, cold, and broken, but inside they are alive: "Pero como los troncos, el hombre en la pelea / seco, amarillo, frío, mas por debajo, verde" (*El poeta en la calle* 85). Just as the city in Alberti's "Madrid-Otoño" hides the seed of victory inside its broken body, so the trees, emblems of the soldiers, survive the approaching winter by holding on to green, the color of spring and hope. In "Madrid-Otoño" the promise of ecologic resurrection is also suggested in the personified leaves of the fallen trees; soldiers seem to defy death through nature's cycle.

However, these poems evoke the Benjaminian need not to believe in history as a norm that will take us to a progressive future. On a more optimistic tone, Alberti's "Madrid-Otoño" also defies that vision of lineal progress through his critique of the devastation produced by our technological modern warfare, and by holding on to a hope that evokes circular time and a natural cycle of life. Unlike Vallejo, Cernuda, and Hernández, who feminized the country of Spain as a mother, Alberti evidently places his poem "Madrid-Otoño" in the besieged capital, where the urban center is portrayed as the broken body of a pregnant mother, giving birth in the end to victory.

After July 1936, Madrid became a battleground and one of the symbols of the Republican resistance. Through the apostrophe in Alberti's "Madrid-Otoño," the speaker personifies the city in ruins, reveals its injured body, and revitalizes her as a mother, pregnant with the future. The speaker addresses the city in the first verse: "Ciudad de los más turbios siniestros provocados... / yo quisiera furiosa, pero impasiblemente / arrancarme de cuajo la voz, pero no puedo" (*El poeta en la calle* 67). From the livid, anguished city emerges the furious voice of the poet, who wants to impose silence, and at the same time, merge his cry and his song with "la sangre tirada" of the dead.[38] The text begins and ends with a voice, a cry, a product of the city's catastrophic outcome.

In the modern topos of ruins, we frequently find that the speaker identifies with a passerby, who walks by the streets, the monuments, the fragments of the past. In "Madrid-Otoño," the speaker describes himself as a witness of a historical present. From the impossibility of remaining silent, of "arrancarme de cuajo la voz," Alberti's poem begins.[39] Peter Wesseling in his book on Alberti, *Revolution and Tradition*, indicates that a change in his poetic trajectory is fictionalized in "Madrid-Otoño": "The images that begin and end it symbolize the process of change Alberti felt he was undergoing during the war and that he saw mirrored in the social, cultural and political crisis of the twenties and thirties" (67).[40] This poetic change was a gradual process, influenced by Marxist ideals, and it coincides with the Avant-garde poets' disillusionment at the end of the "roaring twenties."[41] The poetic structure, as it has been analyzed before by Salvador Jiménez Fajardo, seems to follow "concentric circles," where the speaker's journey goes from the outskirts of the city, "los barrios en ruinas," the empty houses, into the interior of the city, its wounded body and its hopeful womb.[42]

In Alberti's poetry book *Capital de la Gloria*, the metaphor of autumn reveals a vision of war and death as part of a natural, ecological cycle. Considering the Fascists' monopoly of the spiritual world through their religious discourse, maybe the only hope of an atheist like Alberti is to think that the dead bodies will be recycled, and they will be reintegrated in this process of ecological renewal. Madrid is naked as a tree in autumn, and the speaker explores its periphery: "voy las hojas difuntas pisando entre trincheras, / charcos y barrizales" (67). The personified fallen leaves suggest a parallelism with the dead bodies of the soldiers in the trenches. From the trees to the buildings, the "cielo temeroso de explosiones y llamas" threatens to destroy everything.

The historical and artistic memory is also in danger of erasure in the poems on ruins: "avenidas de escombros y barrios en ruinas, / corre un escalofrío al pensar tus museos / tras de las barricadas" (67). Alberti, as secretary of the Alianza de Intelectuales Antifascistas, his wife María Teresa de León, and José Bergamín were always worried about the masterpieces in the Museo del Prado. They had the immense responsibility of carrying out the order to empty the museum to protect it from the constant bombardments.[43] But in this poem, Alberti does not privilege the artistic heritage over the human loss of the war. In the topos of ruins we traditionally find the poet's gaze imagining the daily life of the inhabitants of the houses that lay in ruins:

> Hay casas cuyos muros humildes, levantados
> a la escena del aire, representan la escena
> del mantel y los lechos todavía ordenados,
> el drama silencioso de los trajes vacíos… (67)

These verses reveal the theater of ordinary, daily life, interrupted by the bombs. Through the metonymy of the "trajes vacíos," we can visualize the absent bodies, the ghosts of the ruined houses. In the topos of ruins, the macrohistorical space is represented in the broken, abandoned, empty house, full of moss and reptiles. Here, a bomb disrupted the bubbling life of the house: the play, the theatrical course of daily life, is broken in half and comes to a tragic, abrupt end—where we can see backstage.

The apostrophe in the final stanza of the first part of the text intensifies the defiant presence of the wounded city:

> Ciudad, ciudad presente,
> Guardas en tus entrañas de catástrofe y gloria
> El germen más hermoso de tu vida futura.
> Bajo la dinamita de tus cielos, crujiente,
> Se oye el nacer del nuevo hijo de la victoria.
> Gritando y a empujones la tierra lo inaugura. (68)

The city and the earth are joined in this poetic space, where the natural and the cultural elements are not opposed, but become allies against the barbarism of modern technological warfare. "Madrid-Otoño" culminates with a vision in which the feminized city, so close to death, paradoxically gives birth to the "nuevo hijo de la victoria," a vital response, a cry that silences "la dinamita de tus cielos." The poet's role is then to help the city give birth to its future: "Ciudad, quiero ayudarte a dar a luz tu día." Here, life is not born from the bodies that nurture the earth and from which plants, and trees, will grow; life is, paradoxically, emerging from the earth and from words, but born in and by the modern urban space, full of rubble and crumbled buildings.

The feminization of the city is a trope that can be connected to a well-established tradition in art and literature that depicts the ideal female body as one that signifies purity as in the allegory of justice as a blind woman, symbol in itself of the state, and therefore, the city's commitment to order. Nonetheless, the ideal nude or the naked woman as the emblem of the modern city and its allegorical meanings can also come to symbolize the impurity of Modernity, as in Edouard Manet's paintings or Charles Baudelaire's poetry. For example, in Eugène Delacroix's famous *Le 28 Juillet: La Liberté guidant le peuple*, the allegory of freedom is represented by the heroine who does not care if she shows her breasts while leading the battle. That painting also defies the notion of purity in the urban center, since some critics saw in her both a whore, a representative of the modern city worker, and a political leader. By exposing her breasts and carrying the flag, she is both vulnerable and fierce. In poetry, the *madre patria*, the fatherland, or the nation tends to be feminized as a mother who gives birth to the citizens, united by the brotherhood of a very polemical bloodstream. The political connotations of this feminization are key in "Madrid-Otoño," but rather than read this as a way of subjugating and delimiting the national body to a victimized, defenseless woman, I believe Alberti aims here to signal a hope of political renewal. This vision of a hope, a light, a sign of life that emerges from the ruins of the city, from its waste, has more to do with his Marxist ideals and the dialectics of history.

The poems to Madrid are countless; the capital became the core of the Republican resistance. "Madrid-Otoño" aims to evoke in the readers a sense of outrage and to incite them to become witnesses to history. The testimonial vein of these texts reiterates their urgency, but also their veracity. In one of the many manifestos by La Alianza de Intelectuales Antifascistas, the authors emphasize the need to give testimony: "Desde Madrid, presenciando la patológica crueldad de los fascistas… queremos denunciar ante vosotros, haceros testimonio de los últimos acontecimientos, asesinatos incalificables…" (Hernández, *Crónicas* 134).[44] In the manifesto they condemn the bombardments of the civilian population, a danger that also threatens the millenary art work in the Museo del Prado. The manifesto ends with a call to action to the international democratic powers. The authors legitimize their accusations by restating their truth: "La verdad está con nosotros y no puede ser falseada… os la decimos nosotros que somos poetas, escritores, artistas y tenemos un alto sentido de nuestro oficio que se halla por encima de la propaganda, de la mentira útil…" (136). They insist that artists are bound to truth, and they deny that their art is propagandistic. They are not politicians; they have no ulterior motives to exaggerate the real drama of Madrid. Among the many artists who signed this are: Bergamín, Cernuda, Aleixandre, Antonio Machado, María Teresa León, Alberti, and Miguel Hernández.

Madrid is also represented as a wounded woman, being slowly killed by Italian and German cannons, in one of Hernández's articles written from the Front: "…la ciudad de Madrid se conmueve y se desangra por todas sus ventanas y todos sus campos: desnuda, muda y serena" (*Crónicas* 30). The city and its countryside are graceful victims, serene, naked, and thus, vulnerable. Hernández could voice his outrage: he volunteered in 1936 and was one of the very few intellectuals and poets who actually fought in the trenches. He was only twenty-one when he first arrived in Madrid in 1931. In the early thirties, his poetic works were greatly influenced by his friendship with Ramón Sijé and their Catholic convictions, but in 1934 and 1935 when he meets Neruda and Aleixandre, already well-recognized poets who would become his close friends, his poetry finds another voice. Hernández was rooted to the land, always proud of being "el pastor de Orihuela," a shepherd for most of his life, who studied through scholarships with the Jesuits and on his own, "un autodidacta."[45] As Alberti has mentioned, "Pablo Neruda fue quien lo vio mejor. Solía repetir: '¡Con esa cara que tiene Miguel de patata recién sacada de la tierra!'" ("Imagen primera" 18). The metaphor was an homage to Hernández's countryman demeanor; his skin showed his energy, his internal glow, and the traces of years of manual work. Just like Alberti and Vallejo, he was a politically committed poet, a Communist, whose war poetry expressed an internal music, a sense of dignity and strength seldom found. As Alberti states: "Miguel Hernández fue el mejor y más auténtico poeta de la guerra" (*La arboleda* 112). I usually dislike those types of generalizations, especially the claim of authenticity. But here I agree with Alberti: Hernández was exceptional. Not merely committed to the Republican cause and the people's plight, he *was* one of the people, one of the exploited workers, who knew what was at stake. It is hard to discuss his work because it is remarkably *moving*, in every sense of the word, and yet it is also remarkable that he is not as well known internationally as Vallejo, Neruda, Alberti, and Cernuda. Antonio Buero Vallejo, the famous Spanish playwright, met him in one of the many prisons he was subjected to after the end of the war. Buero Vallejo compares Hernández's work and his deep intuition to the mystical poet San Juan de la Cruz, among other poets, and stresses that he, unlike so many, was "un poeta *necesario*" (33). Miguel Hernández died in an Alicante prison, vomiting pus and blood, in 1942, just thirty-one years old.[46]

So far, we have seen various ways of representing Spain, often feminized and vindicated as the *cause*, the *source* of unity. Antonio Machado depicted a divided country, torn between a caricaturesque reactionary and dull society, and a liberal and self-complacent vision; but from the ruins of those vain yesterdays would emerge the "young" and vibrant, revolutionary Spain. Manuel Machado, during the war, decided to voice the diatribe of the Francoist regime and chose a Spain that saw the future tied to its glorious, imperial tradition. César Vallejo treats Spain as a book, a mother, and a teacher, who instead of being bound by its national borders transgresses those frontiers, defies its ruined state, and becomes a symbolic utopia, from which a new social order of justice should and would emerge. Even though their poetic works are dramatically diverse, in both Vallejo and Alberti we realize that from the modern city or the vision of a Spain in ruins springs a need, a hope for resurrection: cultural, political, or even ecological. In Alberti and Hernández, though not so much in Vallejo, this hope is rooted in the land and the Baroque promise of a natural renewal, where life is born from death. This need to cling to an optimistic outcome for the war was also a way for these poets to distance themselves from a Romantic aesthetics of ruins, where the melancholic self only saw himself reflected in the external destruction. There may be a nostalgic tone in many of these texts, in particular in Antonio Machado's last poems, but it is not solipsistic and self-obsessed. In a thought-provoking essay on the changing depictions of Spain in Antonio Machado, Hernández, and Cernuda, Marina Mayoral compares the first two poets:

> In sum, in Machado's work the term "España" first stood for a principle of unity; then, for a harsh and bellicose land haunted by the roaming shadow of Cain; and finally, for a fractured entity comprised of two irreducibly opposed societies challenged by yet another society that, aligned with the finest part of Spanish heritage, sought to forge a third way.
>
> In the hands of Miguel Hernández, "España" was to take an altogether different meaning. In the Civil War poems, "España" emerges as a great mother, as home and country... Spain essentially means Republican Spain. (304)

Mayoral argues that unlike Machado, who saw a divided Spain, Hernández mainly portrayed Spain as the motherland of the Republicans, of the proletarian class, and condemned the Fascists as traitors and therefore not deserving of being called Spaniards. In a way, he is reversing the "Nationalist's" rhetorical discourse of calling the Republicans, the *Anti-españoles*, the "barbarians."

196

The demonization of the other is prevalent in the war poetry of both ideological camps. Spain is portrayed as a cemetery, a grave in itself, as Hernández suggests in "Recoged esta voz": "España no es España, que es una inmensa fosa, / que es un gran cementerio rojo y bombardeado: / los bárbaros la quieren de este modo" (*Obra poética* 324). Just as in Alberti's "Madrid-Otoño," the bombardments of the city bound it to ruins: "Ciudades... cuerpos de potencia / yacen precipitados en la ruina" (Hernández, *Obra poética* 323). But obviously, Hernández in times of war does not claim to have an objective perspective. The victims are always Republicans; the cemetery is both red with blood and ideologically red. These ruins are clearly the product of war and technological progress, and they are part of his denunciation and his attempt to instill sympathy in the international community for the Republican cause: "Hombres, mundos, naciones / atended, escuchad mi sangrante sonido" (322). This poem is divided into two parts, and while the first one focuses on a Spain in dramatic turmoil, the second defies the pessimistic depiction and avows that the committed Republican youth offer a promise of ecological and political renewal: "Ellos harán de cada ruina un prado, / de cada pena un fruto de alegría" (325). The ruins of Modernity are therefore replaced by the natural utopia of meadows and fruits; this may sound like the neo-Romantic pastoral attempt to return to the goodness of the earth, and in a way it is, but it is also Hernández's impulse to unite the new social and political order and the workers' land. However, Hernández's poetics are more heterogeneous, and nature is not always the only answer. "La fábrica-ciudad" is a result of his experience of watching the birth of a tractor, during his trip to the Soviet Union in the fall of 1937: "La fábrica-ciudad estalla en su armonía... / Y a un grito de sirenas, arroja sobre el día, / en un grandioso parto, raudales de tractores" (366). Here, the industrial city is feminized and depicted as a mother whose sirens are the cries that announce the birth of the tractors. Tractors will ultimately become the tools of the working class to construct their ideal city.

Nonetheless, in most of Hernández's poems the industrial city is seldom idealized. Rather than imagery that solidifies and exalts the modern factory, metaphors of the soldiers and the speaker as seeds, plants, and trees abound in Hernández's work. In "Recoged esta voz," nature clears the destruction of modern warfare, and the comparison of the youth to a seed reiterates that they were fighting for the freedom to grow without being submitted to the ruling classes: "la juventud de España saldrá de las trincheras / de pie, invencible como la semilla… / que jamás se somete ni arrodilla" (325). The motif of nature's freedom reappears in many of his poems, which famous Catalan singer Joan Manuel Serrat made into popular songs of resistance in the seventies. In the second part of "El herido," Hernández's speaker explains why he joined the war effort:

> Para la libertad sangro, lucho, pervivo.
> Para la libertad, mis ojos y mis manos,
> como un árbol carnal, generoso y cautivo,
> doy a los cirujanos…
> Retoñarán aladas de savia sin otoño
> reliquias de mi cuerpo que pierdo a cada herida.
> Porque soy como el árbol talado, que retoño:
> porque aún tengo la vida. (377–78)

The speaker stresses that freedom motivates his struggle to fight in the war and survive. The sacrifice of the self and the body in ruins is only worthwhile if freedom guides it, and for his ideals he lets go of himself and his possessions: "me desprendo a golpes de mis pies, de mi brazos, / de mi casa, de todo." He is willing to offer his body, his eyes, his hands, his feet, his arms, his house, and his being. Through the metaphor of the tree there is always the hope of ecological resurrection. From the smashed parts of the tree, new branches will sprout, the blood will become sap, and salve; and from the "carne talada," the relics of the wounded body, life will emerge. Just as Alberti in "El otoño y el Ebro" explores the metaphor of the soldier as a tree, strong, resistant, hopeful, and green inside, in Hernández's text, the soldier is the wounded speaker, and fall is not tangible. The body can reappear because of the "aladas de savia sin otoño"; instead of being a threatening stage in the natural cycle that precedes the barren winter and the promising spring, fall disappears.

The metaphor of the speaker as a tree rooted and clinging to the earth materializes once again in Hernández's "Madre España." It is mainly in this poem that he conveys the feminization of Spain as a mother figure, who unites all her children. As Agustín Sánchez Vidal avows: "Y es que España es concebida como un lugar de convergencia de todas las sangres, huesos y raíces, una especie de fosa común que, a través de esa sacrosanta entidad que es el Pueblo, supone una especie de Comunión de los Santos, tal como se expresa en 'Madre España'" (263). The critic refers here to the fourth stanza of Hernández's poem, where the speaker deciphers what *mother* means: "Decir madre es decir *tierra que me ha parido*; / es decir a los muertos: *hermanos, levantarse*" (*Obra poética* 390). In a move similar to Vallejo's *España, aparta de mí ese cáliz*, where mother Spain replaces God as the Father, Hernández gives mother earth the power of resurrection. However, this poem transforms the spiritual language of resurrection and tinges it with strong visceral imagery: entrails, blood, bones conglomerate in the pit of the earth. The mother earth, thus, exemplifies an oxymoron, both the womb and the tomb of Spain.

The title of the text clarifies that through the apostrophe, the speaker addresses not his individual mother, but his country. This may seem obvious, but it is worth pointing out, since the speaker in the first stanzas assumes almost a fetal position, the role of a child who clings to the protective womb. The rhetorical questions intensify the metaphorical hug: "Abrazado a tu cuerpo como el tronco a su tierra, / con todas las raíces y todos los corajes / ¿quién me separará, me arrancará de ti, / madre?" (Hernández, *Obra poética* 390). Through the simile, the speaker clings to the body of the mother as a tree to the land: "Abrazado a tu vientre, que es mi perpetua casa." The metonymy of the womb that represents the national body is once more reinstated in the female organ as the house no one can take away. The speaker even differentiates his physical mother from the metaphorical motherland: "La otra madre es un puente, nada más, de tus ríos. / El otro pecho es una burbuja de tus mares" (390). The metaphor of a mother as a bridge that connects the self with the land and the image of the breast round as a bubble of its seas situate the literal mother as a vehicle of the metaphorical mother's will. Spain, here, is not so much a social map and its national frontiers, as its rivers and seas, its natural landscape. The poem becomes more than a lament; through the apostrophe, the poetic voice demands: "Hermanos, defendamos su vientre acometido" (390). The Civil War symbolizes the fight for the womb that unites them; but the brothers here are not fighting each other, they are mainly the ones fighting together, implicitly on the Republican side. This language may seem generic and vague, but the speaker tries to materialize the patriotic feeling: "Una fotografía y un pedazo de tierra, / una carta y un monte son a veces iguales. / Hoy eres tú la hierba que crece sobre todo, / madre" (391). The love for Spain can be felt both in the memories of mountains and in cultural products that soldiers cling to, such as a photo and a letter, transmitters of a visceral nostalgia. Structurally, the poem has thirteen stanzas, often using the *alejandrino* or Spanish alexandrine, and always finishing each stanza with one word, *madre*, which is only replaced a few times, by *nadie*, *sangre*, *aires*, and *grande*. The repetition of the word *mother* intensifies the pathos of the poem; the addressee is present in every stanza, and the poem's tone evokes that of a prayer. The final stanza serves as a plea, and the wish of the speaker, facing a very probable death, is to inhabit the same corner of her womb, of the ground, with his wife and son.

The feminization of Spain in "Madre España" strengthens the patriotic feeling, the pathos, and the empathy Hernández wants to inspire in his readers. One could argue that this text has a nationalist vein, and yet, Spain could be any other country. There are no particularities that characterize it, and in a way, its feminization, the depiction of Spain as a womb, erases its facial features. This is interesting if we read what Hernández thought of racial differences and national borders: "La verdad es que no existen razas, pensad en que la muerte nos hace a todos de la misma raza… La tierra no es de aquellos cuya raza es el gusano, que esgrimen las fronteras, los idiomas como armas con que despreciarse y odiarse. No existen varias razas, sino una sola especie…" (Hernández, in Sánchez Vidal 255). Similar to Langston Hughes in his speech "Too Much Race," Hernández tries to empty the discourse of segregation, in which land and power are divided by arbitrary racial, national, and cultural frontiers. He argues that death serves as a bed to all, as we all share the same ground, the same ditch once we are dead.

The political and the erotic codes merge in the imagery of the land, the earth, in Hernández's poetry. The presence of the earth as both a cradle and a grave seems to be in many of his poems. Cano Ballesta points out the sexual meanings behind the representation of the mother in "Madre España": "En el poema *Madre España* es también el elemento instintivo-sexual el que informa y da sentido al vocablo *madre*... El mismo motivo metafórico de la 'madre' como 'tierra' y, al contrario, de la 'tierra' como 'madre' abierta y fecundada por el arado, se repite en *El niño yuntero* y en la *Canción del esposo soldado*" ("Miguel Hernández" 158, 160). Cano Ballesta refers to two very different poems: in "El niño yuntero" the protagonist is the exploited child, who works the land and treats it with the respect he would give to his mother: "levantando la corteza de su madre con la yunta" (*Obra poética* 313), while the erotic discourse and the desire of the young soldier for his wife predominate in "Canción del esposo soldado." Both poems reveal the splendor and depth of Hernández's pen. The metaphor of the earth as a womb reappears in "Canción del esposo soldado"[47]

> He poblado tu vientre de amor y sementera,
> he prolongado el eco de sangre a que respondo
> y espero sobre el surco como el arado espera:
> he llegado hasta el fondo.
>
> Morena de altas torres, alta luz y ojos altos,
> esposa de mi piel, gran trago de mi vida,
> tus pechos locos crecen hacia mí dando saltos
> de cierva concebida. (341)

The speaker addresses his loving wife from the very beginning and compares her womb full of his semen and love with the plowed land. In dialogue with the tradition of the *Song of Songs* and San Juan de la Cruz, the depiction of the wife as a pregnant deer captures the desire and the ecstasy of reaching the ultimate heights: "ojos altos." Hernández conveys the *eros* and *thanatos* of the war's extreme situations: "sobre los mismos muertos sin remedio y sin fosa / te quiero, y te quisiera besar con todo el pecho" (342). Furthermore, the speaker's passion for his wife, and future child, also nurture his political commitment and his desire to survive: "Es preciso matar para seguir viviendo" (342). The wife's struggle in giving birth is parallel to the soldier's solitude in the battleground: "Tus piernas implacables al parto van derechas... y ante mi soledad de explosiones y brechas / recorres un camino de besos implacables" (342). Their kisses have replaced the bullets. Just as in "Madre España," in this poem the imagery of the young mother evokes the comfort, the strength, and the vibrant life that gives hope to the ailing soldiers in the battlefield.

A Spain in ruins or the body in ruins is not only portrayed by destroyed buildings, or broken bones; in "Carta," the residues of the dead, their only remains, are their love letters. The first verses seize the motif of the letter like a messenger pigeon, carrying the news: "El palomar de las cartas / abre su imposible vuelo" (378). The poem intensifies with the personification of the letters, which have a beating heart as they travel to their goal, or die in the muteness of amnesia. The repetition of the *estribillo* or refrain connects all those letters to the particular letter that the poem becomes: "Aunque bajo la tierra / mi amante cuerpo esté, / escríbeme a la tierra, / que yo te escribiré" (378). The earth will therefore be only a threshold between lovers; as the literary convention suggests, love triumphs over death, reminiscent of Quevedo's "Amor constante más allá de la muerte." However, in "Carta," love-making is replaced by writing: the love letter embodies the passion also expressed in "Canción del esposo soldado": "Cuando te voy a escribir / se emocionan los tinteros: / los negros tinteros fríos / se ponen rojos y trémulos" (379). The personified ink transports and transmits the heat evoked by the words of desire, just as the letters retain the life of the dead writers: "Cartas que se quedan vivas / hablando para los muertos" (380). Finally, the speaker alludes to the love letter he awaits, which he will receive asleep or awake: "Y mis heridas serán / los derramados tinteros" (380). The imagery suggests that his wounded body materializes the page, his blood inspires the ink, and his wounds become the mouth from which he speaks and declares his love. In "Carta" writing serves as a form of resurrection, just as in Vallejo's "Pequeño responso" we find cultural transmission through the metaphor of the sprouting book; in Vallejo's poem to Pedro Rojas, the dead man still writes and signs in the air "¡Viban los compañeros!," leaving his footprint, with the *b* that characterizes his signature and voice, inscribed in the political memory of his comrades and in the oral history of the war. But in Hernández's "Carta" the letters, rather than being political manifestos in defense of the war, are clearly transmitters of love; they are cultural remnants, keepers of the emotional memory of those soldiers, relics of the *real*.

The letters serve as witnesses of those loves and lost lives, just as the speakers of these poems encourage the readers to become witnesses, to be conscious of their own "historical awakening." Jean Franco reflects upon the astonishing quality of Vallejo's *España, aparta de mí ese cáliz*: "The poet… does not assume the role of the prophet but is simply a witness who bears the marks of a past which has been superseded by the events he describes" (*César Vallejo* 233). The role of the witness is prevalent in the works of most of these poets, from Vallejo and Neruda to Alberti and Guillén, and yet as Manuel Durán reiterates: "la poesía de guerra de Miguel es única: si en algún momento el poeta ha sido, plenamente, testigo, esto se da en su caso. Testigo que participa y vive cada instante…" (39). This is not to say that Hernández's poetry supersedes in value Vallejo's or Neruda's works, but Durán's statement stresses what other critics have continued to indicate: "César Vallejo asume el papel del observador comprometido que está haciendo una crónica de la guerra mientras que Hernández es actor y participa desde dentro" (Pulgarín and Calvillo 134).[48] The insistence on Hernández as both a first-hand witness and an actor, an active participant in the war front, seems to give his work a stamp of authenticity. However, I consider that regardless of their particular life stories, all these poets *lived* the war and were fully committed in their own ways to a poetics of solidarity and political agency.

The feminization of Spain as a mother in the poems about the ruins of the war strengthens the political message and *moves* the reader. One could argue that it also reduces women to the role of mothers and wives. A feminist critique of these poets should point out that while there were many *milicianas* at the beginning of the war fighting with the soldiers on the battlefield, women were ultimately relegated in literature and in the war effort to the traditional gender roles: cooking, cleaning, sewing, and giving birth. Still, poems like Hernández's "Rosario, dinamitera" or Vallejo's homage to Lina Odena in "Himno a los voluntarios de la República," among the many poems to *la Pasionaria*, show that these writers also saw in women role models of bravery and vigor. Few women poets wrote about the war, in comparison with the overwhelming number of men poets, known and unknown. Therefore, it is a difficult task to determine why the feminization of Spain is particularly embraced by male poets. The reception of the war by women poets sympathetic to the Republican cause is varied. Concha Méndez's *Lluvias enlazadas* (1939), poems on exile, nostalgia, and the anguish of time, clings to the memory of Spain, which seems to be an unspoken presence in these texts, while Carmen Conde's book of prose poems, *Mientras los hombres mueren* (1938–39), testifies to the pain and horrors of the war and its most vulnerable victims: children. Unlike Méndez, Conde, in the text XXI, advocates that the mothers nurture an amnesia of the war: "¡Madres jóvenes de España, pedid a vuestros hijos! No les habléis de la guerra. Que olviden… cuánto lloramos por ellos" (Miró 416).[49] Although motherhood and fertility are motives that prevail in many of the poetic works of women poets such as Méndez, Conde, Ernestina de Champourcín, and Josefina de la Torre, I have not found that any of their poems written during the Civil War explore the representation of Spain as a mother. Rosa Chacel's "Alarma" is definitely one of the most valuable contributions to the urban poetics of the war. She personifies the alarm that announces any attack on the city, feminizing the "Alarma" whose shouts or cries save the lives of many who seek protection from the air raid. The "Alarma" serves as a protective force, a watchful dog, a vigilant soldier: "Sabiendo que ella vigila, / la ciudad duerme segura," but she is not represented as a mother, nor as Spain (Miró 228). So, why do poets such as Vallejo, Alberti, Hernández, and as we will see in the next section, Cernuda, depict Spain as a mother figure?

As Antonio and Manuel Machado showed us, there are multiple conflicting versions of Spain that suggest diverse ideological ways of defining the nation: from an old hag to a young, vigorous Spain; from the epitome of division to the emblem of unity in a glorious tradition. The feminization of the nation should be read as literary convention by now, but what does it contribute to the transatlantic poetics of solidarity? It obviously creates empathy among the readers, but it also implies that men, in particular, the soldiers, and the children, must save their own mother, the mother land. The depiction of women as vulnerable and innocent victims comes into play in these texts, where Spain as a mother is at the same time the source of life, the protective shield, and the cemetery, the target of death, the earth that must be defended. Still, as we perceive in poets like Vallejo and

Guillén, among others, Spain is not only the mother of Spaniards, it has transcended its Spanishness to become a symbol of a new social and political order. The poetry of Vallejo, Alberti, and Hernández may be dramatically distinct from one other, but the feminization of Spain serves a common aim: to project a poetics of hope for the Republican cause. They all see poetry as a metaphorical weapon; and in most of their poems, a Spain in ruins reemerges like the phoenix, which opens up possibilities of a political, spiritual, and ecological resurrection. In the works of most of the poets who write about the Spanish Civil War there is a consistent commitment to the truth, an ethical imperative to give their testimony and contribute to the annals of history. As Giorgio Agamben explains in reference to Primo Levi's testimonies: "El testigo testimonia de ordinario a favor de la verdad y de la justicia, que son las que prestan a sus palabras consistencia y plenitud" (34). These poets validate their voices through the claim of giving a truthful testimony of the war, and yet since these are not judicial manuscripts, the poems voice "lo intestimoniable"; they also speak for the integral, *real* witnesses that Primo Levi refers to, the ones who cannot testify because they died. The representation of Spain as a mother touches and recomposes that common thread of humanity that the war so successfully tries to steal.

Cernuda's Clouds and Paz's Voices: The Elegies to Spain

Cernuda, Paz, and Neruda met in Spain in the nineteen thirties and participated in literary and political movements in support of democracy and against fascism during the Spanish Civil War. The sixteenth-century poet Rodrigo Caro in his "Itálica" evokes a city in ruins in a very different historical context, and yet, the poems to the ruins of the Spanish Civil War reread present destruction while constantly alluding to that foundational text and to the Baroque topos.

Although ruined cities only give a deformed vision of the past, modern poems on ruins reinscribe historical memory, by which I mean that the texts also become historical documents. Caro's "Itálica" searches for the past as if the poem were an archaeological project; it reconstructs and remembers the buildings and the monuments of the Roman city, its military heroes, and its Christian martyrs. Caro's poem is a foundational text in the Spanish topos of ruins, and twentieth-century poets seem to go back to "Itálica" to rethink their contemporary, wrecked Spain.

Cernuda's "Noche de luna" in *Las nubes* (1937–40) develops an allegory of history's violent paths and represents ruins as products of war. He establishes an intellectual dialogue with Caro and with his own contemporaries, Eliot and Neruda. For instance, Cernuda's morbid imagery of fertility and sterility is reminiscent of Eliot's "Whispers of Immortality" and *The Waste Land;* and as in Caro's "Itálica," Cernuda represents the ruins as signifiers of history, and the moon as the historical eye, the witness.

Caro's "Itálica" is treated as a literary monument, and perhaps another ruin of tradition, in Cernuda's "Noche de luna."[50] Yet, unlike "Itálica," this poem to the Spanish Civil War does not depict Spanish ruins; it conveys the imminent threat of fascism through apocalyptic visions of history. Nonetheless, Cernuda's *Las nubes* is also written from the nostalgic perspective of the political exile, impotent and empty. "Elegía española" I and II and "Lamento y esperanza" nationalize the ruined landscape, and in contrast to most of the poems I examine, reveal a nostalgic and a melancholic portrayal of the motherland.

In the second chapter, I analyzed the representations of the modern city in ruins by Baudelaire and Cernuda and their critique of progress; I mainly focused on Cernuda's early work from *Un río, un amor* (1929) and *Los placeres prohibidos* (1931). Cernuda's poems of the Civil War reveal a poetic transformation into a voice more moved by a collective plight. Among his poems in *Las nubes,* "Noche de luna" reveals Cernuda's reading of history as one that constantly fluctuates between cycles of violence.

In "Theses on the Philosophy of History," Benjamin's notion of the angel of history faces a vision of wreckage and debris. Benjamin's angel, as a modern subject, feels torn between the past and the future. Cernuda's "Noche de luna" and Neruda's "Canto sobre unas ruinas" culminate in apocalyptic visions of history, connected to Benjamin's materialist critique, which instill a sense of urgency in the reader. Nationalistic and nostalgic tones permeate three other poems by Cernuda, "Elegía española" I and II and "Lamento y esperanza." In contrast to Neruda's poem, these texts express the anguish of political exile and idealize the Spanish historical past, once glorious and now in ruins. "Noche de luna" and these texts project a "cultural mourning," a pessimistic reading of history as ultimately leading to a state of destruction and nothingness. The end of the poem, and of the world, can be analyzed as part of Cernuda's critique of modern versions of progress, yet it also conveys the aestheticization of nothingness and the moon's nostalgic gaze.

In his essay on Cernuda's ruins, Antonio Colinas remarks that there is a transition in the Andalusian poet's favorite symbols from walls to ruins.[51] Colinas comments on how the walls represent a closed door on reality. Throughout his essay, he identifies the various forms of ruins in Cernuda's work, from the Romantic tradition to the ruins of war and the body in ruins: "Al principio, la ruina se muestra en los versos de Luis Cernuda junto a otros temas arquetípicos de la antigüedad clásica: las estatuas… los elfos, la fuente… La ruina es casi un cliché literario pues aún no ha sido deshecha por la guerra, por la sangre" (136). "Noche de luna" introduces *Las nubes*, the collection of poems where ruins are stained with blood and marked by war.

"Noche de luna" portrays the moon as the witness to history, not the river that is the common trait in the Baroque topos of ruins. The moon represents the eternal eye, the survivor of time—and it is also the Romantic symbol for the nostalgic gaze. "Noche de luna" demonstrates Cernuda's intertextual dialogue with the Romantic and the Baroque traditions of ruins and inserts his work into a modern historical critique. Cernuda's poem distances itself from the Baroque topos by not naming a specific vanished city like Itálica or Rome. While Caro described a city in ruins and transported us to its antique past, Cernuda instead travels through history from the conquest of the land and its early civil wars to the emergence of agriculture and a feudal system.

"Noche de luna" begins by describing the passage of time and the way in which people started to forget pagan gods.[52] The beginning of history is marked by violence. The second and third stanzas present the violence of the conquest of the land as analogous to rape, which will lead to the reproduction of the species and the establishment of the community. The poem advances a notion of history characterized by generalizations and incompleteness. Nonetheless, Cernuda's time-traveling experience proves to be in touch with Eliot's, Paz's, and even Neruda's questionings of progress and their apocalyptic visions of war.

Paradox, oxymoron, and antithesis also abound in Cernuda's evocation of the voices of the past:

> El sordo griterío,
> Todo el horror humano que salva la hermosura,
> Y con ella la calma,
> La paz donde brota la historia. (*PC* 252)

The serenity of the moon is contrasted with the silenced cries of the dead, the horror that paradoxically saves and protects beauty. In the poem, peace, unlike war, produces history because it allows the spectator to interpret and transcribe what is happening and what has happened.[53] Yet ruins seem to be the text from which history is written.

In the fifth stanza, the speaker narrates the development of society into an agricultural community. Cernuda also exploits the paradox that I discussed earlier in reference to Eliot's *The Waste Land* and "Whispers of Immortality," that out of war and death, life and the fertility of the land bloom:

> También miro el arado
> Con el siervo pasando
> Sobre el antiguo campo de batalla,
> Fertilizado por tanto cuerpo joven… (252)

The dead bodies nourish the land—reminiscent of Eliot's references to a corpse that might sprout and bloom in "The Burial of the Dead" (55). Nature takes over but only to a certain extent because it is still private property: as the owner runs freely through his territories, "la hierba, ortiga y cardo / Brotaban por las vastas propiedades" (*PC* 252).[54] As Jiménez Fajardo states: "Images of sterility prevail in these last lines; young blood first fertilized the land, but once won, the fields were left fallow. Time begins to assert its grasp: there is now history—'the ancient battlefield'—established by war" (*Luis Cernuda* 52). History is in constant battle with itself.

In the sixth stanza, the futilely spilled blood and semen highlight the analogy of war and sexual reproduction:

> Cuánta sangre ha corrido
> Ante el destino intacto de la diosa.
> Cuánto semen viril…
> De cuerpos hoy deshechos
> En el viento y el polvo,
> Cuyos átomos yerran en leves nubes grises...
>
> (*PC* 252)

As Freud maintains in *Civilization and Its Discontents*, the human drive is divided between the aggressive, the death instinct, materialized in war, and the instinct for life, represented in sexual love. But in Cernuda's verses blood and semen, which epitomize both death and life, are wasted. War produces a wasteland of bodies, a landscape that echoes Eliot's imagery of destruction. The bodies in ruins are transformed into clouds, a metaphor developed by Cernuda throughout his collection and in its title. The clouds symbolize both the dreams of men and the shadows they have become. *Las nubes* refers also to Baudelaire's prose poem "L'étranger." The stranger in Baudelaire's text has no family, no friends, no God, no country, no desire for gold, but what characterizes him is his fascination with clouds: "J'aime les nuages… les nuages qui passent… là-bas…" (*OC* 1: 277). Clouds reflect his state of being—his sense of self as a nomad, a foreigner, a traveler, and a constant passerby. Yet in Cernuda's poem, the clouds also signify the "hoy cuerpos deshechos"; they are the ultimate disintegration of the body in ruins. In response to all this violent history, the goddess of the moon remains aloof and tranquil. Her distance seems to protect the moon but it also shows her as an unsympathetic witness, unlike the moved and moving speaker in Caro's "Itálica."

The seventh stanza alludes to Caro's "Itálica." The repetition of *cuántas* increases the elegiac, dramatic tone, and metaphorically connects the blood and the semen to the ruins of the cities:

> Cuántas claras ruinas,
> Con jaramago apenas adornadas,
> Como fuertes castillos un día las ha visto;
> Piedras más elocuentes que los siglos…
>
> (*PC* 252–53)

The allusion to Caro's "Itálica" perhaps resides in the word *jaramago*, the break-through of nature, the yellow plant, which usually grows among the rubble. Cernuda describes the plant as an adornment, a yellow dress for the naked ruins. The yellow of the plant is similar to the color of dust, pointing to the passage of time and the abandonment of the ruins. Nature grows without human control. Ruins are swallowed by nature in both Caro's and Cernuda's poems. Caro uses the same plant *jaramago* to dress the destroyed amphitheater:

> Este despedazado anfiteatro,
> impío honor de los dioses, cuya afrenta
> publica el amarillo jaramago,
> ya reducido a trágico teatro,
> ¡oh fábula del tiempo! representa
> cuánta fue su grandeza, y es su estrago.
>
> (Caro, in Rivers, *Poesía lírica* 290)

Caro's speaker complains about this irony: the tragic passage of time is represented literally and metaphorically by the structure of the theater, which once stood tall and is now unrecognizable. Both Cernuda and Caro contrast the state of the destroyed castle and the amphitheater in ruins with their past grandeur and strength. This contrast underscores once more the fugitive nature of the seemingly permanent and solid products of culture—the didactic way of reminding the reader that history repeats itself and that empires rise and fall easily. Cernuda's poems of the Civil War carry a sense of nostalgia that is difficult to pigeonhole in Boym's categories of "restorative" or "reflective" nostalgia; it has elements of both. While these poets seek a historical reconstruction of the past, they also see themselves as nostalgic and do not pretend to reveal the truth about the past.

Cernuda reads in the stones the voices of the past, the historical memory of the cities in ruins: "Piedras más elocuentes que los siglos." Paradoxically, the poet makes the stones, the concrete and immobile remnants, speak more eloquently of history and time than the abstract centuries themselves. In marked contrast, Caro's stones remain silent. The archeologist in "Itálica" laments that there is no written record, not even in the stones that paid homage to the political leaders of the city: "Casas, jardines, césares murieron / y aún las piedras que de ellos se escribieron" (290). In "Itálica" nothing remains of the powerful men, their houses, and their histories in stone. Unlike Caro, Cernuda uses the analogy of the stones as traces of the past that tell a story. Cernuda's "Noche de luna" treats Caro's poem as a monument itself, a literary cornerstone, which speaks of history's turmoils and the desolate city in ruins.

Poems on ruins recall the voices of the past, the *vox populi*. Caro's "Itálica" cries for the lost city, but he is clearly mourning the nobles, the heroes, the Caesars, and not the workers: "el gemido de mil sombras nobles en su ruina" (291). The nobility of the specters could also refer to their sense of decency, but their dignity is linked to their privileged social status in the context of "Itálica." In the fourth stanza of "Noche de luna," Cernuda's "sordo griterío" proves to be a muted cry, that does not listen to itself, and the social background of those voices is undetermined.[55]

The world, "la antigua morada de los hombres," abandoned by the goddess of fertility, the moon, is mute, empty, and sterile (*PC* 253). The moon, a symbol of the Romantic narcissistic self, is probably lonely, since without the human gaze no one can admire her, no one can acknowledge her: "Sin que ningunos ojos humanos / Hasta ella se alcen a través de las lágrimas" (254). "Noche de luna" ends with the moon's self-engrossed, nostalgic vision of the world, now a world of silence and nothingness: "El silencio de un mundo que ha sido / Y la pura belleza tranquila de la nada" (254). The sordid imagery of the uninhabited earth recalls Eliot's deserted spaces; and the final sense of nothingness also associates Cernuda's text with the verses of Neruda's "Canto sobre unas ruinas": "todo reunido en nada, todo caído / para no nacer nunca" (*Tercera Residencia* 54). But Cernuda's final aestheticization of nothingness stresses the beauty of ruins, while Neruda's text emphasizes its sordid hopelessness. Still, Cernuda's and Neruda's poems on ruins portray a somber site of destruction and share Eliot's pessimistic vision of history and modern progress. But Cernuda and Neruda not only echo Eliot's post-World War I poem, as I have suggested they also look back to the Baroque topos of ruins and recall the elegiac tone in Caro's "Itálica," the use of apostrophe, anaphora, and paradoxes, the enumeration of destroyed elements or monuments, and the incorporation of the *vox populi*.

In both Cernuda's "Noche de luna" and Neruda's "Canto sobre unas ruinas," their cities in ruins are not specified; they could be anywhere; but there are many allusions in their collections of poems pointing to the Spanish Civil War as the imminent historical context. In his brief commentary on "Noche de luna," Derek Harris also mentions that the nameless place in Cernuda's poem is easily associated with Spain: "...la luna ha sido testigo del desarrollo confuso y muchas veces sórdido de la raza humana en un país sin nombrar pero fácilmente reconocible como España" (*La poesía de Luis Cernuda* 112). In Neruda's and Cernuda's texts, ruins, products of war, become part of an apocalyptic vision of the world. These two texts may seem ahistorical because of their lack of specific references; but instead, they historicize Spanish ruins by expanding their repercussions to a universal phenomenon, by evoking their existential dilemmas and a general historical cycle of violence and war, which culminates in emptiness and nothingness.

Cernuda's and Neruda's poems reveal a vision of utter destruction comparable to the one faced by Benjamin's angel of history. In his "Theses on the Philosophy of History," Benjamin projects his materialist reading of history into his interpretation of the angel depicted in Paul Klee's painting *Angelus Novus*.[56] The face of the angel of history turns to the past and its ruins, but his body and his wings are controlled by the "storm" of progress, which "propels him into the future." Cernuda's and Neruda's portrayals of decay and wreckage in these two texts do not explicitly accuse progress as the tornado that leaves everything empty and deserted, but progress has many faces.

Benjamin's angel is similar to Cernuda's moon or Neruda's speaker, a witness to the destruction, a reader of the past, overpowered by the storm of progress, and the inevitability of the future. Nonetheless, Cernuda's poem, in contrast to Neruda's text, shows the moon as a very narcissistic witness of history; facing the end of the world, she can also see a reflection of herself and a vision of the pure, "eternal" beauty of nothingness. Cernuda, just like Neruda, provokes the reader into a political reading of the ruins. Cernuda and Neruda want the readers to feel threatened by the evanescence of material reality, for which ruins are the perfect mark. They want readers to be moved by the lessons of the past and to see the urgency of action in the present, especially in and after 1937.

Benjamin considers progress as a menacing force because in the name of progress many atrocities are committed and permitted. The fetish of progress disillusioned the materialist historian. Just before he explains his notion of the angel of history, Benjamin addresses the contemporary crisis in Europe threatened by fascism:

> The tradition of the oppressed teaches us that the "state of emergency" in which we live is not the exception but the rule. We must attain to a conception of history that is in keeping with this insight. Then we shall clearly realize that it is our task to bring about a real state of emergency, and this will improve our position in the struggle against Fascism. One reason why Fascism has a chance is that in the name of progress its opponents treat it as a historical norm. ("Theses," in *Illuminations* 257)

Cernuda's "Noche de luna" and Neruda's "Canto sobre unas ruinas" do not name the destructive force, the storm of progress, or the nightmare of war; yet in *España en el corazón* and *Las nubes,* fascism is clearly present as the enemy, not a historical norm, but a threat to everything they know and believe in. Cernuda's elegies in *Las nubes* convey both a sense of emergency and of despair. *España en el corazón* explicitly called for political and military action in the fight against the Fascist uprising. While *Las nubes* also expresses a state of urgency, it is not driven toward a revolutionary end in the same way as Neruda's book. A great part of *Las nubes* was written during Cernuda's exile, and nostalgia and cultural mourning mold these texts.[57] A feeling of despair predominates in Cernuda's poems, carried through the elegiac tone and the metaphors of darkness and death.

The preliminary version of "Noche de luna," entitled "Elegía a la luna de España," was published in 1937 in the anthology of Republican poetry *Poetas en la España leal.*[58] The change in title demonstrates that the poem was originally intended to be an elegy to Spain, but that Cernuda later decided not to identify the ruins as particularly Spanish. Just as Neruda does in "Canto sobre unas ruinas," Cernuda chooses not to specify the nationality of the ruins, perhaps because he wanted to project an apocalyptic vision not limited to the Spanish soil, a vision that acknowledged the general threat of fascism in Europe and the beginning of World War II. The title of the collection itself also went through a transformation.[59] Cernuda at first intended it to be *Elegías españolas*, but later settled on *Las nubes*.

The original title of the collection persists in the titles of two of its main poems, "Elegía española I" and "Elegía española II." In these two elegies, Spain is openly evoked through the apostrophes to the mother and the land, respectively. While "Elegía española I" focuses on the disasters of the Civil War, "Elegía española II" recaptures the anguish of the exiled poet. In both poems the apostrophe to Spain emphasizes a feminization of the country in ruins, commonly portrayed by the epithet *madre patria*. The apostrophes to the mother in "Elegía I" and the repetition of the imperative verbs demand an answer or a story.[60] In the same poem, the repetitions of "Dime, háblame" and "Háblame, dime" highlight the desire to establish a dialogue with history, or in this case, with Spain.

The mother in "Elegía I" and the moon in "Noche de luna" are witnesses, survivors of history, and thus they are the Romantic epitome of what is eternal. For instance, the speaker of "Elegía I" stresses at the end when he refers to the motherland: "Porque tú eres eterna" (*PC* 261). The mother and the moon share a similar distance reproached by the speaker of the elegy: "No te alejes así, ensimismada" (259). The mother is depicted as enigmatic and loving—she is self-engrossed because she is in mourning. She represents the cultural mourning of the nation, as an alter-ego of the poet. Cernuda's elegy to Spain interestingly uses the nationalist discourse: a national past, from which generations of sons emerge, is loved by the speaker. This disputes the Francoist propaganda that Republicans were anti-nationalist and anti-Spanish. Unlike the unmovable moon, the first-person speaker in "Elegía I" is moved by the ruined site and the dead children of the motherland:

> No sé qué tiembla y muere en mí
> Al verte así dolida y solitaria
> En ruinas los claros dones
> De tus hijos, a través de los siglos;
> Porque mucho he amado tu pasado,
> Resplandor victorioso entre sombra y olvido.
>
> (*PC* 260)

The last verses denote a nostalgic idealization of Spain's glorious past. The speaker's nationalistic tone sheds light on the forgotten past, "la gloria de su estirpe."

In the poem, the historical path defines the nation:

> Tu pasado eres tú
> Y al mismo tiempo eres
> La aurora que aún no alumbra nuestros campos.
> Tú sola sobrevives
> Aunque venga la muerte;
> Sólo en ti está la fuerza
> De hacernos esperar a ciegas el futuro. (*PC* 261)

The motherland, the Spanish nation, embodies the past and the future; like Benjamin's angel of history, the nation faces the successes and the wreckage of the past but it is propelled into the uncertain future. However, Cernuda's verses do not depict a Benjaminian future, moved by the storm of progress. The future is portrayed as hopeful, a dawn, "la aurora que aún no alumbra nuestros campos"; and it is something to wait for, not to transform and reconstruct. In her essay "Nostalgia and Exile," Noël Valis does not specifically refer to Cernuda but her insights explain very well what lies behind the nostalgia in these verses:

> In the context of the *fin de siglo*, nostalgia as a sign of modernity seems to be mourning not only of the past but also, strangely enough, the future. The nostalgic is, metaphorically and affectively, truly an "out of place"... In the case of the Spanish Civil War and the Republican exiles, the passage of time has not only intensified such feelings but also created them. (124)

The speakers of Cernuda's *Las nubes* are out of place; the title of the collection announces the metaphor—they are nomads, traveling shadows, like the clouds. Valis stresses that modern forms of nostalgia can be seen as mourning for the past and the future, the anguish that Benjamin's angel of history expresses. Cernuda develops two approaches to the ruins of the war, one nationalistic and hopeful, and another more nihilist and existentialist. "Elegía I" conveys the idea of a hopeful future, while "Noche de luna" ends with the lack of a future, with a state of nothingness. "Elegía I" ends on a very different note; instead of focusing on the destroyed site, the poem concludes by stating the timelessness of the nation, the motherland. The final verses of "Elegía I" sound contradictory: "Algo advierte que tú sufres con todos. / Y su odio, su crueldad, su lucha, / Ante ti vanos son, como sus vidas." The motherland seems to be an aloof spectator like the moon in "Noche de luna," and yet it suffers with everyone. The nation is elevated: "Porque tú eres eterna / Y sólo los creaste / Para la paz y gloria de su estirpe" (*PC* 261). The last verse could be read as ironic because the poem suggests that the nation, with its glory and its peace, is never eternal. "Elegía I" in general manifests a nationalistic and a nostalgic vision of the past, not characterized by poetic irony.

The nationalistic tone in "Elegía I" can also be found in another poem in *Las nubes*, "Lamento y esperanza." Cernuda is not a particularly nationalistic poet, but war and exile instensify the feelings of nostalgia, which nurture a nationalistic idealization of the lost Spain. In "Lamento y esperanza," the speaker narrates the story of his generation, whose dreams of justice and revolution were crushed by the war. The dreamers in "Lamento y esperanza" are anywhere but in the clouds; they are stepping on death and destruction: "Pisando entre ruinas un fango con rocío de sangre" (268). The poem portrays a singular violence and stillness, where the brown and the red are disturbed only by the footsteps among the ruins. The imagery in the verse denotes an aestheticization of ruins, by combining what is considered impure, mud, with the symbols of crystalline purity, dew and blood.[61] In the next stanza, the lyric voice angrily denounces the national and the international commercial interests in the Civil War of those who aim to: "arrancar jirones de su esplendor antiguo." Cernuda stresses that Spain's "essence" or mark of identity is defined by its history, not always glorious and prosperous, "su propia gran historia dolorida." The final verses underscore a hopeful redeeming suffering; just as the title "Lamento y esperanza" suggests, the pain of the exile dwells between the nostalgic recollections of the past, his homesickness, and his hope to return.

In "Elegía española II" the speaker transports himself as if in a cloud to reach "mi tierra"; his body remains empty and lost in a permanent state of exile. Unlike Neruda's *España en el corazón*, this poem reflects both a sense of nostalgia for the homeland and an overwhelming melancholic feeling. In the final stanza, Spain is paradoxically depicted as a strong tower in ruins: "Tú nada más, fuerte torre en ruinas, / Puedes poblar mi soledad humana" (*PC* 271). There are two paradoxes: the tower in ruins remains strong, and the land inhabits the speaker's body. As Colinas denotes: "El pasado, con sus glorias y con sus dogmas es pura contradicción, es esa *fuerte torre en ruinas* que representa al propio país" (136). Cernuda's *Las nubes* represents the history of Spain in ruins and conveys his traumatic experience of exile in England.

In this section, I have demonstrated how Cernuda's references to Caro's, Eliot's, and Neruda's works situate his poetry in an intertextual dialogue that redefines the modern topos of ruins. Cernuda's *Las nubes* is marked by war and later on by his political exile. His texts evoke a nostalgic and a nationalistic imagery. His poems are not always narcissistic and predominantly melancholic; sometimes they are contradictory and puzzlingly nationalistic and nostalgic. In Cernuda's *Las nubes* there is a longing for the past, a desire to return to what seems unreachable and lost.

The Voices of the Dead in Paz's Poetry

Elegies and poems on ruins are mournful laments for the dead, for the lost city or the destroyed nation. Cernuda's elegies personified Spain and grieved for the devastation of the country and its inhabitants; these poems performed a nostalgic cultural mourning for the past. Cernuda and Neruda wrote poetry collections to the Spanish Civil War, while Paz included in *Calamidades y milagros* (1937–47) just a few poems that allude to the war, in particular one elegy. As for so many artists of his time, the Spanish Civil War proved to be for Paz a transforming political experience. Paz's "Elegía a un compañero muerto en el frente de Aragón" and parts of *Piedra de sol* voice the traumatic experience of war, his depiction of human ruins, and the poet's identification with the victims of the war. In this elegy, Paz, only twenty-three when he visited Spain in 1937, chooses to identify himself with a young Republican soldier who paradoxically dies "en el ardiente amanecer del mundo" (*Obra poética* 99). Unlike Neruda's workers in *Alturas,* Caro's noble shadows, and

Cernuda's "sordo griterío" in "Noche de luna," Paz addresses in this text only one person, one anonymous soldier, and this intensifies the reader's identification with the dead.[62]

Paz's "Elegía a un compañero muerto en el frente de Aragón," which is divided into three parts, begins with a verse that will be repeated throughout the text: "Has muerto, camarada" (*Obra poética* 99). The apostrophe to the anonymous dead soldier intensifies the undertones of the poem, and the speaker's eagerness to listen to the voices of the dead calls upon the absent ones in the poetic present. Death has immobilized the soldier's voice: "Parada está tu voz." Still, the poem aims to give it back in a ventriloquist attempt to identify the speaker with the dead man:

> Y alzándote,
> llorándote,
> nombrándote,
> dando voz a tu cuerpo desgarrado,
> labios y libertad a tu silencio,
> crecen dentro de mí,
> me lloran y me nombran,
> furiosamente me alzan,
> otros cuerpos y nombres... (100)

Paz's "Elegía" gives voice to the voiceless through memory and imagination. Through the act of naming the nameless, Paz pretends to give the speaker the power to reconstruct his "cuerpo desgarrado." By restoring his lips, the poet's metonymy gives him back his voice. The identification is stressed in this stanza by the change of pronouns, from *te* to *me*, from "llorándo*te*" to "*me* lloran." The elegy is more than a lament for his death; it is an exaltation of his life, and the recovery of his voice is a way of keeping the historical memory of the war alive. The speaker is able to identify with other bodies, other names: the dialogue between "yo" and "tú" is extended, opened to a collectivity of victims.

In the second part of the poem, the first- and second-person singular pronouns change to a first-person plural, *nosotros*. They were both blinded by the burning light and they fall together: "hundiéndonos." The repetition of "Yo recuerdo tu voz" associates the soldier's voice with the light, and hope, but also evokes the violence and fervor of the soldier: "Yo recuerdo tu voz, tu duro gesto, / el ademán severo de tus manos" (*Obra poética* 100). The dead soldier's strength and youth are broken: "Tu corazón, tu voz, tu puño vivo / detenidos y rotos por la muerte" (101). The imagery of the body in ruins, mutilated, contrasts with his undisturbed, genuine smile, analogous to the dawn of life: "un claro sonreír, un alba pura" (101).

In the third part of Paz's "Elegía," remembrance leads to imagining the body in ruins and the revival of the violent scene: "Te imagino cercado por las balas," and "Te imagino tirado en lodazales, / sin máscara, sonriente" (*Obra poética* 101). The final verses underline that he did not die alone or in vain: "Has muerto entre los tuyos, por los tuyos" (101). Unlike so many of his contemporaries reviewed here, Paz's vision of history is not apocalyptic. Despite its tragic tone and the fact that Paz was never at the front fighting with the International Brigades, the poem aims to be a vehicle of communication, a way of preserving historical memory. "Elegía a un compañero muerto en el frente de Aragón" has not been critically analyzed and yet it is one of Paz's few poems about the Spanish Civil War. By remembering the dead man's voice and pretending to give voice to the voiceless, Paz seeks to construct more than just an elegy, a historical document. Paz's elegy to one man is expanded in his 1957 *Piedra de sol* to multiple women and children, victims of the Spanish Civil War.

Piedra de sol centers on a poetics of the instant. The speaker begins his poetic journey, searching for the poetic instant, in which time ceases to exist: "*Piedra de sol* puede verse como una corriente temporal que vuelve sobre sí misma. Es un círculo y su centro es el instante... En *Piedra de sol* la vida humana es un proceso hecho de años y días en torno a un punto, un instante en el que arden y se apagan, aparecen y desaparecen todos los tiempos" (Ulacia, "Octavio Paz: Poesía, pintura" 629). Paz stresses the circular structure of the poem, and alluding to Mircea Eliade's *The Myth of the Eternal Return*, he remarks how individual and collective histories are inserted in the "circular time of the myth."[63] The text has no periods, only commas, colons, and semicolons, and it begins and ends with the repetition of the same verses. It is the personal journey of the speaker, and yet the "I" merges with the "you." By doing so, the poem distances itself from what García Montero calls the Avant-garde "yo en crisis" and voices "un nosotros rehumanizado" (*Los dueños del vacío* 120).

Neruda's "Explico algunas cosas," among other poems in *España en el corazón*, denounces the bombardments of Madrid and the suffering of innocent civilians. Twenty years later, Paz brings to mind the Madrid of 1937 in *Piedra de sol*. The main stanza dedicated to the Civil War emerges suddenly like a traumatic memory from the rubble. The stanza paints a scene of daily life in the center of Madrid, but the songs of the women and children are interrupted by the noise of the siren, the shouts, the bombs:

> Madrid 1937
> en la Plaza del Ángel las mujeres
> cosían y cantaban con sus hijos,
> después sonó la alarma y hubo gritos,
> casas arrodilladas en el polvo,
> torres hendidas, frentes escupidas
> y el huracán de motores, fijo...
>
> (*Obra poética* 268–69)

The scene reinstates the interruption of daily life within the context of *Piedra de sol* and accentuates the speed of war and death. Women and children are introduced in a harmonious scene of happiness, sewing, and singing. But the alarm disrupts their happiness and stops the music, warning them of the Fascist aerial attack. The contrasting imagery highlights the symbol of the fallen towers, alluding to Eliot's *The Waste Land*: "casas arrodilladas en el polvo, / torres hendidas, frentes escupidas" (*Obra poética* 269). Destruction takes over both the houses and the people who inhabit them, all transformed into dust. The airplanes bombing the Spanish capital are portrayed as a hurricane, "huracán de motores." The sound of their engines engulfs and digests the cries of the people. The hurricane of the airplanes, like Benjamin's storm of progress, devastates as it propels a totalitarian, technocratic future.

The verses that follow this scene of destruction underscore their contrast with it with a hopeful tone. The two naked bodies become one when they make love, defying war and death, time and identity: "no hay tú ni yo, mañana, ayer ni nombres, /

verdad de dos en sólo un cuerpo y alma, / oh ser total..." (*Obra poética* 269). The lovers, whom Paz also evokes in *Homenaje y profanaciones,* otherwise serve as an optimistic answer: the traces of the eternal in combat with the war scenes. It seems the poem idealizes love as an answer to military power, and it obviously simplifies the context of the Civil War with the contrast between history and a mythical, eternal love. In contrast with "Elegía a un compañero muerto en el frente de Aragón," the pronouns are supposedly obliterated, the union of the two lovers seems to erase time and space, and it also erases the memory of the victims. In an anti-Marxist, a-historical move, love is the transforming force—Paz's rhetoric joins neo-Platonic aesthetics and the mystical poetic tradition. In a zigzag move, the next stanza recalls once again the flashback of the Spanish Civil War and the verses that precede it: "cuartos a la deriva / entre ciudades que se van a pique, / cuartos y calles, nombres como heridas" (269). Rooms and cities in ruins are depicted as sinking ships; public streets and private rooms are broken, and the memory of the names of the streets and the rooms is as painful as wounds. The imagery serves as a poetic transition between the union of the lover's bodies in their room and the decay of the rooms, the destruction of space by modern progress in the shape of capital speculation and German airplanes. José Emilio Pacheco remarks: "*Yo* prosigue su camino, su desvarío. Pero está acompañado de *Tú* y el poema se remansa durante unos endecasílabos felices, hasta que otra vez irrumpe la historia en el reino de los amantes y en la morada interior para traerles el testimonio de una infinita catástrofe" ("Descripción de *Piedra de sol*" 141). This cycle repeats itself: in Paz's vision of history, ruins are an inevitable outcome, but the *nosotros* dominates *Piedra de sol.*

In an interview with Manuel Ulacia, Paz stressed that: "... desde mis comienzos, he intentado insertar en mis poemas: la historia. La ciudad es la gran creación de la historia y, a su vez, ella misma es creadora de historia. Cuando se dice historia se habla de creación pero también de destrucción. La historia produce ruinas..." (Ulacia, "Octavio Paz: Poesía, pintura" 618). Paz signals that history functions on the dialectics of creation and destruction, from which ruins emerge. Paz implies that cities in ruins, like Madrid in 1937, are the outcome of history's wars and the cycle of destruction and reconstruction. But this is precisely what Benjamin criticizes when he claims that fascism has a chance of prevailing if it is treated as a historical norm.

Piedra de sol privileges mythical time; rather than provoking a historical awakening as I have discussed in other poems, the historical scene of the war interrupts and is inserted into the poem. The text tends to allude to historical figures such as Moctezuma, Robespierre, Lincoln, and Madero, in the form of a pastiche. This does not mean that the poem *historicizes* the ruins; quite the contrary, the stanza dedicated to the Spanish Civil War is just the interruption of history, the decorative presence of context in the text. Moreover, Paz's *Piedra de sol* finally opts for a hopeful message through his poetics of the instant:

> cada día es nacer, un nacimiento
> es cada amanecer y yo amanezco,
> amanecemos todos, amanece
> el sol cara de sol, Juan amanece
> con su cara de Juan cara de todos,
> puerta del ser, despiértame, amanece…
> adonde yo soy tú somos nosotros,
> al reino de pronombres enlazados… (276–77)

In what seems a cliché, sunrise is the symbol of a hopeful future. Paz's Juan represents the anonymous man, but unlike Juan Cortapiedras, Juan Comefrío, and Juan Piesdescalzos in Neruda's *Alturas*, his social class is not specified, only his gender—an absence that can also be read as anti-Marxist. In *Piedra de sol*, written more than a decade after *Alturas,* Paz is clearly not identifying Juan with the working class. Still, his play with pronouns coheres with his ahistorical poetics of the instant and the abstract "nosotros rehumanizado," as envisioned by García Montero. As Pacheco indicates: "La experiencia de la soledad desemboca en el anhelo de la solidaridad" ("Descripción de *Piedra de sol*" 142). Neruda's *Alturas* and Paz's *Piedra de sol* share a sense of solidarity with the other, although Neruda's "nosotros" has a clearer political and historical referent. As Pacheco notes, Paz shows an "anhelo," a wish, but in my view this solidarity does not materialize in the poem.

Paz's "Elegía" and the excerpt from *Piedra de sol* exhibit two different strategies of inserting history in his poetic project:

one focuses on one soldier's death and the other reconstructs through flashback the attack on Madrid in 1937 that transforms it into a city in ruins. In these two poems there is a sense of loss and the representation of a collective trauma, just as in Cernuda's and Neruda's works. In his "Elegía" the young soldier paradoxically dies "en el ardiente amanecer del mundo" (99), while in *Piedra de sol*, at the end we are all born with each sunrise: "cada día es nacer, un nacimiento / es cada amanecer y yo amanezco, / amanecemos todos..." (276). Paz's perspective changes from a disillusioned "Elegía" written in 1937 to a more hopeful *Piedra de sol* written in 1957.

In comparison with Paz's poems of the Spanish Civil War, Neruda's *España en el corazón* bares a clearer political conscience of the historical, and it is a fundamental piece in mapping the topos of ruins in modern poetry. Neruda's poems on the Spanish Civil War mark a crucial development in his poetic style that can also be traced back to *Residencia en la tierra II*, but it is appalling how little critical commentary they have received in comparison with some of his other poetry collections. There are just a few close readings of the main texts of *España en el corazón*. Still, the poems that Neruda wrote during the Spanish Civil War, after his close friend Federico García Lorca had been assassinated, remain a critical part of his political and literary evolution.[64]

Chapter Five

Pablo Neruda's Cities in Ruins

Poetic Histories from
Madrid to Machu Picchu

Historicizing Ruins

Modern poetry on ruins yields a map of how to read the historical and the literary pasts through its metaphors of destruction. Baroque poems on ruins commemorate Classical ruins and meditate on the decay of a historical space that has lost its grandeur. This evocation becomes a didactic enterprise that laments the power of time and nature over cultural products. In turn, Romantic poems on ruins tend to *dehistoricize* this seemingly unreachable past. Romantic poets express the melancholic feelings that those symbols of death and decay cause in the speaker, the overriding poetic *I*. While in marked contrast, modern texts on ruins *historicize* the past, ancient and recent. Poems on modern ruins are often products of progress or war. But as I have suggested earlier, ruins' representations in modern poetry are not limited to war poetry. For instance, Pablo Neruda's *Alturas de Macchu Picchu* (written and published in 1945 and as part of *Canto General* in 1950) transports the reader to the lost past of the Inca city.[1]

To evoke the Amerindian, pre-Columbian past, Neruda engages the seventeenth-century tradition of Francisco de Quevedo's and Rodrigo Caro's poetry and also establishes a dialogue with the Romantic poetic tradition. These two distinct traditions confirm and reinforce Neruda's modern voice rather than separate it from Modernity. In this chapter, I analyze Neruda's poems on the Spanish Civil War and Madrid's ruins in *España en el corazón* (1936–38) and examine their relation to the collections *Residencia en la tierra I y II* (1925–35) and *Alturas de Macchu Picchu*. The poems about the Spanish Civil War or the pre-Columbian era link the past and the present and reflect upon their historical gaps.

In my analysis of *España en el corazón* within the context of Avant-garde poetry, I explain why Neruda distances himself from narcissistic, nostalgic, and melancholic feelings in his representation of war ruins.[2] I analyze the political significance of ruins in Neruda's *España en el corazón*, in particular "Canto sobre unas ruinas," and how he invokes the sense of urgency, "the state of emergency," and "cultural pessimism."[3] Nostalgia and melancholia have no grounds in the politicization of the ruins. The political and historical indignation that provokes *España en el corazón* strengthens *Alturas de Macchu Picchu*. The contemporary ruins of Spain and the aerial attacks on Guernica and Madrid foreshadow World War II battles and mold Neruda's political reading of the present and the past when he visits the Inca ruins. The dead of the Inca city are buried, petrified in the past. As I maintain in my discussion of *Alturas*, Neruda inserts his poetic homage to the Inca city in ruins in the tradition of the Baroque topos of ruins, and yet the poem stresses its own artificiality, as well as Neruda's modern quest for the forgotten in Latin American history—in this poem he privileges working men as the main subjects of history.

The Spanish Civil War provoked a "historical awakening" that politically ignited the generation of Neruda, Cernuda, and even Paz, although he was ten years younger. But Neruda and Cernuda, just like other Spanish Avant-garde poets such as Alberti and García Lorca, were increasingly politicized throughout the late nineteen twenties by the demise of the dictatorship of Primo de Rivera (1923–29), the 1929 economic crisis, and all the turmoil during the first years of the Second Republic. None of these poets lived in a historical vacuum prior to the beginning of the war; Neruda, Paz, and Cernuda did not suddenly wake up to political reality when they saw Madrid bombed. The existential and literary frustrations of the Avant-garde movement and its "yo en crisis" led them to look for a poetic sensibility that was less narcissistic, less melancholic; they were still very interested in the literary recognition of Góngora, but Quevedo became a more influential figure because of his political engagement.

Neruda's poems of ruins avoid a melancholic and a narcissistic vision of both the Spanish present and the Inca past to highlight his solidarity with the exploited community. In contrast with Simmel's and Starobinsky's readings of Romantic ruins, which project a melancholic representation of the city in ruins and a yearning for a harmonious return to nature, Neruda's project aims to *historicize* the ruins. By this I mean that instead of erasing the ruins' historical background, he is reflecting upon the historical events that led to destruction.

Against the Nostalgic Self

After returning from a Spain in ruins in the fall of 1937, Neruda traveled through Chile giving lectures and reciting his poems. In Vega Central he met a group of workers: "Sólo tenía mi libro *España en el corazón* conmigo… No se me ocurría qué decirles… Leí casi todo el libro" ("Algo sobre mi poesía" 11). Neruda described the silence of that audience and his astonishment when he finished reading his poems dedicated to the Spanish Civil War: "Entonces se produjo el hecho más importante de mi carrera literaria. Algunos aplaudían. Otros bajaban la cabeza." From the crowd, a man approached him: "'Compañero Pablo, nosotros somos gente muy olvidada… nunca habíamos sentido una emoción tan grande. Nosotros queremos decirle...' Y rompió a llorar, con sollozos que lo sacudían" (11). The outburst of emotion demonstrated a moving sense of solidarity—those Chilean workers felt a bond with the Spanish victims of the war because they were also "gente olvidada." Neruda's *España en el corazón* consciously aims to keep the historical memory of the Civil War by honoring its forgotten victims, symbolized by the abandoned handkerchief in "Canto sobre unas ruinas:" "Esto que fue creado y dominado, / esto que fue humedecido, usado, visto, / yace —pobre pañuelo— entre las olas…" (*Tercera Residencia* 53). These poems on ruins do not move the spectator into a melancholic search of self; these poems aim to be testimonies, witnesses, interpreters, and agents of history.

España en el corazón marks a subtle evolution in Neruda's poetry, rather than a drastic change in his aesthetic and political ideas. The poems dedicated to the Spanish Civil War crystallize an aesthetic positioning that Neruda had started to develop in the second part of *Residencia en la tierra*. *España en el corazón* represents an effort to merge oneiric, surreal imagery, unexpected metaphors, and frequent enumerations with a prosaic tone and a clear political message. Such an evolution is palpable in poems like *Crepusculario*'s "Pantheos" and *Residencia en la tierra I*'s "Unidad," where death is the source of the speaker's melancholic mood. In contrast, *Residencia en la tierra II*'s "La calle destruida" and *España en el corazón*'s "Canto sobre unas ruinas" show history, not time or death, in the abstract, as the agent of destruction: "una lengua de polvo podrido se adelanta" (*Residencia en la tierra II* 76). Both the literary Avant-garde discourses and Neruda's experiences in Spain shift his poetry from a self-centered endeavor to a political and aesthetic project more in touch with a large community of readers—with the "people." The speaker stops representing his own anguish, angered by the abuses of war and in solidarity with the pain of its victims.

Luis García Montero synthesizes aptly the lyrical evolution produced by the internal crisis of the Avant-garde poets:

> Fue la crisis del propio callejón sin salida de la sublimación intimista, radicalizado en sus contradicciones por la vanguardia, la que provocó una búsqueda de alternativas en la intención social. El yo en crisis que forma parte de una multitud hueca intenta recuperarse a sí mismo a través de un nosotros rehumanizado. Por eso no creo que deba entenderse el acercamiento de los vanguardistas a la política como una infección exterior a sus procesos creativos, motivada por las circunstancias extremas de la época. (*Dueños del vacío* 120)

García Montero underscores the fact that historical circumstances are not the main determining factor behind the literary development of the Avant-garde poets. Their interest in social issues, their change of pronouns, and of perspective, also came from an "internal" literary trajectory. García Montero continues his argument: "La búsqueda de amparo social surge también dentro del proceso lógico de una lírica que ya se había encontrado en sus paseos interiores con los vertederos de un callejón sin salida. El Neruda de la *Tercera Residencia* necesitaba como poeta y como ciudadano una *Reunión bajo las nuevas banderas*" (120). *España en el corazón* is not a sudden creative outburst nor does it represent a drastic change in the political and literary path of Avant-garde poetry. *Tercera Residencia*, *Las nubes,* and even the earlier *Poeta en Nueva York* express the frustration with the failures of Modernity and its notions of progress after World War I and the 1929 market crash. Baudelaire, Eliot, Cernuda, Neruda, and Paz realized that the Romantic project had run its course. These poets' search for alternatives and responses to the identity crisis, provoked by the modern cultural and economic crisis, led them to a search for other origins, away from the Romantic "yo en crisis" and toward "un nosotros rehumanizado."[4] This is not to say that the Avant-garde poets' solipsistic, and sometimes narcissistic, projects lacked a political and social message; the diverse movements that emerged from the Avant-garde were connected by an irreverent attitude toward authority and a challenge to the conservative values of the bourgeoisie. Furthermore, Avant-garde artists presented themselves as revolutionaries, even though their visions of radical change and liberation were mainly centered in aesthetic projects.

The Spanish Civil War and World War II inevitably transform Neruda's political vision and radicalize his participation when he found an intellectual home in communist ideology. Roberto González Echevarría stresses that Neruda's *Canto General* responds to the devastation of post–World War II Europe. The poem comes from "the hope that out of the ruins of Europe and Western civilization in general, Latin America would emerge as a new, vital force, untainted by the errors and sins of the Old World" ("Introduction to Neruda's *Canto General*" 2). *Canto General* embarks on a metaphoric journey through Latin American history, from its beginnings redolent with a natural exuberance and peopled by Amerindian pyramidal societies to European colonization and contemporary political corruption. Neruda's integration of the mythical and the historical and his combination of epic and lyrical elements bring to light a poetics of synthesis.

In the context of this historical exploration of Latin America, Neruda visits the Inca ruins. Nature has protected Machu Picchu for centuries. The natural surroundings of the Inca city kept it "undiscovered" by modern society until 1911, when Hiram Bingham and his team found it in his explorations in Perú. Machu Picchu was untouched by Spanish conquest and colonization; nature was strikingly intertwined with the ruined site. *Alturas de Macchu Picchu* expresses Neruda's desire to recover the buried America and its human histories that lie under its stones, its trees, its earth, its rivers. The speakers in poems from *España en el corazón* to *Canto General* reveal a reflective nostalgia that signals how the poetic "I" lingers on "the patina of time and history" (Boym 41).

Nostalgia and melancholia are related concepts, but they are not equivalent terms. The ruins of Madrid and Machu Picchu, portrayed in Neruda's poems, have eliminated the melancholic feelings of Romantic ruins and his previous melancholic meditations on death and solitude. The etymological definition of melancholy indicates its association to black bile and a pensive mood—it also means a serious depressive state. However, nostalgia is etymologically a desire to return home, either to one's former life or to a former time. Nostalgic feelings may be accompanied by melancholic feelings, but they are different concepts. In *España en el corazón* the speaker is nostalgic for the progressive aspects of the Republican era, Boym's idea of a "reflective nostalgia," but there is no trace of melancholia.[5] In his essay "Mourning and Melancholia," Freud explains the mental features of melancholia as "painful dejection, cessation of interest in the outside world, loss of capacity to love, inhibition of all activity… self-reproaches…" (244). The main difference between someone in mourning and a melancholic person resides in their view of the self; melancholic feelings tend to be narcissistic. Thus, political poetic projects such as *España en el corazón* and *Canto General* could not run the risk of sounding narcissistic through a melancholic mood.

When Georg Simmel discussed the melancholic feelings that overwhelm the spectator of ruins, he mostly alluded to the eighteenth and nineteenth centuries or to a Romantic spectator of ruins. Simmel remarked that the decay of buildings or monuments highlights the overpowering force of nature taking over the cultural or the spiritual:

> The balance between nature and spirit, which the building manifested, shifts in favor of nature. The shift becomes a cosmic tragedy which, so we feel, makes every ruin infused with our nostalgia; for now the decay appears as nature's revenge for the spirit's having violated it by making a form in its own image. ("The Ruin" 259)

Art has been transformed by nature; it has not just been altered, but conquered. Simmel refers to a new form of unity within the disharmony of nature and culture. Nature feels angry and violated because art made a form based on nature's own image. The destruction of buildings or monuments leads to a return to nature, to nature's reclaiming its space. The fascination of the ruin for Simmel resides in a paradoxical reunion, in which the origin of things is put into question: "the work of man appears to us entirely as a product of nature" (261). Simmel points to a particular ecology of ruins, the final integration of human culture into nature. Jean Starobinski alludes to Simmel's essay and emphasizes that ruins become nature's creatures: "Un équilibre s'établit, où les puissances antagonistes de la nature et de la culture se réconcilient derrière notre passage, au moment où se défont les traces de l'effort humain, et où la sauvagerie regagne le terrain perdu" ("La mélancolie dans les ruines" 180). From the tension provoked by the encounter of nature and culture, Starobinski reads in Simmel a harmonious reconfiguration of forces.

Art and civilized works seem to be destined to destruction or death in the paradoxically vital embrace of Mother Nature. Nonetheless, those whom Starobinski defines as the spectators of ruins in the eighteenth century evade the conceptualization of a ruined site where history and nature merge. "La poétique de la ruine est toujours une rêverie devant l'envahissement de l'oubli... On l'a remarqué, pour qu'une ruine paraisse belle, il faut que la destruction soit assez éloignée et qu'on en ait oublié les circonstances précises...: l'Histoire, le Destin" ("La mélancolie dans les ruines" 180). Starobinski claims that the spectator of ruins aestheticizes the remnants of cities to the point of forgetting the causes that brought those buildings to destruction. For ruins to be beautiful, the spectators of the eighteenth century and part of the nineteenth century had to forget their uncomfortable past; ruins had to be de-historicized. Thus, the melancholic representation of the ruins as externalizations of the speaker's internal turmoil empties the ruins of their historical signification: "La poésie de la ruine est poésie de ce qui a partiellement survécu à la destruction... Sa mélancolie réside dans le fait qu'elle est devenu un monument de la signification perdue" (180). These fashionable ruins would become decorative elements of bourgeois households or gardens, in need of the prestige of heritage provided by their broken columns and statues.

Neruda's *Alturas de Macchu Picchu* does precisely the opposite. In his homage to the Inca ruins and his journey into the self and the land, Neruda intends to rescue the history that "speaks" through the Inca city. Although Neruda's speaker has some Romantic traits, he is not Simmel's or Starobinski's melancholic spectator of ruins. Neruda's political and aesthetic project is much closer to Walter Benjamin's politicized reading on Baroque allegories, in which he underlines how "in the ruin, history has physically merged into the setting" ("Allegory and Trauespiel" 177). I would argue that modern poems on ruins do not read the ruins as products of waste, but rather as history's signature. In Neruda's political and aesthetic work, the historical subject is the main protagonist of the poem; and the poetic *I* is not only an individual, with his own existential dilemmas, but a historical agent, able to interpret the past and modify the course of history.

Neruda's *España en el corazón* and *Alturas de Macchu Picchu* lack the Romantic melancholic introspection that can be found in the first book of *Residencia en la tierra*. We may find traces of melancholia in the first part of *Alturas*, but Neruda's political stance generally has to neglect the melancholic vision of the ruins. However, the notion of melancholia is processed through diverse stages in his multifaceted poetic journey. In his reading of Neruda's "Arte poética" in *Segunda Residencia*, García Montero argues that there is a displacement of melancholia that appears to be associated with the prophetic: "la melancolía pasa a ser un sentimiento relacionado con el futuro, con la falta de futuro" (*Los dueños del vacío* 111). He discusses the final verses where the wind, the night, and the sounds demand of the speaker something "prophetic": "me piden lo profético que hay en mí, con melancolía." But Neruda does not offer any prophetic answer; quite the contrary, his speaker is overwhelmed by the internal crisis of the modern poet, tied to "un nombre confuso." However, García Montero's adequate rendering stresses that this "arte poética… ensucia y ridiculiza la melancolía" (110). Further on, he indicates that this leads to a dumping ground, a sort of wasteland.[6] There is a poetic voyage from the exhausted feelings of the Romantic ruins to the "yo en crisis" and the modern frustrations with a stale language, for instance in Eliot's *The Waste Land,* among other works. But the notion of the wasteland not only sullies the melancholic Romantic feelings, it also empties them. The Avant-garde poet needs to erase melancholy from its poetic discourse to be able to approach a "collectivity," a sense of *nosotros* or even a plurality of voices as in Eliot's case. Although the accumulation of abandoned objects in both *Segunda Residencia* and *España en el corazón* may be read as a melancholic vision of the future, a response to the nothingness and emptiness of the Modernist project, I would propose that the pessimistic and cynical vision excludes melancholia altogether. Thus, melancholia immobilizes and brings the poet to a standstill, producing a solipsistic, dark vision of reality, which reflects the poet's internal crisis. Romantic ruins exemplify well this melancholic vision of reality, one that openly alienates the spectator of ruins from the historical context. If we read Spanish and Latin American poetry from the late twenties and early thirties as critical of modern progress, running away from Romantic ruins, the poems on the Spanish Civil War or on modern wars in general must be analyzed within the wider context of Modernity's failures and the poetics of disillusionment.

Nonetheless, Enrico Mario Santí underscores the ironic sense of the word *melancolía* in "Arte poética." Similarly to what García Montero denotes, Santí remarks: "Instead of discrediting the role of melancholy, the shift of images affirms it by attributing it to a prophetic function" (*Pablo Neruda* 40). However, Santí's reading emphasizes that this poem clarifies Neruda's use of Romantic irony and prophecy. The word *melancholy* is thus interpreted as a self-conscious ironic stance. Santí's interpretation of "Arte poética" follows the meta-literary guidelines of a poem whose very title indicates its purpose within the collection. He convincingly argues that despite the fact that the associations of melancholy and prophecy seem to lead to contradiction and confusion, prophecy in Neruda is actually a rhetorical move: "For prophecy is, finally, the fiction that identifies the visionary act. Once the visionary subject acknowledges his own facticity and discloses the degree to which his status depends on fiction, all visions are exposed as similar constructs…" (42). In the poems on ruins that I discuss here, the ironic stance that stresses the speaker's disclosure of the text as a metaliterary move is not as evident as in "Arte poética."

The representation of ruins in modern poetry links the historical and the mythical, the fugitive and the eternal, the urban and the natural landscapes. In the seventeenth century, Caro's "Canción a las ruinas de Itálica" uses the imagery of the Roman ruins to reflect upon the literary and archeological search for the past and the origins of the Spanish nation. Meanwhile, Neruda's *Alturas de Macchu Picchu* evokes the motif of the ruins in the context of the twentieth-century rethinking of Latin America's cultural heritage and its literary tradition. Neruda situates the beginning of Latin American history in Machu Picchu; the Inca city leads us to the "origins" of the modern Latin American city. Just like Caro's "Canción a las ruinas de Itálica," these texts intend to become a medium for the production of a historical memory, a means to read and translate the stones and the voices of the past.

Caro's "Itálica" and the Traces of the Past

Between 1595 and 1647, Rodrigo Caro, archeologist and antiquarian, wrote five versions of his "Canción a las ruinas de Itálica." I will only deal with his final and best-known version. Relics, ashes, residues abound in the first stanza of Caro's "Itálica." The poem begins with an apostrophe to a Fabio, to whom the speaker shows the ruins: "Estos, Fabio, ¡ay, dolor!, que ves ahora / campos de soledad… / fueron un tiempo Itálica famosa."[7] The poem transports the reader to an empty place, but the speaker's imagination tries to reproduce almost archeologically the plaza, the temple, the theater, and the city walls: "*Este* llano fue plaza, *allí* fue templo… / *Este* despedazado anfiteatro" (in Rivers, *Poesía lírica* 289, line 12; emphasis added). The immediacy created by the apostrophe is reinforced by the demonstrative adjectives and the series of adverbs in the first stanzas: *ahora, este, allí, aquí*. Apostrophe and anaphora are common figures in the topos of ruins, and as Caro's text demonstrates, they highlight the presence of what seems absent.

The echoes of Caro's "Itálica" are felt in most poems on ruins throughout Latin American and Spanish twentieth-century poetry. Cedomil Goic and Erik Camayd-Freixas state that both Caro's "Itálica" and Neruda's *Alturas* make use of anaphora to portray the ruins. In Caro's poem we perceive this: "*Mira* mármoles y arcos destrozados… / *Mira* estatuas soberbias." In *Alturas* there is a similar repetition to stress the imaginary description of the past: "*Aquí* los anchos granos de maíz ascendieron… / *Aquí* la hebra dorada… / *Aquí* los pies del hombre…" (23, canto 6; emphasis added). Camayd-Freixas interestingly associates the topos of ruins with this formal feature: "Si hay algo que puede considerarse privativo de la elegía de ruinas es el uso anafórico de la indicación conmemorativa" (407). The anaphora serves as a sign that guides the readers through the map of the city in ruins; it underlines the gaps between the past and the present state of things.

The tragedy of time is represented in the decomposed body of "El despedazado anfiteatro." The amphitheater, painted in "amarillo jaramago," denotes the putrid and dusty nature of the "fábula del tiempo," the real tragedy of the city (290, lines 20–22).[8] In this scene, the joyful voices of Roman spectators are silenced; they are replaced by phantasmagoric murmurings: "las voces de dolor (que) el alma siente" (line 34). Paradoxically, "la noche callada" inspires Caro to listen to the voices of the past, much as Neruda addresses them later on in *Alturas*: "habladme toda esta larga noche" (30, canto 12). Caro's speaker listens to the echoing lament "Itálica" repeated with anguish and nostalgia (lines 76–84). But stones do not speak by themselves; both the grandeur of the statues and the fame of their heroes lie "en alto silencio sepultado" (56). And yet "el gemido de mil sombras nobles en su ruina" can still be heard in the poetic present (lines 83–84).

There are two alternative readings of this poem's ideological significance. A traditional approach has tended to place Caro's "Itálica" in a tradition of poems that portray ruins as a reflection of the national decadence of Spain in the seventeenth century, emphasizing a historical circularity in the rise and fall of powerful empires.[9] Even though Ferri Coll's reading of the text is not limited by its reference to national decadence, he does point out that by Caro's time the motif of the ruins had been intensely nationalized. Through the use of the apostrophe, Caro plays on the vanishing nature of Classical cities:

> Y a ti, Roma, a quien queda el nombre apenas,
> Oh, patria de los dioses y de los reyes:
> Y a ti, a quien no valieron justas leyes,
> Fábrica de Minerva, sabia Atenas. (61–64)[10]

Gods, kings, and laws are all figures of authority, vulnerable to the power of time and fate. In a very different tone from Caro's admiration for Greek and Roman societies, these symbols of authority are also evoked in Neruda's *Alturas* when the speaker denounces Machu Picchu's power structure as unjust.

David Darst convincingly offers a different reading of "Itálica": "For Caro, but not for Lope and Quevedo, the glorious past now fallen into ruins and turned to ashes is not a reflection on the present destruction... quite simply because the past is not Christian" (15). Darst's analysis of "Itálica" as a poem of the Counter-Reformation is mostly based on the last stanza and affirms that all pagan, man-made things are destroyed, except Geroncio's corpse, the only remnant of the past that should be whole and everlasting because he was a Christian martyr.[11] This very persuasive claim would explain the disdain for the pagan gods and kings and the religious connotations of the last stanza. However, for the sake of his argument, Darst seems to leave the third stanza aside, avoiding a discussion of the role of the national heroes. Yet, in the text both Geroncio's and Trajano's remains are buried in Itálica, the cradle of the religious and the political origins of the Christian kingdom of Spain. The conclusion is part of Caro's desire to insert the past into the present Christian tradition, uniting in a conciliatory manner Antiquity with Christianity.[12] Caro's conciliatory intention differs from Neruda's reiteration that the common grounds between the Inca past and the contemporary world lay in a violent and easily erased history of exploitation and injustice.

The catalogue of heroes in both Caro's and Neruda's poems expresses an anxiety for lost origins. Caro's review of Spain's national history through the topos of ruins projects both a restorative and a reflective nostalgia. The third stanza in Caro's poem signals a particular interest in the hero's birthplace: "Aquí nació... gran padre de la patria, honor de España... triunfador Trajano" (35–37). The prestige of the national history, represented by Trajano, Adriano, Teodosio, and Geroncio, is rooted in those ruins, but only "zarzales" are left of the gardens. In

Baroque aesthetics, nature overcomes history; this is an image that could also be read from the Counter-Reformation theological statement about the vanity of human endeavor as opposed to God's power.

The Baroque obsession with opposites and paradoxes present in Caro's poem confirms Orozco Díaz's proposal that "en las ruinas se ha realizado esa asimilación completa entre lo artificial y lo natural."[13] In Caro's "Itálica," lizards invade the houses and their long forgotten gardens, a sign that nature has overcome the city. Thus, the poem confirms Simmel's and Starobinski's arguments that ruins merge the natural and the cultural, meaning both the spiritual and the artificial. Caro's poem must be placed in the context of the formal characteristics that define the Baroque topos of ruins: apostrophe, anaphora, paradoxes, and the catalogue of heroes, among others. I will frequently refer to these formal features to analyze how modern poets use and manipulate metaphoric language in their intention to read the historical past in the poetic ruins.

Similar to Quevedo's *Salmo XVII* "*Miré los muros de la patria mía*," Caro's "Itálica" portrays the passage of time as a process that moves from the general to the particular, from the nation and the natural to the house and the body:

> La casa para el César fabricada
> ¡Ay! Yacc de lagartos vil morada.
> Casas, jardines, césares murieron,
> Y aún las piedras que de ellos se escribieron. (48–51)

Death and destruction surprise the caesars and their houses. Still, how can we narrate Itálica's history if we do not even have "las piedras que de ellos se escribieron"? History is set in motion by written records. Without the memory of the written stones, the poet reconstructs the past through an act of imagination. Like Caro's "Itálica," Neruda's "Canto sobre unas ruinas" and *Alturas* reveal a similar vision of the poet as an archeologist who reconstructs the historical past through poetic imagination.

Spain in Ruins: Neruda's Political Commitment

Neruda arrived in Spain as a diplomat in May 1934. He had already been in Spain in the late twenties, but this was the first time he had lived there as the Chilean consul at Barcelona. In February 1935 he was appointed consul at Madrid. Boiling political tensions constantly threatened the Spanish Republic. The brutal military repression of the revolutionary outburst of the mineworkers in October 1934 in Asturias, where General Franco's atrocities against the strikers and the civil population in general are well documented, marks a terrible period for the Republic. Pedro Gutiérrez Revuelta eloquently synthesizes the critical state of things and the profound impact it had in the Spanish intellectual sphere: "El nacimiento de España de movimientos pro-Fascistas como la Falange (1933); la victoria de las derechas en las elecciones de noviembre de ese mismo año y el compromiso político de muchos intelectuales europeos aceleró la politización de los jóvenes intelectuales españoles. Politización no exenta de crisis de identidad" (300). Spain was galvanized; it was a time of growing factions and divisions in the political and social sphere.

Neruda's *España en el corazón*, and in particular "Explico algunas cosas," exposes the political implications of his aesthetic work, and "Canto sobre unas ruinas" echoes what Theodor W. Adorno called the era's "cultural pessimism." Spanish ruins reveal the traumatic experiences of the war and its horror through surreal imagery. These ruins transform Neruda's insight and lead him to read in the future a historical allegory of social injustice in the Inca ruins. But already before the war, in his first prologue to *Caballo Verde para la Poesía*, "Sobre una poesía sin pureza," Neruda argues for an aesthetics of the concrete, the impure, the artificial: "una poesía impura como un traje, como un cuerpo… con arrugas… Y no olvidemos nunca la melancolía, el gastado sentimentalismo… la luz de la luna, el cisne en el anochecer… Quien huye del mal gusto cae en el hielo" (*OC* 637). Neruda ironically advocates a pastiche of Romantic moons, like the ones in Cernuda's and Lorca's poems, of *Modernista* imagery like Darío's swans, and of Symbolist aesthetics with Baudelaire's melancholic and disturbed swans. His life in Spain and the events leading up to the Spanish Civil War gradually changed Neruda's perspective: "El contacto con España me había fortificado y madurado. Las horas amargas de mi poesía debían terminar. El subjetivismo melancólico de mis *Veinte poemas de amor* o el patetismo doloroso de *Residencia en la tierra* tocaban su fin" (*Confieso* 196). In his note in 1939 to "Las furias y las penas," a Quevedesque poem in *Tercera Residencia*, Neruda describes his makeover, both personal and public; the war transformed him and the world:

> En 1934 fué escrito este poema. ¡Cuántas cosas han sobrevenido desde entonces! España, donde lo escribí, es una cintura de ruinas. ¡Ay! Si con sólo una gota de poesía o de amor pudiéramos aplacar la ira del mundo, pero eso sólo lo pueden la lucha y el corazón resuelto.
>
> El mundo ha cambiado y mi poesía ha cambiado. Una gota de sangre caída en estas líneas quedará viviendo sobre ellas, indeleble como el amor.
>
> Marzo de 1939. (*OC* 244)

Avant-garde poets abandoned the one-way street into the self. The Spanish Civil War provoked a collective awakening against the growing power of totalitarian regimes, and poetry was another political tool. *España en el corazón* and *Canto General* intend to fight against fascism, colonialism, and neo-colonial forms of capitalism.

These books were meant to incite the reader's mind politically and aesthetically; these poems participate in the conceptualization of the Spanish and the Latin American historical and cultural heritage. Neruda abandons his anti-intellectual pose and searches in literary culture, in books, for what the Romantics sought in nature: "Me pareció encontrar una veta enterrada, no bajo las rocas subterráneas, sino bajo las hojas de los libros. ¿Puede la poesía servir a nuestros semejantes? ¿Puede acompañar las luchas de los hombres?" (*Confieso* 196). Poetry was a public service for Neruda, and modern poets, like the minstrels in medieval times, had to preserve the historical memory of their communities.

España en el corazón is a book that emerges literally from the traces of the war. The ruins of the poems are materialized in the manufacture of the book itself. *España en el corazón* was made by the victims and the soldiers to whom it is inscribed. The book was printed under very difficult circumstances toward the end of the Civil War. Neruda describes his collection of poems to the Spanish Civil War as having a strange history: "Creo que pocos libros... hayan tenido tan curiosa gestación y destino" (174). Neruda recalls that years after the end of the war, he saw the 1938 Spanish edition: "vi un ejemplar de esta edición en Washington, en la Biblioteca del Congreso, colocado en una vitrina como uno de los libros más raros de nuestro tiempo" (174). Manuel Altolaguirre printed it in the Monastery of Monserrat in Catalonia with the help of Republican soldiers. They had no paper to print Neruda's book, so they had to manufacture some materials and they used what they had. Altolaguirre tells the story:

> El día que se fabricó el papel del libro de Pablo fueron soldados los que trabajaron en el molino. No sólo se utilizaron las materias primas (algodón y trapos) que facilitó el Comisariado, sino que los soldados echaron en la pasta, ropas y vendajes… trofeos de guerra, una bandera enemiga y la camisa de un prisionero moro. (908–09)

In a symbolic moment, the remainders of war materialize in the poems that show the ravages of war; the material shape of the book offers an uncanny continuity with its historical referent. The physical book itself, a recycled product, a promise of ecological renewal, is born from waste, transforming the nothingness of war into poetry of defiance.

Critics have often underestimated *España en el corazón*, preferring to celebrate the aesthetic achievement of the first parts of *Residencia en la tierra*. Robert Pring-Mill indicates that what concerns him in *España en el corazón* is "its failure to achieve any real distancing from the immediacy of war" (xxxvii). Pring-Mill establishes that "Explico algunas cosas" and "Canto sobre unas ruinas" exemplify a more successful attempt to express the harshness of war, but that parts of the collection "degenerate into raucous diatribe, such as 'Sanjurjo en los infiernos'" (xxxvii). Granted "Sanjurjo" is not a great satirical short poem; however, the following "Mola en los infiernos" is a fierce and funny text in honor of Quevedo's humorous wordplays and Dante's *Inferno*. Pring-Mill's insistence on Neruda's lack of detachment from the immediacy of the war is not a persuasive line of criticism. Poets do not need critical distance to think about a historical moment. Contrary to Pring-Mill's argument, the imminence of the war and Neruda's innovative metaphoric language give these poems a particular emotional and political force—as "Explico algunas cosas" demonstrates.

In *España en el corazón*, Neruda portrays Madrid as a city in ruins and Spain as a country in flames. In "Explico algunas cosas," the speaker addresses the Fascist generals, and the readers themselves, demanding that they face the ruins:

> mirad mi casa muerta
> mirad España rota…
> pero de cada niño muerto sale un fusil con ojos,
> pero de cada crimen nacen balas
> que os hallarán un día el sitio
> del corazón.
>
> *(Tercera Residencia* 41)

The ruined house, the divided country, and the dead child: Neruda's analogies carry the dramatic force of immediacy and desperate feelings in the face of annihilation. These texts present the destruction of the war as it is taking place. Therefore, these poems to modern Spanish ruins have to instill a particular sense of horror and reality. There is a clear evolution of style from the more melancholic, surreal, and obscure imagery of the first book of *Residencia en la tierra* toward a politically charged figurative language in *España en el corazón*. Manuel Durán and Margery Safir address this change: "The poet who had once described the ecstasy of love and the anguish of loneliness must now tell of battlefields and city streets drenched in blood."[14] They highlight that this poetry had to be clear and direct to be accessible to a majority of readers: "To attain its goal, the poetry must reach a vast public, it must be clear, direct, unequivocal" (Durán and Safir 79). In my view, this collection of poems combines simple, prosaic language with difficult, surreal metaphors. Neruda himself acknowledges that he never considered this book to be "easy-reading": "Yo nunca pensé que *España en el corazón* fuera un libro fácil" ("Algo sobre mi poesía y mi vida" 11). This book is far from being transparent and easy to analyze. Instead of revealing clarity in language, these poems demonstrate clarity in political conscience.[15]

Most modern poems on ruins reveal a pessimistic, even apocalyptic vision of history. In Cernuda's case, I suggest that his nostalgic poems are products of a major cultural mourning, an anguish intensified by his political exile. In Eliot's case, I highlighted how his interpretation of history as a disintegrating, degenerating process was condensed in his critique of modern progress, a critique that led him to increasingly entrenched and reactionary positions. These poets from Baudelaire to Neruda project in their poems on ruins a poetics of disillusionment, interpreted through Weber's ideas on the "disenchantment of the world" and connected to Adorno's notion of "cultural pessimism." There are gradations and differences among the poets I discuss, of course; for example, Paz is much more optimistic with his poetics of reconciliation than Cernuda's poem on ruins.

España en el corazón voices both the pessimism of apocalyptic visions and the need to remain hopeful to fight the Fascist forces; his book goes beyond the poetics of disillusionment; because it was made during a "state of emergency," this historical vision aims to provoke that sense of urgency in the reader. When rationality fails to depict the real, Neruda resorts to surreal imagery to express the horrors of war. Adorno stresses that suffering in times of crisis cannot be conceptualized and cannot be processed through knowledge. Adorno goes on to explain how Hegel's aesthetics can be read in post-Hitler Germany:

> Hegel's thesis that art is consciousness of plight has been confirmed beyond anything he could have envisioned. Thus his thesis was transformed into a protest against his own verdict on art, a cultural pessimism that throws into relief his scarcely secularized theological optimism, his expectation of an actual realization of freedom. The darkening of the world makes the irrationality of art rational: radically darkened art. (18–19)

Neruda's *España en el corazón*, and in particular "Canto sobre unas ruinas," reflects that "cultural pessimism" in the accumulation of destroyed objects that culminate in dust, in nothingness. Eliot's *The Waste Land* epitomizes how art embodies the "darkening of the world," and to a certain degree, Neruda's poems to the Spanish Civil War use surreal imagery to parody the Fascists as deformed and abominable. For instance, in "Madrid 1936" he denounces the alliance between the military insurgents and the Church: "Un hipo negro / de generales, una ola / de sotanas rabiosas..." broke into and attacked the personified capital. The surreal metaphors criticize the cold rationality, the economic interests, and the political, and military ambitions that provoked and financed the war. In particular, Neruda parodies and condemns the political alliances between part of the bourgeoisie, the Church, the Moorish mercenaries, and Hitler's and Mussolini's military support of Franco's army.[16]

Poems on ruins generally use a ventriloquist discourse to reach "history," either through rivers, or moons, or just a predominant speaker. *España en el corazón* wants to be a witness to history, to politically engage the reader and provoke a "historical awakening." In "Explico algunas cosas," Neruda asks the reader to become a witness through the repetition of the final verses, "venid a ver la sangre por las calles." The running blood of dead children takes the place of the river in other poems on ruins, characteristically portrayed as the witness of history. Poems on ruins need a witness of history, a vehicle of communication with the past—it is their way of authenticating their portrayal of history. Writing with blood and through blood becomes Neruda's aesthetic claim, a point already advanced by García Lorca when he introduced him at a conference to literature students in Madrid as "un poeta… más cerca de la sangre que de la tinta" (*Presentación de Pablo Neruda, OC* 147).

In 1934, when García Lorca described Neruda as closer to blood than to ink, to death than to philosophy, he was commenting on *Residencia en la tierra* and Neruda's aesthetics of an impure poetry, in which he privileged the representation of the concrete. There was a need in his poetry to react against Juan Ramón Jiménez's defense of abstract, pure poetry.[17] In his third prologue to *Caballo verde para la poesía,* Neruda describes his poetics in a visceral way: "en casa de la poesía no permanece nada sino lo que fue escrito con sangre para ser escuchado por la sangre" ("Conducta y poesía," *OC* 639). Neruda confirms his poetic and political position in this 1935 prologue with bloody imagery in *España en el corazón.* Blood evokes emotion, violence, and desire as well as a connection with those who can "listen through blood." The verses of "Explico algunas cosas" illustrate the violence he sees in Madrid's streets, and with heated indignation the poem calls for action. In Neruda's poetry, intensified by his visceral imagery and bloody metaphors, war not only mutilates the bodies of men, women, and children, but it is also described as a cannibalistic ritual. Neruda satirizes the Church and the military's roles in the war as if they were voraciously eating at a feast. In "Almería" the Church and the rich receive a dish with the remains of the poor, the victims of the war:

un plato para el obispo, un plato de sangre de Almería…
un plato con mejillas
de niños del Sur feliz, un plato
con detonaciones… ruinas y espanto.

(Tercera Residencia 49)

The surreal metaphor of the poem, as a dish with body parts and ruins that the clerical Fascists have to digest, denounces the anthropophagous aspect of the war. Adorno's argument that "the darkening of the world makes the irrationality of art rational" explains why Neruda insists on surreal metaphors to parody and satirize the Fascists. By representing the Fascist enemy as an irrational, visceral, cannibalistic force, he conceptualizes the darkening of the real, the ruins as effects of the real.

In "Explico algunas cosas," resistance emerges from the battered bodies in the shape of weapons, a rebirth that foreshadows *Alturas de Macchu Picchu.* John Felstiner maintains that the aesthetic change noted in *España en el corazón* is fundamental for the new forms of *Alturas de Macchu Picchu.*[18] For instance, the use of imperatives in "Explico algunas cosas" stresses the anxious, challenging tone that also characterizes parts of *Alturas de Macchu Picchu,* particularly canto 10 when the speaker addresses the city and demands answers.

The speakers in Caro's "Itálica" and Neruda's "Canto sobre unas ruinas" are less demanding of the ruins than the speaker in *Alturas.* The absence of verbs in the imperative in Caro's "Itálica" indicates a very different tone, similar to Neruda's "Canto sobre unas ruinas" in *España en el corazón.* Neruda's "Canto" has no apostrophe to a particular city like Machu Picchu or Itálica, and the poem is not an attack against a hierarchical system. Just like Neruda's "Canto," Caro's poem does not attack Itálica's social structure. Caro's tone of admiration for the glorious past and despair at the ruined site explains the absence of verbs in the imperative. In contrast, Neruda's attitude of defiance and his use of verbs in the imperative serve as ways of condemning the Inca social structure in *Alturas.*

Amado Alonso and Enrico Mario Santí have each commented on the connections between Caro's "Itálica" and Neruda's "Canto sobre unas ruinas." Alonso considered it the best poem of Neruda's "nueva poesía política," probably because it is clearly less explicit and less prosaic than the other poems in

España en el corazón, although this does not necessarily make it the best poem of the collection. In contrast with "Explico algunas cosas," this text tells a story of ruins that are not temporally nor spatially identified. "Canto sobre unas ruinas" alludes to the Baroque topos of ruins, in which nature overpowers culture, and destruction annihilates walls and words.

Alonso concludes the first scholarly book on Neruda's poetry and style remarking on "Canto sobre unas ruinas" and its clear echoes of Caro's poem: "considero un acierto artístico el de iniciarlo con una resonancia de la canción de Rodrigo Caro *A las ruinas de Itálica*" (365). In both Caro's text and Neruda's "Canto sobre unas ruinas," the first verses introduce the ruined space, once inhabited. Alonso acknowledges an important difference between the two poets: "Neruda... no sigue la línea de monumentalidad y lejanía de nuestro clásico, sino una recogida intimidad y presencia" (366). Alonso stresses the poem's intimate evocations to relate them to Neruda's neo-Romantic style. Caro monumentalizes the ruins as an allegory of the past's grandeur, while Neruda's "Canto" does not treat ruins as monuments of or to the past. Ruins are not reconstructed in the poem with a restorative nostalgia; they are remains of the past, historical documents to be read and interpreted. The critic simplifies the significance of the poem as a mere evocation of pain and anguish at the site of destruction: "Aquella vista de formas destruidas le despierta como un rayo (su estilo siempre) el dolor básico..." (367). Alonso insists on a neo-Romantic Neruda, whose poetic inspiration hits him like lightning, and he states the obvious: the ruins symbolize "la Vida destruida." The ruins are not mere traces of death and destruction; they are the product of historical events, as war and progress, and they are cultural emblems in themselves that speak of the social, political, and economic structure of the city that once stood there.

Santí underscores the absence of a clearer differentiation between the two poets in Alonso's rendering. He then sets off to establish a set of differences between Caro's text and Neruda's "Canto sobre unas ruinas":

> The most important among these differences are the
> nature of ruins and the events that occasioned them.
> Whereas Caro's poem provides a moral argument on the

> vanity of history through ruins decayed by the weathering
> of time, Neruda's is a lament for human fate through
> the spectacle of ruins destroyed by human intervention.
> (*Pablo Neruda* 139)

"Canto sobre unas ruinas" projects an apocalyptic vision of history, determined by human intervention, but time and fate also participate in the destruction of the site. In "Canto sobre unas ruinas," the verse "todo por una rueda vuelto al polvo" makes fate, an epitome of time, appear in a circular shape, a cyclical motion that represents its repetitive nature. In the destructive force, even the wheel of fortune loses its magical aura, encircled in a series of objects that disappear, from urine and glasses to leather and perfumes. Santí emphasizes a relevant aspect of this poem: the evasion of a historical referent. Although "Canto" does not specify its historical referent, the poem is part of a collection where the historical context of the Spanish Civil War cannot be overlooked.

In their readings of "Canto sobre unas ruinas," both Alonso and Santí generalize from different perspectives. Santí argues that in "Neruda's bombed wasteland the destruction was so complete that little if any trace of human intention was left standing and therefore the ruins of the poem's title hardly existed" (*Pablo Neruda* 139). A close reading of the poem reveals that the ruins of the title, despite Santí's final suggestion, are visible and that the reader is called upon as a witness. Still, I agree with Santí's Benjaminian emphasis on the historical significance of ruins: "Ruins are not simply the wasteland that occasions nostalgic laments but historical signs that, being marks of transience, render their presence paradoxical and their meaning far from certain" (140). Because Neruda's "Canto sobre unas ruinas" does not simply portray a rootless wasteland, it is relevant to consider the historical traces and the details that modernize this text.

The Spanish Civil War is literally and metaphorically present in all of the poems in *España en el corazón*. Nonetheless, "Canto sobre unas ruinas" describes a more universal ruined landscape that could be identified with any ruined site. In addition, "Canto sobre unas ruinas" was the first poem published along with Nancy Cunard's "Para hacerse amar" (translated by Vicente Aleixandre) in the famous magazine *Les Poètes du*

Monde Défendent le Peuple Espagnol, which was created by Neruda and Cunard to help the Republican militants. Rafael Osuna posits that the ideological and thematic route of this magazine is set by this poem: "'Canto sobre unas ruinas' abría simbólicamente la ruta ideológica y temática al resto de las composiciones de la revista."[19] The readers of Neruda's poem in this magazine knew that the ruins addressed the Spanish Civil War, but by not underlining its specificity, Neruda is also envisioning the possibility of a ruined Europe, not just a ruined Spain. He could be suggesting to the readers of the magazine and those who collaborated with the international effort to aid the Spanish Republic that they should take into consideration the imminent threat of Nazism and Fascism throughout the continent.

"Canto sobre unas ruinas" conveys the era's "cultural pessimism," but it does not give us a nostalgic or a melancholic rendering of the ruins, although there are some instances of a reflective nostalgia for the peaceful days. Further, the lack of a resurrection in "Canto sobre unas ruinas" contrasts with the possibility of a rebirth in *Alturas*. Both texts aim to become historical agents, but they approach history from different viewpoints.

"Canto sobre unas ruinas" begins with the metaphor of the ruins as a used, old handkerchief, lying abandoned and forgotten.[20] The storm of modern progress seems to have consumed society; the poem denounces the politics of obsolescence and dereliction: "Esto que fué creado y dominado... yace —pobre pañuelo— entre las olas / de tierra y negro azufre." The first stanzas describe the genesis of things and life, just as Neruda will do later in the opening of *Canto General* with "La Lámpara en la Tierra." In "Canto sobre unas ruinas," life appears from dust, from death:

> ... como la flor que sube
> desde el hueso destruído, así las formas
> del mundo aparecieron. Oh párpados,
> oh columnas, oh escalas.
> Oh profundas materias
> agregadas y puras: cuánto hasta ser campanas!
> cuánto hasta ser relojes!
>
> (*Residencia en la tierra* 53–54)

The apostrophes in Neruda's poem intensify the elegiac tone as they narrate a creative process: the transformation of nature into cultural products like columns, bells, and clocks.[21] "Canto sobre unas ruinas" underlines the spatial and temporal symbols that appeared and disappeared: the columns that buttress the buildings we inhabit, and the bells and clocks with which we measure time.[22]

In her analysis of "Canto sobre unas ruinas," Concha Meléndez reads in the verses "Aluminio… cemento / pegado al sueño de los seres" the introduction to the destructive force depicted in the poem:

> Podría comentarse ya la química poética de Neruda, que se desdobla de su frecuente símbolo metales. El "aluminio de azules proporciones," "el cemento pegado al sueño de los seres," son elementos inconfundibles en ruinas de hoy. Los seres dormidos por la muerte sueñan ahora adheridos a las materias rotas. (301)

The relevance of metals in the text as a sign of a mechanized Modernity is key for the discussion of how the city is constructed and later on destroyed. In my view, aluminum and cement are materials of construction. Meléndez claims that they can be read as traces of the ruins, foreshadowing the next stanzas. Still, they signal the creation of cities, buildings and houses. Aluminum and cement are attached to people's dreams because they girdle the structures of their future houses.[23]

In the following stanza, nature becomes a metaphor of how social and cultural objects expand and grow. The imagery is ambiguous and can be confusing: "El polvo se congrega, / la goma, el lodo, los objetos crecen." The formation of cities is characterized by a symbol of its destruction: dust. The accumulation of dust and objects is paradoxically represented as a "darkening of the world." Progress is not portrayed with a clean, shiny look; it is made of dirt, rubber, and mud—Neruda's ecological critique of modern progress. The walls are not crumbling but, on the contrary, they are erected: "las paredes se levantan / como parras de oscura piel humana." The walls of cities expand limitlessly. The image insists on the expansive nature of vine leaves as similar to the growth and reproduction of humans and houses, the emergence of civilizations. The metaphor of the human vine leaves represents nature in alliance with humans, in contrast with the traditional antagonistic relation in the Baroque topos of ruins between nature and culture.

The poem goes from the general to the particular, from the creation of things to a nocturnal scene in a modern social space:

> Allí dentro en blanco, en cobre,
> en fuego, en abandono, los papeles crecían,
> el llanto abominable, las prescripciones
> llevadas en la noche a la farmacia mientras
> alguien con fiebre,
> la seca sien mental, la puerta
> que el hombre ha construído
> para no abrir jamás.
> Todo ha ido y caído
> brutalmente marchito. (54)

Paper grows like people and buildings, as if the passing of time and history could be recorded with the accumulation of abandoned papers. These verses mark a change; they introduce the ruined space. Modern war is not explicitly present in these verses, but pain and disease come together in a modern setting: the desperate person who goes to the pharmacy with a prescription. The fever is a symptom of disease, a foreshadower of death. The fever can refer to the frenzy of war through the dried mental capacity to manage reality. The metaphorical door is constructed like a barrier or a wall; its function of opening and closing in the passage of ideas or persons is destroyed.

"Todo ha ido y caído / brutalmente marchito" is the first verse in "Canto sobre unas ruinas" that captures the movement, the process of falling and disappearing, and the ruins themselves.[24] Ironically, the ruins are portrayed not as a product of human intervention as Santí suggested, but as nature's brutality: everything has fallen, faded, "brutalmente marchito," withered like a flower. The next stanza shows traces of the destructive force, and it introduces the core of the decayed space.

The catalogue of heroes, easily recognizable in both Caro's "Itálica" and Neruda's *Alturas*, and which characterizes the topos of ruins, appears in "Canto sobre unas ruinas" in a surreal spectacle of violence. Throughout this work, I have noted that the catalogue of heroes indicates the subjects of history the poem privileges and the voices of the past with which it wants to communicate. The catalogue of heroes in "Canto sobre unas ruinas" is not clearly determined; it is constituted by a conglomeration of metaphors, metonymies, personification of elements, and symbols, which portray a surreal, dreamlike experience. For example, the personification of tools, "utensilios heridos," serves also as a metonymy, in which the tools become one with the wounded workers in the Spanish Civil War. Similar to Picasso's landscape of body parts in "Guernica," instead of the generic catalogue of heroes, the poem offers a long list of body fragments like "mejillas," and residues, "espuma sucia," and "orines." The closets of the city seem to have been bombarded, spreading around all their intestines: "telas nocturnas," "vidrio, lana, / alcanfor, círculos de hilo y cuero" (54). The text explores the body in ruins as metonymy of the rooms, the houses, the city, the nation, and the world.

Fate is shaped like a wheel, suggesting that circular time takes everything back to dust: "todo por una rueda vuelto al polvo" (54). Although this vision of Baroque ruins as a spectacle of the rise and fall of cities and empires is often accompanied by the notion of circular time, in "Canto sobre unas ruinas" there is no resurrection: "todo reunido en nada, todo caído / para no nacer nunca" (54). Despite the poem's interconnections with Caro and the Baroque tradition, Neruda's lack of faith in the resurrection of things and bodies aligns "Canto sobre unas ruinas" with the Modernist and Surrealist aesthetics and an atheist ideology. There is a dramatic tone in the assertion that in the end everything turns into dust, which recalls Quevedo's "Amor constante más allá de la muerte."[25] As Alonso acknowledges: "Quevedo, antes y ahora su antepasado poético más directo, parece haberle prestado su léxico de estallidos…" (362). Neruda explains in his essay *Viaje al corazón de Quevedo* regarding "Amor constante más allá de la muerte": "Nunca en nuestro idioma alcanzó la palabra acumular pólvora tan desbordante… Polvo serán, más polvo enamorado… Está en este verso el eterno retorno, la perpetua resurrección del amor" (*Viaje* 24).[26] Although there are similarities between the sonnet and "Canto," Neruda's poem is much more pessimistic than Quevedo's "polvo enamorado" and than his own future *Alturas de Macchu Picchu.* In "Canto sobre unas ruinas," there is no love or resurrection: "Ved cómo se ha podrido / la guitarra en la boca de la fragante novia." Therefore, in contrast with the tradition of Caro and Quevedo, Neruda's poem reveals no consolation. The future is like a wasteland. The circular time of the wheel of fate is smashed on the ground just like everything else—an immense conglomeration of objects and bodies that will not return to life.

In the context of the Spanish Civil War, it is understandable for Neruda to nostalgically portray his thirst for peace as a "sed celeste" and the early days of the Republic, before the right acquired power, as "épocas de polen y racimo." The natural metaphors of peaceful, democratic days are contrasted with the metaphors of death in the destroyed wood and the rotten guitar. "Sed" is obviously joined to "ved" by its internal rhyme. The repetition of the imperative verb *ved* is not as drastic and intense as the accumulation of imperatives in *Alturas*, but it does serve to ask the reader for an active participation as a witness of history and of the poem as an image of what is happening:

> … *ved* cómo
> la madera se destroza
> hasta llegar al luto: no hay raíces
> para el hombre: todo descansa apenas
> sobre el temblor de lluvia.
> *Ved* cómo se ha podrido
> la guitarra en la boca de la fragante novia:
> ved cómo las palabras que tanto construyeron,
> ahora son exterminio… (54–55)

The poem is not only an evocation of ruins but of the movement itself of the collapse, the process of destruction and putrefaction. The speaker demands that the reader see, open his or her eyes to what is happening. The destroyed wood could stress the wooden coffins as expressions of the mourning of the land and its multiple dead. Santí and Alonso signal the rootless waste land in the verses "no hay raíces / para el hombre." Unlike the human vine leaves in its metaphor of growth and expansion, humans have become rootless. The wooden coffins go back, submerged into the earth, but not as seeds from which roots and trees will grow. War uproots its victims as it destroys their sense of belonging, of *nostos*, because they end up either dead or in exile, internal and external, inside and outside of Spain.

In his analysis of "La calle destruida" and "Canto sobre unas ruinas," Gutiérrez Revuelta asserts that in both texts there is death, a time "in retroceso," where the historical agents play a crucial role. He argues that *España en el corazón* develops what is already present in *Residencia en la tierra II*. Gutiérrez Revuelta focuses on the symbol of wood:

> La madera en *España en el corazón* ya se percata como tiempo fecundo: tiempo social, tiempo de trabajo. Pero la fuerza que destruye la madera en "Canto sobre unas ruinas" es una fuerza aniquiladora de la materia... La fuerza que ha destrozado la madera ha desmaterializado también el tiempo: "un temblor de lluvia." Esta desmaterialización del tiempo fecundo —entendida como regresión... (se) encuentran semejantes planteamientos poéticos y vitales entre *España en el corazón* y *Residencia en la tierra*. (306)

The notion of time "en retroceso," turning backward, is also a trend of Baroque poems of ruins like Caro's "Itálica," where nature recovers the space once inhabited. Civilization seeks to control nature, by organizing it and devastating it: "los jardines... ahora son zarzales y lagunas" (290, lines 46–47). Nature's control over its own habitat is demonstrated precisely by a creative chaos, a lack of deadly human control. Neruda's "Canto sobre unas ruinas" is a song, a cry, and, like Orpheus's songs, it seeks to move nature, whose tears are echoed in "un temblor de lluvia." The final footprint symbolizes the human reminder of pain. Through moss, nature once again penetrates the footprints of the dead: "la huella —ya con musgos— del sollozo." In the "huella... del sollozo," one finds the text's poetic function, a lament, a product of cultural mourning.

In this somber depiction of a ruined site, there is no hope and no music: the bridegrooms are dead; and in a surreal image, the brides remain with a rotten guitar in their mouths.[27] Concha Meléndez proposes that the guitar is a symbol of poetry: "La imagen de la guitarra asociada siempre por Neruda a la poesía, puede ser aquí visión material o creación imaginaria. En la segunda posibilidad "guitarra" es la poesía de las palabras amorosas cortadas por la muerte" (301). In "La calle destruida" from *Residencia en la tierra II,* the guitars also symbolize a destroyed hope, an assassinated poetic song: "Oh herida en donde caen / hasta morir las guitarras azules!" The destroyed guitars silence the mouths of the young brides; they cannot sing, speak, or mourn their dead.

The imagery of "La calle destruida," "metal destrozado," "tomates asesinados," "una lengua a polvo podrido... un sabor mortal a retroceso," foreshadows the urban scene in "Explico algunas cosas."[28] In "Canto sobre unas ruinas," the personified words, that built so much, also refer to the Spanish Republic's rhetoric and democratic days. Words, like the people who have uttered them, have been exterminated. The ruins in the title "Canto sobre unas ruinas" are ultimately evoked by shattered pieces of lime and marble, a possible metaphor for the broken buildings and the broken tombs: "mirad sobre la cal y entre el mármol / deshecho / la huella —ya con musgos— del sollozo" (*Residencia en la tierra* 55). The final imperative verb changes, and although there may not seem to be a great difference between *ver* and *mirar*, the verbs point to diverse forms of observing. The spectator has to look to notice the footprint of pain, covered by moss, dressed by nature. The typical iconography of ruins in both painting and poetry emphasizes the shattered buildings, their broken columns, overpowered by nature, and transfigured by ivy, moss, and trees that surround them. Ruins usually merge nature and culture and represent the remnants of the historical past, buried in the natural landscape. "Canto sobre unas ruinas" epitomizes the poetics of disillusionment and cultural mourning—here we only find "la huella... del sollozo." The organic metaphors of the poem convey an unstoppable process of human destruction and natural putrefaction, in which even the roots are destroyed: "no hay raíces para llegar al hombre."

Alturas de Macchu Picchu projects a totally different vision; from the start, the journey to the Inca city is introduced as a path toward the roots of Latin America. Neruda moves away from the pessimistic tone of *España en el corazón* and insists on the power of poetry to instill life in the lifeless, in a rebirth that emerges from the shackles, from the ruins of the Inca city. The distant Inca voices seem easier to recover than the cries in *España en el corazón*; perhaps the Spanish dead are too close to

Neruda's personal experience for him to pretend to be the voice of the voiceless.

Journey to the Center of the Past: Neruda's *Alturas de Macchu Picchu*

Alturas de Macchu Picchu wants to rescue the "lost voices" of the Inca workers; it is an intrinsic part of *Canto General* —Neruda's alternative narration of Latin American history.[29] Caro's and Neruda's texts claim to give voice to the voiceless.[30] Cedomil Goic, in his comparative analysis of Caro's "Itálica" and Neruda's *Alturas*, shows that in these texts the speaker becomes a mediator between the past and the present, the dead and the living.[31] These poems want to grasp the authentic voices of the past in tension with Western tradition and its historical accounts. The transition from silence to language also points to the Inca's lack of written history. Therefore, the speaker must translate, imagine, and interpret the voices petrified in the city of stones.

Most of Neruda's major critics discuss the prophetic tone of his poetry. Rodríguez Monegal relates Neruda's prophetic tone in *España en el corazón* and in *Alturas de Macchu Picchu* to the discovery of his own "vocación de poeta: a partir de este momento, por su boca hablarán los hombres que no tienen voz" (*Neruda: El viajero inmóvil* 458). Neruda's poetics of *vox populi* manifests itself in his desire to give voice to the voiceless, to the dead victims of modern or colonial times of Spain or Latin America. Rodríguez Monegal reacts against Alonso's first proposition that the prophetic in Neruda is associated with his hermetic language and with his Romantic notions of poetic inspiration.[32] They both allude to Neruda's "Arte poética" in his first book of *Residencia en la tierra* and the speaker's claim that the nights "me piden lo profético que hay en mí, con melancolía." The sense of the prophetic inevitably changes with Neruda's experiences in Spain and in Machu Picchu. Rodríguez Monegal asserts that the last lines in "Arte poética" become a meta-literary reflection, where the revelation of his prophetic mode leads him to change his melancholic mood. Even if I agree with Rodríguez Monegal's criticism of Alonso's insistence on the inspirational to find the Romantic vein of "Arte poética," I would highlight that in the cited line the prophetic and the melancholic are joined; the future or the lack of future, the prophecy or, in my view, the lack of prophecy are marked by melancholy.[33] While there are strong connections between *Residencia II* and *España en el corazón*, Neruda's aesthetics in *Residencia I* are more centered in his melancholic notion of self than in the role of the other or in the community.

The prophetic tone in Neruda's work is rooted in the Romantic tradition. Santí synthesizes this rhetorical argument as follows: "Neruda's formal adoption of the prophetic mode" is "mediated by the Romantic tradition" (*Pablo Neruda* 15). Santí's study is closer to Rodríguez Monegal's formal analysis than to Hernán Loyola's work. Nonetheless, Loyola, who published his book on Neruda in 1967 before Rodríguez Monegal's, also stressed the depiction of Neruda as a Romantic poet prophet: "… los poetas eran los adelantados, los agentes, los representantes de la vida, los profetas de la fecundidad oculta" (90). Loyola follows Alonso's line of thought where the prophetic is connected to the obscure, the "truth" submerged in the poetry. Loyola develops his argument by alluding to "Significa Sombras": "Sea, pues, lo que soy… / ardiente testigo, / cuidadosamente destruyéndose y preservándose incesantemente, / evidentemente empeñado en su deber original" (*Residencia en la tierra II* 59). In Loyola's characterization of Neruda's work as testimonial, the poet is a witness. However, he sees in these lines Neruda's self-portrait as a prophet: "Un testigo leal a sus deberes, a su responsabilidad de poeta y profeta, a su obediencia…" (Loyola 100). Although this statement may seem religiously charged, Loyola does not suggest that Neruda is obedient to God but rather to himself and his Romantic role of poet of the people.

However, Neruda is no prophet. The word *prophet* carries diverse meanings, from a visionary or a person who speaks for God or deities, for someone or for some thing, to a foreteller of the future or spokesperson of some doctrine. Neruda does not speak for God nor claim to, nor does he aim to foretell the future, so why label him a prophet? Does speaking with and for the dead make him a prophet? What are his prophecies? To describe Neruda as a prophet is a way of idealizing his social role as a poet, with the intention of making his work useful and sacred in a scholarly way. The notion of the poet priest who speaks for the people and in the people's idiom is deeply rooted in nineteenth-century English and German Romanticism. Moreover, to assume that Neruda is a prophet whose verses have magical powers is an elusive way of dismissing the imagery or the figurative language characterized by a complex web of meanings and associations. *Alturas* may evoke a prophetic mode and tone by stressing that the poet is the spokesperson of the dead and the forgotten victims of history, yet it returns to the past not the future. Eliot reacts against the Romantic notion of the poet prophet with his allegoric character in *The Waste Land*, Tiresias. An old, blind, wise, foreteller of the future, Tiresias is the visionary of Sophocles' trilogy, *Oedipus the King, Oedipus at Colonus,* and *Antigone,* as well as the poet in Eliot's text, who is lost in Modernity and its ruins. Tiresias is "multiplied" through the poetic voices of *The Waste Land*, just as Whitman's speaker in *Leaves of Grass* and Neruda's speaker in *Alturas* are "multiplied" to be able to see themselves in everyone. I insist, as Santí does in his introduction, that the prophetic mode is a rhetorical move. Neruda may dress himself as a prophet and may transgress the role itself, but the criticism regarding his works need not reduce his poetics to Romantic versions of the poet.

In Neruda's poems on ruins, his neo-Romantic vein in search of a different poetic idiom is not as significant as his interest in Quevedo. When the intimist sensibility was becoming stale and the Romantic metaphors exhausted, the Spanish Generation of '27 and Latin American poets like Vallejo, Neruda, and later on Paz, found challenge and innovation in Baroque aesthetics. The search for literary and historical origins led the Spanish and Latin American Avant-garde poets to reread their Golden Age poets: Caro, Góngora, and Quevedo. It is possible that, among other things, Neruda's rereading of Quevedo, revealed in his selection of *Sonetos de la muerte* published in *Cruz y Raya* in December 1935, as well as *Viaje al corazón de Quevedo*, a lecture he gave in 1943 in Santiago, offered a transition from his more self-centered poems in *Residencia I* to his gradual immersion in social and political causes in *Residencia II* and *III*. Pring-Mill explains how in his *Viaje* "Neruda makes clear that Quevedo's neo-stoicism seemed to offer a way out of his personal horror at the inexorable quality of time and death, which dominated many poems of *Residencia*" (xxiv). In *Viaje*, Neruda actually describes his reading of Quevedo as "una experiencia viva." Furthermore, he maintained a poetic dialogue with the Spanish poet until the end of his life, as exemplified by "Con Quevedo, en primavera" from the posthumous collection *Jardín de invierno* (1974). Neruda distinguishes the stoic teachings of Quevedo's poems on death: "Quevedo me dio a mí una enseñanza clara y biológica… Si ya hemos muerto, si venimos de la profunda crisis, perderemos el temor a la muerte. Si el paso más grande de la muerte es el nacer, el paso menor de la vida es el morir" (*Viaje al corazón de Quevedo* 14). As I will discuss in further detail, *Alturas de Macchu Picchu* revives the personal crisis in the beginning of the speaker's journey, in which death overwhelms him. Throughout his ascent and his immersion in the collective historical conscience of the place, he is able, with Quevedo's teachings, to embrace death as a form of revelation and integration with the other, the dead, the workers. *Alturas de Macchu Picchu* uses the natural metaphors of rebirth with the seeds that will bloom again, but Neruda's sense of rebirth reveals his materialist vision of history in which the workers re-emerge in the work itself and in their identification with contemporary workers. In this way, Quevedo's stoicism serves as a powerful tool against the melancholic entrapment of personal anguish and fear of death, and it is easily integrated in Neruda's poetic search for a "nosotros," the community.[34]

In *Alturas de Macchu Picchu,* Neruda penetrates the earth searching for the roots, the origins of American society, to delineate what Latin American society should not forget: its historical past.[35] The disillusioned poet, traumatized by the Spanish Civil War and World War II, wants to find solace in the overwhelmingly secluded site of the Inca ruins. Unlike the European ruins, the Inca ruins seem alienated from the modern world and protected from modern wars, and they motivate the speaker to embrace a journey toward the past. The search for the origins of Latin American history is portrayed through the initial image: "como una espada envuelta en meteoros, / hundí la mano turbulenta y dulce / en lo más genital de lo terrestre" (canto 1, 19). The act of knowledge is represented as a sexual act, where the sword and the hand are the means of penetrating the earth in a sensual, violent way. The speaker manifests his pursuit for the "eternal," the cultural and natural roots of

Latin America, in his desire to reach the core of things. Slowly, "descendí como gota... como un ciego, regresé al jazmín de la gastada primavera humana" (19). The descent necessary for reaching the heights is also a return to the sources, to death, almost a Platonic enterprise of self-reflection. His descent and his blindness will allow him to ascend and to truly "see," as the foreteller Tiresias, but Neruda's speaker is closer to Dante's traveler, who gets lost in the beginning of his journey only to find his way with Virgil's help in the *Divine Comedy*.[36]

In Neruda's *Alturas*, we find the speaker seeking the "eternal" in both the modern city and in the ancient ruins: "cuántas veces en las calles de invierno de una ciudad o en un autobús en el crepúsculo... me quise detener a buscar la eterna veta insondable..." (canto 2, 20). In the Baudelairean city of dusk, authenticity is unattainable, and the speaker only encounters "un racimo de rostros o de máscaras" (21). His quest for "lo indestructible, lo imperecedero, la vida" (21) has to leave behind his melancholic wanderings around the modern city, his own *Residencia en la tierra,* to be able to integrate himself into the natural and the historical landscape of Machu Picchu. In canto 3 the speaker evokes the "muerte pequeña" of everyday life in contrast with the "muerte poderosa" in canto 4. The "muerte pequeña" entangles the speaker in the anguish of empty events that fall into oblivion: "El ser como el maíz se desgranaba en el inacabable / granero de los hechos perdidos..." (21). The presence of Quevedo's stoic vision of death is recaptured in these verses where people spend their lives waiting for death: "todos fallecieron esperando su muerte, su corta muerte / diaria..." (21). La "poderosa muerte" allows him some sort of transformation or renovation. The personal and poetic crisis expressed in the poems of *Residencia en la tierra* pushes him to the pit: "por calle y calle, río y río, / ciudad y ciudad... rodé muriendo mi propia muerte" (canto 4, 22). The petrification of the speaker is elaborated as paradoxical: the speaker, immobilized, dies like a stone that moves, a rolling stone in agony. By the end of canto 5, the speaker is able to liberate himself from the anguish of an insignificant and unredeeming death.

The tripartite structure of *Alturas* has been thoroughly commented upon by critics; I will, therefore, only mention briefly how the speaker's journey is linked to Dante's *Divine Comedy*.

From canto 1 to canto 5, Neruda's speaker remembers, using the past tense, his poetic phase as a neo-Romantic poet entrapped in the *Hell* of melancholia, and he descends into the tempting net of death. From canto 6 to canto 9 we find the speaker's ascent to *Purgatory*, and we encounter both the present perfect ("he subido") and the present "miro." Hence, he has to sweat to reach *Paradise* and he exhorts the reader to join him: "Sube conmigo, amor americano" (canto 8, 25). *Paradise* is closer when he joins the dead from canto 10 to canto 12, but it is only truly experienced with a moment of illumination, the anagnorisis, emblematized by a collective rebirth: "Sube a nacer conmigo, hermano" (canto 12, 30).

The final rebirth in *Alturas* is preceded by what we may call "una muerte empática," when the speaker empathizes with the dead and the forgotten and is able to feel their pain, as modeled on the epic tradition.[37] The elegiac tone and the meditation on death characterize both Caro's and Neruda's texts—particularly the first part of *Alturas*. Goic suggests that a tone of lamentation predominates in Caro's "Itálica," while in Neruda there is a tone of consolation, marked by a sudden "rebirth." The echo "Cayó Itálica" underlines the nostalgic tone that permeates Caro's poem, while in *Alturas* the city is very much there; what has disappeared is not so much Machu Picchu but its objects: "porque todo ropaje, piel, vasijas, / palabras, vino, panes / se fue, cayó a la tierra" (canto 6, 24). The fall in both poems has different connotations. In Caro's text, Itálica falls from greatness into almost historical oblivion; the only possible rebirth is that of San Geroncio's remains if they were to be miraculously found by the archaeologist. In Neruda's poem, the rebirth is a moment of anagnorisis, a kind of revelation provoked by his ascent to the Inca city and his encounter with the lost but recovered pre-Columbian origins—no traces of nostalgia remain in the last cantos.

In his biographical account of his visit to Machu Picchu, Neruda also mentions his emotional reaction once he visited the ruins: "En la soledad de las ruinas la muerte no puede apartarse de los sentimientos" ("Algo sobre mi poesía y mi vida" 13). In Machu Picchu the lyrical voice senses the eternal side of things, "una permanencia de piedra y de palabra" (canto 7, 24) and sees in the ruins the representation of a collective death:

"os desplomasteis como en un otoño en una sola muerte." The implacable death of *Residencia en la tierra* and *España en el corazón* prepares the ground for *Alturas de Macchu Picchu*. The poem is not only an allegory of his journey to the center of Latin American history, but it is also an allegory of his own poetic oeuvre and the evolution through which it went. *Alturas* is an allegory that takes one through a poetic and a historical journey to the Latin American past, the pre-Columbian past. Machu Picchu embodies a "petrified history."[38]

In Machu Picchu, Neruda realizes that his *Canto General de Chile*, which he had started after his father's death in 1938, had to be expanded and opened to the rest of Latin America to transcend national frontiers to other regions that were themselves the product of a colonial history. Neruda recalls how reaching the ruined Inca city made him feel part of a lost past, a center of culture that was now in the margins, covered by jungle:

> Me detuve en el Perú y subí hasta las ruinas de Macchu Picchu. Ascendimos a caballo... Desde lo alto vi las antiguas construcciones de piedra rodeadas por las altísimas cumbres de los Andes verdes. Desde la ciudadela carcomida y roída por el paso de los siglos se despeñaban torrentes. Masas de neblina blanca se levantaban desde el río Wilcamayo. Me sentí infinitamente pequeño en el centro de aquel ombligo de piedra; ombligo de un mundo deshabitado, orgulloso y eminente, al que de algún modo yo pertenecía. Sentí que mis propias manos habían trabajado allí en alguna etapa lejana, cavando surcos, alisando peñascos. (*Confieso que he vivido* 235)

Neruda's narration of his personal experience in the Inca city signals the structure of the poem after he ascends and encounters the ruins and the river, the empty city of stones, which carries the presence of the workers who constructed its buildings. Neruda's identification with the working people in the Inca past motivates him to identify with the working people in other parts of contemporary Latin America: "Me sentí chileno, peruano, americano. Había encontrado en aquellas alturas difíciles, entre aquellas ruinas gloriosas y dispersas, una profesión de fe para la continuación de mi canto" (235).

In *España en el corazón*, the speaker is the witness to the atrocities of the Civil War, the communicator, and he demands that we also become witnesses. Throughout *Alturas*, the speaker wants to become a witness, a translator, and an interpreter. The river Urubamba, known by its Andean name of Wilkamayu, precedes the lyrical voice in this task. In canto 8, the river Wilkamayu is evoked as a vehicle of communication with the past and the entrails of the earth. Neruda's apostrophe to the river alludes to the poetic use of rivers as the only permanent witnesses to history and the passage of time in the topos of ruins. For example, in Góngora's "A Córdoba ¡Oh excelso muro, oh torres coronadas!" the Guadalquivir is described and apostrophized as "¡Oh gran río, gran rey de Andalucía...!"; and in Quevedo's "A Roma sepultada en sus ruinas" the river is evoked in a more solemn, tragic tone as the sole survivor of history, whose waters also serve as a metaphor of the tears, the pain of a ruined Rome: "Sólo el Tíber quedó, cuya corriente, / si ciudad la regó, ya sepultura / la llora con funesto son doliente." The paradox is that although the river's fluency reminds us of the brevity of life, the constant presence of the Tiber or the Guadalquivir in both Rome and Córdoba, respectively, makes them metaphors of the "eternal."[39] In *Alturas,* Neruda stresses the ability of the river to speak through the alliteration of *o* in "Oh, Wilkamayu, de sonoros hilos," trying to recapture the rhythm of the river. Its musicality is suggestive especially when the speaker transforms its sounds into a language he must decipher: "qué idiomas traes a la oreja apenas / desarraigada de tu espuma andina?" (25). The river is the blood of the land, the artery that gives it life:

> Qué dicen tus destellos acosados?...
> Quién va rompiendo sílabas heladas,
> idiomas negros, estandartes de oro,
> bocas profundas, gritos sometidos
> en tus delgadas aguas arteriales? (26)

The personified river has the power to reveal and conceal—witnessing means remembering. The lyrical voice wants to hear through the river the cries that were drowned in its waters. But no voices emerge from the river, and only the poet's imagined community of drowned cries remains.

The river in Neruda's poem represents the conjunction of nature and history; it embodies the presence of the past. Saúl Yurkiévich reads in *El Canto General* two creative forces: the mythical that suggests a return to the past; and the historical, which embraces a lineal notion of progress. Yurkiévich convincingly argues that Neruda wants his text to develop from: "el mito a la historia, de la oscuridad a la claridad, …de la soledad a la solidaridad" ("Mito e historia" 207). The poem moves from the loneliness of the wanderer through the dark streets that lead nowhere at the beginning of *Alturas* to the ascent and the commemoration of the Incan city, with all the epithets and surreal images of canto 9; and finally, reaching the realization that the city is the product of an unjust, pyramidal society in a sign of solidarity with the dead Inca laborers in canto 10: "Macchu Picchu, pusiste piedras en la piedra, y en la base, harapo?" (28).

The search for origins comes close to Caro's archaeological endeavors: "roer… rascar… la entraña hasta tocar al hombre" (28). The topos of *ubi sunt*, so embedded in the traditional poems of ruins, is evident in Neruda's text. In *Alturas* we perceive it through the initial question "Qué era el hombre?" (21) and in various occasions through the form of a penetrating hand that seeks: in canto 1 when the speaker sinks his hand into the core of the earth; in canto 5 when he sinks his hands into the wounds of death: "y no encontré en la herida sino una racha fría / que entraba por los vagos intersticios del alma" (23); and finally, in canto 11 where he asks: "déjame hundir la mano / y deja que en mí palpite… / el viejo corazón del olvidado!" (29). The speaker's hand digs through land, death, dead bodies, and the self, seeking to find something to hold on to. He recognizes the dangers of idealizing the past and acknowledges that "la América enterrada" is also based on poverty and hunger. The apostrophes to the city in canto 10 show his challenge to the unjust society Machu Picchu also represented. Therefore, the imperatives acquire a particular force: "Devuélveme al esclavo que enterraste!" (28). Neruda implies that the slaves who constructed the city are also buried in its grounds, if not literally, metaphorically.

In his essay on *Alturas de Macchu Picchu*, Erik Camayd-Freixas traces the connection of Neruda's poem to the elegy. He remarks how the elegiac poems are characterized by three functions: exhorting the reader or passerby to stop, to honor the dead, and to meditate on death itself. Camayd-Freixas indicates that "Lo conmemorativo es casi tautológico, y la intención exhortatoria se advierte en el uso persistente del modo imperativo, ubícuo en toda la poesía elegíaca desde la baja Edad Media" (405). Thus, the imperative mode in *Alturas de Macchu Picchu* serves as a rhetorical tool to intensify feeling in the demand "Devuélveme al esclavo que enterraste!," as well as to establish communication with the dead: "Mírame desde el fondo de la tierra... / Mostradme vuestra sangre y vuestro surco" (30).

In the last stanza of canto 10, the apostrophized Antigua América is also personified as a "novia sumergida," a bride to the gods, a sacrificed woman; and the rite is characterized by the thunder of "tambores y lanzas" (29). This refers to the possibility that Machu Picchu was a place for adoration of the gods, where virgins were sacrificed.[40] América, submerged, drowned, or buried, is portrayed as a female victim, but more importantly these verses demonstrate that at the origin of Latin America lies a crime, and in the intestines of the antique past lies hunger. Neruda's Marxist ideological discourse developed in *Canto General* begins to find a poetic expression with the latent criticism in *Alturas* of a theocratic society and its closed hierarchical structure; this obviously distances Neruda's poem from Caro's "Itálica."

Neruda's *Alturas* uses some of the trademarks of the Baroque topos of ruins shared with Caro's "Itálica," but the best example that helps us differentiate the political implications of these two seventeenth- and twentieth-century poems is the catalogue of heroes. Caro's "Itálica," immersed in the rhetoric of the Renaissance, sings to the Roman emperors and authors, while Neruda's "catálogo de heroes" is made of "anónimos obreros."[41] Both poems encounter in the ruins the voices of the past, but each chooses to listen to a different social class. Neruda decides to dissociate himself from the nostalgic tone of the elegy and pays homage to the real forgotten figures buried in the ruins, in a very idealistic rebirth.

However, the individual identity of the workers is lost. They can only be identified through their work and their pains. Therefore, the speaker names his brothers as Juan Cortapiedras, Juan Comefrío, and Juan Piesdescalzos. The invitation to ascend in this collective journey is addressed to his "brother," but it is also an invitation to the reader in the hope that he or she will identify as well with the forgotten worker. Neruda wants to reach the lost Inca workers and wants to become them through poetry, just like Whitman becomes the oppressed when he asserts in "Song of Myself": "I am the hounded slave" (C.33, 225). Although I have privileged Neruda's revision of Baroque aesthetics and poems on ruins, I want to emphasize that the speaker in *Alturas* also represents himself in a rhetorical move as the Romantic poet priest aiming to be a voice of the voiceless through the poem: "Yo vengo a hablar por vuestra boca muerta" (30). Neruda has already used language with religious connotations—for example, he characterizes canto 9 with the rhythm of a prayer—but at the end of the poem it is clear that he depicts himself as a democratic prophet, in a rhetorical strategy to sound more truthful, more convincing.[42]

In canto 12, the speaker uses the imperative to ask for the story of the anonymous workers: "mostradme, decidme, señaladme, contadme…" (30–31). They are all homogenized into one death, one body, one voice, but the speaker's mission is to change their silence and their absence into language and presence that will keep them alive in the historical memory of the continent. In his essay on the apostrophe, Jonathan Culler asserts the capacity of the trope to invoke a creator of "potential presences": "…a poem may invoke objects, people, a detemporalized space with forms and forces which have pasts and futures but which are addressed as potential presences" (*The Pursuit* 149). Just as the ruins of Machu Picchu and "la América enterrada" are apostrophized, the Inca workers are invoked with imperatives that accentuate their "potential presence." Neruda intends to write through his own body: "afilad los cuchillos que guardasteis / ponedlos en mi pecho y en mi mano" (30–31). These verses reveal an ambiguous message: by taking the weapons of rebellion he becomes the vehicle of change or justice, as well as the victim who is sacrificed, the Christ figure. Furthermore, in the same final canto, Neruda has also recognized the many Christ figures that remain forgotten and unknown among the dead workers: "señaladme la piedra en que caísteis / y la madera en que os crucificaron" (30). The rebirth means a symbolic incarnation of the dead through the speaker's voice and body: "Hablad por mis palabras y mi sangre" (31). Neruda is not searching like Dante and Caro for God's redemption or even for a spiritual religious rebirth. Neruda's integration of the mythical and the historical, the epic and the lyric, has a political purpose, and in this sense, the collective renewal he seeks is not a religious but a historical, a political, and an aesthetic rebirth.

Although both Caro's and Neruda's poems end on a hopeful note that consoles the reader of ruins, they rely, nevertheless, on different notions of the "eternal" and the "original." In Caro's "Itálica" one may argue like Darst that the "eternal" is a religiously charged concept, represented in the undiscovered remains of a Christian saint. I would add that Spain's cultural "origins" in Caro's poem are not only found in Geroncio's traces but also in the memory of "los padres de la patria," Trajano and his lot. In Neruda, the eternal is attached to the mythical, violent origins of Latin America and all the nations it unites, which he places in Machu Picchu. Even if he suggests that the indigenous heritage is the "authentic" root of the continent, he integrates his poem in the Hispanic literary tradition of cities in ruins. In dialogue with both Baroque and Romantic traditions, Neruda situates *Alturas* within the literary legacy of poets like Caro and Quevedo, Dante and Whitman.

I have traced the connections between *Alturas de Macchu Picchu* and the Baroque poems of ruins, in particular Caro and Quevedo, to reflect upon Neruda's incorporation of tradition as well as his forms of experimenting and renovating the topos of ruins. Although I analyze *Alturas* mostly as a poem of ruins, I do not want to imply that its only subject is the ruined city itself. Neruda's poem combines elements from the epic and the lyric tradition, from the elegy and the topos of ruins. Hence, it is crucial to connect *Alturas* to Neruda's previous works like *Residencia en la tierra* and *España en el corazón*. His vision of Latin American history embodied in the Inca ruins is molded by the fresh memory of the ruins he faced during the Spanish Civil War.

Paz, Cernuda, and Neruda turned to the Baroque sensibility to look for a metaphoric language that would help them face death with its various manifestations and also criticize the destructive forces in their portrayal of a decadent, sordid scenario. However, as I have discussed in my second chapter, the Baroque is approached with a sense of ironic distance and in a parodic form. I do not argue that Neruda's *Alturas* is a parody of Baroque aesthetics, but by highlighting its major political and poetic differences in comparison with Caro's "Itálica," I underscore how Neruda establishes the critical distance necessary for the text to become a political and literary challenge to tradition. It is obvious that Neruda's *Alturas* is a modern poem, with philosophical and political concerns determined by twentieth-century wars. His teachings are not from the moral sphere, which condemns human vanity and its lack of consciousness of the fugitive nature of greatness.

In her book on Benjamin, Susan Buck-Morss indicates that the Baroque allegorists considered that: "the ruin was... emblematic of the futility, the 'transitory splendor' of human civilization, out of which history was read as a 'process of relentless disintegration'" (164). Buck-Morss quotes Benjamin to comment on how the Baroque ruin differs from his use of the ruin in *The Arcades Project* as "an emblem not only of the transitoriness and fragility of capitalist culture, but also its destructiveness" (164). Although this is the political discourse developed in *Canto General*, I cannot propose that a criticism of capitalist culture is evident in *Alturas*. But I do consider that Neruda's *Alturas* criticizes the pre-Columbian theocratic, pyramidal society to establish a historical connection with his criticism of contemporary capitalist culture.

Neruda's "message" is evidently a political criticism of a hierarchical society, what Camayd-Freixas refers to as his "conciencia social." However, when I discuss the echoes of canonical poets like Quevedo and Caro in Neruda, it is not a way of praising or attacking the Chilean poet as Juan Larrea does.[43] When I compare Neruda to the seventeenth-century poets, I aim to understand how in his search for origins he reads the nature and the history of Machu Picchu. Moreover, his quest into the past also delves into the literary and historical tradition that has molded his ways of seeing and perceiving, and therefore, has contributed to a vision of Latin American cultural identity. Neruda's poetic critique of Baroque allegories through the topos of ruins is mainly a political stance, similar to Benjamin's positioning when he re-evaluates his ideas on the German Baroque plays in his final and unfinished work, *The Arcades Project*. As Buck-Morss points out:

> But whereas the Baroque dramas were melancholic reflections on the instability of decay and disintegration, in

the *Passagen-Werk* the devaluation of (new) nature and its status as ruin becomes instructive politically... The crumbling of the monuments that were built to signify the immortality of civilization becomes proof, rather, of its transiency. And the fleetingness of temporal power does not cause sadness; it informs political practice. (170)

In their materialist reading of history, both Neruda and Benjamin share a political philosophy that criticizes a capitalist society in which they see that the modern economic system and its promises of progress are bound to follow the path of "natural decay," although Neruda's Marxist ideological discourse would not want to wait for natural decay to disrupt the voracious social and economic structure he attacks in *Canto General*. In the German Baroque dramas or in the English Romantic poems on ruins, melancholic feelings accompany these portrayals of the passage of time and history's ravages. Nonetheless, as I have examined in my study of Cernuda's, Paz's, and Neruda's texts, the modern poems of ruins that face the destruction of the Spanish Civil War, or in the case of *Alturas* that reacts to the remains of the Inca civilization, demonstrate that there is no place for melancholy in their revision of the topos, even if sometimes there is a reflective nostalgia that distinguishes the texts.

In Cernuda's, Paz's, and Neruda's poems, the speakers search for the eternal in the ruins they evoke, but usually not in a melancholic way. In their quest for the eternal, they find themselves as the interpreters of history, the witnesses that will rescue the hidden, unknown stories from oblivion. Cernuda, Paz, and Neruda are merging nature and history through their apostrophes, just as Benjamin and Simmel suggest in their reflections on ruins. The apostrophes to the moon, the river, the dead soldiers, and the dead workers seek to recover the lost origins, the lost ideals. Therefore, paradoxically nature and the victims buried in its earth illuminate the historical signification of the ruins. The poems dedicated to the Spanish Civil War convey a cultural mourning and portray their poetics of disillusionment, a desolate, pessimistic vision of history that will lead to emptiness and nothingness. In comparison to his representation of the modern Spanish ruins, Neruda's *Alturas de Macchu Picchu* offers a different interpretation of the topos, in which hope emerges from the "petrified" violent historical past.

The revelation of a common death in *Alturas de Macchu Picchu* gives the speaker a sense of a hopeful eternity. Neruda's message of solidarity and rebirth is clearly linked to the Marxist ideology he supports. Although the poem should not be read as a mere reproduction of his political positions, it privileges the workers as the main subject of history. While he realizes the social injustice of the Inca Empire, he also idealizes the indigenous working community. Is there an irrevocable continuity between all exploited workingmen? Could poetry really be a "medium" of communion with the past? Reaching the past through cities in ruins is always a fragmented, incomplete endeavor. Sometimes even the recent historical past is difficult to reconstruct through poetry. Yet these poems on ruins recapture the presence of the past, the forgotten history. In Neruda's *Alturas de Macchu Picchu,* the speaker and the reader culminate their journey with a vision of Latin American cultural identity, embedded in a poetics of solidarity and rebirth.

Chapter Six

The Effects of the Real

Reading Ruins in Modern Poetry

Ruins unveil the uncomfortable historical legacy of the city. Ruins are often treated as disposable waste or as valuable sites for the tourist gaze, but modern poems ultimately see ruins as the effects of the real. Echoing Baudelaire and Eliot, the modern city is dressed as the "Unreal city," constantly changing its wardrobe. Buildings are demolished and facades are remodeled according to economic speculation, architectural fashion, and urban planning. The poetic representation of the modern city in ruins is a paradox in itself. The modern urban landscape has always been in a process of destruction and reconstruction; its promises of progress contain its "unreality." The ever-shifting margins of the new city, its remnants, its derelict neighbor-hoods, its abandoned buildings, constitute the real casualties of modernization and the roads to progress. The map of the modern topos of ruins in poetry *historicizes* the remains of the past in a political and ethical critique of progress or war.

September 11, 2001, marked the beginning of the twenty-first century and is imprinted into the American psyche as a day of national mourning. Terrorists attacked New York's symbol of economic pride and power with airplanes, products themselves of modern progress. The attacks in New York and Washington, DC, prompted a collective shocking experience and exposed American vulnerability. The ruins of the World Trade Center signified a "historical awakening" to the real that installed a state of emergency.[1] But the historical awakening was a temporary wake-up call; life continues after the disruption.[2] After the collapse of the Twin Towers, the war on terrorism produced wreckage in other countries, not only in the United States. However, many saw in the destruction the need to "rise up," expressed in Bruce Springsteen's song, "My City of Ruins" —the ruins stirred a sense of solidarity with the people of New York.

How do ruins shape our ways of reading reality and representing history? Are ruins always a sign of finitude? The attacks in Madrid on March 11, 2004, provoked political indignation and defiance when a majority of the Spanish people felt manipulated by the terrorist attacks, and simultaneously, by the response of politicians in power, three days before the national elections. The destruction of the trains meant the death of many innocent civilians, but in the atrocious face of terrorism, it also enfused a firm political response in the people, whose general cry became "queremos saber."

Contemporary historical events determine the modern representation of ruins. Madrid's ruins during the Spanish Civil War made Neruda, a few years later, see beyond the natural and cultural communion of the isolated Machu Picchu. The overwhelming beauty of the site moved Neruda, but he decided not to evoke the past in a nostalgic restorative project. On the contrary, in his search for origins and his desire to reach the Inca past, he recognized the injustices and the violence buried among the stones. Though poetic ruins may divulge an apocalyptic vision of history and a poetics of disillusionment, in Neruda's *Alturas de Macchu Picchu*, they also became a source of redemption, hope, and solidarity with the victims of the past.

Modern poems on ruins can be read as historical allegories. By representing the destruction of a past, a city, an empire, they seek to rethink the historical traces of Modernity. In Latin American poetry, the main historical past that tends to be buried in the layers of ruins is the indigenous legacy. Rosario Castellanos's "Silencio cerca de una piedra antigua" presents the dilemma of the Latin American poet as the "voice of the voiceless," even when the speaker's "words" seem to be themselves fragmented and in ruins. The first verses of the poem depict words as ripe and untouched: "Estoy aquí, sentada, con todas mis palabras / como con una cesta de fruta verde, intactas" (61). Words are like fruits, not ready to eat, not ready to communicate. Words are also comparable to the stones of the past, the fragments of the ancient ruins that want to speak through her:

Los fragmentos
de mil dioses antiguos derribados
se buscan por mi sangre, se aprisionan, queriendo
recomponer su estatua.
De las bocas destruidas
quiere subir hasta mi boca un canto… (61)

The ruins of the Aztec and Mayan empires are projected in the fragments of the lost gods. Like Ozymandias's statue, the lost gods lie broken and forgotten, but want to be reconfigured and reconstructed into the statues they once were. Castellanos underlines the oral nature of the text with the mouths of the dead just as does Neruda in *Alturas de Macchu Picchu* to legitimize the poem as a song that speaks for the eroded and erased past. Yet the speaker in Castellanos's poem realizes that she cannot pretend to be the voice of the past, of historical memory. The speaker identifies with la Malinche and with a silent nature that has forgotten its own sounds: "Pero soy el olvido, la traición, / el caracol que no guardó del mar / ni el eco de la más pequeña ola" (61). The poem reinforces the frustrating incapacity to communicate with the past, the silence that permeates the ruins. When she sees nature taking over the ruins, the speaker understands that she is not a witness to history: "Yo no miro los templos sumergidos / sólo miro los árboles que encima de las ruinas / mueven su vasta sombra…" (61). History's layers are covered by trees, and the speaker decides to seek the lost humanity in its ghostly presence: "Pero yo sé: detrás / de mi cuerpo otro cuerpo se agazapa" (61). Unlike Neruda's *Alturas*, where the poet pointedly identifies the workingmen as the subjects of history, Castellanos's poem avoids a direct identification of the exact bodies, voices, or "antepasados" she refers to. However, "Silencio cerca de una piedra antigua," like many of the poems I have discussed here, from Caro's "Itálica" to Paz's "Petrificada petrificante," is a performance of a reflective nostalgia, and the presence of the voices of the dead in the ruins are ambiguously accessible, yet difficult to grasp and comprehend. These ruins, instead of merely representing the lost place of the dead, suggest that their inhabitants still live in them and haunt the poet: "Pero yo no conozco más que ciertas palabras / en el idioma o lápida / bajo el que sepultaron vivo a mi antepasado"

(61). The ancestors, who are buried alive, remind the poet of the tortures and massacres of the colonization of the Americas and the never-ending cycles of violence and oppression that preceded it. Castellanos's final verses reiterate the irony and the futility of a poem that sings to and for the ancestors using the words, the language that was used to silence them. Castellanos's poem depicts a random stone, which can also signify a tomb or a temple, a buried city of ancestors. In *Cities in Ruins*, I analyzed the diverse poetic representations of ruins, which like Castellanos's text often underscore the futility of attempting to reach and reconstruct the past as it was.

Another Mexican poet, José Emilio Pacheco also evokes the Aztec and Mayan ruins as emblems of the lost past, for example in "Ruinas del Templo Mayor," and "Ciudad maya comida por la selva"; but it is in his prose poem "A las puertas del Metro" where we find one of his most poignant criticisms of a devouring Modernity and of the dehumanized way in which modern city dwellers treat the homeless.[3] The poem depicts how this body in ruins in the doors of the metro is treated as waste: "Quisieran borrarlo como se barren latas de cerveza y envolturas de plástico, desechos deshechos de una sociedad capaz de producir estas imágenes" (*Tarde o temprano* 222). Modern society produces this situation of living in the margins, poor, ageless, and abandoned by the society, an idea reinforced by "las señoras de bolso y los señores de traje" who would rather eliminate his bothersome presence. His body in ruins, "desechos deshechos," is the ethical and political reminder of their complicity with an unjust, violent, unequal society. The homeless man, chanting rock songs with a broken voice, dressed in torn jeans and a run-down t-shirt that epitomizes commercial culture, saying *Have a Pepsi*, is looked at as if he were a used can. But as the speaker in the poem finally suggests: "Si lo viera Ernesto Cardenal le diría que se levante, que en él están los frutos de cuatro siglos de hambre, violencia y opresión; pero también el genio que construyó las pirámides e hizo posible Machu Picchu, el calendario maya, los códices nahuas, la escultura azteca y la obra de Nezahualcóyotl" (222). This anonymous man, a body in ruins in the doors of the metro, standing there in the margins, unable to get into the train of progress, symbolizes the priceless cultural legacy of the Aztec, Inca, and Mayan pasts. Pacheco establishes continuity between the modern ruins of an urban Latin America, in this case Mexico City, and the traces and treasures of pre-Colombian history. Though their poetry has not been studied here in detail, Castellanos and Pacheco confirm some of the patterns I have pointed out in the Latin American topos of ruins. They establish a symbolic continuity between their texts to the Aztec and the Mayan ruins and their poems on the modern city, to strengthen their political and ethical critique of a Modernity that treats its "wasted" subjects and the ruins of the past as mere waste.[4]

Throughout *Cities in Ruins*, I have argued that the poetic portrayal of the modern city in ruins is part of an aesthetic, ethical, and political critique of the new versions of progress, the process of modernization, the brutality of war or the erasure of the historical traces of the past. Jean Franco suggests that contemporary Latin American reality defies us to rethink our notions of community, identity, and subjectivity "from fragments and ruins" (*The Decline and Fall* 190). In response to this quote, Michael Lazzara and Vicky Unruh present their recent collection of essays, *Telling Ruins in Latin America*, as one that "forcefully argue(s) that ruins are dynamic sites… palimpsests on which memories and histories are fashioned and refashioned. Ruins, for these authors, do not invite backward looking nostalgia, but a politically and ethically motivated 'reflective excavation' (Unruh, "It's a Sin" 146) that can lead to a historical revision and the creation of alternative futures" (Lazarra and Unruh 3). The ruin as a palimpsest of sorts reveals the multiple cultural connections and intertextual allusions present in the texts I discuss. Just as in the essays in *Telling Ruins*, in *Cities in Ruins* we find that these poets' critique of progress resides in how "ruins challenge modernity's imposed narratives" (Lazarra and Unruh 8). As I have maintained, Baudelaire, Cernuda, Eliot, Paz, Neruda, and the other Spanish Civil War poets I have studied here, see in ruins "a material embodiment of change" (Lazarra and Unruh 1), political, historical, emotional, cultural; and they resist the possible temptations of a backward-looking nostalgia to transform their indignation and their reflections into constructive and critical readings of the present and the process of modernization.[5]

Throughout this book I have looked at how Baudelaire, Cernuda, Eliot, Paz, and Neruda use modern ruins to reread and rewrite their historical and literary traditions. These modern poems on ruins convey a poetics of disillusionment, close to Weber's "disenchantment of the world," and Adorno's "cultural pessimism." And yet, in most cases, their poems cannot be reduced to apocalyptic visions of history: for example, Paz's insistence on the reconciliation of opposites in *Homenaje y profanaciones* and *Piedra de sol* reinforces a mythical notion of time as circular. As Paz's poems demonstrate, not all poems historicize ruins in the same way. Paz's and Eliot's poems on ruins are more preoccupied with their intertextual dialogues, their parodic re-evaluation of the Baroque and the Metaphysical poets, that is, with becoming palimpsests of textual ruins, than with ruins as the stage of historical conflicts and contradictions.

Modern poems on ruins redefine themselves in relation to the Baroque and the Romantic literary traditions, but in different degrees and with distinct political intentions. As I have suggested, Baroque poems on ruins moralize about humanity's vain confidence on material existence, and Romantic poems project in ruins a reflection of a devastated self. In contrast, modern poems often represent ruins as historical allegories in their critique of progress or war. Drawing upon Simmel's and Starobinsky's essays, I have maintained that the Romantic sensibility erased the historical background of ruins to depict a harmonious meeting of nature and culture that stirred melancholic and nostalgic visions of the past. Modern poems parody or distance themselves from the Baroque and the Romantic topoi because the modern ruins are evoked as effects of the real, the semblance of "la mémoire du présent," that voices a political critique. As Žižek explains:

> The Real which returns has the status of a(nother) semblance: *precisely because it is real, that is, on account of its traumatic / excessive character, we are unable to integrate it into (what we experience as) our reality, and therefore are compelled to experience it as a nightmarish apparition.* This is what the compelling image of the collapse of the WTC was: an image, a semblance, an "effect," which, at the same time, delivered "the thing itself." (*Welcome* 19)

These poems project the ruins of the modern city as an effect, an image, and the object of destruction, the "thing itself." Being *in ruins* the city integrates into its landscape the continuous action of the destruction; Modernity embraces the idea of a city constantly in ruins with the prospects that it will become at some point "complete."[6] The ruins of the Twin Towers seemed *too real*, and therefore, they needed to be experienced as "a nightmarish apparition." In this book, I have analyzed how ruins have been represented as inhabited by ghosts or voices of the past as in the case of Caro's "Itálica" or Neruda's "Alturas," or they have been symbolized by a body in ruins in the modern urban scene, "a nightmarish apparition," as in Baudelaire's and Cernuda's poetry. The current memory boom and its fascination with ruins, recycling and reshaping them as artifacts of the past, respond to this spine-chilling effect of experiencing ruins as something that goes beyond the image, beyond the evocation, and the effects, to become the product of the Real itself.

Modern poems on ruins, especially the ones that emerge from the Spanish Civil War, tend to avoid a narcissistic, melancholic reading of destruction. There are, of course, some exceptions: Cernuda's *Las nubes* conveys a nationalist, nostalgic idealization of Spain's glorious past, tainted with melancholia and pain, typical of his political exile. As Noël Valis argues, nostalgia can signal survival, but "the effects of nostalgia tend to deterritorialize and dematerialize the original object or event, mythifying and enveloping it in an aura" ("Nostalgia" 130–31). Cernuda's historical allegory in "Noche de luna" deterritorializes the ruins. There is no specific site of destruction, no historical context that determines the ruins, and the moon and the speaker are the only ones who can appreciate the aura of the desolate landscape. The poem closes with the moon's melancholic gaze and an apocalyptic vision of earth.[7] This tension with the melancholic self is also projected in Cernuda's earlier works.

Baudelaire's and Cernuda's urban poetics manifest a tension with melancholic visions of the past in their ambivalent reactions to the changes of the modern city. They show in diverse ways both fascination and disgust with the new faces of the city. While Baudelaire privileges the beauty of the ugly faces of old women, blind men, hungry prostitutes, mad swans and lonely flâneurs, Cernuda's urban subjects are phantomlike, more abstract, more elusive figures of desire and disgust.

Baudelaire and Cernuda both project a poetics of disillusionment that represents a historical awakening in the face of the erasure of the past and its margins, and with the intention of reshaping how their present will be remembered. Benjamin's reading of the shock experience in Baudelaire's poetry led me to review the poetic city in ruins and its marginalized human ruins as producers of a traumatic historical awakening. Baudelaire's nightmarish apparitions are politically charged with a critique of Baron Haussmann's versions of progress and the endeavors of the late 1850s and early 1860s to reconstruct Paris, ostracizing and dehumanizing the city's poor, disposable subjects. The disintegration and dislocation of time and space are a result of the aesthetic contradictions that characterize Modernity, also prevalent in the Surrealist imagery of Cernuda's Avant-garde poetics and the aesthetics of a collective "yo en crisis" during the 1920s and early 1930s. Baudelaire's "Le cygne," "La chambre double," and "Rêve parisien" as well as Cernuda's "En medio de la multitud" and "Habitación de al lado," in their need to escape the effects of the real, highlight that art captures modern reality through memory and imagination—blurring the borders between the real and the ideal, the eternal and the transient, the external and the internal. In the second chapter, I find that Baudelaire and Cernuda show a strong preoccupation with the "mémoire du présent," the historical and aesthetic definitions of the present. While Baudelaire clearly reacts to Haussmann's transformation of Paris and how this transgresses into the aesthetic sphere, Cernuda does not refer to a particular city and is more concerned with the poet's historical role in the cosmopolitan city than in defining Modernity's aesthetic claims. These poems on the modern city in ruins are allegories of the continuous process of modernization and the possible destruction of the fugitive past.

Cernuda and Baudelaire are European poets questioning the present and the city's future outcome. In contrast, Eliot and Paz are two American poets, eager to recuperate the sixteenth century in the first half of the twentieth century, and hence, inscribe their works in the context of their European forefathers, in a poetics of a "return to the origins."[8] Moreover, while Paz conceptualizes his poetics of reconciliation as part of a Mexican neo-Baroque aesthetics, a cultural meeting point between the pre-Columbian legacy and the European tradition, Eliot considered himself closer to the European canon than to the American literary world. Eliot and Paz share poetics of disenchantment and the critique of modern progress in their poems on ruins, but instead of finding Baudelaire's and Cernuda's contradictory mixture of fascination and disgust, their urban poetics entangle an ironic, burlesque tone to concretize their own integration into the literary canon. Eliot articulates a conservative outlook on modern history as a process of disintegration. Paz's texts occasionally convey the need to insert history into his mythical, egocentric poetic discourse. Nonetheless, their works also offer an elitist critique of bourgeois conventions and capitalist progress. Ranging from works of the 1920s to the 1960s that emerge as a critique of the post–World War order and the Cold War in the case of Paz, the third chapter showed how Eliot and Paz merge their respective critiques of war and its very real ruins with their visions of the unreal, where poetry is the key to reach immortality. Eliot in "Whispers of Immortality" and *The Waste Land* and Paz in "Homenaje y profanaciones" reread their different though related English and Spanish traditions, the Metaphysical poets and the Baroque Golden Age, particularly Donne and Quevedo, and revisit the topos of ruins in diverse, burlesque ways. Interestingly, certain poems by Paz are more playful and erotic, more in tune with Donne's poems, than with Eliot's and Quevedo's complex intellectual web of metaphors and allusions. Eliot's and Paz's consciousness of the "presence of the past" in ruins shapes their intent to reconcile Modernity and Antiquity, the Baroque and the Modern, the European and the American literary canons to write the text that will become a literary museum, the precious repository of all those previous textual ruins.

In contrast with these priorities, the texts that emerge from the transatlantic poetics of solidarity during the Spanish Civil War aim to move the readers to political action and to provoke an ethical and a political awakening. Some of these texts may establish an intertextual dialogue with the tradition of the Baroque topos of ruins, but rather than portraying the urban scene as one of fascination or repulsion, and rather than assuming a burlesque, distant attitude toward the destruction, these war poems want to be read as historical testimonies. This traumatic historical event not only shaped Spanish history, but also changed and strengthened the bonds that connect Latin American and Spanish transatlantic poetics. The Spanish war transformed the conceptualization of the topos of ruins—writers from all over felt moved to take action and saw in those ruins the emblems of an imminent, very real threat. From Hughes's and Guillén's critiques of Fascism through its racist and imperialist discourse to the feminization of the city in ruins or of the Spain in ruins in Alberti, Vallejo, and Hernández, these texts in solidarity with the Republican cause serve as cornerstones for the cultural memory of the war, so fragmented and distorted by decades of Francoist dictatorship. These poems underline the need to testify as an ethical imperative, and through the use of the apostrophe, the poetic voices speak directly to other poets, to the Fascists, to Spaniards, and to their international readers, encouraging more political and economic support for the Republican cause. They exemplify what Merewether suggests with: "ruins stand for an ethical acknowledgment of that which has been" (34), and in the case of the war, what was happening at that very moment. These poems are not and should not be buried in the collective imagination as artifacts from the past; in the current debate of the memory boom, these texts serve as historical testimonies that defy the politics of amnesia and silence.

Modern poetry represents ruins as "concretizing" historical change. Twentieth-century poetry historicizes ruins in different modes. The modern poem on ruins also draws on formal conventions, unabashedly using apostrophe, anaphora, and paradoxes, and reformulating commonplaces in the topos, such as *memento mori*, *ubi sunt*, and *vox populi*. The apostrophes to the moon, the river, the dead soldier, or the dead workers symbolize the poem's desire to communicate with the "witness of history" and recover the lost past. However, the tone and the apostrophe to the moon in Cernuda's "Noche de luna" is much less demanding and defiant than the speaker's imposing tone in Neruda's *Alturas de Macchu Picchu* when he addresses the calm city in ruins and questions its buried violent past.

Initially, my examination of Cernuda's, Paz's, and Neruda's poems to the Spanish Civil War appeared to reinforce their literary connections, their formal approaches to the topos, their allusions to Caro's "Itálica," and their solidarity with the Spanish Republicans in the fight against Fascism. But throughout my analysis of their war poems, the complexities that differentiate them became more obvious. Cernuda's *Las nubes* revealed a poetics of disillusionment, very different from Paz's and Neruda's; his poems on ruins are melancholic, nationalistic, and nostalgic of an idealized past, a mythified glorious Spain. Paz's "Elegía" also expressed "cultural mourning," a form akin to Cernuda's work; but "Elegía" does not nostalgically remember the dead soldier, and the speaker's identification with the "tú" eludes a self-engrossed poetic discourse, trying to preserve the historical memory of the war victims. Nearly twenty years later, *Piedra de sol* alludes to the memories of the Spanish Civil War as an interruption of history, a pastiche that disrupts the neo-Platonic union of the lovers and Paz's final poetics of reconciliation. In contrast to Paz's ambivalent positions, Neruda's poetry aims to promote historical and political agency. Neruda's poems to ruins and his aesthetics of disillusionment ultimately convey a hopeful message; he insists on the poetic power of "un nosotros rehumanizado" and the working class as the main subject of history.

Madrid's ruins in *España en el corazón* (1938) transform Neruda's eyesight and insight, an "awakening" that is more a process than an abrupt change, a process that will culminate several years later in 1945 in *Alturas de Macchu Picchu*, as part of the beginning of his ambitious and thoroughly studied *Canto General*, which poeticizes his literal and metaphoric journey through Latin America. Neruda's poem to the Inca ruins enacts a search for the literary and historical origins of Latin America. Through my analysis of the modern topos of ruins, unexplored territory until now in a monograph, I underscore the ways in which these texts aim to become a medium for the production of historical memory, a means to read and translate the stones and the voices of the past.

Nostalgia lingers around ruins like the brown fog of the "Unreal City." Whether melancholic or nostalgic, subversive or ideologically conservative, representations of the modern city in ruins distort the past and deform the present. Nevertheless, Baudelaire, Cernuda, Eliot, Paz, and Neruda, in their own ways, uncover ruins as the effects of the real. Modern poetry on ruins can project an apocalyptic vision of history, a poetics of disillusionment and of cultural mourning, but it also produces a historical awakening that empowers these texts with political and historical agency. The shadow of progress does not always propel toward the future; the poetic modern city in ruins reanimates what falls in the margins, the buildings, the pieces that have until then remained forlorn.

Notes

Chapter One
Introduction

1. Slavoj Žižek alludes to Roland Barthes's term "L'effet du réel" to differentiate between how he describes the attacks of September 11, 2001, and Barthes's discussion: "… in contrast to the Barthesian *effet du réel*, in which the text makes us accept its fictional product as 'real,' here, the Real itself, in order to be sustained, has to be perceived as a nightmarish unreal spectre" (Žižek, *Welcome* 19). The Real also refers to the Lacanian term, which often seems elusive and enigmatic, but it is crucial in psychoanalysis to aim at an encounter with the real to understand the deepest roots of traumatic behavior. The repetition of "the nightmarish visions of catastrophe" (17), images that express our collective fears of destruction, suddenly become a *happening*, and those images or effects become *real*, demanding that we do not "mistake reality for fiction" (19). Although I do not use psychoanalytic theory to study the poetic representations of ruins, I often refer to the effects of the real to signal how ruins provoke in the spectator/reader an encounter with the consequences of modern progress or warfare—an awakening to reality.

2. Owen Barfield has thoroughly described the epistemological development of the word *ruin*: "In the classical contexts themselves it nearly always carries with it a larger sense of swift, disastrous movement 'ruit arduus aether' of a deluge of rain… In any case it is noticeable that, when the substantive 'ruina' came to be formed, it contains this last part only of the meaning of the verb… it could now mean, not only the falling itself, but the thing fallen" (113, 115).

3. José María Ferri Coll summarizes well the evolution of the topos (21).

4. Bruce Wardropper also discusses how *Le sentiment des ruines* is not found in the Spanish Baroque topos: "The love of ruins is something which arises in the eighteenth century, and reaches its climax in the Romantic period. It is not until the seventeenth century that the English garden begins to sprout artificial ruins… But in this as in so much else Spain avoids contamination with the Romantic tradition of the north" (305). The English and the French *sentiment des ruines* may not be manifested in the Spanish Baroque poems, and nineteenth century Spain did not exploit the Romantic topos of ruins, yet Spanish poetry was also fascinated by relics and abandoned monuments, and Bécquer's obsessions with human ruins and the metaphor of ruins and stones are notorious (see *Rimas* XLV).

5. See M. Morel, R. Foulché-Delbosc, and J. G. Fucilla.

6. For another relevant revisionist essay on the topic, see Begoña López Bueno.

7. "If Garcilaso's enormous influence in the sixteenth century turned poets' attention from Rome to Carthage, the baroque poets of the seventeenth century brought their vision back to Rome itself" (Wardropper 300).

8. Du Bellay's poem creates a chain of allusions, referring to Janus Vitalis's verses "Qui Romam in media quaeris novus advena Roma / Et Romae in Roma nil reperis media..."

9. As Gonzalo Sobejano indicates: "Del engaño de lo firme, en la primera sección, se pasa al desengaño de lo fugitivo, en la segunda" (106).

10. Emilio Orozco Díaz states that "las dos ruinas que con más frecuencia cantan nuestros poetas son las de Itálica y las de Sagunto" (134). Among the poets who write to Itálica's ruins are el Conde de Villamediana, Rodrigo Caro, Francisco de Medrano, Francisco de Rioja, and Pedro de Quirós.

11. Jean Starobinski reiterates that in the eighteenth century: "La poétique de la ruine est toujours une rêverie devant l'envahissement de l'oubli... On l'a remarqué, pour qu'une ruine paraisse belle, il faut que la destruction soit assez éloignée et qu'on en ait oublié les circonstances précises...: l'Histoire, le Destin" ("La mélancolie" 180). This effort to erase the historical traces of the ruined site is also prevalent in the English eighteenth-century fascination with ruins. Goldstein also refers to Lord Kames and his *Elements of Criticism* (1762) to emphasize how English Gothic Revival had a political purpose within the evolution of the topos of ruins. For Lord Kames, Gothic ruins were better than Classical ruins, placed in parks and gardens, because they "symbolize the triumph of time over art without the uncomfortable suggestion of military conquest" (*Ruins and Empire* 7).

12. Christopher Woodward clarifies that Byron inherited "the mouldering ruin of Newstead Abbey, a thirteenth century Priory near Mansfield, when he was ten years old... Pride in that inheritance was inseparable from a consciousness of his family's decay..." (57–58). Woodward maintains that this personal experience was formative and crucial for his development as a poet. He concludes: "It was not the warm south which made Byron a poet but the clammy mists of a ruined English abbey. His genius germinated in the damp shadows of ancient decay" (62).

13. The verses that follow this section corroborate this interpretation:

> ...And ever since, and now, fair Italy!...
> Thy very weeds are beautiful, thy waste
> More rich than other climes' fertility;
> Thy wreck a glory, and thy ruin graced
> With an immaculate charm which cannot be defaced.
> (Byron XXVI, Canto the Fourth)

14. Just as I consider that in the Spanish Golden Age ruins bloomed and thrived in poetry, I recognize that the Spanish Romantic poets did not dwell on ruined sites as much as did English Romantics. I do not mean to underestimate Gustavo Adolfo Bécquer's and Rosalía de Castro's works or their immense influence on the poets I discuss, in particular on Cernuda; however, it is key to note that Carolina Coronado is one of the Spanish Romantic poets who wrote an interesting poem on ruins, "En el castillo de Salvatierra," which I discuss briefly.

15. Among the Romantic poems on ruins, I would remark Wordsworth's "Composed among the Ruins of a Castle in North Wales," "Among the Ruins of a Convent in the Apenines," and "Lines Composed a Few Miles above Tintern Abbey."

16. Starobinski in his revision of the historical evolution of nostalgia, remarks that in the eighteenth century it was regarded as a mortal illness ("Le concept" 97).

17. Sophie Thomas argues in reference to the late eighteenth-, and early nineteenth-century reception of ruins that: "The ruins create a pleasurable illusion of a historical encounter—of an encounter with the historical as a leisure pursuit—while articulating the absence of history" (185).

18. Valis also refers to this part of Jean Starobinski's essay "Le concept de nostalgie."

19. Valis stresses that "the nostalgic possesses an intrinsically historical character, which is expressed through metaphorical properties. Nostalgia conveys metaphorically and emotionally historical change by signaling that something or someone is gone. It registers the past as past through a special form… of remembrance" (120).

20. Restorative nostalgia thinks of itself as "truth and tradition;" it feeds on nationalist sentiments with a desire to "return to the origins"; while reflective nostalgia "explores ways of inhabiting many places at once and imagining different time zones" (Boym xviii)

21. This is part of an essay called "Science as Vocation," originally a speech at the University of Munich in 1918 (see Weber, *From Max Weber* 155).

22. Weber's statement is in the context of this reasoning: "The tension between religion and intellectual knowledge definitely comes to the fore wherever rational, empirical knowledge has consistently worked through to the disenchantment of the world… For then science encounters the claims of the ethical postulate that the world is a God-ordained and hence somehow meaningfully and ethically oriented cosmos" (Weber, "Religious Rejections of the World and Their Directions," in *From Max Weber* 350).

Chapter Two
Urban Ruins in Baudelaire's and Cernuda's Poetics

1. Luis T. González del Valle provides an insightful analysis of Baudelaire and Spanish writers from the turn of the century, in particular Unamuno, Valle-Inclán, Martínez Ruíz, Antonio and Manuel Machado. Therefore, he does not discuss Cernuda's work. However, Emilio Barón discusses Baudelaire's presence in Cernuda's poetry in his *"Odi et Amo."*

2. See, for example, Friedrich.

3. I want to clarify that in this chapter I do not thoroughly analyze the "psychoanalytical awakening," although I mention it, as Benjamin's theoretical reasoning considers it fundamental. However, I have focused on the Benjaminian conceptualization of the term, since pursuing the Freudian or the Lacanian readings of "awakening" would take me on a different route.

4. Whether it was a success or a failure is debatable and has been the object of extensive research, for example in the works by T. J. Clark and Marshall Berman. Clark in his exemplary *The Painting of Modern Life* analyzes the historical and political transformations of Paris under Haussmann's rule. Clark recognizes that "By the end of the 1860s he (Haussmann) could boast that Paris had twice as many trees as in 1850… it had policemen and night patrols, bus shelters, tap water…" (38). However, Haussmann's project also failed due to his lack of faith in electric light, the cholera outbursts in 1867, and the imminent threat of tuberculosis. Clark continues to indicate its failures: "Haussmannization was unpopular in Paris: the defeat of the official slate in the city in the 1869 elections was bound to that fact, as was the decisive no which Paris gave the emperor's plebiscite in 1870…" (41).

5. Clark incorporates this quote in his first chapter of *The Painting of Modern Life,* in which he gives both versions of the journal entry. The 1860 version is not dramatically different from the edited version of 1891. However, the old version links London with the future Babylon, and in the 1891, Edmond de Goncourt rewrites it as the future American Babylon (34–35).

6. Sharpe affirms, "The city as representative woman forms an integral part of the contrast between heavenly and earthly states, and reveals much about the Western male views of the city as a female space to be mastered or seduced by, a space in which actual women are often rigorously controlled" (9).

7. As Richard Burton clarifies, "In Book III of the Aeneid the exiled Aeneas comes to Chaonia… where he encounters Andromache bewailing her late husband Hector beside an empty tomb that she has constructed beside the waters of a mock Simoïs…" Also see Burton for a more detailed analysis of the historical references to Andromache and the river.

8. Ross Chambers points to this reading of the river when discussing the structure of the poem: "For it is a 'stream poem' or 'poème fleuve' itself a 'Simoïs menteur' … that it is remarkable for the double openness of its structure" (156).

9. In "Le peintre de la vie moderne," memory is the defining factor, which molds perception and motivates the harmonious reunion of opposites: "Il dessine de mémoire, et non d'après le modèle" (Baudelaire, *OC* 2: 698).

10. Victor Brombert stresses the nostalgia of the text and how this stanza immobilizes Andromache: "Slave, widow, and wife—all are telescoped in one image. The stanza, in its powerful figuration of pain, mourning, and beauty, immobilizes a statuesque Andromache in a pose that continues into an eternal present" (99). The immobility of Andromache also suggests that she is a symbol of melancholia, literally and metaphorically paralyzed in time.

11. The references to the new Paris, the new Carrousel of the Second Empire, also situate the speaker in the margins, as an exile in his own city. Terdiman explains the historical implications of the allusion to the new Carrousel: "The Carrousel remembered in 'Le Cygne' in 1859 had been abruptly razed in 1852. Indeed, its demolition was the first, the founding act in the transformations that remade Paris under the Second Empire." The Second Republic wanted to demolish the old Carrousel for low-cost housing for workers, while Napoleon III did it for the grand remodeling of the rue de Rivoli. The old Carrousel, however, was "where a group of artists who had made a strategic investment in representing themselves as figuratively homeless in Paris *felt at home*. For this segment of the nascent avant-garde, the razing of the quartier was a symbolic eviction—an exile" (116).

12. Jauss pinpoints the urban estrangement and the emotional chaos, produced by the modern city in ruins: "After the paradoxical and abrupt change in expectation aroused by the sentimentally evoked 'vieux Paris' (ll. 7–8), that world appears as chaotic, smashed 'forme d'une ville,' as the disorderly, desolate burial ground of a vanished past..." ("On the Question of 'Structural Unity,'" *Aesthetic Experience* 249).

13. Starobinski analyzes the poem as an epitome of Baudelaire's aesthetics of melancholia: "'Le Cygne,' ce grand poème de la mélancolie, conjugue l'acte de pensée et l'image de la figure penchée" (*La mélancolie au miroir* 56).

14. Claude Pichois, in the edited notes on this poem, indicates that in 1846 there was a newspaper story in which four wild swans entered les Tuileries searching for the pond, and they stayed there until it was filled with water (in Baudelaire, *OC* 1: 1005).

15. As Hugo Friedrich proposes, "Baudelaire knew that a poetry suitable to his time could be achieved only by seizing the nocturnal and the abnormal: they constitute the only place where the self-estranged soul can produce poetry and escape the triviality of 'progress,' the disguise of a terminal era... Baudelaire defined progress as 'the progressive decay of the soul and the progressive domination of matter'" (25).

16. Terdiman also emphasizes that in 1859 Napoleon III offered amnesty to the opponents of the regime. Hugo could return but he *chose* exile. As Terdiman so eloquently suggests, "Amnesty thus attempts to induce a State-mediated *amnesia*, to upset the process of rememoration, the story told about the past, the very substance of signification itself" (108).

17. Baudelaire's melancholia plays a crucial role in his critique of progress, which some critics like Elizabeth Wilson have read as hostility

to urbanization that was felt by people from diverse political standpoints. "Hostility to urbanization was more likely to come from opposite ends of the political spectrum. On the Left, Engels was deeply critical not only of the slum and factory conditions... but equally of the indifference and selfishness... Right-wing critics of urban life equally harked back to an organic rural community. They feared the way in which the break-up of traditions in cities led to the undermining of authority, hierarchy and dignity" (91).

18. Paul Valéry, in an essay on Baudelaire, indicates that he grew up as a poet under the umbrella of Romantic icons like Lamartine and Hugo, and yet, "His literary existence provoked and nourished by them... is however, necessarily dependent upon negation, upon the overthrow and replacement of those men" (8).

19. Rousseau, Coleridge, and Hugo, among others, explore diverse notions of the grotesque beauty that determines Baudelaire's own aesthetics of the bizarre and the grotesque. But as Virginia E. Swain argues, "Baudelaire builds on and yet departs from Rousseau's theory and practice to create a new, modernist idiom... Both Baudelaire and Rousseau wrote under repressive governments whose censorship practices affected them directly, and both adopted a stance toward the grotesque that reflected their opposition to these regimes. But if Rousseau wanted to do away with the grotesque and, implicitly, the absolute monarchy that sponsored it, Baudelaire welcomed the grotesque, which he understood as a principle of instability or a destabilizing force. For Baudelaire, the grotesque was a subversive force in oppressive times" (6–7).

20. José Miguel Serrano de la Torre indicates that Cernuda's fusion of the mythical and the epic with his personal experience in his lyrical work links him to the Romantic techniques (100–01).

21. For Cernuda's vision of ruins, Bécquer and Eliot are also key readers of Modernity, whose works serve as bridges among different time periods and cultural backgrounds.

22. Cernuda's gaze "podría parecer anacrónica, si no aportara su propia variante... su propia adopción de la multiplicidad" (Fernández Cifuentes, "Miradas" 167).

23. Eliot's influence on Cernuda's work is evident and it has been thoroughly examined by critics from Fernando Ortiz and C. G. Bellver to Octavio Paz. Both Ortiz in "Eliot en Cernuda" and Paz in "La palabra edificante" discuss the relevance of Eliot's work in Cernuda's poetry. In one of her endnotes, Bellver also connects the two poems as I suggested: "When Cernuda went to England after his exile, he fell prey to the same shallow, staid society that Eliot endured and describes it much in the same way, as we can see if we compare passages from the 'Love Song of J. Alfred Prufrock' and from Cernuda's 'Lázaro' and 'Otras ruinas'" ("Luis Cernuda and T. S. Eliot" 107n3).

24. Emilio Barón also studies the connection between Baudelaire, Eliot, and Cernuda, yet he compares poems without analyzing them. See his "Retrato del poeta."

286

25. This is according to the Derek Harris and Luis Maristany edition, *Luis Cernuda: Poesía completa* 809.

26. This also resembles the situation of the speaker at the end of "Les sept vieillards," where the speaker's soul is like a small boat without masts in a limitless sea, overtaken by the monstrous city.

27. Francisco Ruiz Soriano emphasizes the destructive side of the modern city and how Baudelaire, Eliot, and Cernuda evade it through a melancholic gaze: "La ciudad moderna aparece… como elemento destructor… por eso los poetas proyectan su ideal y amor hacia el pasado mítico o lugares lejanos: en 'Le Cygne' de Baudelaire, la negra tísica busca con la mirada los ausentes cocoteros…; Eliot en *The Waste Land*, mira hacia los jardines de Munich donde se tomaba café…; y Cernuda en *Un río, un amor,* proyecta su amor hacia lugares lejanos como Daytona o Nevada…" (49). There is a nostalgic vein in these poems, yet they are also characterized by an ironic distance that recognizes the impossibility of reaching the past, mythic or not.

28. For excellent thorough studies on Baudelaire's prose poems and their connections with French literary tradition, see Jonathan Monroe, Barbara Johnson, and Fabienne Moore.

29. A few critics have mentioned the connection between "Rêve parisien" and "La chambre double," although I have not found a thorough and detailed comparative analysis. Some of the critics who have connected the two texts are Claude Pichois in the notes to Baudelaire's *Œuvres complètes* and Jean-Claude Susini in his "*Rêve parisien* de Baudelaire," p. 349.

30. In the Corominas dictionary it appears that *cataratas* has been used in Spain since the sixteenth century as a medical term to specify opaque, blurred vision.

31. The images of ponds, where the nymphs "se miraient" and the ices "reflétaient," are some of the examples that lead us to read this text as a visual poem. The metaphor of the dream, of the poem as a "tableau," is suggested by the text itself in the third stanza and by his ultimate cry of aesthetic exaltation: "Tout pour l'œil, rien pour les oreilles!" (Baudelaire, *OC* 1: 103).

32. In "On Some Motifs in Baudelaire," Benjamin states: "Baudelaire placed the shock experience at the very center of his artistic work" (163).

33. In a Lacanian reading of this text, the knocking at the door by the specter may be seen as the interruption of the Real in the fictional text. The imperative to face reality as discussed by Freud and Lacan is manifested in this prose poem, because in the end the dictatorship of Time takes over, and the speaker feels himself to be a slave of Life, of consciousness, of the repetitive knocking at the door. There is also the imperative that forces him to see his room, his social reality, as one marked by poverty and by isolation. Still, Baudelaire does not see awakening as an ethical imperative as would Lacan and Benjamin; the speaker in the prose poem wants to flee to the a-temporal sphere of the other room.

34. An extended study of this essay is provided in his book "*Odi et Amo.*" Barón has also published a biographical reading of Cernuda's work in *Luis Cernuda, poeta*, a revised edition of his book *Luis Cernuda, vida y obra*.

35. "Las imágenes del poema por su hermetismo hacen muy difícil su análisis y es por lo que sólo pretendo dar un sentido aproximado" (Capote Benot 154).

36. Capote Benot also refers to this line, "No estrechéis la mano," and considers it a part of the poem's surreal aesthetics: "La mano que aparece en la línea 9 es característica de la estética surrealista. Acordémonos de aquella mano cortada que aparece en 'El ángel exterminador' de Luis Buñuel. La mano que no se debe estrechar representa un oscuro temor, que cierra al poema más aún a la desolación" (87).

37. Although neither Silver nor Eloy Sánchez Rosillo clarify where they find out that Cernuda evokes Pompey's ruins, Sánchez Rosillo also proposes that "Las ruinas" alludes to a poem by Leopardi: "'Las ruinas'... describe una imaginaria visita a Pompeya (y que, a mi entender, está indudablemente inspirada, de una manera muy directa en 'La ginestra o il fiore del deserto' de Giacomo Leopardi)..." (151).

38. See, among others, Sánchez Rosillo and Villena (79).

39. Silver theorizes upon Cernuda's solipsistic vision, also pointing to personal traits like the ones suggested by Villena and Sánchez Rosillo and specifically to the frustrated desire that triggers so many of his poems: "Hence, on the ontic level desire is eros, failure, and solitude, whereas on an ontological level, separation, which is permanent, produces melancholy and eventually leads Cernuda to write poetic allegory" (*Ruin and Restitution* 104).

40. I will discuss in detail Caro's poem in the fourth and fifth chapters, in comparison with both Cernuda's and Neruda's works.

41. Miguel García Posada also indicates the influence of Caro and Bécquer in Cernuda's work: "Cernuda venía de Bécquer, pero asimismo de... Francisco de Rioja, y de Rodrigo Caro, es decir, de una lírica sensórea pero grave, plástica pero penetrante en los temas de la belleza y el tiempo" ("Cernuda" 40).

42. Although I denote many similarities between Neruda's *Alturas de Macchu Picchu* and Cernuda's "Las ruinas" (1941), I am conscious of the fact that Neruda wrote his poem around 1945 after Cernuda had published his. Even though there is the possibility that Neruda read it, I am not certain that he did. I actually believe that the similarities that unite both poems have more to do with their respective readings of Caro and Quevedo.

43. Although I agree with Colinas in finding a connection between the monumental ruins, the tombstones, and the human ruins, I consider that Cernuda's cemetery poems, to which he is referring as well, portray a different vision of death—one that is closer to and more harmonious with nature, suggested in the garden (Colinas 136).

44. Jiménez, *El Sol*, qtd. in Díez de Revenga 148.

45. Valéry signals Baudelaire's visceral reaction against French Romanticism: "He arrived at man's estate when Romanticism was at its height; a dazzling generation was in possession of the Empire of Letters. Lamartine, Hugo, Musset, Vigny, were masters of the day… He has been brought up on the authors whom his instinct imperiously orders him to wipe out" (8).

Chapter Three
Cities in Ruins: The Burlesque Baroque
in T. S. Eliot and Octavio Paz

1. Helmut Hatzfeld gives a detailed description of how the *pérola barroca*, a pearl with an irregular shape, comes from the commerce of pearls by the Portuguese in the early 1600s. At first the term had pejorative connotations of fraud, since it was a cheaper, less valuable type of pearl. But the word *barroco* evolved, and it is in the nineteenth century that it acquires a more positive and modern significance, associated with bizarreness and artificiality (418). The etymological meaning of *baroque* as an irregular pearl is also suggested in Corominas and Pascual (529).

2. Nelson Lowry opposes this etymological theory of the word *barroco,* arguing that it was a term used by Schoolmen to describe a kind of syllogism. Although I will allude to the definition of *baroque* as an irregular pearl for the purpose of my chapter and its structure, I consider that the different, various etymological theories of the word point to its slippery and ambivalent characteristics as a term. As both Hatzfeld and Lowry acknowledge, the term *barroco* has evolved historically and its definitions vary through time. Frank Warnke also summarizes all the controversial definitions of *barroco* and adheres to the reading of the term as a complex series of different styles joined in a period between the late sixteenth century and the middle of the seventeenth century. He indicates how the term is at first associated with art history, and later on in the late nineteenth century appropriated by literary historians (*Versions of Baroque* 3).

3. All of Paz's poem that I discuss are in his *Obra poética (1935– 1988);* quotes from Eliot's poems (including *The Waste Land*) are taken from his *Collected Poems 1909–1962.*

4. René Wellek openly criticizes Hatzfeld's argument, where the Baroque and "lo hispánico" become practically identical: "The metaphysicals are not reducible to Spanish influence, even though Donne may have traveled in Spain besides taking part in the burning of Cadiz. There was simply no Spanish poetry at the time which could have served as model for Donne" (105). I am convinced that Quevedo and Donne share common traits in their respective poetic sensibilities. Wellek reacts against the suggestion that Spanish seventeenth-century poetry is more valuable and therefore more influential than other European literary spheres.

5. In contrast, Eliot in his Clark Lectures in 1926, proposes that Spanish poets, especially Santa Teresa and San Juan de la Cruz, exert much more influence on Richard Crashaw than on Donne ("The Clark Lectures," *Varieties* 162).

6. Although Paz does not specify where this quote comes from, he does mention in the first part of his essay the biography of Edward Le Comte, *Grace to a Witty Sinner: A Life of Donne* (New York, 1965).

7. Thomas Docherty also confirms Paz's statements on Donne's interest in European artistic context, not just English literature: "In his travels he must have been exposed to the literatures of Spain and Italy, France and the Netherlands... He was the product of the culture of Europe as much as of the English and Catholic background..." (148).

8. "Las afinidades entre los 'metafísicos' ingleses y los poetas españoles es uno de tantos temas apenas tocados por la crítica... Aquí subrayo que los estilos nunca son nacionales... No hay una escuela poética inglesa, española o alemana: hay la poesía barroca, la neoclásica, la romántica, la simbolista" (Paz, "Un poema de John Donne" 96).

9. Michel Foucault stresses the obsession of modern thought with origins: "Dans la pensée moderne... ils ne pouvaient pas donc jamais énoncer véritablement leur origine... c'est l'historicité qui dans sa trame même laisse se profiler la nécessité d'une origine qui lui serait à la fois interne et étrangère" (340).

10. See Adriana Méndez Rodenas 36.

11. Roberto González Echevarría discusses Paz's aesthetic of the bizarre with regards to Lunarejo's reflection on deformity and what it means to be an "indiano" (*Celestina's Brood* 164–65).

12. Lois Parkinson Zamora avows that Carpentier's and Paz's recovery of the Baroque poets is comparable to Eliot's revival of the English Baroque, the Metaphysical poets (in contrast to the American transcendentalists' connections with the Romantics) (*The Usable Past* 208).

13. Jameson states that "the familiar split between avant-garde art and left-wing politics was not a universal but merely a local, Anglo-American phenomenon... In their attitudes toward history... the Formalists may be seen to have a far more positive and dialectical attitude than the American New Critics" (45–47).

14. Reyes also includes in his *Cuestiones gongorinas* an essay "Góngora y América" (1929). Also see: Dámaso Alonso's "Góngora y América" as well as Luis Alberto Sánchez.

15. Julio Ortega explains how the neo-Baroque narrative "no surge como una renovación de la estética barroca del siglo XVII, si no que supone una instauración de un orden nuevo, heterodoxo y vital." He asserts that "En la renovación poética de la prosa neobarroca... influye poderosamente la Generación del 27" (*La estética neobarroca* 6).

16. See Gerardo Diego's "Un escorzo de Góngora" and *Antología poética en honor de Góngora* and Jorge Luis Borges.

17. Borges mentions in "Examen de un soneto de Góngora" Zidlas Milner's *Góngora y Mallarmé,* and Reyes refers in *Cuestiones gongorinas* to two seminal essays by Gourmont in *Prómenades Littéraires* (4th, Paris, 1912) and by Francis de Miomandre in *Hispania* (1918).

18. Sen stresses how poets like Baudelaire and Donne mark Eliot's poetry (91).

19. Paz specifies that he read the translation of *The Waste Land* when he was 17 years old and it appeared in the literary magazine *Contemporáneos* in 1930 with a prologue by the translator, Enrique Munguía. He reaffirms his interest in the poem by recalling how he searched for another translation, published in Madrid. Although Paz does not clarify which translation he is referring to, it is probably Angel Flores's *Tierra baldía* ("La vuelta de los días, T. S. Eliot" 40).

20. Paz emphasizes that: "Toda visión de la historia… contiene un metahistoria. La que anima a *The Waste Land* estaba y está en abierta oposición a mis ideas y creencias… Pero la fascinación persistía, ¿Qué me unía a *The Waste Land*? El horror al mundo moderno. Ante los desastres de la modernidad, el conservador y el rebelde comparten la misma angustia" ("La vuelta de los días" 41).

21. Eliot continues to write about Donne in the thirties. In an essay that commemorates the tercentenary of Donne's death in 1931, "Donne in Our Time," Eliot distances himself from his earlier commentaries on Donne, signaling Donne's lack of organization, which he also underlines in his Clark Lectures in 1926.

22. All references to Eliot's poems will be found in his *Collected Poems 1909–1962.* His poem "Whispers of Immortality" is on pages 45–46.

23. In "Eliot Re-Donne," Aileen Shafer draws attention to the imagistic similarities between Eliot's "Love Song of Alfred Prufrock" and Donne's "Valediction: Forbidding Mourning" (40).

24. Quevedo also exploits this double meaning of sense, and love is as a force of ruinous power in Soneto 109: "Amor me ocupa el seso y los sentidos… Todo soy ruinas, todo soy destrozos…" (*Poemas escogidos* 183).

25. Philipp Wolf traces back the modern crisis of memory to Donne's poetics (41).

26. Northrop Frye clarifies that: "In the age of Donne what Eliot calls sensibility was called wit, and what he calls an objective correlative was called a conceit, or something conceived. 'Wit' has a more intellectual sound than 'sensibility' or 'emotion,' and indicates why poetry of Donne's school is called 'metaphysical.' Its 'metaphysical' quality is actually a technique of fusing images and ideas which is deliberately strained and forced. Hence there is a latent irony in its conceits, a suggestion of the grotesque which seems conscious, and so intellectual" (30–31).

27. See Eliot's Clark Lecture III, "Donne and The Trecento," and Lecture IV, "The Conceit in Donne" (*Varieties*).

28. S. A. Cowan offers a hypothetical reading of the dog as an echo of Donne's work (97).

29. All references to Donne's poems are from his collection *The Complete English Poems*.

30. Eliot and Paz identify themselves with poets like Donne and Quevedo, since the threat to a masculinist order is even more acute in the twentieth century. The exclusion of women from their poetic canon, with a few exceptions like Sor Juana Inés de la Cruz, is just one of the symptoms that derive from their masculinist epistemology.

31. In the interviews and writings in which Paz discusses Eliot's legacy, he stresses Eliot's insertion of his poetry into *history*, responding to both the cultural and political context of the twenties, and to a very modern sense of anguish. Among other interviews, see Roberto González Echevarría and Emir Rodríguez Monegal's "Interview to Octavio Paz" and Manuel Ulacia's "Octavio Paz: Poesía, pintura, música, etcetera. Conversación con Octavio Paz."

32. Paz maintains that Lope and Donne are the greatest love poets from the seventeenth century, even if "Unir los nombres de Lope y de Donne puede parecer forzado: (ya que) el *wit* del poeta inglés está más cerca del ingenio de Quevedo que de la escritura de Lope... (y) que Donne fue un intelectual y un polemista como Quevedo..." Paz stresses in this essay his disappointment at Quevedo's moral pettiness and political ambitions. Quevedo "era un oportunista que cambió de bando varias veces, un escritor cuyos ataques y adulaciones estaban dictados por el interés... Falla moral pero también intelectual: el conceptismo oculta a la realidad, siempre irregular, con la simetría de los conceptos. El Quevedo político y el Quevedo moralista me decepcionaron..." ("Quevedo, Heráclito y algunos sonetos" 129).

33. Paz meticulously analyzes his own poem in "Reflejos: Réplicas. Diálogos con Francisco de Quevedo" (78–79).

34. In his essay on Donne and Quevedo, González Fernández de Sevilla discusses "Amor constante más allá de la muerte," affirming that the sonnet is structured around these antitheses (556).

35. This sonnet, "Amor constante más allá de la muerte," is included in Paz's poems (340), but all of Quevedo's poems come from his *Poemas escogidos*.

36. In *La Llama doble,* Paz analyzes closely Quevedo's "Amor constante más allá de la muerte," and he underlines that the final verses enact the "Derrota del cuerpo: ese polvo está animado y siente" (67).

37. All references to Rodrigo Caro's poem "Itálica" come from Elías Rivers's *Poesía lírica del Siglo de Oro*.

38. John Fein also signals Paz's allusions to Neruda's and Caro's poems in his essay on "Himno entre ruinas": "De inmediato todo parece sugerir la afiliación del poema con una tradición literaria que se extiende desde los clásicos griegos al barroco español (por ejemplo, *A las ruinas de Itálica* de Rodrigo Caro hasta llegar al Neruda de *Alturas de Macchu Picchu)*" ("Himno entre ruinas" 165).

39. Ramón Xirau sees in the juxtaposing stanzas the contrast between a "solitary" attitude and one that calls for a "communion" with others (ex. 5th stanza). I could connect this with Neruda's passage from "soledad a solidaridad" (Yurkiévich), but unlike Xirau, I do not read in Paz's poem a message of social communion. The end of "Himno entre ruinas" in a hopeful tone sings to the power of words, of fables, of poetry that may grow like flowers and fruits, and become actions.

40. Jason Wilson also points to Paz's move, dismissing "lyrical obscurity to seek intellectual lucidity," very much in the vein of Góngora and Sor Juana (50). José Quiroga also has an excellent discussion of Octavio Paz's work.

41. Fein also explains very accurately the transition between these two stanzas: "La transición a la caduca sociedad de hoy es anticipada por la referencia a los muertos en vida" (166).

42. Of the two critics who analyze "Petrificada petrificante," Martha Nandorfy is the only one who mentions but does not develop the poem's allusion to Eliot's work (Nandorfy 572). Alejandro González Acosta begins his analysis indicating that it is a poem of "profunda mexicanidad," which may be too complex for a critic who is not Mexican or who is not deeply familiarized with Mexican history (519–20). He does not comment on the relevance of Eliot's *The Waste Land* in "Petrificada petrificante," although he alludes to a very wide range of echoes, from Aristophanes' *Frogs* and Posada's dead imagery to general references to the Civil War and the Mexican revolution (522–23).

43. See Severo Sarduy.

44. José J. Arrom acknowledges that the "Barroco de Indias" "al saltar a su pasado… se topó con el mundo prehispánico… el barroco tenía esenciales rasgos en común con la visión estética y religiosa de los aztecas, mayas, e incas, en América se le aceptó como un inesperado reencuentro con lo propio" (66–67).

45. Peter Ackroyd in his biography of Eliot traces his famous self-portrait to Charles Maurras "who in 1913 was described as the embodiment of three traditions—'classique, catholique, monarchique'" (41).

46. See Celeste Olalquiaga.

Chapter Four
The Spanish Civil War:
A Transatlantic Vision

1. Also see Paul Preston, *¡Comrades!* and Preston, *Revolution and War in Spain 1931–1939,* as well as Edward Malefakis.

2. For a thorough analysis of the Soviet Union's role during the civil war, consult *Spain Betrayed: The Soviet Union in the Spanish Civil War,* ed. Ronald Radosh, Mary R. Habeck, and Grigory Sevostianov.

3. Sebastian Balfour has an excellent analysis of the connection between the Moroccan war and the Spanish Civil War, entitled *Deadly Embrace: Morocco and the Road to the Spanish Civil War.*

4. The volume *Víctimas de la guerra* avows that 140,000 Republicans were executed, victims of the war and of Franco's state repression. The number of casualties is still hard to ascertain not only because the undocumented are as important as the documented, and during the war the chaos of violence reigned, but also because contemporary scholars should not trust Francoist historiography, and the numbers in their archives (Juliá, *Víctimas de la guerra* 411).

5. Of the immense bibliographical sources on the civil war and the dictatorship, I recommend as a concise introduction Carolyn P. Boyd's article. For more thorough studies on Franco, the Civil War, and the dictatorship: Gabriel Jackson, *The Spanish Republic and the Spanish Civil War, 1931–1939*; Enrique Moradiellos, *La España de Franco (1939–1975)*; Raymond Carr and Juan Pablo Fusi, eds., *Spain: Dictatorship to Democracy.* In *The Franco Regime (1936–1975)*, Stanley G. Payne gives different numbers for the casualties of war and political repression, based on Ramón Salas Larrazábal's *Pérdidas de la Guerra* (Barcelona, 1977, pp. 428–29), (219).

6. This quote of Francisco Franco appears in Raymond Carr and Juan Pablo Fusi, eds., *Spain: Dictatorship to Democracy* (17). They also explain how the regime had three main institutionalized families: the "Nationalist" Army, the Falange, and the Catholic Church, and their political families were the integral Francoists, the monarchists, the technocrats, and the professionals (18).

7. José Alvarez Junco discusses how both ideological camps used and manipulated the nationalist discourse. Spanish Republicans also argued that the "Nationalists" represented foreign Fascist interests and were therefore "anti-Spanish." The use of the word *traitor* or *leales* versus *desleales* was also reappropriated by the "Nationalists," since Republicans always saw themselves as "leales a la República" and the traitors were the ones who had forced a military coup ("La guerra civil como Guerra nacional" in Malefakis).

8. F. González, "El Alcázar."

9. F. González, "El Alcázar."

10. Marín, "Las ruinas de Belchite," *La Vanguardia* 9 Oct. 2002.

11. For excellent accounts on the role of Spanish intellectuals in exile, see: Sebastiaan Faber, *Exile and Cultural Hegemony: Spanish Intellectuals in Mexico, 1939–1975;* and Michael Ugarte, *Shifting Ground: Spanish Civil War Exile Literature.* For a historical reconstruction of the complexities of the Spanish exile in diverse areas of study, review: José Luis Abellán, ed., *El exilio español de 1939.*

12. The memory boom in Spain and the polemic on the *pacto del silencio* has been amply discussed and analyzed. Among the many historians and critics, consult Paloma Aguilar Fernández's *Memoria y olvido de la* *guerra civil española*; Helen Graham's "The Uses of History" in *The Spanish Civil War* and "Coming to Terms with the Past: Spain's Memory Wars"; and Joan Ramon Resina's "Short of Memory: The Reclamation of the Past since the Spanish Transition to Democracy," *Disremembering the Dictatorship*.

13. José Alvarez Junco explains how the Republican newspapers and posters allude to the threat of the colonization of Spain. For example, he quotes the *ABC* on July 25th, equating the war with 1808, as the "Segunda Guerra de Independencia": "los rebeldes… ganosos de convertirnos en una colonia del más repugnante fascismo negro" ("La guerra civil" 586–87).

14. In her book on the representation and the role of Moroccans in the Civil War, Madariaga not only discusses the Insurgents' rhetoric trying to unite Islam and Christianity against atheism, she also analyzes something that has not been thoroughly studied before: the racist and xenophobe discourse that arises among the left with regards to the fear of the Moors (Madariaga 345–80).

15. On the fifteenth anniversary of the beginning of the Spanish Civil War on July 19, 1951, in Paris, Paz echoes Neruda's statements: "La fecha que hoy reúne a los amigos de los pueblos hispánicos preside como un astro fijo, la vida de mi generación. Luz y sangre" (*Obras completas* 433). Paz gave this speech in a meeting with Republican exiles, in which Albert Camus also spoke in solidarity with their political cause.

16. Among the many writers Neruda mentions, he distinguishes Paz: "Entre noruegos, italianos, argentinos, llegó de México el poeta Octavio Paz… En cierto modo me sentía orgulloso de haberlo traído. Había publicado un solo libro que yo había recibido hacía dos meses y que me pareció contener un germen verdadero. Entonces nadie lo conocía" (*Confieso que he vivido* 183).

17. In that book, Cernuda published "Elegía Española 1937" and "Elegía a la luna de España." I will examine the final versions of these poems published in *La realidad y el deseo*.

18. Although Philip W. Silver does not explain well why he questions Cernuda's commitment to the Republican cause, he stresses that: "La nostalgia por el Edén de Andalucía, Cernuda no dejó nunca de expresarla en su poesía, pero su patriotismo por la España republicana fue de corta duración" (*Luis Cernuda* 242). He might refer to Cernuda's exile in England and his lack of explicit poetic homages to the Republican cause, especially after *Las nubes,* although I think this does not make him less committed as an anti-Fascist. It is true that his nationalist phase (I am not referring to the Francoist nationalism) was short-lived.

19. Although I will not discuss it, W. H. Auden's "Spain" is one of the most famous examples of how the war was an event that not only affected Spaniards.

20. See Iván Jaksic, *Ven conmigo a la España lejana.*

21. Michael Thurston discusses Hughes's role as a reporter during the Civil War in "Bombed in Spain." Also see Barbara Dale May's "Poetry and Political Commitment: Alberti, Guillén, and Hughes" and "The Endurance of Dreams Deferred: Rafael Alberti and Langston Hughes."

22. Franz Fanon in reference to the Second World War scenario also declares that "an Anti-Semite is inevitably an Anti-Negro" (60).

23. Paul Gilroy, in *Against Race*, asks: "What place should the history and memory of past conflicts with fascism have in forging the minimal ethical principles on which a meaningful multiculturalism might be based?" (5–6).

24. See Mary Nash's *Rojas: Las mujeres republicanas en la guerra civil*.

25. Here Ugarte signals that the text is "anything but propaganda," in response to Arnold Rampersad, who condemns the poem as "maudlin," and in connection with Cary Nelson, who defends its complexity.

26. For a more thorough analysis of *El laberinto del fauno*, see my article "La guerra civil española: Entre fantasmas, monstruos y faunos."

27. For more thorough reflections on Transatlantic Studies and the redefinitions of Hispanism, see Sebastiaan Faber's "Fantasmas hispanistas," Brad Epps and Luis Fernández Cifuentes's *Spain beyond Spain*; Francisco Fernández del Alba y Pedro Pérez del Solar's "Hacia un acercamiento cultural"; Joseba Gabilondo's introduction to *Arizona Journal of Hispanic Cultural Studies*; Julio Ortega's "Post-teoría"; Joan Ramon Resina's "Cold War Hispanism"; and Jill Robbin's "Globalization."

28. He establishes a difference between literary and political discourses, arguing that in contrast to poetry, the language of politics "freezes identities into static definitions" (25–26).

29. The cartoons and prints are published and discussed by José Alvarez Junco in *Mater Dolorosa*.

30. Only one of the plays, *El hombre que murió en la guerra*, had a premier in 1940, when Antonio Machado had already died (Albornoz 12).

31. There are particularly three poems in Antonio Machado's *Campos de Castilla* that precede "El mañana efímero" and criticize the decadent bourgeoisie, product of the *Restauración*, and provincial Spain in ruins: "El hospicio," "Campos de Soria," and "El mañana efímero" (*Campos de Castilla* 108, 135, 213). In *Historia de las dos Españas,* the well-recognized historian Santos Juliá offers a thorough, provocative historical reading of the two opposing visions of Spain, the "old" and the "new."

32. In *Poesías de guerra de Antonio Machado*, Aurora de Albornoz publishes along with her essay his poems on the Civil War, including nine sonnets. The sonnet I discussed earlier (#77), is numbered in this volume as Sonnet 6.

33. Sara M. Saz explains the religious allusions and language in the collection as part of his cultural baggage, and she stresses that this is part of his Marxist aesthetics (1092).

34. Julio Vélez asserts that "España es el símbolo de la utopia siempre presente en César Vallejo." In this way he argues for the book's continuity with Vallejo's other poetry collections ("Vallejo, Neruda, Guillén: España y sus constelaciones en la poesía de 1937" 109).

35. Sara M. Saz discusses more fully Vallejo's, Juan Marinello's, and Nicolás Guillén's interventions in the Congress and how they reiterated the relevance of the Spanish Civil War to Latin Americans in her "'Yo, hijo de América… muero por ti': Repercusiones de la guerra civil española en la poesía iberoamericana."

36. In reference to Xavier Abril's *Vallejo*, Marlene Gottlieb compares Neruda's *España en el corazón* and Vallejo's *España, aparta de mí ese cáliz* to conclude that "mientras que Neruda concibe la guerra civil como algo fuera de sí, algo que le conmueve y le incita a actuar, Vallejo ve la guerra como el reflejo más fiel de su propia vida" (153). She has argued that in contrast to Neruda, "Para Vallejo, en cambio, la guerra no le arranca de un ensimismamiento egocéntrico" (146). Gottlieb reads them as neo-Romantics who are both committed to the Republic, although Neruda manages to break free from his solipsistic stage, while Vallejo sees in the war—as Romantics often do in their poems on ruins—"su propia tragedia humana" (147). Although I appreciate her critical work, I disagree with this reading of Vallejo's *España*, since a tormented first-person speaker (evident in Neruda as well) is not the protagonist in most of the poems of this collection, where the texts try to give voice and to establish a dialogue with a varied community: from volunteer militiamen and anonymous children to Pedro Rojas, an emblem of the Republican worker and soldier, victim of the Fascist repression.

37. Georgette de Vallejo asserts that the collection *España, aparta de mí ese cáliz* was written from September to November, 1937 and not also into 1938 as has been asserted in print (5).

38. Salvador Jiménez Fajardo emphasizes in his analysis of this poem: "It is the city that gives birth to the poet as it gives birth to its own new being" ("Icons of War" 124).

39. Robert Havard suggests that this violence against the self reveals a desire to be "impersonal": "whether out of a feeling of inadequacy in the face of such momentous events, or a reluctance to intrude upon the grief of others, he seeks to lose his poetic persona, 'arrancarme de cuajo la voz'… As a communist, he knows that mass suffering is not to be appropriated by an individual… Only by identification with those who suffer is the poet validated" (223).

40. Wesseling argues that "the poet wants to leave the 'sótanos lívidos' of the alienation of the past in order to 'walk the city' ('pisarte')" (64).

41. Luis García Montero notes the "paulatina toma de postura política" in Alberti's work ("La poesía de Rafael Alberti" 71). For an excellent introduction and analysis of how these poets' social and political commitments develop throughout the nineteen thirties, see Anthony Geist.

42. Jiménez Fajardo also shows the relevance of the poetic structure in this journey: "the poet's gaze identifies, incorporates the multiple wounds of war. The exploration follows concentric circles from the city's outer limits (stanza 2), to streets and neighborhoods (stanza 3), to vacant homes (stanza 4), and then outwardly, as vulnerable body on the plain, extended for death or for birthgiving (stanza 5)" ("Icons of War" 125).

43. Rafael Alberti narrates this experience in his memoir, *La arboleda perdida* (98–101). For a fascinating analysis of the Communist memoirs that emerge after the Spanish Civil War, see Gina Herrmann.

44. See also "A los intelectuales antifascistas del mundo entero," *El Sol* [Madrid], 19 Nov. 1936.

45. Vicente Aleixandre recalls how he first came across Hernández's name. Hernández wrote to Aleixandre asking very respectfully for a copy of his book, since Hernández could not afford it, and signed the letter "Miguel Hernández, pastor de Orihuela" ("Evocación de Miguel Hernández" 20).

46. See Agustín Sánchez Vidal's *Miguel Hernández, desamordazado y regresado*.

47. Agustín Sánchez Vidal in *Miguel Hernández, desamordazado y regresado* comments on these allusions along with references to Jorge Manrique, Neruda, and Espronceda. He discusses as well the metrical complexity of the text: "La métrica, sin embargo, es harto complicada, lejos del tópico e inevitable romance al uso: alejandrinos que se agrupan en serventesios de pie quebrado de rima consonante y organizados al compás de un ritmo de auténtico virtuoso…" (252).

48. In response to their argument, Vallejo expresses the need to see poetry as a weapon in his speech in the congress in Valencia, 1937, "La responsabilidad del escritor," and although both Hernández and Vallejo are clearly using poetry as a voice for Republican propaganda, neither reduces their work to merely propagandistic.

49. These poems by Concha Méndez, Carmen Conde, and Rosa Chacel can be found in Emilio Miró, ed., *Antología de Poetisas del 27*. And for a more complete study and selection of Concha Méndez, see her *Poemas (1926–1986)*.

50. Neruda's "Canto sobre unas ruinas" also refers to Caro, and I will analyze it in close detail in the fifth section of this chapter.

51. "No es raro… que en un primer momento de… juvenil desasosiego, sea el muro (y no las ruinas) el signo que presida las horas del poeta" (Colinas 135).

52. In the first stanza, Cernuda introduces the moon as "aquella diosa virgen," and although the goddess is not named, it is an obvious reference to Roman and Greek mythology. Diana and Artemis, respectively the Roman and the Greek goddesses of the moon, are also the deities that look after fertility, childbirth, and the hunt. In the poem, the goddess of the moon comes to symbolize the creation of society, by protecting the literal and metaphorical nutrition of the body: the hunt for food and sexual reproduction.

53. Silver remarks on the new significance of history in Cernuda's poetry because of the Spanish Civil War and its traumatic impact on the poet and his generation: "'Noche de luna,' el poema que inicia *Las nubes* señala el comienzo de una nueva dirección semántica de la palabra *historia* en el vocabulario de Cernuda" (*Luis Cernuda* 240).

54. The feudal system in which the serf worked the land is replaced by the "dueño orgulloso" who owns the land for his recreation.

55. The moon is the only one that prevails; the shadows, represented before as the clouds, quickly disappear as "sombras efímeras." In consonance with the tradition of ruins, Cernuda acknowledges the fugitive, oral quality of the song, which in comparison to the apparent eternity of the written poem, is always menaced and never certain. Jiménez Fajardo comments that in these verses: "His dream may abstract deeds from time and give them a measure of eternity... History has been written. It will but repeat itself continuing a cycle of death until the virgin goddess sees in the earth a reflection of herself" (*Luis Cernuda* 53).

56. "His eyes are staring, his mouth is open, his wings are spread. This is how one pictures the angel of history. His face is turned towards the past. Where we perceive a chain of events, he sees one single catastrophe which keeps piling wreckage upon wreckage and hurls it in front of his feet... a storm is blowing from Paradise...This storm irresistibly propels him into the future to which his back is turned, while the pile of debris before him grows skyward. This storm is what we call progress" (Benjamin, "Theses on the Philosophy of History," *Illuminations* 257–58).

57. Valis talks about how nostalgia can be considered a "particular secularized form of cultural mourning," expressing a sense of loss (121).

58. Besides the title, the main difference between the two versions of the poem is that in the first one there are two extra stanzas toward the end, which Cernuda considered unnecessary in a final edited version.

59. Derek Harris indicates that: "Cernuda tuvo la intención original de poner el título de *Elegías españolas* a los poemas escritos durante la Guerra Civil." Harris continues in his footnote: "véase la nota a 'Elegía a un poeta muerto,' *Hora de España*, núm. VI (1937): 36. El borrador de 'Noche de luna,' conservado en los archivos familiares de Sevilla, lleva el título de 'Elegía a la luna de España'" (*La poesía de Luis Cernuda* 112n22).

60. "Háblame, madre" is also used a few years later in Neruda's *Alturas de Macchu Picchu*—both respond to the tradition of the elegy.

61. This is also prevalent in Cernuda's "Elegía I" with the comparison between fallen soldiers and "pétalos rotos entre sangre y lodo" (259).

62. Paz did not write a poetry collection about the Civil War but he wrote a few essays narrating his experience in 1937. In his speech commemorating the Congress of writers in Valencia (1937–87), Paz ponders upon how the Republican defeated cause is now victorious: "La historia es un teatro fantástico: las derrotas se vuelven victorias, las victorias derrotas, los fantasmas ganan las batallas... En el caso de la Guerra civil española, la victoria de nuestros enemigos se volvió ceniza pero muchas de nuestras ideas y proyectos se convirtieron en humo." Paz suggests that with the democratic period, the victory of the Fascists was defeated, turned to ashes, and also some of the Republican ideals they fought for had dissipated ("El lugar de prueba" 440).

63. See Mircea Eliade, *The Myth of the Eternal Return: Or, Cosmos and History*. In an interview by Roberto González Echevarría and Emir Rodríguez Monegal, Paz signals that *Piedra de sol* speaks of "the history of one man, who belongs to a generation, a country and an epoch... inserted into the circular time of myth" (González Echevarría and Emir Rodríguez Monegal, "Interview to Octavio Paz" 40). I did not discuss *Piedra de sol* in my third chapter, not only because I think much has been written already on the text, but mainly because, as Paz points out in this interview, it is difficult to compare it to Eliot's *The Waste Land*: "*Piedra de sol* is a linear poem that ceaselessly turns back upon itself, it is a circle or rather a spiral. *The Waste Land* is much more complex. It has been said that it is a collage, but I would say that it is an *assemblage de pièces détachées*" (35). Although one may read the influence of *The Waste Land* in Paz's paradoxes and imagery, he does argue very well that *Piedra de sol* presents "another vision of the world. The word *pleasure* is one of the axes of *Piedra de sol*. A word that doesn't exist in Eliot's poetry" (36).

64. Among other critics, Emir Rodríguez Monegal remarks "el profundo viraje de su poesía desde la guerra civil española" (*Neruda: El viajero inmóvil* 149).

Chapter Five
Pablo Neruda's Cities in Ruins
Poetic Histories from
Madrid to Machu Picchu

1. Pablo Neruda titles his poem *Alturas de Macchu Picchu* and highlights his version of Macchu with a double *c*, distancing from the mainstream way of writing it as Machu Picchu. For a more detailed discussion on the double *c*, consult Enrico Mario Santí's *Pablo Neruda: The Poetics of Prophecy*. All quotes from *Alturas* are taken from *Canto General*.

2. Neruda's *España en el corazón* has already been examined in relation to Miguel Hernández's and Rafael Alberti's poetic works, but Cernuda's and Paz's poems to the Spanish Civil War have not been compared to Neruda's work. For a more thorough analysis on Neruda and Hernández, see Juan Cano Ballesta's "Miguel Hernández."

3. Here I refer to Walter Benjamin's "Theses on the Philosophy of History" (in *Illuminations*) and Theodor W. Adorno's *Aesthetic Theory*.

4. However, one must also acknowledge the subtleties and the diversity of each poet's complex works. For instance, Cernuda is not always as inclined to "un nosotros rehumanizado," as Paz is in *Piedra de sol*.

5. I am not convinced by Orringer's argument that Neruda wanted to restore a bourgeois capitalist system, but what is apparent is that his poems manifest nostalgia for the Republican era, idyllic in comparison with any fascist regime. Orringer affirms: "...Neruda anhela restaurar el equilibrio burgués de la sociedad española... no mira hacia delante como los utópicos marxistas, sino hacia atrás con nostalgia... el mercado de frutas vendibles que llegaban al horizonte... en resumen, un comendio de una sociedad capitalista en armonía" (203).

6. García Montero also points out that in "*Residencia en la tierra...* Neruda busca los signos de la existencia en los hierros oxidados, las cáscaras, los objetos rotos... y las ridículas formalidades de unas apariencias que sólo sirven para ocultar el vacío interior" (*Los dueños del vacío* 119).

7. Jonathan Culler in his essay on the apostrophe asserts that it serves to underline a kind of poetic immediacy: "a poem may invoke objects, people, a detemporalized space with forms and forces which have pasts and futures but which are also addressed as potential presences" (*The Pursuit of Signs* 138). The spaces in Caro's poem are evidently marked by temporality and decay, but the glorious past can become a "potential presence" through those apostrophes.

8. E. M. Wilson indicates that there is a connection between the tragedy of the amphitheater in ruins and the stanza that remembers the heroes of Itálica: "un príncipe es el protagonista más indicado para una tragedia; de aquí la posibilidad de que no sea accidental la enumeración de glorias de Itálica que ocurre en la estancia siguiente." I agree with Wilson's explanation of this transition, although I do not support his critique of the poem as monotonous and with "epítetos sin valor" ("Sobre la *Canción a las ruinas de Itálica* de Rodrigo Caro" 382).

9. José María Ferri Coll comments on Caro's fascination with the Classical world: "todo lo que escribió el erudito utrerense... tiene razón de ser en la Antigüedad... La idea de continuidad entre el pasado y el presente alienta su obra" (91).

10. The verse "Roma, a quien queda el nombre apenas" is an allusion to Quevedo's *A Roma sepultada en sus ruinas.*

11. Darst maintains that "...the poem plays with the idea of a noble lord (Itálica) giving some kind of gift to the poet in payment for dedicating the poem to him... Ironically all man-made, material things of pagan Itálica have turned to ashes and dust... but the body of a simple Christian remained whole, incorruptible and permanent. Geroncio's corpse is, in truth, the only thing Itálica has to give to Rodrigo Caro" (14).

12. Ferri Coll alludes to Caro's prose, *El memorial de Utrera* and *Antigüedades*, to recall how the poet uses "los falsos Cronicones" to prove the dubious existence of martyrs like Geroncio in Itálica. In his two archaeological works, Caro dedicates as well various chapters to the "hijos ilustres de Itálica," Trajano, Adriano, and Teodosio.

13. In his essay about ruins and gardens, Orozco Díaz links the revival of these poetic motifs in the Baroque to the development of scientific areas like archeology and botany (123).

14. Although in this instance, Durán and Safir were able to eloquently express the poetic function of *España en el corazón* and its political relevance, their book sometimes tends to underestimate the readers with simplistic comments like: "Pablo Neruda is one of the few literary figures who, for the most part, has been able to be both ideological and poetical" (105). It is obvious that every poetic stance is also an ideological one (79).

15. I concur with Jaime Alazraki, although I would not ascribe this to a political "conversion": "La poesía de Neruda abandona los antros oscuros de la inconsciencia para elevarse a la claridad de la conciencia" (189).

16. Amid such dark events and cultural pessimism, there is still some hope in Neruda's poems of the Spanish Civil War. Neruda's last lines of the collection, in "Oda solar al ejército del pueblo," reveals this fight for hope, and how it resides in the people's army: "… tu definida estrella, / clava sus roncos rayos en la muerte, / y establece los nuevos ojos de la esperanza."

17. For a more detailed account of Neruda's polemic debate with Juan Ramón Jiménez, see Ricardo Gullón, "Relaciones Pablo Neruda–Juan Ramón Jiménez," where he refers to Juan Ramón Jiménez, "Carta a Pablo Neruda" (1942) and Juan Ramón Jiménez, "¿América sombría?" (August 14, 1943).

18. Felstiner avows that: "A stark parallelism 'look at my dead house, / look at broken Spain'—aligns the poet ineluctably with the history of the place and time, as does the sequence of tenses in his poem, from past to present to future. At the end, Neruda shapes his imperatives with line breaks that show a stronger, simpler touch… All these points of technique manifest a new purpose, a sense of what to speak for and whom to speak to, without which *Alturas de Macchu Picchu* is inconceivable" (*Translating Neruda* 118). Durán and Safir also coincide with Felstiner and they remark on the transitional role of *España en el corazón*: "The lyrical and the poetic forms present in *Spain in My Heart* are extended and expanded, this time to embrace the epic, a collective and historical vision of an entire continent, in which immediate feelings and events are replaced by a broader, all-encompassing vision of America" (Durán and Safir 81).

19. Osuna also reiterates what has been pointed out by Alonso and Santí about "Canto sobre unas ruinas": "Los versos que compone Neruda laten con pulsaciones exclamativas… (con) tono decididamente elegíaco. El tema de las ruinas, ahora no destruidas por el tiempo como en la lírica barroca sino por el impacto mortífero de la maquinaria moderna, alienta en todos sus versos, comenzando por el mismo principio en el que a todas luces se reconoce una vinculación con la famosa 'Canción a las ruinas de Itálica'" (76–77).

20. As suggested before, the first verses recall Caro's first address to Fabio in "Itálica."

21. The flower born from a bone which has paradoxically served as fertilizer may allude to Eliot's *The Waste Land*: "April is the cruelest month, breeding / Lilacs out of the dead land," which in itself is also a reference to Whitman's elegy to President Lincoln, "When Lilacs Last in the Dooryard Bloom'd."

22. Therefore, "Canto sobre unas ruinas" does not describe a ruined city like Caro's architectural and archeological journey through Itálica.

23. Alazraki underlines this point in his reading of these verses: "'Las formas del mundo' que van apareciendo… todo aquello es obra del brazo humano, levantando tras la paciente laboriosidad de siglos y generaciones, creado con la fuerza constructiva del músculo y la ilusión del sueño" (197).

24. Owen Barfield explains how the word *ruin* pointed to the movement of falling and destruction and how it also came to convey the collapse itself. Barfield affirms that the Latin verb *ruo* is translated as "rush" or "fall," and he stresses that "in the classical contexts themselves it nearly always carries with it a larger sense of swift, disastrous movement…" (113).

25. Juan Manuel Marcos argues that César Vallejo's *España, aparta de mí ese cáliz* and Neruda's *España en el corazón* are joined by their utopic representations of Spain and by Quevedo's influence: "El emblema retórico en que Vallejo y Neruda convergen en la tradición quevedesca es el oxymoron" (219).

26. Robert Pring-Mill, in his introduction to an anthology of Neruda's work after Neruda died in 1973, remarked that Quevedo had been much more influential than Góngora: "Quevedo's influence went deeper. It endured throughout Neruda's life, to be reflected in a poem called 'Leyendo a Quevedo junto al mar' in his very last political pamphlet (Incitación al nixonicidio y alabanza de la revolución chilena, 1973), and in the haunting 'Con Quevedo, en primavera' of the posthumous *Jardín de invierno* (1974)" (xxiv).

27. Neruda's surrealist imagery confirms his aesthetic ties with the French Surrealist movement, but it does not determine his poetry collection or his work in general as Surrealist. There are strong narcissistic intentions behind the Surrealist fascination with dreams and wordplays, from which Neruda distances himself when he redefines his poetic principles in the context of an international state of emergency during the Civil War.

28. Gutiérrez Revuelta has already examined how "Canto sobre unas ruinas" relates to "La calle destruida" and to Caro's "Itálica."

29. Since I am focusing on the topos of ruins, I will mainly analyze *Alturas,* not addressing *Canto General*'s multiple dimensions.

30. Rodríguez Monegal states in reference to *Alturas de Macchu Picchu* that the poet's solidarity with the dead is established through a "proceso de vocalización" ("El sistema del poeta" 82).

31. "El poeta aspira ser el intermediario de la voz auténtica de lo originario, el vocero vinculado a los enterrados que quiere arraigar su voz" (Goic 241).

32. Rodríguez Monegal indicates that "…la llamada de lo profético que hay en el poeta queda reducida para Alonso a la *inspiración*… La poesía que Neruda propone en 'Arte poética' es, pues, una poesía profética. No una poesía sólo hermética, como cree Alonso" (*Neruda* 453–54). He is alluding to Amado Alonso's analysis of this poem: "Su poesía es el viento repentino que azota el pecho y le pide lo profético que hay en él. El acento se pone en esta afirmación y exaltación de sí mismo y de su chispa sagrada. Por eso la atmósfera de melancolía…" (A. Alonso 72) Alonso's description of Neruda's inspiration as a "chispa sagrada" is precisely what disturbs Rodríguez Monegal.

33. In the first part of this chapter, I discussed how Santí and García Montero interpret this verse as the seemingly contradictory union of the melancholic and the prophetic.

34. In her essay on the poem "Con Quevedo, en primavera," Amarilis Ortiz connects Seneca's stoic vision with Quevedo's sonnets and recognizes the connections between Neruda and Quevedo and the ideological differences between their versions of death and rebirth: "Para Quevedo, la religión determina el renacer, y para Neruda, el factor que lo determina es la naturaleza" (13).

35. Pring-Mill makes a fundamental point when he affirms that Neruda believed Machu Picchu to be a city of cities, where the Incas began to establish their cultural empire: "Present-day archaeological opinion regards it as late Inca foundation, but part of the symbolic significance which it assumed in the poem undoubtedly came from the fact that Bingham took it to be the birthplace of the Inca race. Neruda treats it, indeed, almost as the source of all Amerindian culture" (xxxiv).

36. Many critics discuss the comparison between *Alturas de Macchu Picchu* and the *Divine Comedy* and argue that Neruda incorporates Dante's structure into his own text. It would be interesting to study other connections between the two poems, such as the role of the rivers in both "Purgatories." Yet, Santí makes a relevant commentary regarding this comparative analysis that precisely deals with the blindness both protagonists must transcend: "Whereas in the *Commedia* the pilgrim expiates the sins of moral blindness, in *Alturas* he atones for the errors of cultural alienation, a blindness that has kept him from seeing the true way of pre-Columbian origins" (*Pablo Neruda* 149). Unlike Dante's, Neruda's quest does not search for God's illumination, but for the light within himself and within the historical past that has had the working collectivity in the dark for centuries.

37. I allude to Camayd-Freixas's eloquent argument and his use of the "muerte empática" to explain the collective rebirth in *Alturas*: "…el más importante de los tópicos del planto épico es aquel mediante el cual el héroe experimenta una suerte de muerte empática por sus compañeros para sentir de manera más inmediata su dolor y comprender mejor la muerte… La muerte empática será para Neruda la vía de la iluminación, de la anagnórisis, de la conciencia histórica" (408).

38. I am referring to Benjamin's notion of "petrified history" which he relates to the "fossil," as Susan Buck-Morss explains: " (the fossil) is the emblem of 'petrified history,' then nature too has a history, so that the historical transiency (the ruin) is the emblem of nature in decay" (161). Although in Neruda's *Alturas* the depiction of nature is exuberatingly vibrating; thus, in this case, the city in ruins is the emblem of "petrified history," merging the natural and the historical settings.

39. Camayd-Freixas also points to the similarities between Quevedo's sonnet and Neruda's *Alturas*, although he stresses that both poems correspond more to the genre of the funereal elegy than to the topos of ruins: "En el soneto 'A Roma sepultada en sus ruinas' de Quevedo, puede verse que 'Alturas' guarda cierta afinidad con la retórica de la elegía de ruinas. Sin embargo, esta afinidad se debe gran parte a que la elegía de ruinas remeda la retórica de la elegía fúnebre. De ella tomas los tópicos tradicionales del *ubi sunt?*, del catálogo de héroes, de la falacia patética, de la presencia organizadora del peregrino, así como el tema barroco del desengaño del mundo, el del olvido, la fugacidad y otros más" (407).

40. As suggested by Hiram Bingham, *Lost City of the Incas* (1948), pp. 190–99.

41. Also see Goic, *"Alturas de Macchu Picchu:* La torre y el abismo" 237.

42. Fernando Alegría underlines Neruda's incorporation of Whitman's self-assigned role of the democratic poet-prophet: "Poseído del mismo papel editorialista máximo que Whitman usa en *Democratic Vistas*, Neruda mezcla sus avisos políticos con sus apóstrofes líricos." This is particularly evident when in *"Alturas de Macchu Picchu... al* levantar de las ruinas incaicas al hombre sacrificado, Neruda da una resolución política..." ("¿Cuál Whitman?" 10). For other readings comparing Whitman and Neruda's work, consult: Enrico Mario Santí, "The Accidental Tourist: Walt Whitman in Latin America"; Didier Jaén, "Walt Whitman: Tema literario,"; and Doris Sommer, "Supplying Demand: Walt Whitman as the Liberal Self."

43. For Larrea, Neruda's *Alturas* resonates too strongly with Caro's "Itálica" and Darío's "Visión"; he accuses him of imitating these works.

Chapter Six
The Effects of the Real:
Reading Ruins in Modern Poetry

1. As Slavoj Žižek underscores: "reactionary proclamations of a state of emergency are a desperate defence against the true state of emergency itself" (*Welcome to the Desert of the Real!* 108). The continuous state of emergency reinforces the state's power, which recalls Benjamin's advice in the fight against Fascism: "The tradition of the oppressed teaches us that the 'state of emergency' in which we live is not the exception but the rule... our task (is) to bring about a real state of emergency" ("Theses on the Philosophy of History," in *Illuminations* 257).

2. Žižek refers to the state of war that President Bush declared after the attacks and points to two main paradoxes: on the pretext of defending

American "freedom," the people's civil rights have been curtailed; and the United States government insists that they are in a state of war, but America is not really at war in the conventional sense, "for the great majority of people, daily life goes on" (*Welcome* 107).

3. José Emilio Pacheco has written multiple, moving poems on ruins. For a thorough analysis of his poems on Tlatelolco, see Sandra Messinger Cypess's "Tlatelolco: From Ruins to Poetry."

4. Antonio José Ponte is also a Cuban "ruinologist," whose book of short stories presents the ethical concerns that contemporary ruins trigger. As Esther Whitfield suggests in her prologue: "'Un arte de hacer ruinas' sugiere que las ruinas representan una estética históricamente enraizada, una pantalla al estancamiento de la ideología actual" (28). For a meticulous analysis of Cuban ruins in connection with Ponte and with other texts and films, see Vicky Unruh's "All in a Day's Work: Ruins Dwellers in Havana."

5. I have argued this previously in my articles "Broken Presents" and "Reaching the Past through Cities in Ruins."

6. Sylvia Molloy intelligently points out: "Something 'in ruins' can be remembered, if not personally at least collectively. A ruin—or the lack it represents—can only be conjectured or, more precisely, evoked" (52). As I have argued throughout this book, a city in ruins can be reconstructed, and it is precisely the goal of the modern city to refashion itself constantly as part of its economic and social growth.

7. I do not constrain Cernuda to the label of neo-Romantic, but I acknowledge the influence of poets like Holderlin, Bécquer, and Leopardi in his poems on ruins, especially in *Las nubes*.

8. Paz's *Sor Juana Inés de la Cruz, o las trampas de la fe* highlights Sor Juana as the main intellectual figure of Latin American colonial literature as part of his poetics of a "return to origins."

Bibliography

Abellán, José Luis, ed. *El exilio español de 1939*. Madrid: Taurus, 1977.

Abril, Xavier. *Vallejo*. Buenos Aires: Front, 1958.

Ackroyd, Peter. *T. S. Eliot: A Life*. New York: Simon and Schuster, 1984.

Adorno, Theodor W. *Aesthetic Theory*. Ed. and trans. Robert Hullot-Kentor. Minneapolis: U of Minnesota P, 1997.

Agamben, Giorgio. *Lo que queda de Auschwitz: El archivo y el testigo*. Trans. Antonio Gimeno Cuspinera. Valencia: Pre-textos, 2000.

Aguilar Fernández, Paloma. *Memoria y olvido de la guerra civil española*. Madrid: Alianza, 1996.

———, and Katherine Hite. "Historical Memory and Authoritarian Legacies in Processes of Political Change: Spain and Chile." *Authoritarian Legacies and Democracy in Latin America and Southern Europe*. Ed. Katherine Hite and Paola Cesarini. Notre Dame: U of Notre Dame, 2004. 191–231.

Alarcón Sierra, Rafael. "La ciudad y el domingo, el poeta y la muchedumbre (de Baudelaire a Manuel Machado)." *Anales de la Literatura Española Contemporánea* 24 (1999): 35–64.

Alazraki, Jaime. *Poética y poesía de Pablo Neruda*. New York: Las Americas, 1965.

Alberti, Rafael. *La arboleda perdida 2 (1931–1987)*. Madrid: Alianza, 1998.

———. "Imagen primera y definitiva de Miguel Hernández." *Miguel Hernández*. Ed. María de Gracia Ifach. Madrid: Taurus, 1975. 18–19.

———. *Poesía (1920–1938). Obras completas*. Ed. Luis García Montero. Vol. 1. Madrid: Aguilar, 1988.

———. *El poeta en la calle*. Colección Ebro 9. París: Librairie du Globe, 1966.

Albornoz, Aurora de. *Poesías de guerra de Antonio Machado*. San Juan, Puerto Rico: Asomante, 1961.

Albornoz, Aurora de, and Elena Andrés, eds. *Chile en mi corazón: Homenaje a Pablo Neruda*. Barcelona: Península, 1975.

Aldiss, Brian. *Ruins*. London: Hutchinson, 1987.

Alegría, Fernando. "¿Cuál Whitman?: Borges, Lorca y Neruda." *Texto Crítico* 22–23 (1981): 3–12.

———. *Walt Whitman en Hispanoamérica*. Colección Studium 5. México, DF: Studium, 1954.

Aleixandre, Vicente. "Evocación de Miguel Hernández." *Miguel Hernández*. Ed. María de Gracia Ifach. Madrid: Taurus, 1975. 20–21.

———. "Luis Cernuda en la ciudad." *Homenaje a Luis Cernuda*. Valencia: La caña gris, 1964. 11–12.

Alighieri, Dante. *The Divine Comedy: Purgatorio*. Ed. and trans. Robert M. Durling. Introd. Ronald L. Martinez and Robert M. Durling. Vol. 2. Oxford: Oxford UP, 2003.

Alonso, Amado. *Poesía y estilo de Pablo Neruda (Interpretación de una poesía hermética)*. 1940. Madrid: Gredos, 1997.

Alonso, Carlos J. "The Burden of Modernity." *The Places of History: Regionalism Revisited in Latin America*. Ed. Doris Sommer. Durham: Duke UP, 1999. 94–103.

Alonso, Dámaso. *Ensayos sobre la poesía española*. Madrid: Revista de Occidente, 1944.

———. "Góngora y América." *Estudios y ensayos gongorinos*. Madrid: Gredos, 1955. 381–92.

———. "Notas a la *Antología en honor a Góngora*, recogida por Gerardo Diego." *Revista de Occidente* 18 (1927): 396–401.

———. *Seis calas en la expresión literaria española*. Madrid: Gredos, 1951.

"A los intelectuales del mundo entero." By La Alianza de Intelectuales Antifascistas. *El Sol* [Madrid], 19 Nov. 1936.

Altolaguirre, Manuel. "Carta a José Antonio Fernández de Castro." *Obras completas*. Vol. 3. By Pablo Neruda. Buenos Aires: Losada, 1957. 908–09.

Álvarez, Francisco R. "Octavio Paz: Hacia una metapoética de la modernidad." *Hispania* 81 (1998): 20–29.

Álvarez Junco, José. "La guerra civil como Guerra nacional." 1986. *La guerra civil española*. Ed. Edward Malefakis. Madrid: Taurus, 2006. 579–620.

———. *Mater Dolorosa: La idea de España en el siglo XIX*. Madrid: Taurus, 2001.

Amate Blanco, Juan José. "Análisis histórico-literario de un texto de Neruda: 'Explico algunas cosas' de España en el corazón." *Actas del III Simposio del Séminaire d'Etudes Littéraires de l'Université de Toulouse*. Toulouse: Le Mirail and Universidad Complutense de Madrid, 1980. 75–85.

Arias, Arturo. "Fernando Vallejo's Ruinous Heterotopias: The Queer Subject in Latin America's Urban Spaces." *Telling Ruins in Latin America*. Ed. Michael Lazzara and Vicky Unruh. New York: Palgrave Macmillan, 2009. 229–40.

Arrom, José Juan. *Esquema generacional de las letras hispanoamericanas.* Bogotá: Instituto Caro y Cuervo, 1977.

Artigas, Miguel. *Don Luis de Góngora y Argote, biografía y estudio crítico.* Madrid: Revista de Archivos, 1925.

Bachelard, Gaston. *The Poetics of Space.* Trans. Maria Jolas. Introd. John R. Stilgoe. Boston: Beacon, 1994.

Balfour, Sebastian. *Deadly Embrace: Morocco and the Road to the Spanish Civil War.* Oxford: Oxford UP, 2002.

Balibar, Étienne. "Is There a Neo-Racism?" *Race, Nation, and Class: Ambiguous Identities.* Ed. Étienne Balibar and Immanuel Wallerstein. London: Verso, 1988. 17–28.

Balmer, Pierre Maurice. "El mediodía en la poesía de Octavio Paz." *Thesaurus: Boletín del Instituto Caro y Cuervo* 46 (1991): 245–89.

Bann, Stephen. *The Inventions of History: Essays on the Representation of the Past.* Manchester: Manchester UP, 1990.

———. *Romanticism and the Rise of History.* New York: Twayne, 1995.

Barfield, Owen. *Poetic Diction: A Study in Meaning.* 1st ed., 1928. Rpt. 3rd ed. Middletown, CT: Wesleyan UP, 1973.

Barón, Emilio. "Baudelaire en Cernuda." *Revista de Literatura* 59.117 (1997): 67–87.

———. *Luis Cernuda, poeta.* Sevilla: Alfar, 2002.

———. *Luis Cernuda, vida y obra.* Sevilla: Andaluzas, 1990.

———. *"Odi et Amo": Luis Cernuda y la literatura francesa.* Sevilla: Alfar, 2000.

———. "Retrato del poeta: Baudelaire visto por (Eliot y) Cernuda." *Revista Hispánica Moderna* 48.2 (1995): 335–48.

Barthes, Roland. *Image, Music and Text.* Trans. Stephen Heath. New York: Hill and Wang, 1977.

Baudelaire, Charles. *Journaux intimes.* Paris: Georges Crès, 1919.

———. *Œuvres complètes.* Vols. 1 and 2. Ed. Claude Pichois. Paris: Gallimard. 1975.

Baudrillard, Jean. *Simulacra and Simulation.* Trans. Sheila Faria Glaser. Ann Arbor: U of Michigan P, 1994.

Bécquer, Gustavo Adolfo. *Desde mi celda: Cartas literarias.* Ed. José Montero Padilla. Salamanca: Anaya, 1970.

———. *Rimas.* Ed. Rafael Montesinos. Madrid: Cátedra, 2000.

Bell, Clive. "T. S. Eliot." *The Nation and the Atheneum* 22 Sept. 1923, 772–73.

Bibliography

Bellini, Giuseppe. *Quevedo y la poesía hispanoamericana del Siglo XX: Vallejo, Carrera Andrade, Paz, Neruda y Borges.* New York: Torres, 1976.

Bellver, C. G. "The City as Antagonist in the Poetry of Luis Cernuda." *Romance Notes* 19 (1978): 156–63.

———. "Luis Cernuda and T. S. Eliot: A Kinship of Message and Motifs." *Revista de Estudios Hispánicos* 17.1 (1983): 107–24.

Benjamin, Walter. *The Arcades Project.* Trans. Howard Eiland and Kevin McLaughlen. Cambridge, MA: Belknap Press of Harvard UP, 1999.

———. *Baudelaire: A Lyric Poet in the Era of High Capitalism.* Trans. Harry Zohn. Norfolk: Thetford, 1976.

———. *Illuminations.* Ed. Hannah Arendt. Trans. Harry Zohn. New York: Schocken, 1968.

———. *The Origin of German Tragic Drama.* Trans. John Osborn. London and New York: Verso, 1998.

Berman, Marshall. *All That Is Solid Melts into Air: The Experience of Modernity.* New York: Penguin, 1982.

Bernard, Judith. "Myth and Structure in Octavio Paz's *Piedra de sol.*" *Symposium* 21 (1967): 5–13.

Bewley, Marius. *Masks and Mirrors.* New York: Atheneum, 1970.

Bingham, Hiram. *The Lost City of the Incas: The Story of Machu Picchu and Its Builders.* New York: Duell, Sloan and Pearce, 1948.

Blackmur, R. P. "Irregular Metaphysics," *T. S. Eliot, A Collection of Critical Essays.* Ed. Hugh Kenner. Englewood Cliffs, NJ: Prentice-Hall, 1962. 58–64.

Blood, Susan. *Baudelaire and the Aesthetics of Bad Faith.* Stanford: Stanford UP, 1997.

Bloom, Harold. *The Anxiety of Influence: A Theory of Poetry.* 1973. Oxford: Oxford UP, 1997.

———. *The Best Poems of the English Language.* New York: Harper Collins, 2004.

Borges, Jorge Luis. "Examen de un soneto de Góngora." 1926. *El tamaño de mi esperanza.* Barcelona: Seix Barral, 1994.

Boyd, Carolyn P. "History, Politics, and Culture 1936–1975." *The Cambridge Companion to Modern Spanish Culture.* Ed. David T. Gies. Cambridge: Cambridge UP, 1999. 86–103.

Boym, Svetlana. *The Future of Nostalgia.* New York: Basic Books, 2001.

310

Bradbury, Malcolm, and James McFerlaine, eds. *Modernism 1890–1930*. Atlantic Highlands, NJ: Humanities, 1978.

Bradford, Richard. "Richard Lovelace and Eliot's 'Whispers of Immortality.'" *Trivium* 22 (1987): 103–12.

Breton, André. *Manifestes du surréalisme*. Paris: Gallimard, 1972.

Brombert, Victor. *The Hidden Reader: Stendhal, Balzac, Hugo, Baudelaire, Flaubert*. Cambridge: Harvard UP, 1988

Brooks, Peter. *Body Work: Objects of Desire in Modern Narrative*. Cambridge: Harvard UP, 1993.

Brunel, Pierre. *Charles Baudelaire: Les Fleurs du Mal, entre fleurir et défleurir*. Paris: Editions du temps, 1998.

Bruton, Kevin J. "Luis Cernuda's Exile Poetry and Coleridge's Theory of Imagination." *Comparative Literature Studies* 21 (1984): 383–95.

———. "The Cemetery Poems of Luis Cernuda." *Anales de la Literatura Española Contemporánea* 13.3 (1988): 189–208.

———. "Symbolical Reference and Internal Rhythm: Luis Cernuda's Debt to Holderlin." *Revue de Littérature Comprarée* 58 (1984): 37–49.

Buci-Glucksmann, Christine. *La raison baroque: De Baudelaire à Benjamin*. Paris: Galilée, 1984.

Buck-Morss, Susan. *The Dialectics of Seeing: Walter Benjamin and the Arcades Project*. Cambridge: MIT P, 1989.

Buero Vallejo, Antonio. "Un poema y un recuerdo." *En torno a Miguel Hernández*. Madrid: Castalia, 1978. 23–33.

Burton, Richard. *The Context of Baudelaire's "Le Cygne."* Durham: U of Durham, 1980.

Byron, George Lord. *Childe Harold's Pilgrimage*. London: Cassell, 1899.

Camayd-Freixas, Erik . "'Alturas de Macchu Picchu': Forma y sentido en su retórica elegíaca." *Romance Languages Annual* 7 (1995): 405–12.

Cano, José Luis, ed. *Cartas inéditas de Jorge Guillén, Luis Cernuda, Emilio Prados*. Madrid: Versal, Cátedra, 1992.

Cano Ballesta, Juan. *Las estrategias de la imaginación: Utopías literarias y retórica política bajo el franquismo*. Madrid: Siglo XXI, 1994.

———. *Literatura y Tecnología, las letras españolas ante la revolución industrial (1890–1940)*. Valencia: Pre-textos, 1999.

311

Cano Ballesta, Juan. "Miguel Hernández y su amistad con Pablo Neruda." *Pablo Neruda, el escritor y la crítica*. Ed. Emir Rodz. Monegal and Enrico Mario Santí. Madrid: Taurus, 1980. 143–74.

———. *La poesía de Miguel Hernández*. Madrid: Gredos, 1962.

Cañas, Dionisio. "The Poet and the City: Lorca in New York." *Lorca's Legacy*. Ed. Manuel Durán and Francesca Colecchia. New York: Peter Lang, 1991. 160–67.

———. *El poeta y la ciudad: Nueva York y los escritores hispanos*. Madrid: Cátedra, 1994.

Capote Benot, José María. *El surrealismo en la poesía de Cernuda*. Sevilla: Universidad de Sevilla, 1976.

Cárcamo-Huechante, Luis E. "La economía poética del mar: Patrimonio y desbordamiento en 'Maremoto' de Neruda." *Revista Iberoamericana*. 72.215–16 (2006): 587–605.

Cardwell, R. A . "The Persistence of Romantic Thought in Spain." *Modern Languages Review* 65 (1970): 803–12.

Carnero, Guillermo. "Luis Cernuda y el purismo poético: *Perfil del aire*." *Vuelta* 12.144. (1988): 63–64.

Caro, M. A. *La "Canción a las ruinas de Itálica" del Licenciado Rodrigo Caro*. Bogotá: J. M. Rivas Sacconi, 1947.

Carpenter, Peter. "Taking Liberties: Eliot's Donne." *Critical Survey* 5.3 (1993): 278–88.

Carpentier, Alejo. "Presencia de Pablo Neruda." *Pablo Neruda, el escritor y la crítica*. Ed. Emir Rodz. Monegal and Enrico Mario Santí. Madrid: Taurus, 1980. 53–59.

Carr, Raymond, and Juan Pablo Fusi, eds. *Spain: Dictatorship to Democracy*. 2nd ed. London: Allen and Unwin, 1981.

Castellanos, Rosario. *Poesía no eres tú (1948–1971)*. México, DF: Fondo de Cultura Económica, 1995.

Castro, Rosalía de. *En las orillas del Sar*. Ed. Mauro Armiño. Colección Austral. Madrid: Espasa-Calpe, 1997.

Cernuda, Luis. "Baudelaire y el centenario de *Las flores del mal*." 1959. *Prosa completa*. Ed. Derek Harris and Luis Maristany. Barcelona: Barral, 1975. 1037–47.

———. "Historial de un libro" (*La realidad y el deseo*) (1958). *Prosa completa*. Ed. Derek Harris and Luis Maristany. Barcelona: Barral, 1975. 898–939.

———. "Bécquer y el poema en prosa español." 1959. *Prosa completa*. Ed. Derek Harris and Luis Maristany. Barcelona: Barral, 1975. 984–93.

——. *Epistolario inédito.* Ed. Fernando Ortiz. Sevilla: Compás, 1981.

——. "Goethe y Mr. Eliot." 1959. *Prosa completa.* Ed. Derek Harris and Luis Maristany. Barcelona: Barral, 1975. 1048–57.

——. "Notas sobre Holderlin." *Cruz y raya* [Madrid] 32 (1935): 115–18.

——. *Poesía completa.* Ed. Derek Harris and Luis Maristany. Madrid: Siruela, 2002.

——. *La realidad y el deseo (1924–1962).* México, DF: Fondo de Cultura Económica, 1995.

Cervantes, Miguel de. *El ingenioso hidalgo Don Quijote de la Mancha.* Ed. Luis Andrés Murillo. Madrid: Castalia, 1978.

——. *The Ingenious Hidalgo Don Quixote de la Mancha.* Trans. John Rutherford. Introd. Roberto González Echevarría. New York: Penguin, 2000.

Cervera Salinas, Vicente. "Temor y temblor en la ciudad grande." *Anthropos* 169 (1995): 61–67.

Chambers, Ross. *The Writing of Melancholy: Modes of Opposition in Early French Modernism.* Trans. Mary Seidman Trouille. Chicago: U of Chicago P, 1987.

Chase, Cynthia. *Decomposing Figures: Rhetorical Readings in the Romantic Tradition.* Baltimore: John Hopkins UP, 1986.

Clark, T. J. *The Painting of Modern Life.* 1984. Princeton, NJ: Princeton UP, 1999.

Coleman, Alexander. "The Ghost of Whitman in Neruda and Borges." *Walt Whitman in Mickle Street.* Ed. Geoffrey Sill. Knoxville: U of Tennessee P, 1994. 257–69.

Colinas, Antonio. "Luis Cernuda: La lección de las ruinas." *Actas del Primer Congreso Internacional sobre Luis Cernuda (1902–1963).* Sevilla: Universidad Internacional Menéndez Pelayo, 1988. 135–38.

Concha, Jaime. *Neruda (1904–1936).* Santiago: Universitaria, 1972.

Conteris, Hiber. "Octavio Paz: Crítica de la Revolución." *Siglo XX* 10.1–2 (1992): 143–63.

Corominas, J., and J. A. Pascual. *Diccionario crítico etimológico castellano e hispánico.* Madrid: Gredos, 1980.

Coronado, Carolina. *Poesías.* Ed. Noël Valis. Madrid: Castalia, 1991.

Cortines, Jacobo, ed. *Historial de una vida: Homenaje a Luis Cernuda en el centenario de su nacimiento (1902–2002).* Sevilla: Fundación José Manuel Lara, 2003.

Coven, Jeffrey. *Baudelaire's Voyages: The Poet and His Painters*. Boston: Little, 1993.

Cowan, S. A. "Echoes of Donne, Herrick and Southwell in Eliot's *The Waste Land*." *Yeats Eliot Review* 8 (1986): 96–102.

Crary, Jonathan. *Techniques of the Observer: On Vision and Modernity in the Nineteenth Century*. 1990. Cambridge: MIT P, 1999.

Culler, Jonathan. "On the Negativity of Modern Poetry: Friedrich, Baudelaire and the Critical Tradition." *Languages of the Unsayable*. Ed. Sanford Budick and Wolfgang Iser. New York: Columbia UP, 1989. 189–208.

———. *The Pursuit of Signs: Semioticism Literature and Deconstruction*. Ithaca: Cornell UP, 1981.

Darst, David. "The Conceptual Design of Rodrigo Caro's *Itálica*." *Hispanófila* 109 (1993): 11–17.

Davis, Mike. *Dead Cities and Other Tales*. New York: New Press, 2002.

De Man, Paul. *Blindness and Insight*. Trans. Wlad Godzich. Minneapolis: U of Minnesota P, 1971.

Del Paso, Fernando. "Elogio de un poeta." *Vuelta* 21.255 (1998): 6–10.

Derrida, Jacques. *Mémoires d'aveugle, l'autoportrait et autres ruines*. Paris: Reunión des musées nationaux, 1990.

des Goncourts, Edmond and Jules. *Journal des Goncourts: Mémoires de la vie littéraire*. Vol. 1. 1851–61. Paris: Bibliothèque-Charpentier, 1895.

Diego, Gerardo. *Antología poética en honor de Góngora*. Madrid: Revista de Occidente, 1927.

———. "Don Luis de Góngora y Argote." *Revista de Occidente* 16 (1925): 246–51.

———. "Un escorzo de Góngora." *Revista de Occidente* 7 (1924): 76–89.

Díez de Revenga, Francisco Javier. "Trayectoria poética de Luis Cernuda." *Cervantes* 3 (2002): 143–56.

Docherty, Thomas. *John Donne, Undone*. London and New York: Methuen, 1986.

Donne, John. *The Complete English Poems*. London: Penguin, 1996.

———. *Devotions upon Emergent Occasions*. Cambridge: Cambridge UP, 1923.

Durán, Manuel. "Miguel Hernández, barro y luz." *En torno a Miguel Hernández*. Madrid: Castalia, 1978. 34–52.

Durán, Manuel, and Margery Safir. *Earth Tones: The Poetry of Pablo Neruda*. Bloomington: Indiana UP, 1981.

Eagleton, Terry. *The Ideology of the Aesthetic*. Oxford: Blackwell, 1990.

Earle, Peter. "Octavio Paz y España." *Revista Iberoamericana* 53 (1987): 945–53.

Edo, Miguel. "T. S. Eliot, crítico y poeta." *Quimera* 122 (1994): 53–59.

Edwards, Jorge. "Octavio Paz y la crítica: Dos o tres conjeturas." *Siglo XX* 10 (1999): 5–9.

Edwards, Michael. "*Renga*, Translation, and Eliot's Ghost." *PN Review* 16 (1980): 24–28.

Eliade, Mircea. *The Myth of the Eternal Return: Or, Cosmos and History*. Trans. Willard R. Trask. Princeton, NJ: Princeton UP, 1954.

Eliot, T. S. *Collected Poems 1909–1962*. New York: Harcourt Brace, 1991.

———. "Donne in Our Time." *A Garland for John Donne (1631–1931)*. Ed. Theodore Spencer. 1931. Gloucester, MA: Meter Smith, 1958. 1–19.

———. "John Donne." *The Nation and Atheneum* 33, 9 June 1923, 331–32.

———. "The Metaphysical Poets." 1921. *Selected Prose*. London: Penguin, 1953. 111–20.

———. *The Sacred Wood*. London: Methuen, 1972.

———. *Tierra Baldía*. Trans. and prologue Angel Flores. Barcelona: Cervantes, 1930.

———. *The Varieties of Metaphysical Poetry: "The Clark Lectures," at Trinity College, Cambridge, 1926, and "The Turnbull Lectures" at the Johns Hopkins University, 1933*. Ed. and introd. Ronald Schuchard. London: Faber and Faber, 1993.

———. *The Waste Land, A Facsimile and Transcript of the Original Drafts Including the Annotations of Ezra Pound*. Ed. Valerie Eliot. New York: Harcourt Brace Jovanovich, 1971.

Elizondo, Salvador. "Cernuda y la poesía inglesa." *Luis Cernuda en México*. Ed. James Valender. México, DF: Fondo de Cultura Económica, 2002. 165–69.

Elliott, John H. *Do the Americas Have a Common History? An Address*. Providence: John Carter Brown Library, 1996.

Eng, David, and David Kazanjian. *Loss: The Politics of Mourning*. Berkeley: U of California P, 2003.

Enjuto Rangel, Cecilia. "Broken Presents: The Modern City in Ruins in Baudelaire, Cernuda and Paz." *Comparative Literature* (2007): 140–57.

———. "Cities in Ruins: The Recuperation of the Baroque in T. S. Eliot and Octavio Paz." *How Far Is America from Here? Proceedings of the International American Studies Association* (IASA) Leiden, 2003. Ed. Paul Giles, Theo D'Haen, Djelal Kadir, and Lois Parkinson Zamora. Amsterdam, New York: Rodopi, 2005. 283–96.

———. "La guerra civil española: Entre fantasmas, monstruos y faunos." *Vanderbilt e-Journal of Luso-Hispanic Studies* 5 (2009): 37–55.

———. "Huidobro's Voices in the Transatlantic Poetics of the Spanish Civil War." *Rereading Huidobro: 21st Century Approaches.* Ed. Scott Weintraub and Luis Correa Díaz. U of Minnesota P, 2010. http://hispanicissues.umn.edu/Spring2010.html.

———. "Petrified Pasts: Octavio Paz and the Representation of Ruins." *Ciberletras,* July 2004. http://www.lehman.cuny.edu/ciberletras/.

———. "Reaching the Past through Cities in Ruins: *Itálica* and Machu Picchu." *Colorado Review of Hispanic Studies* 2 (2004): 43–60.

Epps, Brad, and Luis Fernández Cifuentes, eds. *Spain beyond Spain: Modernity, Literary History and National Identity.* Lewisburg: Bucknell UP, 2005.

Faber, Sebastiaan. *Exile and Cultural Hegemony: Spanish Intellectuals in Mexico, 1939–1975.* Nashville: Vanderbilt UP, 2002.

———. "Fantasmas hispanistas y otros retos transatlánticos." *Cultura y cambio social en América Latina.* Ed. Mabel Moraña. Madrid: Iberoamericana/Vervuert, 2008. 315–45.

———. "'El norte nos devora': La construcción de un espacio hispánico en el exilio anglosajón de Luis Cernuda." *Hispania* 83.4 (2000): 733–44.

Fanon, Franz. *Black Skin, White Masks.* Trans. Charles Lam Markman. London: Pluto, 1986.

Fein, John. "Himno entre ruinas." *Aproximaciones a Octavio Paz.* Ed. Angel Flores. México, DF: Mortiz, 1974. 165–70.

———. "La estructura de *Piedra de sol.*" *Revista Iberoamericana* 38 (1972): 73–93.

Felstiner, John. "La danza inmóvil, el vendaval sostenido, *Tour Quartets* de T. S. Eliot y *Alturas de Macchu Picchu* de Neruda." *Anales de la Universidad de Chile* [Santiago] No. 157–60 (Jan.–Dec. 1971): 177–95.

———. *Translating Neruda: The Way to Macchu Picchu.* Stanford: Stanford UP, 1980.

Fernández del Alba, Francisco, y Pedro Pérez del Solar. "Hacia un acercamiento cultural a la literatura hispano-americana." *Iberoamericana* 6.21 (2006): 99–107.

Fernández Cifuentes, Luis. "Lorca en Nueva York: Arquitecturas para un poeta." *Boletín de la Fundación Federico García Lorca* 4.10 (1992): 125–34.

———. "Miradas sobre el cuerpo (Fragmento para una historia literaria de la modernidad en España)." *Anales de la Literatura Española Contemporánea* 30.1–2 (2005): 153–78.

Fernández, Teodosio. "*Canto General:* Lírica y épica, mito e historia." *Nerudiana* [Sassaria, Italy] (1995): 46–59.

Ferrero, Mario. *Neruda, voz y universo.* Santiago de Chile: Logos, 1988.

Ferri Coll, José María. *Las ciudades cantadas, el tema de las ruinas en la poesía española del Siglo de Oro.* Alicante: Universidad de Alicante, 1995.

Forgues, Roland. "'Salid, niños del mundo': Vallejo y la guerra civil española." *César Vallejo: Al pie del orbe. Artículos y poemas en homenaje al primer centenario de su nacimiento (1892–1991).* Ed. Nestor Tenorio Requejo. Lambayeque, Perú: Lámpara de Papel, 1992. 57–59.

Foucault, Michel. *Les mots et les choses.* Paris: Gallimard, 1966.

Foulché-Delbosc, R. "Notes sur le sonnet *Superbi colli.*" *Revue Hispanique* 11 (1904): 225–43.

Fox-Genovese, Elizabeth. "Literary Criticism and the Politics of New Historicism." *The Postmodern History Reader.* London: Routledge, 1997. 84–88.

Franco, Jean, and Christiane Tarroux Follin, eds. *Des avant-gardes à l'engagement: "Residencia en la tierra" et "Canto General" de P. Neruda.* Collection Études Américaines. Montpellier: ETILAL, 2000.

Franco, Jean. *César Vallejo: The Dialectics of Poetry and Silence.* Cambridge: Cambridge UP, 1976.

———. *The Decline and Fall of the Lettered City: Latin America in the Cold War.* Cambridge, MA and London: Harvard UP, 2002.

Freedman, Stanley. "The Attitudes of John Donne and T. S. Eliot toward Experience and Religion." Honors Thesis. Harvard U, 1942.

Freud, Sigmund. *Civilization and Its Discontents*. 1930. New York: Norton, 1989.

──────. "Mourning and Melancholia." *On the History of the Psycho-Analytic Movement. Papers on Metapsychology and Other Works*. Vol. 14 (1914–16). London: Vintage, 2001. 243–58.

Frey, Hans-Jost. *Studies in Poetic Discourse, Mallarmé, Baudelaire, Rimbaud, Holderlin*. Trans. William Whabrey. Stanford: Stanford UP, 1996.

Friedrich, Hugo. *The Structure of Modern Poetry, from the Mid-nineteenth to the Mid-twentieth Century*. Trans. Joachim Neugroschel. Evanston, IL: Northwestern UP, 1974.

Frye, Northrop. *T. S. Eliot*. Edinburgh and London: Oliver and Boyd, 1963.

Fucilla, J. G. "Notes sur le sonnet *Superbi colli* (Rectificaciones y suplemento)." *Boletín de la Biblioteca Menéndez Pelayo* 31 (1955): 51–93.

Fuentes, Carlos. *Tiempo mexicano*. 2nd ed. México, DF: Mortiz, 1972.

Gabilondo, Joseba. Introduction. *Arizona Journal of Hispanic Cultural Studies* 5 (2001): 91–113.

Gai, Mijal. "El arte de imitar con ingenio: Análisis comparativo de un soneto de Quevedo." *Revue Romane* 21.2 (1986): 208–28.

García Lorca, Federico. "Baeza." *Prosa 1*. Ed. Miguel García Posada. Madrid: Akal, 1994. 132–39.

──────. "Homenaje a Luis Cernuda." *Luis Cernuda, el escritor y la crítica*. Ed. Derek Harris. Madrid: Taurus, 1977. 25–26.

──────. "La imagen poética de Don Luis de Góngora." *Prosa 1*. Ed. Miguel García Posada. Madrid: Akal, 1994. 236–59.

──────. *Poeta en Nueva York*. Colección Austral. Madrid: Espasa-Calpe, 1989.

──────. *Presentación de Pablo Neruda*. Madrid, 1934. Rpt. *Obras completas*. Madrid: Aguilar, 1960.

──────. *Primer Romancero gitano*. Ed. Miguel García Posada. Madrid: Castalia, 1988.

García Montero, Luis. *Los dueños del vacío: La conciencia poética entre la identidad y los vínculos*. Barcelona: Tusquets, 2006.

──────. "La poesía de Rafael Alberti." *Poesía (1920–1938) de Rafael Alberti. Obras completas*. Vol. 1. Madrid: Aguilar, 1988. 31–133.

García Posada, Miguel. "Cernuda y las tradiciones andaluzas." *Historial de una vida*. Sevilla: Fundación José Manuel Lara, 2003. 39–57.

———. *Lorca: Interpretación de Poeta en Nueva York*. Madrid: Akal, 1981.

Garro, Elena. *Memorias de España 1937*. México, DF: Siglo veintiuno, 1992.

Gautier, Théophile. Preface to *Paris Démoli*. By Edouard Fournier. 2nd ed. Paris: Auguste Aubry, 1855. 1–59.

Geist, Anthony. *La poética de la generación del 27 y las revistas literarias: De la vanguardia al compromiso (1918–1936)*. Madrid: Guadarrama Punto Omega, 1980.

Gelman, Juan. Acceptance speech of *Premio Cervantes*, 2007. April 2008. http://www.elpais.com/elpaismedia/ultimahora/media/200804/23/cultura/20080423elpepucul_1_Pes_PDF.pdf.

Gibbons, Reginald, ed. and trans. *Selected Poems of Luis Cernuda*. Los Angeles: U of California P, 1977.

Gil de Biedma, Jaime. "El ejemplo de Luis Cernuda." *Luis Cernuda, el escritor y la crítica*. Ed. Derek Harris. Madrid: Taurus, 1977. 124–28.

———. "Prólogo a una traducción catalana de los *Cuartetos* de T. S. Eliot." *Revista de Occidente* 110–11 (1990): 161–81.

Gil Iriarte, María Luisa. *Debe haber otro modo de ser humano y libre, —la obra de Rosario Castellanos*. Huelva: Universidad de Huelva, 1997.

Gilbert, Sandra. "'Now in a Moment I Know What I Am For': Rituals of Initiation in Whitman and Dickinson." *Walt Whitman of Mickle Street*. Ed. Geoffrey Sill. Knoxville: U of Tennessee P, 1994. 168–78.

Gilroy, Paul. *Against Race: Imagining Political Culture beyond the Color Line*. Cambridge: Belknap Press of Harvard UP. 2000.

Goic, Cedomil. "*Alturas de Macchu Picchu*: La torre y el abismo." *Pablo Neruda, el escritor y la crítica*. Ed. Emir Rodz. Monegal y Enrico Mario Santí. Madrid: Taurus, 1980. 219–44.

Goldstein, Laurence. *Ruins and Empire: The Evolution of a Theme in Augustian and Romantic Literature*. Pittsburg: U of Pittsburg P, 1977.

Góngora, Luis de. *Sonetos completos*. Ed. Biruté Ciplijauskaité. Madrid: Castalia. 1985.

González, Felipe. "El Alcázar." Tribuna. *El País.* 18 Oct. 1998.

González Acosta, Alejandro. "En la raíz mexicana: *Petrificada petrificante* de Octavio Paz." *Revista Iberoamericana* 57 (1991): 519–20.

González del Valle, Luis. *La canonización del diablo: Baudelaire y la estética moderna en España.* Madrid: Verbum, 2002.

González Echevarría, Roberto. *Alejo Carpentier, the Pilgrim at Home.* 2nd ed. Austin: U of Texas P, 1990.

———. *Celestina's Brood: Continuities of the Baroque in Spanish and Latin American Literature.* Durham: Duke UP, 1993.

———. "Guerra de los poetas." Prologue to *Los poetas del mundo defienden al pueblo español.* By Pablo Neruda and Nancy Cunard. Sevilla: Renacimiento, 2002.

———. "Introduction to Neruda's *Canto General*: The Poetics of Betrayal." *Canto General.* By Pablo Neruda. Trans. Jack Schmitt. Los Angeles: U of California P, 1993. 1–12.

———. *Isla a su vuelo fugitiva.* Madrid: Porrúa Turanzas, 1983.

———. *Myth and Archive: A Theory of Latin American Narrative.* Durham: Duke UP, 1998.

———. *La prole de Celestina: Continuidades del barroco en las literaturas española e hispanoamericana.* Madrid: Colibrí, 1999.

González Echevarría, Roberto, and Emir Rodríguez Monegal. "Interview to Octavio Paz." *Diacritics* 2.3 (1972): 35–40.

González Fernández de Sevilla, José Manuel. "La poesía metafísica de John Donne y Francisco de Quevedo." *Neophilologus* 95 (1991): 548–61.

González Martín, Jerónimo Pablo. "Significación de la poesía de Rafael Alberti durante la Guerra Civil." *Los escritores y la Guerra de España.* Ed. Mar Hanrez. Barcelona: Libros de Monte Avila, 1997. 155–67.

González, Eduardo G. "Octavio Paz and the Critique of the Pyramid." *Diacritics* 2 (1972): 30–34.

———. "The Lyre, the Mire and Laughter." *Diacritics* 4.4 (1974): 18–21.

Gottlieb, Marlene. "La guerra civil española en la poesía de Pablo Neruda y César Vallejo." *Perfil de César Vallejo. Litoral* 76–77–79 (1968): 143–54.

Graham, Helen. "Coming to Terms with the Past: Spain's Memory Wars." *History Today* 54.5 (2004): 29–31.

———. *The Spanish Civil War: A Very Short Introduction.* Oxford: Oxford UP, 2005.

Gramsci, Antonio. "The Historical Role of Cities." *Selections from Political Writings 1910–1920.* Trans. John Mathews. London: Lawrence and Wishart, 1997. 150–53.

Grandes, Almudena. "Razones para un aniversario." *Memoria del Futuro (1931–2006).* Madrid: Visor, 2006. 121–27.

Guillén, Nicolás. *Obra poética.* Ed. Angel Augier. La Habana: Letras Cubanas, 1980.

Gullón, Ricardo. "Relaciones Pablo Neruda–Juan Ramón Jiménez." *Hispanic Review* 39 (1971): 141–66.

Gutiérrez Revuelta, Pedro. "Neruda en España: 'La calle destruida.'" *Ideologies and Literature, Journal of Hispanic and Lusophone Discourse Analysis* 4.1 (1989): 299–316.

Habermas, Jurgen. *The Philosophical Discourse of Modernity.* Trans. Frederick Lawrence. Cambridge: MIT P, 1991.

Hart, Stephen, ed. *¡No pasarán! Art, Literature and the Spanish Civil War.* London: Tamesis, 1988.

Harris, Derek, ed. *Luis Cernuda, el escritor y la crítica.* Madrid: Taurus, 1977.

———. *La poesía de Luis Cernuda.* Granada: Universidad de Granada, 1992.

Harris, Derek, and Luis Maristany eds. *Luis Cernuda. Poesía completa.* Madrid: Siruela, 2002.

Harrison, Regina. "Machu Picchu Recycled." *Telling Ruins in Latin America.* Ed. Michael Lazzara and Vicky Unruh. New York: Palgrave Macmillan, 2009. 63–75.

Harvey, David. *Paris: Capital of Modernity.* New York: Routledge, 2003.

Hatzfeld, Helmut. *Estudios sobre el Barroco.* Madrid: Gredos, 1964.

Havard, Robert. *The Crucified Mind: Rafael Alberti and the Surrealist Ethos in Spain.* Rochester, NY: Tamesis, 2001.

Heckscher, William S. "Heliotropes and Romantic Ruins, Recent Emblematic Acquisitions." *Princeton University Library Chronicle* 15 (1983): 33–40.

Hernández, Miguel. *Crónicas de la guerra de España.* Ed. Fundación Domingo Malagón. Barcelona: Flor del Viento, 2005.

———. *Obra poética completa.* Introd. and notes Leopoldo de Luis and Jorge Urrutia. Madrid: Alianza, 1982.

Herrmann, Gina. *Written in Red: The Communist Memoir in Spain.* Urbana Champaign: U of Illinois P, 2010.

Hiddleston, J.A. *Baudelaire and the Art of Memory*. Oxford: Oxford UP, 1999.

Holmes, Richard. *Shelley: The Pursuit*. London: Weidenfeld and Nicolson, 1974.

Homenaje a Don Luis de Góngora y Argote. Special Issue of *Boletín de la Real Academia de Ciencias, Bellas Artes y Nobles Artes de Córdoba* 6.18 (1927).

Hoover, Elaine L. *John Donne and Francisco de Quevedo: Poets of Love and Death*. Chapel Hill: U of North Carolina P, 1978.

Hoover, Judith Myers. "The Urban Nightmare: Alienation Imagery in the Poetry of T. S. Eliot and Octavio Paz." *Journal of Spanish Studies Twentieth Century* 6.1 (Spring 1978): 13–28.

Hugo, Victor. *Œuvres poétiques III*. Paris: Gallimard, 1974.

Huyssen, Andreas. "Nostalgia for Ruins." *Grey Room* 23 (2006): 6–21.

———. *Present Pasts, Urban Palimpsests and the Politics of Memory*. Stanford: Stanford UP, 2003.

———. *Twilight Memories: Marking Time in the Culture of Amnesia*. New York and London: Routledge, 1995.

Jackson, Gabriel. Introduction. *The Spanish Civil War: Domestic Crisis or International Conspiracy?* Boston: Heath, 1967.

———. *The Spanish Republic and the Spanish Civil War. 1931–1939*. Princeton, NJ: Princeton UP, 1965.

Jaén, Didier. "Walt Whitman: Tema literario." *La Torre* 60 (1968): 77–100.

Jaksic, Iván. *Ven conmigo a la España lejana: Los intelectuales norteamericanos ante el mundo hispano, 1820–1880*. Chile: Fondo de Cultura Económica. 2007.

Jameson, Fredric. *Prison House of Language: A Critical Account of Structuralism and Russian Formalism*. Princeton NJ: Princeton UP, 1972.

Jauss, Hans Robert. *Aesthetic Experience and Literary Hermeneutics*. Minneapolis: U of Minnesota P, 1982.

———. "Reflections on the Chapter 'Modernity' in Benjamin's Baudelaire Fragments." *On Walter Benjamin: Critical Essays and Recollection*. Ed. Gary Smith. Cambridge: MIT P, 1988. 176–84.

Jelin, Elizabeth. *State Repression and the Labors of Memory*. Trans. Judy Rein and Marcial Godoy-Anativia. Minneapolis: U of Minnesota P, 2003.

Jiménez, José Olivio. "Desolación de la Quimera." *Luis Cernuda, el escritor y la crítica*. Ed. Derek Harris. Madrid: Taurus, 1977. 326–35.

———. "Emoción y trascendencia del tiempo en la poesía de Luis Cernuda." *Homenaje a Luis Cernuda*. Ed. Jacobo Muñoz and J. L. García Molina. Valencia: La caña gris, 1962. 45–83.

Jiménez Fajardo, Salvador. "¿América sombría?" *Repertorio Americano* 24, 14 Aug. 1943, 209–11.

———. "Carta a Pablo Neruda." *Repertorio Americano* 23, 17 Jan. 1942, 12.

———. "Icons of War in Alberti: 'Madrid–Otoño.'" *The Spanish Civil War in Literature*. Ed. Janet Pérez and Wendell Aycock. Lubbock, TX: Texas Tech UP, 1990. 121–28.

———. *Luis Cernuda*. Boston: Twayne, 1978.

———. *The Word and the Mirror: Critical Essays on the Poetry of Luis Cernuda*. Rutherford: Farleigh Dickinson UP, 1989.

Johnson, Barbara. *Défigurations du langage poétique: La seconde révolution baudelairienne*. Paris: Flammarion, 1979.

Juliá, Santos, ed. *Historia de las dos Españas*. Madrid: Taurus, 2004.

———. *Víctimas de la Guerra*. Madrid: Temas de Hoy, 1999.

Lacan, Jacques. "Tuché et automaton." *Les quatre concepts fondamentaux de la psychanalyse*. 1964. Paris: du Seuil, 1973. 61–75.

Laguardia, Gary. "The Butterflies in Walt Whitman's Beard: Lorca's Naming of Whitman." *Neophilologus* 62 (1978): 540–54.

Larrea, Juan. *Del surrealismo a Macchu Picchu*. México, DF: Mortiz, 1967.

Lawrence, D. H. *The Symbolic Meaning, Uncollected Versions of Studies in Classic American Literature*. Ed. Arnin Arnold. London: Centaur, 1962.

Lazzara, Michael, and Vicky Unruh. "Introduction: Telling Ruins." *Telling Ruins in Latin America*. Ed. Michael Lazzara and Vicky Unruh. New York: Palgrave Macmillan, 2009. 1–9.

Lehan, Richard. *The City in Literature: An Intellectual and Cultural History*. Berkeley: U of California P, 1998.

Lezama Lima, José. "Soledades habitadas por Cernuda." *Luis Cernuda, el escritor y la crítica*. Ed. Derek Harris. Madrid: Taurus, 1977. 49–52.

———. *La expresión americana*. Santiago de Chile: Universitaria, 1969.

López Bueno, Begoña. "Tópica literaria y realización textual: Unas notas sobre la poesía española de las ruinas en los Siglos de Oro." *Revista de Filología Española* 66 (1986): 59–74.

López Estrada, Francisco. *Estudios de arte español.* Madrid: C.S.I.C., 1974.

Lowry, Nelson, Jr. *Baroque Lyric Poetry.* 1961. New York: Octagon Books, 1979.

Loyola, Hernán. *Ser y morir en Pablo Neruda (1918–1945).* Santiago, Chile: Santiago, 1967.

Ludmer, Josefina. "Las tretas del débil." *La sartén por el mango.* San Juan, Puerto Rico: Huracán, 1984. 47–54.

Macaulay, Rose. *Pleasure of Ruins.* London: Weidenfeld and Nicolson, 1953.

Machado, Antonio. *Campos de Castilla.* Ed. Geoffrey Ribbans. Madrid: Cátedra, 1999.

———. *Poesías completas.* Ed. Manuel Alvar. Madrid: Espasa-Calpe, 2000.

Machado, Manuel. *Poesía de guerra y posguerra.* Ed. Miguel D'Ors. Granada: Universidad de Granada, 1994.

Macías Brevis, Sergio. *El Madrid de Pablo Neruda.* Madrid: Tabla Rasa, 2004.

Madariaga, María Rosa de. *Los moros que trajo Franco… La intervención de tropas coloniales en la guerra civil española.* Barcelona: Martínez Roca, 2002.

Madrid, Leila. "Octavio Paz: La espiral o la línea o la re-escritura del Romanticismo." *Revista Iberoamericana* 56.151 (1990): 393–401.

Malefakis, Edward, ed. *La guerra civil española.* Madrid: Taurus, 2006.

Manguel, Alberto. *The City of Words.* Toronto: Anansi, 2007.

Marcos, Juan Manuel. "Vallejo y Neruda: La Guerra civil española como profecía hispanoamericana." *Cuadernos Hispanoamericanos* 258.1 (1985): 217–24.

Marín, Antonio. "Las ruinas de Belchite." *La Vanguardia,* 9 Oct. 2002. Web.

Marqués de Tamarón. "T. S. Eliot, reaccionario." *Revista de Occidente* 89 (1988): 143–56.

Marx, Karl. *The Eighteenth of Brumaire of Louis Bonaparte.* New York: International, 1963.

Matthiessen, F. O. *The Achievement of T. S. Eliot: An Essay on the Nature of Poetry.* New York: Oxford UP, 1958.

May, Barbara Dale. "The Endurance of Dreams Deferred: Rafael Alberti and Langston Hughes." *Red Flags, Black Flags: Critical Essays on the Literature of the Spanish Civil War*. Ed. John Beals Romeiser. Potomac, MD: Studia Humanitatis, 1982. 13–54.

———. "Poetry and Political Commitment: Alberti, Guillén, and Hughes." *Studies in Afro-Hispanic Literature*. Vols. 2–3. Ed. Clementine C. Rabassa and Gladys Seda-Rodríguez. New York: CUNY, 1979. 14–27.

Mayoral, Marina. "What They Meant to Say When They Said *España* (The Idea of Spain in the Work of Three Twentieth-Century Poets)." *Spain beyond Spain: Modernity, Literary History, and National Identity*. Ed. Brad Epps and Luis Fernández Cifuentes. Lewisburg: Bucknell UP, 2005. 301–17.

McFarland, Thomas. *Romanticism and the Forms of Ruin: Wordsworth, Coleridge and the Modalities of Fragmentation*. Princeton NJ: Princeton UP, 1981.

Meléndez, Concha. "España en el corazón de Neruda." *Repertorio Americano* 27.19–20 (1940): 300–02.

Menand, Louis. *Discovering Modernism: T. S. Eliot and His Context*. Oxford: Oxford UP, 1987.

Méndez, Concha. *Poemas (1926–1986)*. Ed. James Valender. Madrid: Hiperión, 1995.

Méndez Rodenas, Adriana. "Tradition and Women's Writing: Toward a Poetics of Difference." *Engendering the Word*. Ed. T. Berg, A. S. Elfenbein, J. Larsen, and E. K. Sparks. Chicago: U of Illinois P, 1989. 29–50.

Menéndez Pelayo, Marcelino. *Historia de las ideas estéticas*. Vol. 2. Santander: Aldus, 1947.

Merewether, Charles. "Traces of Loss." *Irresistible Decay: Ruins Reclaimed*. Ed. Michael S. Roth, Claire L. Lyons, and Charles Merewether. Los Angeles: Getty Research Institute for the History of Art and the Humanities, 1997. 25–40.

Messinger Cypess, Sandra. "Tlatelolco: From Ruins to Poetry." *Telling Ruins in Latin America*. Ed. Michael Lazzara and Vicky Unruh. New York: Palgrave Macmillan, 2009. 163–74.

Miró, Emilio, ed. *Antología de poetisas del 27*. Madrid: Castalia, 1999.

Molloy, Sylvia. "Translating Ruins: An American Parable." *Telling Ruins in Latin America*. Ed. Michael Lazzara and Vicky Unruh. New York: Palgrave Macmillan, 2009. 51–62.

Monroe, Jonathan. *A Poverty of Objects: The Prose Poem and the Politics of Genre*. Ithaca: Cornell UP, 1987.

Moore, Fabienne. "Baudelaire et les poëmes en prose du dix-huitième siècle: De Fénelon à Chateaubriand." *Bulletin Baudelairien* 40.1–2 (2005): 113–43.

Moradiellos, Enrique. *La España de Franco (1939–1975): Política y sociedad.* Madrid: Síntesis, 2000.

Moreiras, Alberto. *Tercer Espacio: Literatura y duelo en América Latina.* Santiago: LOM, AROIS, 1999.

Moreiras-Menor, Cristina. "War, Postwar, and the Fascist Fabrication of Identity." *Teaching Representations of the Spanish Civil War.* Ed. Noël Valis. New York: Modern Languages Association of America, 2007. 117–29.

Morel, M. "Histoire d'un sonnet." *Revue d'Histoire Littéraire de la France* 1 (1894): 97–102.

Mortier, Roland. *La poétique des ruines en France.* Genève: Droz, 1974.

Mullen, Edward, ed. *Langston Hughes in the Hispanic World and Haiti.* Hamden: Archon, 1977.

Mumford, Lewis. *The Culture of Cities.* New York: Harvest–Harcourt Brace, 1970.

Muñoz, Jacobo, and J. L. García Molina. *Homenaje a Luis Cernuda.* Valencia: La caña gris, 1962.

Myers Hoover, Judith. "The Urban Nightmare: Alienation Imagery in the Poetry of T. S. Eliot and Octavio Paz." *Journal of Spanish Studies* 6 (1978): 13–28.

Naharro-Calderón, José María. "*Dónde habita el olvido*: Falacias críticas y caídas poéticas en el exilio de las 'Posguerra' (1939–1944)." *Anales de la Literatura Española Contemporánea* 18 (1993): 59–68.

Nandorfy, Martha J. "Petrificada petrificante." *Revista Canadiense de Estudios Hispánicos* 16 (1992): 567–86.

Nash, Mary. *Rojas: Las mujeres republicanas en la guerra civil.* Madrid: Taurus, 1999.

Nelson, Cary. *The Wound and the Dream: Sixty Years of American Poems about the Spanish Civil War.* Urbana: U of Illinois P, 2002.

Nelson, Lowry, Jr. *Baroque Lyric Poetry.* New York: Octagon, 1979.

Neruda, Pablo. "Algo sobre mi poesía y vida." *Aurora* 1 (1954): 1–14.

———. *Canto General.* Prólogo by Fernando Alegría. Caracas, Venezuela: Biblioteca Ayacucho, 1976.

———. "César Vallejo ha muerto." *Obras completas.* Vol. 3. Buenos Aires: Losada, 1973. 645–46.

————. "Conducta y poesía." Prólogos to the journal *Caballo verde para la poesía* [Madrid] (Oct. 1935–Jan. 1936). *Obras completas.* Vol. 3. 1957. 4th ed. Buenos Aires: Losada, 1973. 638–39.

————. *Confieso que he vivido. Memorias.* Barcelona: Seix Barral, 1974.

————. *España en el corazón.* 1938. Santiago: Literatura Latinoamericana Reunida, 1988.

————. "Federico García Lorca." 1937. *Obras completas.* Vol. 3. Buenos Aires: Losada, 1973. 640–45.

————. *México florido y espinudo.* México, DF: Partido Revolucionario Institucional, Comisión Nacional Editorial, 1976.

————. *Miliciano corazón de América.* Cuzco, Perú: Cuadernos Kori-Cancha, 1943.

————. *Obras completas.* 1957. Buenos Aires: Losada, 1973.

————. *Residencia en la tierra.* Ed. Hernán Loyola. Barcelona: Debolsillo, 2003.

————. "Sobre una poesía sin pureza." Prólogo to the journal *Caballo verde para la poesía* [Madrid] (Oct. 1935). *Obras completas.* Vol. 3. 1957. Buenos Aires: Losada, 1973. 636–37.

————. *Tercera Residencia.* Ed. Hernán Loyola. Barcelona: Debolsillo, 2003.

————. *Viaje al corazón de Quevedo.* (*Viajes,* 1955). *Obras completas.* Vol. 2. Buenos Aires: Losada, 1968.

Olalquiaga, Celeste. *The Artificial Kingdom: A Treasury of the Kitsch Experience.* New York: Pantheon, 1998.

Olivares, Julián. "Levity and Gravity: The Interpretation of the Ludic Element in Quevedo's 'Comunicación de amor invisible por los ojos' and Donne's 'The Extasie.'" *Neophilologus* 68.4 (1984): 534–45.

O'Neill, Olivia Ann. "Donne and Eliot: The Compass and the Screen." Honors Thesis. Harvard U, 1974.

Orozco Díaz, Emilio. *Temas del Barroco de Poesía y Pintura.* Granada: Universidad de Granada, 1947.

Orringer, Nelson. "España en el corazón de Neruda y su solidaridad generacional." *La Chispa 87, Selected Proceedings.* Ed. Gilbert Paolini. Eighth Louisiana Conference on Hispanic Languages and Literatures. New Orleans: Tulane U, 1987. 201–09.

Ortega, Julio. *La estética neobarroca en la narrativa hispanoamericana.* Madrid: Porrúa Mudanzas, 1984.

————. "Post-teoría y estudios transatlánticos." *Iberoamericana* 3.9 (2003): 109–17.

Ortega, Julio. *La teoría poética de César Vallejo.* Washington, DC: Library of Congress, Del Sol, 1986.

Ortiz, Amarilis. "La muerte en la obra póstuma de Pablo Neruda: Un modo más de estar con Quevedo." *Mester* 23.2 (1994): 1–16.

Ortiz, Fernando. "Eliot en Cernuda." *Vuelta* 11.124 (1987): 33–38.

Osuna, Rafael. *Pablo Neruda y Nancy Cunard (Les Poètes du Monde Défendent le Peuple Espagnol).* Madrid: Orígenes, 1987.

Pacheco, José Emilio. "Cernuda ante la poesía española (intento de aclaración)." *Luis Cernuda en México.* Ed. James Valender. México, DF: Fondo de Cultura Económica, 2002. 137–39.

———. "Descripción de *Piedra de sol.*" *Revista Iberoamericana* 37 (1971): 135–45.

———. *Tarde o temprano.* México, DF: Fondo de Cultura Económica, 1986.

Paglia, Camille. *Sexual Personae.* New York: Vintage, 1991.

Pariente, Angel, ed. *En torno a Góngora.* Madrid: Júcar, 1986.

Parkinson Zamora, Lois. "Magical Ruins / Magical Realism: Alejo Carpentier, Francois de Nomé and the New World Baroque." *Poetics of the Americas.* Ed. Bainard Cowan and Jefferson Humphries. Baton Rouge: Louisiana State UP, 1997. 63–103.

———. *The Usable Past, The Imagination of History in Recent Fiction of the Americas.* Cambridge: Cambridge UP, 1997.

Payne, Stanley G. *The Franco Regime (1936–1975).* Madison: U of Wisconsin P, 1987.

Paz, Octavio. "Aniversario español." 1951. *Obras completas. Ideas y Costumbres I.* Vol. 9. México, DF: Fondo de Cultura Económica, 1993.

———. *El arco y la lira.* México, DF: Fondo de Cultura Económica, 1956.

———. "La búsqueda del presente (discurso por el Premio Nobel de Literatura en 1990)." *Revista Canadiense de Estudios Hispánicos* 16 (1992): 383–93.

———. "La ciudad y la literatura." 1992. *Obras completas 14. Miscelánea II.* México, DF: Fondo de Cultura Económica, 2001. 32–34.

———. *The Collected Poems of Octavio Paz 1957–1987.* Trans. and ed. Eliot Weinberger. New York: New Directions, 1990.

———. *Los hijos del limo.* Barcelona: Seix Barral, 1974.

———. "Homenaje al 'enemigo más querido': Rescate del discurso de las liras de Pablo Neruda." *Nerudiana* (1995): 23–25.

———. *El laberinto de la soledad.* 10th ed. Madrid: Cátedra, 2003.

———. *La llama doble.* Barcelona: Seix Barral, 1993.

———. "El lugar de prueba (Valencia 1937–1987)." *Obras completas 9. Ideas y Costumbres I.* México, DF: Fondo de Cultura Económica, 1993. 438–46.

———. "Manierismo, barroquismo, criollismo." *Revista Canadiense de Estudios Hispánicos* 1.1 (1976): 3–15.

———. *El mono gramático.* 1970. *Obra poética (1935–1988).* Barcelona: Seix Barral, 1998.

———. *Obra poética (1935–1988).* 1990. Barcelona: Seix Barral, 1998.

———. *Octavio Paz en España.* 1937. Ed. Danubio Torres Fierro. México, DF: Fondo de Cultura Económica, 2007.

———. "La palabra edificante." *Luis Cernuda, el escritor y la crítica.* Ed. Derek Harris. Madrid: Taurus, 1977. 138–60.

———. "La pregunta de Cernuda." *Vuelta* 12.144 (1988): 61–62.

———. "Presencia y presente: Baudelaire, crítico de arte." *Obras completas 6. Los privilegios de la vista I.* México, DF: Fondo de Cultura Económica, 1991. 43–55.

———. "Juegos de memoria y olvido." *Luis Cernuda ante la crítica mexicana.* Ed. James Valender. México DF: Fondo de Cultura Económica, 1990. 154–67.

———. "Un poema de John Donne." 1958, 1965. *Obras completas 2. Excursiones / Incursiones.* México, DF: Fondo de Cultura Económica, 1994. 93–99.

———. "Poesía de soledad y poesía de comunión." 1943. *Obras completas 13. Miscelánea I.* México, DF: Fondo de Cultura Económica, 1999. 234–45.

———. "Quevedo, Heráclito y algunos sonetos." 1981. *Obras completas 3. Fundación y disidencia.* México, DF: Fondo de Cultura Económica, 1994. 125–36.

———. "Reflejos: Réplicas. Diálogos con Francisco de Quevedo." 1996. *Obras completas 14. Miscelánea II.* México, DF: Fondo de Cultura Económica, 2000. 71–90.

———. "El romanticismo y la poesía contemporánea." *Vuelta* 127 (1987): 20–27.

———. "Rupturas y restauraciones." 1994. *Obras completas 14. Miscelánea II.* México, DF: Fondo de Cultura Económica, 2000. 192–204.

———. *Sor Juana Anthology.* Trans. Alan S. Trueblood. Foreword. Cambridge: Harvard UP, 1988.

Paz, Octavio. *Sor Juana Inés de la Cruz, o las trampas de la fe.* México, DF: Fondo de Cultura Económica, 1982.

———. "'La vuelta de los días: T. S. Eliot' (Palabras para recibir el Premio T. S. Eliot)." *Vuelta* 142 (1988): 40–41.

Pemán, José María. *Obras completas.* Madrid: Escelicer, 1947.

———. "El poema de la Bestia y el Angel." *Poesía de la Guerra civil española (1936–1939).* Ed. César de Vicente Hernando. Madrid: Akal, 1994. 307–31.

Peregrín Otero, Carlos. "Cernuda y los románticos ingleses." *Quimera* 15 (1982): 33–38.

Pérez Bowie, José Antonio. *El léxico de la muerte durante la guerra civil española.* Salamanca: Universidad de Salamanca, 1983.

Pérez Firmat, Gustavo. "The Strut of Centipede: José Lezama Lima and New World Exceptionalism." *Do the Americas Have a Common Literature?* Ed. Gustavo Pérez Firmat. Durham: Duke UP, 1990. 316–32.

Pérez Marín, Carmen. "Octavio Paz y el poema en prosa surrealista." *La Torre* 7.26 (1993): 233–67.

Peyre, Henri, introd. *Baudelaire: A Collection of Critical Essays.* Englewood Cliffs, NJ: Prentice-Hall, 1962.

Pfandl, L. *Historia de la literatura nacional española en la Edad de Oro.* Barcelona: Gili, 1933.

Piera, Carlos. "Las personas de Eliot." *Revista de Occidente* 89 (1988): 109–22.

Podestá, Guido A. "Octavio Paz's Poetic Justice: Reading His 'Advertencias.'" *Siglo XX* 10 (1992): 211–20.

Poetas en la España Leal. Madrid-Valencia: Españolas, 1937. Rpt. Madrid: Hispamerica, 1976.

Pollock, Griselda. *Vision and Difference: Femininity, Feminism and the Histories of Art.* London and New York: Routledge, 1988.

Ponte, Antonio José. *Un arte de hacer ruinas y otros cuentos.* Ed. Esther Whitfield. México, DF: Fondo de Cultura Económica, 2005.

Predmore, Michael. *Una España joven en la poesía de Antonio Machado.* Madrid: Insula, 1981.

Prendergast, Christopher. "Codeword Modernity." *New Left Review* 24 (2003): 95–106.

Presley, James. "Langston Hughes, War Correspondent." *Journal of Modern Literature* 5.3 (1976): 481–91.

Preston, Paul, ed. *¡Comrades! Portraits from the Spanish Civil War*. London: Harper Collins, 1999.

———. *Revolution and War in Spain 1931–1939*. 1984. London: Routledge, 1995.

Pring-Mill, Robert, ed. *Pablo Neruda: A Basic Anthology*. Oxford: Dolphin, 1975.

Pujals Resalí, Esteban. "T. S. Eliot y la tierra baldía del siglo XX." *Revista de Occidente* 89 (1988): 123–41.

Pulgarín, Amalia, and Miguel Calvillo. "César Vallejo y Miguel Hernández: Dos poetas ante la guerra civil española." *War and Revolution in Hispanic Literature*. Ed. Roy Boland and Alun Kenwood. Melbourne: Voz Hispánica, 1990. 129–41.

Quevedo, Francisco de. *Obras completas*. Vol. 2. Ed. Felicidad Buendía. Madrid: Aguilar, 1979.

———. *Poemas escogidos*. Ed. José Manuel Blecua. Madrid: Castalia, 1989.

Quiroga, José. *Understanding Octavio Paz*. Columbia: U of South Carolina P, 1999.

Radosh, Ronald, Mary R. Habeck, and Grigory Sevostianov, eds. *Spain Betrayed: The Soviet Union in the Spanish Civil War*. New Haven: Yale UP, 2001.

Rampersad, Arnold. *The Life of Langston Hughes*. New York: Oxford UP, 1986.

Real Ramos, César. "La raíz de *la Diferencia* de Luis Cernuda: La visión mítica de la realidad." *Anales de la Literatura Española Contemporánea* 15 (1990): 109–27.

Reiman, Donald H., and Sharon B. Powers, eds. *Shelley's Poetry and Prose: Authoritative Texts Criticism*. New York: Norton, 1977.

Reimer, A. P. "The Poetry of Religious Paradox—T. S. Eliot and the Metaphysicals." *Sydney Studies in English* 8 (1982–83): 80–88.

Resina, Joan Ramon. "Cold War Hispanism and the New Deal of Cultural Studies." *Spain beyond Spain: Modernity, Literary History and National Identity*. Ed. Brad Epps and Luis Fernández Cifuentes. Lewisburg: Bucknell UP, 2005. 70–108.

———, ed. *Disremembering the Dictatorship: The Politics of Memory in the Spanish Transition to Democracy*. Amsterdam: Rodopi, 2000.

Reyes, Alfonso. *Cuestiones gongorinas*. 1927. *Obras completas de Alfonso Reyes*. Vol. 7. México, DF: Fondo de Cultura Económica, 1958.

Reyes, Alfonso. *Obra poética*. México, DF: Fondo de Cultura Económica, 1952.

———. "Prólogo a Quevedo." 1917. *Capítulos de literatura española. Obras completas de Alfonso Reyes*. Vol. 6. México, DF: Fondo de Cultura Económica, 1957. 74–84.

Richards, I. A. "On T. S. Eliot." *T. S. Eliot, The Man and His Work*. Ed. Allen Tate. Middlesex: Penguin, 1966. 7–15.

Richard, Nelly. "Presentación." *Políticas y estéticas de la memoria*. Ed. Nelly Richards. Santiago: Cuarto Propio, 2000. 9–12.

Rivers, Elías. *Muses and Masks: Some Classical Genres of Spanish Poetry*. Newark, DE: Juan de la Cuesta, 1992.

———. *Poesía lírica del Siglo de Oro*. Madrid: Cátedra, 1997.

Robbins, Jill. "Globalization, Publishing, and the Marketing of 'Hispanic' Identities." *Iberoamericana* 3.9 (2003): 89–101.

Rodríguez García, José María. "John Donne after Octavio Paz: Translation as Transculturation." *Dispositio/n* 21.48 (1996/99): 155–82. Web.

Rodríguez Monegal, Emir. *Neruda: El viajero inmóvil*. Caracas: Monte Avila, 1977.

———. "Relectura de El Arco y la Lira." *Revista Iberoamericana* 37 (1971): 35–46.

———. "El sistema del poeta." *Pablo Neruda, el escritor y la crítica*. Ed. Emir Rodz. Monegal and Enrico Mario Santí. Madrid: Taurus, 1980. 633–91.

Ruiz Soriano, Francisco. "Eliot, Cernuda y Alberti: La ciudad vacía." *Cuadernos Hispanoamericanos* 539–40 (1995): 43–54.

Sainz de Medrano, Luis. *Pablo Neruda, cinco ensayos*. Roma: Bulzoni, 1996.

Sánchez, Luis Alberto. *Góngora en América* and *El Lunarejo y Góngora*. Quito: Imprenta Nacional, 1927.

Sánchez Rosillo, Eloy. *La fuerza del destino: Vida y poesía de Luis Cernuda*. Murcia: Universidad de Murcia, 1992.

Sánchez Vidal, Agustín. *Miguel Hernández, desamordazado y regresado*. Barcelona: Planeta, 1992.

Santayana, George. *Three Philosophical Poets: Lucretius, Dante and Goethe*. 1910. New York: Cooper Square, 1970.

Santí, Enrico Mario. "The Accidental Tourist: Walt Whitman in Latin America." *Do the Americas Have a Common Literature?* Ed. Gustavo Pérez Firmat. Durham: Duke UP, 1990. 156–76.

———. *El acto de las palabras: Estudios y diálogos con Octavio Paz*. México, DF: Fondo de Cultura Económica, 1997.

————, ed. *Luz espejeante: Octavio Paz ante la crítica*. México, DF: Ediciones Era y la Universidad Nacional Autónoma de México, 2009.

————. *Pablo Neruda: The Poetics of Prophecy*. Ithaca: Cornell UP, 1981.

Santos, Boaventura de Sousa. *Toward a New Common Sense: Law, Science and Politics in the Paradigmatic Transition*. New York: Routledge, 1995.

Sardou, Victorien. *Maison neuve*. New ed. Paris: Calmann-Lévy, 1889.

Sarduy, Severo. "El Barroco y el Neobarroco." *América Latina en su literatura*. Ed. César Fernández Moreno. México, DF: Siglo XXI, 1972. 167–84.

Sartre, Jean-Paul. *Baudelaire*. Paris: Gallimard, 1947.

Saz, Sara M. "'Yo, hijo de América… muero por ti': Repercusiones de la guerra civil española en la poesía iberoamericana." *Actas del XXIX Congreso del Instituto Internacional de Literatura Iberoamericana*. Vol. 2. Barcelona: PPU, 1994. 1085–1100.

Sen, Sunil Kanti. *Metaphysical Tradition and T. S. Eliot*. Calcutta: Firma K.L. Mukhopadhyay, 1965.

Serrano de la Torre, José Miguel. *Antiguos y modernos en la poética de Luis Cernuda*. Málaga: Analecta Malacitana, 2002.

Shafer, Aileen. "Eliot Re-Donne: The Prufrockian Spheres." *Yeats Eliot Review* 5.2 (1978): 39–43.

Sharpe, William Chapman. *Unreal Cities: Urban Figuration in Wordsworth, Baudelaire, Whitman, Eliot and Williams*. Baltimore and London: Johns Hopkins UP, 1990.

Shelley, Percy Bysshe. *Shelley's Poetry and Prose: Authoritative Texts Criticism*. Ed. Donald H. Reiman and Sharon B. Powers. New York: Norton, 1977.

Sheridan, Guillermo. "La ciudad de la poesía mexicana." *Vuelta* 18.211 (1994): 65–67.

————. "Entrevista a Octavio Paz: Una apuesta vital." *Vuelta* 21 (1997): 6–9.

————. *Poeta con paisaje: Ensayos sobre la vida de Octavio Paz*. México, DF: Era, 2004.

Sicard, Alain. *La pensée poétique de Pablo Neruda*. Thesis. Université de Bordeaux III. Lille: Reproductions de Theses, 1997.

Sicot, Bernard. *Exilio, memoria e historia en la poesía de Luis Cernuda*. Trans. Tomás Onaindía. Madrid: Fondo de Cultura Económica, 2002.

Silver, Philip W. "Cernuda, poeta ontológico." *Luis Cernuda, el escritor y la crítica*. Ed. Derek Harris. Madrid: Taurus, 1977. 203–11.

———. *Luis Cernuda: El poeta en su leyenda*. Madrid: Castalia, 1995.

———. *Ruin and Restitution. Reinterpreting Romanticism in Spain*. Nashville: Vanderbilt UP, 1997.

Simmel, Georg. *The Conflict in Modern Culture*. Trans. Peter Etzkorn. New York: Teachers College Press, 1968.

———. "The Metropolis and Mental Life." *Classic Essays on the Culture of Cities*. Ed. Richard Sennet. New York: Meredith, 1969. 47–60.

———. "The Ruin." Trans. David Kettler from *Philosophy of Culture*, 1911. *Georg Simmel 1858–1918, Collection of Essays*. Trans. and ed. Kurt H. Wolff. Columbus: Ohio State UP, 1959. 259–66.

———. *The Sociology of Georg Simmel*. Trans. Kurt H. Wolff. London: Free Press of Glencoe Collier-McMillian, 1950.

Sobejano, Gonzalo. "El soneto de Quevedo *A Roma sepultada en ruina*" (esencia y ascendencia)." *Filología* 22.1 (1987): 105–18.

Sola, María Magdalena. *Poesía y política en Pablo Neruda (Análisis del "Canto General")*. Río Piedras: Universitaria de la Universidad de Puerto Rico, 1980.

Sommer, Doris. "Supplying Demand: Walt Whitman as the Liberal Self." *Reinventing the Americas: Comparative Studies of the United States and Spanish America*. Ed. Bell Gale Chevigny and Gary Laguardia. Cambridge: Cambridge UP, 1986. 68–91.

Sontag, Susan. *Regarding the Pain of Others*. New York: Ferrar, Strauss, and Giroux, 2003.

Sor Juana Inés de la Cruz. *Lírica*. Ed. Raquel Asún. Libros Clásicos. Barcelona: Ediciones B., 1988.

Soufas, Christopher. "<Et in Arcadia Ego>: Luis Cernuda, Ekphrasis, and the Reader." *Anales de la Literatura Española Contemporánea* 7.1 (1982): 97–107.

Sourien, Etienne. *La poésie française et la peinture*. London: U of London, Athlone Press, 1966.

Southam, B. C. *A Guide to the Selected Poems of T. S. Eliot*. 6th ed. New York: Harcourt Brace, 1994.

Spears, Monroe K. *Dionysus and the City: Modernism in Twentieth Century Poetry*. New York: Oxford UP, 1970.

Spender, Stephen, and John Lehmann, eds. *Poems for Spain*. London: Hogarth, 1939.

Spengler, Oswald. *The Decline of the West*. Trans. Charles Francis Atkinson. London: George Allen, 1961.

Stainton, Leslie. "¡Oh Babilonia! ¡Oh Cartago! ¡Oh Nueva York!: El europeo ante Manhattan, Manhattan ante el europeo. 1917–1932." *Boletín de la Fundación Federico García Lorca* 4 (1992): 191–212.

Stallybrass, Peter, and Allon White. *The Politics and Poetics of Transgression*. Ithaca: Cornell UP, 1986.

Stanton, Anthony. "Luis Cernuda y Octavio Paz: Convergencias y divergencias." *Luis Cernuda en México*. Ed. James Valender. México, DF: Fondo de Cultura Económica, 2002. 44–59.

———. *Las primeras voces del poeta Octavio Paz (1931–1938)*. México, DF: Ediciones Sin Nombre, Conaculta, 2001.

———. *Inventores de tradición: Ensayos sobre poesía mexicana moderna*. México DF: Fondo de Cultura Económica, 1998.

———. "Octavio Paz and Modern English-Language Poetry." *Tribute to Octavio Paz*. New York: Mexican Cultural Institute, 2001. 68–77.

———. "Octavio Paz, lector de Quevedo." *Más allá del litoral*. Enrique Hülsz Diccona and Manuel Ulacia, eds. México DF: UNAM, 1994. 179–85.

Starkie, Enid. *Baudelaire*. New York: New Directions, 1958.

Starobinski, Jean. "Le concept de nostalgie." *Diogène* 54 (1966): 92–115.

———. *La mélancolie au miroir: Trois lectures de Baudelaire*. (Conférences, essais et leçons du Collage de France). Paris: Julliard, 1989.

———. "La mélancolie dans les ruines." 1964. *L'invention de la liberté (1700–1789)*. Genève: Editions d'Art Albert Skira, 1994.

Susini, Jean-Claude. "*Rêve parisien* de Baudelaire: Vaporisation, concentration et règlements de comptes." *Nineteenth Century French Studies* 26.3–4 (1998): 346–66.

Swain, Virginia. *Grotesque Figures: Baudelaire, Rousseau, and the Aesthetics of Modernity*. Baltimore: Johns Hopkins UP, 2004.

Tarroux-Follin, Christiane. "*Himno entre ruinas*: La réconciliation avec le monde." *Octavio Paz*. Université Paul Valéry, Montpellier III. (1989): 53–71.

Teitelboim, Volodia. "El libro de España." Introd. *España en el corazón*. Santiago de Chile: Literatura Americana Reunida, 1988. 7–10.

———. *Neruda*. Madrid: Michay, 1984.

Terdiman, Richard. *Present Pasts: Modernity and the Memory Crisis.* Ithaca: Cornell UP, 1993.

Thomas, Sophie. "Assembling History: Fragments and Ruins." *European Romantic Review* 14 (2003): 177–86.

Thurston, Michael. "Bombed in Spain: Langston Hughes, the Black Press, and the Spanish Civil War." *The Black Press New Literary and Historical Essays.* Ed. Todd Vogel. New Brunswick: Rutgers UP, 2001. 140–58.

Trapiello, Andrés. *Las armas y las letras. Literatura y guerra civil (1936–1939).* Barcelona: Planeta, 1994.

Trías, Eugenio. *El artista y la ciudad.* Barcelona: Anagrama, 1997.

Trujillo, Patricia. "Los poetas como críticos: Eliot y Cernuda." *Literatura: Teoría, historia, crítica* 4 (2002): 135–69.

"T. S. Eliot: He Knew the Anguish of the Marrow, the Ague of the Skeleton." *Time* 15 Jan. 1965.

Ugarte, Michael. "The Question of Race in the Spanish Civil War." *Teaching Representations of the Spanish Civil War.* Ed. Noël Valis. New York: Modern Languages Association of America, 2007. 108–16.

———. *Shifting Ground: Spanish Civil War Exile Literature.* Durham: Duke UP, 1989.

Ulacia, Manuel. "Francisco de Quevedo y Pablo Picasso en "Homenaje y profanaciones," *El árbol milenario, Un recorrido por la obra de Octavio Paz.* Barcelona: Galaxia Gutenberg, 1994. 207–21.

———. *Luis Cernuda: Escritura, cuerpo y deseo.* Barcelona: Laia, 1984.

———. "Octavio Paz: Poesía, pintura, música, etcétera. Conversación con Octavio Paz." *Revista Iberoamericana* 55.148–49 (1989): 615–36.

Unruh, Vicky. "All in a Day's Work: Ruins Dwellers in Havana." *Telling Ruins in Latin America.* Ed. Michael Lazzara and Vicky Unruh. New York: Palgrave Macmillan, 2009. 197–210.

———. "It's a Sin to Bring Down an Art Deco': Sabina Berman's Theater among Ruins." *PMLA* 122.1 (2007): 135–50.

Valender, James, ed. *Cernuda y el poema en prosa.* London: Tamesis, 1984.

———. "Cernuda y Lezama Lima." *Vuelta* 12.144 (1988): 65–67.

———. *Luis Cernuda en México.* México, DF: Fondo de Cultura Económica, 2002.

————. "Los placeres prohibidos: An Analysis of the Prose Poems." *The Word and the Mirror: Critical Essays on the Poetry of Luis Cernuda*. Ed. Salvador Jiménez Fajardo. Rutherford: Farleigh Dickinson UP, 1989. 81–96.

Valente, José Angel. "Luis Cernuda y la poesía de la meditación." *Homenaje a Luis Cernuda*. Valencia: La Caña Gris, 1962. 29–38.

Valéry, Paul. "The Position of Baudelaire." *Baudelaire: A Collection of Critical Essays*. Englewood Cliffs, NJ: Prentice-Hall, 1962. 7–18.

Valis, Noël. "Introduction." *Teaching Representations of Spanish Civil War*. Ed. Noël Valis. New York: MLA, 2007. 7–20.

————. "Nostalgia and Exile." *Journal of Spanish Cultural Studies* 1.2 (2000): 117–33.

Vallejo, César. *Obras completas: Artículos y Crónicas (1918–1939)*. Lima: Biblioteca Clásicos del Perú, 1997.

————. *Obra poética*. París: ALLCA XX, 1988.

Vallejo, Georgette de. *Apuntes biográficos sobre "Poemas en Prosa" y "Poemas humanos."* Lima: Moncloa, 1968.

Vásquez, Carmen. "Voluntad de un canto: Pablo Neruda y tres poetas de la resistencia francesa." *Les poètes Latino-americains et la Guerre d'Espagne*. Paris: CRICCAL, Service de publications, Université de la Sorbonne nouvelle Paris III, 1986. 149–65.

Vattimo, Gianni. *The End of Modernity*. Trans. Jon Snyder. Baltimore: Johns Hopkins UP, 1988.

Vélez, Julio. "Vallejo, Neruda, Guillén: España y sus constelaciones en la poesía de 1937." *Las relaciones literarias entre España e Iberoamérica. XXIII Congreso del Instituto Internacional de Literatura Iberoamericana*. Madrid: Instituto de Cooperación Iberoamericana y la Universidad Complutense, 1984. 107–14.

Vélez, Julio, and Antonio Merino. *España en César Vallejo*. Madrid: Fundamentos, 1984.

Villegas, Juan. *Estructuras míticas y arquetipos en el "Canto General" de Neruda*. Barcelona: Planeta, 1976.

Villena, Luis Antonio de. *Rebeldía, clasicismo y crisis (Luis Cernuda: Asedios plurales a un poeta príncipe)*. Valencia: Pre-textos, 2002.

Ward, Patricia, ed. *Baudelaire and the Poetics of Modernity*. Nashville: Vanderbilt UP, 2001.

Wardropper, Bruce W. "The Poetry of Ruins in the Golden Age." *Hispánica Moderna: Columbia University Hispanic Studies* 35 (1969): 295–305.

337

Warner, Robin. "The Politics of Pablo Neruda's *España en el corazón*." *Hispanic Studies in Honour of Frank Pierce*. Ed. John England. Sheffield: Sheffield U Print, 1980. 169–80.

Warnke, Frank. *European Metaphysical Poetry*. New Haven: Yale UP, 1961.

———. *Versions of Baroque*. New Haven: Yale UP, 1972.

Warren, Austin. *Connections*. Ann Arbor: U of Michigan P, 1970.

Weber, Max. *The City*. Ed. and trans. Don Martindale and Gertrud Neu-wirth. New York: Free Press, 1958.

———. *From Max Weber: Essays in Sociology*. H. H. Gerth and C. Wright Mills. New York: Oxford UP, 1958.

Webster, John. *The Duchess of Malfi*. 1614. *The Complete Works of John Webster*. Vol. 2. Ed. F. L. Lucas. Boston: Houghton Mifflin, 1928. 3–200.

———. *The White Devil*. 1612. *The Complete Works of John Webster*. Vol. 1. Ed. F. L. Lucas. Boston: Houghton Mifflin, 1928. 67–272.

Weinberg, Kerry. "T. S. Eliot et Baudelaire: 'Whispers of Immortality' et 'Les métamorphoses du vampire.'" *Bulletin Baudelairien* 17.1–2 (1982): 12–14.

Wellek, René. *Concepts of Criticism*. New Haven: Yale UP, 1963.

Wesseling, Peter. *Revolution and Tradition: The Poetry of Rafael Alberti*. Valencia: Albatros, 1981.

Whitfield, Esther, ed. *Un arte de hacer ruinas y otros cuentos*. By Antonio José Ponte. México, DF: Fondo de Cultura Económica, 2005.

Whitman, Walt. *Leaves of Grass*. Library of America ed. New York: Vintage, 1992.

Willard, Charles. *Whitman's American Fame, the Growth of His Reputation after 1892*. Providence, RI: Brown UP, 1950.

Williams, Raymond. *The Country and the City*. London: Hogarth, 1985.

———. *The Politics of Modernism: Against the New Conformists*. London: Verso, 1989.

Williams, William Carlos. "An Essay on *Leaves of Grass*." *Leaves of Grass, 100 Years After*. Ed. Milton Hindus. Stanford: Stanford UP, 1955. 22–31.

Wilson, Edmund. *Axel's Castle*. New York: Scribner's, 1931.

Wilson, Edward M. "Las deudas de Cernuda." *Entre las jarchas y Cernuda, constantes y variables en la poesía española*. Barcelona: Ariel, 1977. 313–31.

Wilson, E. M. "Sobre la *Canción a las ruinas de Itálica* de Rodrigo Caro." *Revista de Filología Española* 23 (1936): 379–96.

Wilson, Elizabeth. "The Invisible Flâneur." *New Left Review* (1991): 90–110.

Wilson, Jason. *Octavio Paz.* Boston: Twayne, 1986.

Wolf, Philipp. *Modernization and the Crisis of Memory: John Donne and Don DeLillo.* Amsterdam and New York: Rodopi, 2002.

Wolff, Janet. "The Invisible Flâneuse: Women and the Literature of Modernity." *Theory, Culture, and Society* 2.3 (1985): 37–46.

Woodward, Christopher. *In Ruins: A Journey through History, Art and Literature.* 2001. New York: Vintage, 2003.

Wordsworth, William. *Poetical Works.* Oxford: Oxford UP, 1936.

Xirau, Ramón. *Octavio Paz. El sentido de la palabra.* México, DF: Mortiz, 1970.

Young, Howard. "Sombras fluviales: *Poeta en Nueva York* y *The Waste Land.*" *Boletín de la Fundación Federico García Lorca* 4.10 (1992): 165–77.

———, and K. M. Sibbald, eds. *T. S. Eliot and the Hispanic Modernity (1924–1993).* Denver, CO: Society of Spanish and Spanish-American Studies, 1994.

Yurkiévich, Saúl. *Fundadores de la Nueva Poesía Latinoamericana: Vallejo, Huidobro, Borges, Girando, Neruda y Paz.* Barcelona: Barral, 1970.

———. "Mito e historia: Dos generadores del *Canto General.*" *Pablo Neruda, el escritor y la crítica.* Ed. Emir Rodz. Monegal y Enrico Mario Santí. Madrid: Taurus, 1980. 198–218.

———. "Octavio Paz: Indagador de la Palabra." *Revista Iberoamericana* 37.74 (1971): 73–95.

Zambrano, María. "La poesía de Luis Cernuda." *Homenaje a Luis Cernuda.* Valencia: La caña gris, 1964. 15–16.

Žižek, Slavoj. "The Two Totalitarianisms." *London Review of Books* 17 Mar. 2005. Web.

———. *Welcome to the Desert of the Real! Five Essays on September 11 and Related Dates.* New York: Verso, 2002.

Index

About the Author

Cecilia Enjuto Rangel, University of Oregon, received her PhD in Comparative Literature from Yale University. Her publications focus on Transatlantic poetics and film. She is currently working on an edition of a historical testimony from the Spanish Civil War.